T0336016

Machine Learning Techniques and Industry Applications

Pramod Kumar Srivastava
Rajkiya Engineering College, Azamgarh, India

Ashok Kumar Yadav
Rajkiya Engineering College, Azamgarh, India

A volume in the Advances in
Computational Intelligence and
Robotics (ACIR) Book Series

Published in the United States of America by
    IGI Global
    Engineering Science Reference (an imprint of IGI Global)
    701 E. Chocolate Avenue
    Hershey PA, USA 17033
    Tel: 717-533-8845
    Fax: 717-533-8661
    E-mail: cust@igi-global.com
    Web site: http://www.igi-global.com

Library of Congress Cataloging-in-Publication Data

CIP Pending

Machine Learning Techniques and Industry Applications
Pramod Srivastava, Ashok Yadav
Engineering Science Reference

ISBN: 979-8-3693-5271-7
eISBN: 979-8-3693-5273-1

This book is published in the IGI Global book series Advances in Computational Intelligence and Robotics (ACIR) (ISSN: 2327-0411; eISSN: 2327-042X)

British Cataloguing in Publication Data
A Cataloguing in Publication record for this book is available from the British Library.

All work contributed to this book is new, previously-unpublished material.
The views expressed in this book are those of the authors, but not necessarily of the publisher.

For electronic access to this publication, please contact: eresources@igi-global.com.

Advances in Computational Intelligence and Robotics (ACIR) Book Series

Ivan Giannoccaro
University of Salento, Italy

ISSN:2327-0411
EISSN:2327-042X

MISSION

While intelligence is traditionally a term applied to humans and human cognition, technology has progressed in such a way to allow for the development of intelligent systems able to simulate many human traits. With this new era of simulated and artificial intelligence, much research is needed in order to continue to advance the field and also to evaluate the ethical and societal concerns of the existence of artificial life and machine learning.

The **Advances in Computational Intelligence and Robotics (ACIR) Book Series** encourages scholarly discourse on all topics pertaining to evolutionary computing, artificial life, computational intelligence, machine learning, and robotics. ACIR presents the latest research being conducted on diverse topics in intelligence technologies with the goal of advancing knowledge and applications in this rapidly evolving field.

COVERAGE

- Cognitive Informatics
- Evolutionary Computing
- Computational Logic
- Cyborgs
- Automated Reasoning
- Natural Language Processing
- Robotics
- Synthetic Emotions
- Machine Learning
- Intelligent Control

IGI Global is currently accepting manuscripts for publication within this series. To submit a proposal for a volume in this series, please contact our Acquisition Editors at Acquisitions@igi-global.com or visit: http://www.igi-global.com/publish/.

Titles in this Series

For a list of additional titles in this series, please visit:
http://www.igi-global.com/book-series/advances-computational-intelligence-robotics/73674

Secure and Intelligent IoT-Enabled Smart Cities
Sushil Kumar Singh (Marwadi University, India) Sudeep Tanwar (Nirma University, India) Rajendrasinh Jadeja (Marwadi University, India) Saurabh Singh (Woosong University, South Korea) and Zdzislaw Polkowski (Wroclaw University of Economics, Poland)
Engineering Science Reference • © 2024 • 434pp • H/C (ISBN: 9798369323731) • US $325.00

Using Real-Time Data and AI for Thrust Manufacturing
D. Satishkumar (Nehru Institute of Technology, India) and M. Sivaraja (Nehru Institute of Technology, India)
Engineering Science Reference • © 2024 • 343pp • H/C (ISBN: 9798369326152) • US $345.00

AI Approaches to Smart and Sustainable Power Systems
L. Ashok Kumar (PSG College of Technology, India) S. Angalaeswari (Vellore Institute of Technology, India) K. Mohana Sundaram (KPR Institute of Engineering and Technology, India) Ramesh C. Bansal (University of Sharjah, UAE & University of Pretoria, South Africa) and Arunkumar Patil (Central University of Karnataka, India)
Engineering Science Reference • © 2024 • 432pp • H/C (ISBN: 9798369315866) • US $300.00

Wearable Devices, Surveillance Systems, and AI for Women's Wellbeing
Sivaram Ponnusamy (Sandip University, Nashik, India) Vibha Bora (G. H. Raisoni College of Engineering, Nagpur, India) Prema M. Daigavane (G. H. Raisoni College of Engineering, Nagpur, India) and Sampada S. Wazalwar (G. H. Raisoni College of Engineering, Nagpur, India)
Engineering Science Reference • © 2024 • 321pp • H/C (ISBN: 9798369334065) • US $335.00

Methodologies, Frameworks, and Applications of Machine Learning
Pramod Kumar Srivastava (Rajkiya Engineering College, Azamgarh, India) and Ashok Kumar Yadav (Rajkiya Engineering College, Azamgarh, India)
Engineering Science Reference • © 2024 • 296pp • H/C (ISBN: 9798369310625) • US $300.00

701 East Chocolate Avenue, Hershey, PA 17033, USA
Tel: 717-533-8845 x100 • Fax: 717-533-8661
E-Mail: cust@igi-global.com • www.igi-global.com

Table of Contents

Detailed Table of Contents

Chapter 1

    Vibhor Sharma, Swami Rama Himalayan University, India
    Deepak Srivastava, Swami Rama Himalayan University, India
    Lokesh Kumar, Roorkee Institute of Technology, India
    Mohit Payal, Graphic Era Hill University, India

Smarter apps and connected devices are now possible because of the proliferation of IoT, which has greatly improved the quality of life in today's urban centers. ML and IoT approaches have been employed in the study of smart transportation, which has attracted a large number of researchers. Smart transportation is viewed as a catch-all word that encompasses a wide range of topics, including optimization of route, parking, street lighting, accident detection, abnormalities on the road, and other infrastructure-related issues. The purpose of this chapter is to examine the state of machine learning (ML) and internet of things (IoT) applications for smart city transport in order to better comprehend recent advances in these fields and to spot any holes in coverage. From the existing publications it's clear that ML may be underrepresented in smart lighting and smart parking systems. Additionally, researchers' favorite applications in terms of transportation system's intelligence include optimization of route, smart parking management, and accident/collision detection.

Chapter 2

    Sambhrant Srivastava, Rajkiya Engineering College, Azamgarh, India
    Vijay Kumar, Rajkiya Engineering College, Azamgarh, India
    Saurabh Kumar Singh, Rajkiya Engineering College, Azamgarh, India
    Pankaj Yadav, Rajkiya Engineering College, Azamgarh, India
    Brihaspati Singh, Rajkiya Engineering College, Azamgarh, India
    Amit Bhaskar, Rajkiya Engineering College, Azamgarh, India

Advances in science and technology are making mechatronic systems more common in mechanical engineering. AI is involved in this transition. Artificial intelligence (AI) is computer software that makes decisions on its own. Simulating professionals' intelligent behaviour boosts efficiency and product quality. Artificial intelligence systems have advanced since their creation. These systems are widely used in mechanical and industrial fields for image processing, intelligent perception, pattern recognition, and virtual reality. Automation and AI are common in industry and mechanics. This study examined AI in mechanical disciplines such heat transfer, production, design, and quality control. Research simulations show a variety of artificial intelligence systems that regulate mechanical manufacturing process components. ANNs, DCNN, CNN, fuzzy logic, and other AI are featured. Thus, new products and system development should be expedited. Mechanical engineering component rejections and faults may be eliminated using AI. Optimised systems can produce higher-quality, more expensive items.

Chapter 3

It is important to recognize that a well-run judicial system contributes to the formation of a favorable atmosphere that fosters national growth. The efficient administration of justice is just as important to the court's efficacy as its capacity to be impartial, firm, and fair at all times. Notwithstanding these vital functions of the court, Nigeria's legal system is sometimes unsatisfactory and sluggish moving. People no longer trust the courts because of this, as most people think that justice postponed is justice denied. In recent times, machine learning methods have been used for predictive purposes in several domains. In this work, the authors used 5585 records of precedent rulings from the Supreme Court of Nigeria (SCN) between 1962 and 2022 to construct a prediction model for the categorization of judgments. Primsol Law Pavilion, an independently owned data repository, provided the data that was gathered from. Following data annotation and feature extraction, three classification methods (Decision Tree, Multi-layer Perceptron, and kNN) were used to construct the model. These techniques allowed for the identification of factors that significantly influence assessments, both from the literature and domain experts. The authors also looked at how two different feature extraction strategies, one based on correlation and the other on information, affected the models; the latter proved to be more successful in identifying pertinent characteristics. According to the study's findings, decision trees are the best machine learning algorithm for predicting how appeal cases that are submitted before the SCN would turn out.

Global cyber dangers related to phishing emails have increased dramatically, particularly after the COVID-19 epidemic broke out. Many companies have suffered significant financial losses as a result of this kind of assault. Even though many models have been developed to distinguish between phishing efforts and genuine emails, attackers always come up with new ways to trick their targets into falling for their scams. Many companies have suffered significant financial losses as a result of this kind of assault. Although phishing detection algorithms are being developed, their accuracy and speed in recognizing phishing emails are not up to par right now. Furthermore, the number of phished emails has concerningly increased lately. To lessen the negative effects of such bogus communications, there is an urgent need for more effective and high-performing phishing detection algorithms. Inside the framework of this study, a thorough examination of an email message's email header and content is carried out. A novel phishing detection model is built using the features of sentences that are extracted. The new dimension of sentence-level analysis is introduced by this model, which makes use of K Nearest Neighbor (KNN). Kaggle's well-known datasets were used to both train and evaluate the model. Important performance indicators, including as the F1-measure, precision, recall, and accuracy of 0.97, are used to assess the efficacy of this approach.

Chapter 5

This research chapter aims to provide a comprehensive overview of cancer cases and rates in the various states of the United States. It explores the trends and patterns of cancer incidence and mortality in the country, as well as the factors such as age, sex/gender, type of cancer whether it is lung or breast cancer and its rates and also the factors that contribute to the development and progression of the disease. The chapter reviews the latest statistics on cancer rates mainly breast and lung cancer in different population groups, including age, sex/gender, and geographical location/ different states of USA. By analyzing the data, the project aims to provide insights and predictions related to the occurrence of cancer in the US. The Python code implements visualizations of cancer data for various states in the USA using Pandas and Matplotlib libraries. The dataset is read into a Pandas data frame and various types of visualizations are produced for the cancer data, including scatter plots, and bar graphs. The scatter plot represents the rate of lung and breast cancer in various states of the USA, and the bar graphs represent the total number of breast cancer and lung cancer, as well as the cancer rates in people of different age groups for each state. The visualizations allow for the comparison of cancer rates and total numbers between different states and age groups, aiding in identifying the states with higher cancer rates and potentially identifying any trends or patterns. The chapter concludes by discussing the challenges and opportunities for cancer prevention, early detection, and treatment in the United States, and the implications for public health policy and practice. Potential applications of this analysis include informing strategies for cancer prevention and treatment in different states and age groups. The project could have implications for public health and policy, as well as for advancing the understanding of cancer and its impact on society. Overall, this chapter aims to provide a comprehensive and up-to-date picture of the burden of cancer in the United States and to identify areas for further research and action.

Chapter 6

Detecting changes in a video sequence or still images is a crucial task in the image processing domain, which aims to distinguish moving objects from static ones. This functionality has a lot of applicability in the image processing domain like mostly in the surveillance cameras in organizations both the government and private. This change detection has captured a lot of attention in recent years due to its use and achievement in the domain. In this work, fast spatiotemporal tree filter (FSTF) method is used to enhance the detection results. It combines the features of the local and global filter that makes it efficient and better in comparison to other filters. Experiments demonstrate that the proposed FSTF filter improves the detection results of various foreground detection approaches, ranging from background modeling to machine learning model.

Chapter 7

Industry 4.0 drives automation, efficiency, and data-driven decision-making. Computer vision plays a pivotal role in Industry 4.0, driving innovation, automation, and efficiency across various domains. This book chapter explores the intersection of computer vision and Industry 4.0, highlighting the intelligence and advancements brought by computer vision in modern industrial settings. The ability of computer vision and its intelligence to extract meaningful information from visual data and understand the surrounding environment is highlighted. Insights into the advanced techniques and technologies, challenges and future directions of this rapidly evolving field are provided. Challenges and limitations are addressed with a view of handling complex industrial environments and variability. Insights into future directions, potential disruptions, and transformative effects in Industry 4.0 are provided. The chapter concludes by highlighting possibilities for future research and development to further unlock the potential of computer vision in driving advancements in industrial sectors.

Arunadevi Thirumalraj, K. Ramakrishnan College of Technology,
    Trichy, India
Rakesh Chandrashekar, New Horizon College of Engineering, India
Gunapriya B., New Horizon College of Engineering, India
Prabhu kavin Balasubramanian, SRM Institute of Science and
    Technology, India

Leaf diseases have a detrimental effect on crop production quality in agriculture. In order to improve agricultural sector output, this has led to a greater emphasis on automating the detection of leaf diseases. In recent years, the process of categorising plant leaves using characteristics and machine learning has advanced. Usually, machine learning is used for supervised training of leaf classifiers using a set of data. Plant illnesses negatively impact both the amount and quality of agricultural goods by causing substantial growth and financial losses. Detecting plant diseases in big agricultural fields within a day has emerged as a critical topic of study. Three processes are used in this study to forecast pepper plant diseases (PPD): picture capture, feature selection, and image classification. The Kalman filter is used to remove noise from images before processing. Feature selection becomes important because it effectively solves the issue by eliminating redundant and unnecessary data, cutting down on computation time, improving learning accuracy, and improving comprehension of the model or data. For feature selection, Tom and Jerry optimisation (TJO) is used, and for final classification, the Modified Swin Transform method (MSTNet) is used. Using TJO, MSTNet's hyperparameters are adjusted to ascertain if a leaf is contaminated. On the Plant Village Dataset, experiments are carried out with different parameter measurements. The suggested MSTNet outperforms the accuracy rates of the current models with a 99.2% classification accuracy.

    Vineet Srivastava, Rajkiya Engineering College, Azamgarh, India
    Pramod Kumar Srivastava, Rajkiya Engineering College, Azamgarh, India
    Ashok Kumar Yadav, Rajkiya Engineering College, Azamgarh, India

Online social networks (OSNs) have emerged as the most convenient platforms for transmitting and communicating media, including news and electronic content. It is imperative to develop technology that can mitigate the spread of fake information/ rumors, which badly harm society. This chapter employs an epidemic approach to develop a model for controlling and examining the dissemination of fake information on OSNs. The model is designed in the form of a system of fractional differential equations, exploring the real-world effects of misinformation propagation in OSNs with memory effect. It incorporates the concept of physics-informed neural networks with approximation based on the theory of functional connection and extreme learning machines. The proposed model elucidates the impact of various measures for correcting misinformation and shows how misinformation spreads across different groups. The validity of the suggested OSN model is confirmed through extensive computational analysis and investigation.

    Kannadhasan Suriyan, Study World College of Engineering, India
    NAgarajan R., Gnanamani College of Technology, India

Character recognition is the technique of identifying characters that have been optically processed (OCR). OCR is a method of converting a wide range of texts, PDFs, and digital pictures into an American Standard Code for Information Interchange (ASCII) or other machine-editable format in which the data may be changed or searched. Many applications, such as OCR, document categorization, data mining, and others, have demanded recent improvements in pattern recognition. Document scanners, character recognition, language recognition, security, and bank identification all rely on OCR. There are two kinds of OCR systems: online character recognition and offline character recognition. Online OCR outperforms offline OCR because characters are processed as they are written, avoiding the first step of character identification. Offline OCR is separated into two types: printed and handwritten OCR. Offline OCR is often performed by scanning typewritten or handwritten characters into a binary or grayscale picture for processing by a recognition algorithm. Scanned papers have become more valuable than typical picture files as OCR technology has advanced, converting them into text contents that computers can identify. Over the traditional process of manually retyping, OCR discovers a superior approach of automatically putting data into an electronic database. The most common issue with OCR is segmentation of linked letters or symbols. The accuracy of the OCR is proportional to the input image.

Chapter 11

Brihaspati Singh, National Institute of Technology, Patna, India
Anmesh Kumar Srivastava, National Institute of Technology, Patna, India
Om Prakash, National Institute of Technology, Patna, India

The increasing scarcity of fossil fuel resources has created a significant need for a clean, inexpensive, and sustainable energy source. Biodiesel, a kind of liquid biofuel, has been discovered to mitigate environmental deterioration, improve engine efficiency, and decrease the release of harmful gases. Biodiesel production and usage processes are complicated and nonlinear, requiring rapid and accurate modelling tools for design, optimisation, and monitoring. Machine learning or other forms of artificial intelligence have been found to be a superior method for modelling biodiesel production. This is due to its ability to make accurate predictions, which is inspired by the auto learning and self-improving capabilities of the brain. Uses of machine learning in biodiesel production range from quality prediction and optimisation to monitoring of process conditions and output quantification. Furthermore, the integration of AI-based solutions from Industry 4.0 with human intelligence is crucial in the context of Industry 5.0 for the biodiesel industry to increase production efficiency, guarantee economic viability, and foster sustainability. This combination facilitates the exploration of reaction mechanisms, specifically in the domain of advanced biodiesel production.

Chapter 12

Sabyasachi Pramanik, Haldia Institute of Technology, India

This chapter examined the profound influence of data science and volunteered geographic information (VGI) on the delivery of public services. Volunteered geographic information (VGI), being material created by users, has had a substantial impact on making geographic information accessible to everybody, enabling people to actively engage in the creation and management of data. The incorporation of volunteered geographic information (VGI) into government operations has introduced novel prospects for enhancing service provision in diverse sectors such as education, health, transportation, and waste management. In addition, data science has enhanced VGI by using sophisticated methodologies like artificial intelligence (AI), internet of things (IoT), big data, and blockchain, thereby transforming the whole framework of government service provision. Nevertheless, in order to effectively use VGI in public sector services, it is essential to tackle significant obstacles such as data accuracy, safeguarding, inclusiveness, technical framework, and specialized expertise. The quality of VGI data may be improved by collaborative endeavors including governments, volunteers, and academics.

Preface

In the continually shifting terrain of technology, few developments offer as much promise and potential as machine learning. As Editors, it is with great pleasure that we introduce this comprehensive reference book, *Machine Learning Techniques and Industry Applications*, which delves into the depths of this transformative field. Machine learning stands as a cornerstone in the journey towards emergence of Industry 5.0, offering unprecedented capabilities in harnessing the power of data to drive innovation and efficiency. Machine learning advances daily as the consequence of innovative approaches, enormous datasets, and widely available low-cost processors.

Machine learning has many uses in a wide range of industries, including finance, healthcare, and agriculture. Through the pages of this book, readers will embark on a journey that explores the conceptual underpinnings of machine learning, while also delving into practical methodologies and various applications that empower individuals and organizations to tackle real-world challenges head-on. Our aim with this book is twofold: to equip both novices and seasoned practitioners with the knowledge and tools needed to navigate the complexities of machine learning, and to illuminate the myriad ways in which this technology can be leveraged for societal good. Within these pages, readers will find a rich diversity of topics, and ranging from basic theory to the implementation of machine learning in epidemiology and beyond. Each chapter is meticulously crafted to provide both a theoretical foundation and practical insights, ensuring that readers emerge with a deep understanding of how machine learning can be wielded as a force for positive change.

As Editors, we extend our heartfelt gratitude to all the contributors who have lent their expertise to this endeavor. It is through their collective wisdom, dedication, and hard work that this book has come to fruition, and we are honored to play a part in its realization.

In closing, we invite readers to embark on this journey with us, as we explore the vast and ever-expanding frontier of machine learning. May this book serve as a beacon of knowledge and inspiration, guiding readers towards new horizons in the realm of technology and innovation.

Chapter 1: A Novel Study on IoT and Machine Learning Based Transportation

This chapter delves into how machine learning and the Internet of Things (IoT) come together in smart transportation. The chapter investigates various applications, including route optimization, smart parking management, and accident detection, shedding light on recent advances and potential areas for further research.

Chapter 2: A Review on Application of Artificial Intelligence in Mechanical Engineering: AI in Mechanical Engineering

This chapter examines how AI is incorporated into mechanical engineering, investigating its impact on improving efficiency and product quality in diverse areas such as heat transfer, production, design, and quality control. It delves into AI's role in streamlining processes and enhancing outcomes, highlighting its potential to revolutionize traditional methods in mechanical engineering. Through case studies and analysis, this exploration aims to illustrate the practical applications of AI within the field, showcasing its ability to optimize operations and drive innovation towards more effective and reliable mechanical systems

Chapter 3: An Anticipatory Framework for Categorizing Nigerian Supreme Court Rulings

This chapter introduces a predictive model for Nigerian Supreme Court judgement categorization. It emphasizes the use of legal predictive analytics through the utilization of machine learning and historical precedent data. This model analyses past rulings to improve understanding and predict legal outcomes. The discussion emphasizes the necessity of using technology to improve legal decision-making, including predictive analytics.

Chapter 4: Analysis Model at Sentence Level for Phishing Detection

This chapter tackles the crucial challenge of identifying phishing attempts in emails. It suggests thoroughly analyzing both email content and headers to improve the effectiveness of phishing detection algorithms. By exploring these elements comprehensively, potential solutions are proposed to reduce cyber threats. The focus is on enhancing email security measures through advanced algorithmic approaches, aiming to safeguard users from falling victim to phishing attacks.

Chapter 5: Cancer Prediction Using Graph Database

This chapter provides an in-depth analysis of cancer rates and patterns using graph databases. By examining factors such as age, gender, and geographical location, the chapter aims to contribute to cancer research and prevention efforts.

Chapter 6: Change Detection Based on Binary Mask Enhancement

This chapter discusses a technique for detecting alterations in video sequences and images. It introduces the Fast Spatiotemporal Tree Filter (FSTF) method to improve detection outcomes, with potential uses in surveillance and image processing fields. The method aims to enhance the accuracy of identifying changes in visual data, offering valuable applications in domains requiring efficient monitoring and analysis of dynamic imagery.

Chapter 7: Computer Vision and its Intelligence in Industry 4.0

This chapter delves into how computer vision contributes to innovation in Industry 4.0. It underscores the intelligence and progress facilitated by computer vision in different industrial sectors, while also addressing the hurdles and potential pathways forward.

Chapter 8: Detection of Pepper Plant Leaf Disease Using Tom and Jerry Algorithm with MSTNet

This chapter discusses a method for identifying plant diseases through machine learning techniques. It introduces the Tom and Jerry optimization algorithm combined with MSTNet for precise disease classification, showcasing its potential uses in agriculture.

Chapter 9: Fractional Order Epidemiological Model of Fake Information Mitigation in OSNs with PINN, TFC and ELM

This chapter has an introduction to a model for controlling fake information dissemination on online social networks. Leveraging fractional differential equations and machine learning techniques, the chapter offers insights into mitigating the spread of misinformation online.

Chapter 10: Recent Trends in Pattern Recognition, Challenges, and Opportunities

This chapter delves into the recent strides made in pattern recognition and their practical implementations. Covering a spectrum from character identification to document organization, it examines the wide-ranging applications and obstacles encountered in this domain. By scrutinizing these advancements, the chapter sheds light on the diverse landscape of pattern recognition, offering insights into both its utilization and the challenges that persist in its advancement.

Chapter 11: Review on Machine Learning as Key Technology Enabler for Sustainable Biodiesel Production

This chapter has a discussion on a comprehensive review of machine learning applications in biodiesel production. The chapter highlights the role of machine learning in optimizing production processes, enhancing efficiency, and fostering sustainability in the biodiesel industry.

Chapter 12: The Impact of Data Science and Participated Geographic Metadata on Improving Government Service Deliveries, Prospects and Obstacles

In this chapter, authors explore how data science and volunteered geographic information (VGI) impact government service delivery. We discuss how VGI has the potential to improve service provision in different sectors and examine the challenges and opportunities involved in its implementation.

Each chapter offers valuable insights and contributes to the broader discourse on machine learning and its applications across diverse domains. We hope that readers will find these contributions insightful and inspiring as they navigate the complex landscape of machine learning and its implications for society.

In concluding this preface, we reflect on the breadth and depth of knowledge encapsulated within the chapters of *Machine Learning Techniques and Industry Applications*. This comprehensive reference book stands as a testament to the transformative power of machine learning in shaping the future of various industries and societal domains.

Throughout these chapters, authored by esteemed researchers and practitioners from around the globe, we have explored the multifaceted applications of machine learning. From the optimization of transportation systems to the detection of plant diseases, from enhancing cybersecurity literacy to mitigating the spread of fake information online, each chapter offers unique insights and innovative solutions to real-world challenges.

As editors, we are deeply grateful to all the contributors who have dedicated their expertise and knowledge to this endeavor. It is through their collective efforts that this book has come to fruition, offering a rich tapestry of theoretical foundations, practical methodologies, and insightful case studies.

We believe that this book will serve as a valuable resource for students, academics, researchers, engineers, and practitioners from diverse domain alike, empowering them to navigate the complexities of machine learning and harness its potential for societal good. As we continue to explore the ever-expanding frontier of technology and innovation, may this book inspire readers to embark on their own journey of discovery and contribute to the advancement of machine learning for the betterment of humanity.

With sincere appreciation and anticipation for the impact of this work, we invite readers to delve into the pages of *Machine Learning Techniques and Industry Applications* and join us in shaping the future of technology and society.

Editors:

Pramod Kumar Srivastava
Rajkiya Engineering College Azamgarh, India

Ashok Kumar Yadav
Rajkiya Engineering College Azamgarh, India

Chapter 1
A Novel Study on IoT and Machine Learning–Based Transportation

Vibhor Sharma
iD https://orcid.org/0000-0002-7365-1846
Swami Rama Himalayan University, India

Deepak Srivastava
iD https://orcid.org/0000-0002-7440-8311
Swami Rama Himalayan University, India

Lokesh Kumar
Roorkee Institute of Technology, India

Mohit Payal
Graphic Era Hill University, India

ABSTRACT

Smarter apps and connected devices are now possible because of the proliferation of IoT, which has greatly improved the quality of life in today's urban centers. ML and IoT approaches have been employed in the study of smart transportation, which has attracted a large number of researchers. Smart transportation is viewed as a catch-all word that encompasses a wide range of topics, including optimization of route, parking, street lighting, accident detection, abnormalities on the road, and other infrastructure-related issues. The purpose of this chapter is to examine the state of machine learning (ML) and internet of things (IoT) applications for smart city transport in order to better comprehend recent advances in these fields and to spot any holes in coverage. From the existing publications it's clear that ML may be underrepresented in smart lighting and smart parking systems. Additionally, researchers' favorite applications in terms of transportation system's intelligence include optimization of route, smart parking management, and accident/collision detection.

DOI: 10.4018/979-8-3693-5271-7.ch001

INTRODUCTION

There has been a steady increase in the intelligence, connectivity, and versatility of mobile devices throughout the past decade. The number of internet-enabled devices has increased dramatically since 2008 (Swan, 2012), when it first topped the number of people on Earth]. Smartphones, embedded systems, wireless sensors, and other gadgets are just few examples of how pervasive network connectivity has become in the Internet of Things era. The more gadgets there are, the more information they will gather. In order to further AI, researchers are turning to machine learning (ML) algorithms to create new programmes that analyses data in order to draw inferences and draw conclusions.

Everything that can be connected to the internet is called a "thing" in the IoT. Embedded systems with a central processing unit are commonplace in things, together with physical sensors and actuators. There needs to be communication between machines since physical objects need to collaborate. Short-range wireless technologies include Wi-Fi and Bluetooth whereas long-range wireless technologies (Vangelista et al., 2015). Since there are so many uses for Internet of Things devices, it's crucial that they don't cost too much. Data collection, M2M connectivity, and even some data pre-processing may also be required of IoT devices, depending on the use case. When designing or purchasing an IoT device, it is essential to strike a balance between price, processing capability, and energy usage. There is no separating the Internet of Things (IoT) from "big data," as IoT gadgets are always collecting and exchanging vast volumes of information. Therefore, methods of processing, storing, and analyzing massive volumes of data (Ibrahim et al., 2016; Naik, 2017) are frequently included into an IoT infrastructure. The use of an IoT platform like Kaa, Thingsboard, DeviceHive, Thingspeak, or Mainflux to facilitate M2M communication using protocols including MQTT, AMQP, STOMP, CoAP, XMPP, and HTTP has become widespread in IoT systems (Naik, 2017). Monitoring, node management, data analysis, storage, data-driven programmable rules, and more are all part of IoT systems. In some use cases, data processing must occur locally on IoT devices rather than at a centralized node, as in the "cloud computing" architecture. So, a new computer paradigm called "edge computing" is developed (Satyanarayanan, 2017) as computation moves to the terminal nodes of networks. Although convenient, low-end devices may not be up to the task of doing complex computations. "Fog nodes" (Tarek, 2018) provided the solution. Fog nodes enable IoT devices to manage massive volumes of data by offering networking, processing, and storage capabilities. The data is then stored in the cloud, where it may be enhanced, evaluated using various machine learning techniques, and shared with other devices; this process ultimately results in the development of new smart apps. In the so-called "smart city," various Internet of Things applications have already surfaced. Smart healthcare, smart transportation, smart monitoring of environmental condition, smart supply chain management, and a smart surveillance system are among the most essential uses (Talari et al., 2017). Figure 1 properly depicts the core components of the IoT infrastructure as they have been utilized in the great majority of applications, despite the fact that much work remains in the area of standardization of IoT design and technology.

Figure 1. Key elements of machine learning-based IoT infrastructure

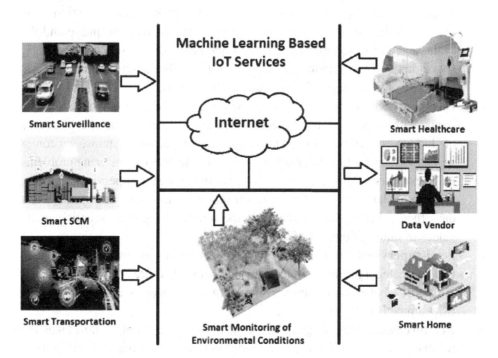

Machine Learning

There is nothing new about machine learning (ML). Artificial Intelligence (AI) and Machine Learning (ML) are closely connected (AI). Through machine learning, feasibility comes to AI. Computers can perform tasks like classification, grouping and prediction using machine learning. For utilizing a variety of algorithms and statistical models to examine sample data in order to preserve the learning process, training is given to systems that are based on historical data. An ML algorithm seeks to identify a link between the features and certain output values known as labels in the sample data, which are often described by quantifiable qualities (Mohammed et al., 2016). It's then utilized to find patterns or make conclusions based on new data that was learned during training. Regression, classification, clustering, and association rule determination can all benefit from ML. Algorithms for machine learning (ML) may be divided into four types based on how they are best learned:

- **Supervised Learning:** In order to forecast things like the weather, people's life experiences, and population increase, supervised learning uses regression techniques like Linear Regression and Random Forest. Many algorithms are used in supervised learning to categories problems like fingerprint recognition, speech recognition, medical diagnosis, and identity theft detection. The two stages that make up supervised learning are the training phase and the evaluation phase. In order to train a model, labelled data sets are necessary. Algorithms are programmes that attempt to predict a set of output values from a given collection of input data. (Kubat, 2017).
- **Unsupervised Learning:** Unsupervised learning has the potential to solve issues with dimensionality reduction, feature extraction, and the discovery of hidden structures. In addition, recommendation systems, customer segmentation, and targeted marketing are all examples of clustering problems that supervised learning is used to address. In contrast to supervised learning, there are no labels to use. These algorithms are designed to find trends in test data, then either group that data into meaningful categories or anticipate its values in future (Kubat, 2017).
- **Semi-supervised Learning:** Both of the preceding types can be found in this sub-category. Both labeled and unlabeled data are used in this study. A part of labeled data improves on unsupervised learning in a similar way (Mohammed et al., 2016).
- **Reinforcement Learning:** In this type of learning, an algorithm takes the result of one calculation as an input for the next, and so on, until the optimal solution is found. This process is repeated until the problem is solved. Later we'll talk about how ANNs and Deep Learning utilize this method of learning. Some of the most popular applications of reinforcement learning in AI games include robot navigation and real-time judgment (Kubat, 2017).

The computational intensity and speed of a specific approach should be taken into account while employing ML techniques. Which machine learning algorithm is used depends on the type of application being developed? There must be an algorithm quick enough to follow changes in input data and generate a timely result if real-time analysis is required.

Machine Learning and IoT

Through the IoT, inanimate things are able to communicate with one another, share knowledge, and continuously collect massive volumes of data. There are several use cases for which data received by IoT devices may be used to trigger predetermined actions. IoT devices, aside from being able to gather data and communicate with one another, must also be capable of functioning independently. They need to be able to evaluate their findings in context and form conclusions accordingly. This is why someone came up with the term "Cognitive Internet of Things" (CIoT) (Xenakis et al., 2019). Smart apps that can allocate resources, communicate without human intervention, and run themselves automatically via the Internet of Things are also essential. Machine learning techniques are extremely useful for Internet of Things applications and infrastructure. Big data cannot be handled by traditional database systems. Massive amounts of structured and unstructured data necessitate a one-of-a-kind framework and specialized methods for analysis (Madden, 2012).

IoT Based Transportation

Using data from the users' mobile devices (Dogra & Kaur, 2022), or with side units placed in specified locations on the road (Lidkea et al., 2019), applications try to estimate traffic congestion and propose optimal route options to minimize traveling times, and therefore reduce car emissions and energy consumption. Using cameras (Wu et al., 2007), or other wireless sensors like magnetic field or IR sensors (Celesti et al., 2019), researchers have proposed new parking reservation systems that allow maximizing a parking lot's availability and capacity and minimizing the searching time. Finally, the IoT M2M communication option has given the opportunity to develop vehicle to vehicle communication and vehicle social networks, where vehicles can exchange useful information with each other and give many more possibilities for new applications (Quadri et al., 2022).

MACHINE LEARNING AND IOT BASED TRANSPORTATION

Because of the size and scope of today's smart cities, transport is at the forefront of academic inquiry due to the myriad challenges it tackles on a daily basis. Machine learning (ML) and the Internet of Things (IoT) may work together to resolve these problems. This analysis is assessing not only the current state of research in one subfield of smart transport but also its breadth. This review thus focuses on cutting-edge studies that employ IoT and/or ML methods to tackle issues in smart transportation (including but not limited to route optimization, parking, lighting, accident detection/prevention, road irregularities, and infrastructure).

Machine Learning Algorithms

In this part, we'll talk about ML-based algorithms:

Ensemble Learning Algorithm

Multiple classifiers are used to solve a problem and their findings are combined in an ensemble approach. Because ensemble techniques are able to enhance weak classifiers into strong classifiers, they are a major benefit. For example, systems can employ weak classifiers that are easy to build and nevertheless have the quality of a powerful classifier (Zhou, 2012). According to Ghosh et al. (2017), a framework for detecting driver's awareness is being developed to reduce road accidents. A camera mounted in front of the driver collects the input data, which is used to track the driver's eye and head movements. Then, the Adaptive Boosting (AdaBoost) method is used to identify Human HAAR features from an extracted integral picture. Combined with other weak classifiers, AdaBoost creates a more robust classifier. Because it can do simultaneous analysis on all of the properties of the research, AdaBoost is a very useful tool. The strong classifiers were organized by the authors into a cascade, with each classifier receiving the features that were processed by the classifier that came before it in the cascade. The Random Forest (RF) method as well as other related ensemble algorithms are becoming increasingly prominent. When working with a large number of decision trees to solve issues involving regression and classification as weak learners, the final output is determined by using the mean or the most sampled values from each tree. When using single decision trees, over-fitting is a much more significant issue than when using RF. Four different models were constructed by the authors of Hou et al. (2015) in order to estimate both current and future traffic patterns in construction zones. The objective of Soultana et al. (2020) is to locate flaws in the pavement. A suite of feature selection and machine learning techniques, along with accelerometer sensors and Arduino microcontrollers, make this possible. The feature selection procedure (PSO) makes use of Particle Swarm Optimization (PSO), Ranker, and the Greedy Algorithm. There is a comparison made between the k-Nearest Neighbor (k-NN), Random Forest (RF), and Support Vector Machine (SVM) algorithms. Three variables were adjusted in the RF algorithm's tuning process. Adjusting factors such as the number of iterations, the seed, and the characteristics can produce the desired outcome. Correctly Classified Rate (CCR) was utilized to evaluate the algorithms. All of the classifiers performed at a rate of 99.9 percent accuracy. The authors of Bokaba et al. (2022) use the RF approach to detect road accidents while contrasting SVM with ANN. In order to gather information for a traffic simulation, SUMO (Behrisch et al., 2011) is employed.

Bayesian Algorithms

Directed acyclic graphs (DAGs) are used to build probability distributions for sets of random variables. To assign labels to new data, the model may be computed with the training data as inputs. All the variables and their connections may be represented in a single Bayesian network. In a Bayesian network, the presence or absence of some variables might provide light on the condition of others (Friedman et al., 1997).

According to Fusco et al. (2015), The Bayesian Network Seasonal Autoregressive Integrated Moving Average- (BN-SARIMA) is a useful tool for making short-term traffic forecasts. The results are predicted using ARIMA models within a Bayesian network. Predictions are made (I) using the change from one point in time to the next in a time series. Using the MA, it is further proved that regression errors are linear mixtures of earlier errors. Two more deep learning algorithms are compared to the BN-SARIMA method. Two primary databases are mined for information on vehicle locations and speeds. For this purpose, we employed the RMSE, MAE, and MAPE measures to compare the various strategies.

Markov Models

In this model, the distribution of the value of a variable at the previous state is all that's needed to calculate the value at the next stage in the chain. The difference between a Markov chain and a Hidden Markov Model is in how the latter makes use of "hidden states" to achieve optimal performance. Each state has its own associated probability function. Each HMM may be characterized by its number of hidden states, its number of system outputs, and its probability distribution of state transitions (Rabiner, 1990). In Zantalis et al. (2019), researchers attempt to solve the issue of motion intention inference by facilitating shared vehicle awareness. Cooperative sensing enables autonomous trigger actions by increasing the vehicles' perceptual range, enhancing perceptual quality, and decreasing response time. To do this, a Coupled Hidden Markov Model (CHMM) is implemented in its rudimentary version. The model is trained using the recorded velocities of a succession of vehicles. Coupled HMMs excel where solo HMMs fail, such as when several processes are concurrently operating. In order to create a parking space detection system, the authors of Wu et al. (2007) use a Support Vector Machine (SVM) and a Markov Random Field (MRF) approach. The authors of this study begin with footage from parking garage surveillance cameras. The first step in further processing photographs is feature extraction. The next step is to use SVM to categories parking spots as either free or occupied; next, MRF is used to settle any discrepancies between the two systems, raising accuracy by 6.84 percent.

Decision Tree

A decision tree is a structure that deals with classification jobs and represents a decision process with a number of alternative outcomes. There are multiple nodes in a decision tree, each of which is either a class or a condition that may be used to push a testing item to a class. In solving classification issues, this is a nave method is used. At each branch of the decision tree, a new sub-process of classification is performed, dividing the primary work into smaller sub-tasks (Utgoff, 1989). When it comes to forecasting traffic congestion, decision trees are examined with four other ML algorithms (RF, MLP, SVM and Logistic Regression) in Devi (2017). A technique called Regression Tree was tried in Hou et al. (2015) for predicting short- and long-term work zone traffic. This type of tree is quite similar to a decision tree, except that it uses numerical values instead of binary ones. To find a regression equation for the dependent variable, a regression tree is utilized. The squared regression error is then determined in a binary recursive partitioning. The branch with the fewest sums of squared errors is chosen for further analysis. The regression tree performed worse at traffic forecasts than the FF-NN or the RF in the aforementioned study.

Clustering

To categorize components into distinct groups based on their commonalities or identified patterns, clustering are an unsupervised approach. In clustering, training a model requires labels, but there are none available, unlike classification approaches. Short-term traffic forecasts may be made using the Fuzzy C-Means clustering algorithm proposed in Kanoh (2005). K-Means is widely used as a clustering method. K-Means is a clustering technique that uses the mean squared error of the data to determine how to break it into groups of k. To achieve this goal, Dogra and Kaur (2022) attempts to optimize the traffic network architecture by estimating the ideal number and placement of processing centers for a variety of providers. The authors use K-Means to calculate supplier distances from central locations in an effort to cut expenditures. To prepare the real-time GIS data for K-Means clustering, a Deep Belief Network method is employed. The DBN is what really locates the initial k values for the k-Means. Accelerometer data from mobile devices is recommended by the authors of Mamun (2017) for detecting road imperfections including bumps, speed bumps, and potholes. The information is sent to the closest fog node for processing. K-Means clustering sorts the data and finds cutoffs that separate unusual roads from normal ones. A similar method is proposed by the authors of Nguyen et al. (2019) to identify road defects.

Artificial Neural Network

ANNs are distinguished by their structure and the way in which they learn. A neural network is made up of neurons connected by weighted connections (Figure 2). Each neuron in each layer of a neural network stands in for a different input variable, and each neuron in each layer of a neural network stands in for a different output label. Between the apparent levels, there might be a concealed one (or many). Since the connections between neurons in a Feed Forward Neural Network (FF-NN) do not loop, it is the simplest type of artificial neural network (ANN).

Figure 2. Example of artificial neural network with interconnected layers

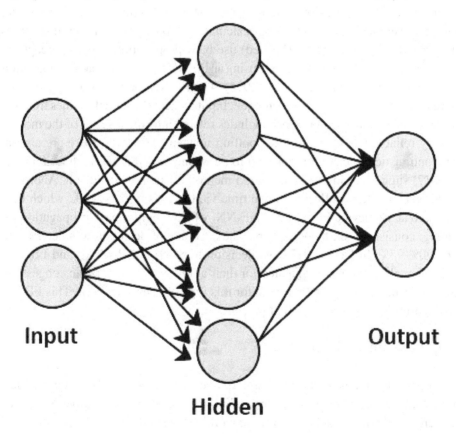

Input   **Output**

Hidden

The proposed FF-NN approach appeared to be less effective, although it did show a little improvement over the other NN algorithm at both the 10- and 15-minute intervals. As was mentioned before, the authors of Hou et al. (2015) looked at four methods for estimating traffic flow in construction zones in the short term. The Multilayer FF-NN method has already been examined. The FF-NN employs a nonlinear function to integrate the input variables in order to extract features. Traffic flow predictions are then made using this nonlinear function. This approach is sometimes referred to as "multilayer NN" since it employs more layers to more accurately represent the calculated properties. According to Simon (2015), an FF-NN is used to forecast travel times. Traffic data, including velocity, travel time, and volume, is collected by roadside sensors. The traffic data is then clustered, and an ANN model is built for each cluster using unsupervised learning techniques. The ANN's FF-NN architecture relies on back-propagation training and a single hidden layer to bring down predicted error (Werbos, 1990). To determine an overall travel time, we sum the differences in travel times between clusters. The back-propagation technique is used for supervised training of an FF-NN, and it employs gradient descent. Using the weighted values, the ANN calculates output error and then distributes it negatively. Neural networks (layered) use back-propagation, just as perceptron. Predicting traffic accidents in real time using an FF-NN trained with back-propagation is also explored in Ozbayoglu et al. (2016). The FF-NN method is analyzed using Regression Trees and the K-NN technique. Input data for the models comes from the road sensors' historical data, which includes related information. All of the models are very reliable when it comes to spotting mishaps. However, there are a great many optimistic forecasts that turn out to be wrong. Another research (Allouch et al., 2017) suggests using an ANN-based method for pothole detection. Android's accelerometer data is collected in real time via the Encog framework, which then feeds it to an on-device FF-NN. The FF-NN, which employs back-propagation for training, consists of six hidden layers. The accuracy of detection was determined to be 90%-95%. In Devi (2017), the decision tree, RF, MLP, SVM, and Logistic Regression algorithms are evaluated for their ability to forecast traffic congestion. Multi-layer perceptron is an acronym for this type of neural network. This FF-NN is composed of numerous layers of perceptron.

Deep Learning Algorithms

Methods of reinforcement learning that can process large amounts of unstructured data are typically classified as "Deep Learning." High-powered graphics processing units are increasingly handling Deep learning workloads. Similar to ANNs, deep neural networks may be built via deep learning. For neural networks, "deep" describes the number of hidden layers that are present. In deep learning, the number of layers is proportional to the number of calculated features. In deep learning, the features are estimated automatically, therefore feature extraction and calculation are unnecessary. More and more options for network topologies are becoming accessible in deep learning as the field develops (LeCun et al., 2015).

The application of CNNs allows for the completion of deep learning. In the academic literature, CNNs are commonly used for image recognition. One crucial aspect of CNN is the reuse of filters across several neurons. The transfer function for each neuron is the sum of its inputs that is weighted. Negative values are converted to zero using non-linear layers that follow the convolutional layer. Then, the number of dimensions is cut down using subsampling layers. Before the input data reaches the FC layer, it is classified by a Multi-Layer Perceptron (MLP). Using smart cameras as input, the scientists employ a Raspberry Pi 2 as a controller to run convolutional neural networks (CNN). On the smart cameras, CNN is implemented using a reduced version of the AlexNet model (Krizhevsky et al., 2012). CNRPark-EXT, a dataset generated by the authors, and PKLot, a well-known dataset, are both used in the assessment (Almeida et al., 2015), with accuracy rates of 98.27% and 90.13 percent, respectively. In addition, a comprehensive study of CNNs and Deeper CNNs (DCNNs)-based deep learning approaches was published in Gopalakrishnan (2018). The author analyzed a number of research that focused on the identification of pavement distress using deep learning. Photos from Google Street View, smartphone images, and 3D models generated using specialist gear are all used in the evaluated research (Daniels, 2005). For example the GPR images, which are constructed using ground penetrating radar (GPR) (Daniels, 2005).

Authors in Kwon et al. (2018) propose the creation of a smart car blind-spot detection system. Based on Fully Connected Networks (FCN), the suggested technique claims to outperform CNNs in real-time image processing. Three cameras positioned on the outside of an automobile would provide the input for the suggested system. Similar to a CNN, an FCN lacks convolution. Each neuron in the previous layer is linked to every node in the next layer, which is called "fully connected." Based on Adam Optimizer and Relu activations, this technique is being researched.

The tool in Dogra and Kaur (2022) is a real-time traffic network assignment tool, as stated before. Deep Belief Network (DBN) pre-processes input data and sets up clustering centers for K-Means, which is used to conduct the necessary clustering in this study, The Restricted Boltzmann machine (RBM) is used to create the two hidden layers of the DBN approach, which makes training simple. RBM is an example of an unsupervised DBN layer. A network like this contains connections between the levels, but not within each layer. Layer by layer, DBNs may also be trained greedily. To aid in the development of digital maps, DBNs are also employed in Wang et al. (2017). This is done by automatically detecting street components like traffic lights and roundabouts. Only GPS data from the user is used to populate the system's database.

Final classifiers are employed after the DBN training to ultimately split input data into classes. Recall is 0.89 and precision is 0.88, according to the findings of the study. Using deep learning, the authors in Ba (2015) were able to sequentially classify several items in an image input. On Google Street view photos, a model dubbed Deep Recurrent Attention Model (DRAM) outperforms CNN in multiple digit recognition, according to the results of the research. While the finest CNNs are quite computationally intensive, DRAM appears to be less so. A Stacked Auto Encoder (SAE) is recommended in Yisheng et al. (2014) to enable large data-based traffic flow forecasts. A Logistic Regression method is employed on top of the SAE to anticipate traffic flow. Unsupervised learning is used to train network layers like Auto Encoding (AE) Auto Encoders, which are fine-tuned utilizing Back Propagation at the end. The MRSE, MRE, and MAE indices are used to evaluate the proposed technique. We may conclude from these data that SAE beats the other comparison methods. An unsupervised reconstruction of the input data is the goal of AEs, which are layered structures. It is possible to stack Auto Encoders, where the output of one is used as input for another. Unsupervised layer-wise training is used to train the AEs until the entire stack has been trained. The weights of the network are then updated using a technique called Back Propagation, which relies on labeled data (Liu et al., 2018).

According to the findings of a study (Ryder & Wortmann, 2017) on traffic accident hot zones, an Inception Neural Network was used to assist in the classification of images. Accident occurrence and location are linked by Swiss Road Authority (FEDRO) data, according to an investigation. As a result, an inception neural network (TensorFlow Inception v3) is trained using Google Maps photos and FEDRO data to identify accident-prone locations. The data reveal that the location–accident connection hypothesis is correct, with a 30 percent accuracy rate. An advantage of the inception network over the CNN is that it is less computationally intensive. The input data is convolutional using a variety of filters. An Inception Network is formed by stacking layers of Inception. Auxiliary classifiers are included in the structure of the inception network. On the inception layers, these structures are employed to compute an auxiliary loss (Szegedy et al., 2015).

Classification of new test data is done using instance-based algorithms, which compare new test data directly to training data. Similarity comparisons are made and the results are placed into a classification function (Aha et al., 1991). It's possible for instance-based algorithms to become memory-intensive as the number of training examples grows.

As discussed in this paper, k-Nearest Neighbor (as opposed to an FF-NN or Regression Tree) is employed in Ozbayoglu et al. (2016) to make real-time autonomous accident detection between the two algorithms. k-NN is based on the idea that comparable data should have the smallest distance from one other. The appropriate k factor for categorizing data is selected by running k-NN many times on the test data. Authors in Soultana et al. (2020) introduced us to the k-NN technique, which uses accelerometer data and algorithms such as k-Nearest Neighbor (k-NN), RF, and SVM to detect irregularities in road surfaces. Finally, in Wang et al. (2017), a DBN-based solution to the challenge of automatic identification of street features was demonstrated.

Regression Analysis

Regression analysis techniques aim to analyses connections between three or more variables. The goal of these models is to represent the interdependencies between the parameters. The results of the system are used as both a dependent and a response variable. It is feasible to determine the associations between the dependent and independent variables (regressors) by employing a regression model. Prediction techniques for gridlock from Devi (2017) are already familiar. Decision Trees (RF), Multi-Layer Perceptron, and Support Vector Machines are the four methods that may be employed in place of Logistic Regression. Logistic Regression performed better than the other methods in this investigation due to the time-dependent nature of the input data.

Non-Probabilistic Approach

There are probabilistic and non-probabilistic approaches to classification problems. Non-probabilistic approaches are often selected when probabilities have no bearing on the classification of the data. An alternative solution may be found by taking into account other factors aside from the problem type. Working with structured data makes non-probabilistic classification useful. Another crucial factor to examine is whether the classification task requires cluster creation or assignment. For example, in Soultana et al. (2020), we saw the comparison of three different methods for finding irregularities in road surfaces: k-NN, RF, and Support Vector Machine (SVM). With a CCR Rate of above 99 percent, linear SVM and the other two classifiers excelled in this test. SVM is a binary classifier that uses a hyper-plane to best segregate labeled data. Hyper-plane must have a maximum distance from both classes' datasets to be effective. Support vectors refer to the data points closest to the hyper-plane, which are important in determining the hyper-plane's orientation and location. The challenge of detecting traffic accidents has also been handled by SVM in Bokaba et al. (2022). Comparisons were made between the SVM algorithm and the Artificial Neural Network and the Random Forest method. In terms of

Specificity, the SVM performed better than the RF, but had the worst accuracy of the three methods. According to studies on traffic congestion forecasts, SVM is the last strategy discovered. An MLP and a decision tree were tested against it, as was an RF as well as a Logistic Regression. When compared to the other algorithms, only the Logistic Regression came out on top of SVM. It was previously mentioned that the MRF technique might be used to rectify SVM classification conflicts in the study on a parking spot identification system (Wu et al., 2007). The standard binary SVM has been modified for the sake of this study. It is possible to create a multi-class SVM classifier by using a one versus one technique. Using picture patches as input, SVM tries to categorize the observed parking spots into eight different categories that it can consider. As a Radial Basis Function (RBF) implementation, the SVM kernel function has been adopted. In Almeida et al. (2015), HD cameras will be placed around parking lots to gather parking lot photographs for use in a dataset (PKLot). To gauge the dataset's usefulness, we used a support vector machine classifier. Local Binary Patterns (LBP) and Local Phase Quantization (LPQ) were used as texture-based features. It was found that the SVM problem was best fitted by a Gaussian kernel. We evaluated the precision of the calculations based on the OER. Two different SVM variations are used in Wang et al. (2017). The purpose of this research is to develop an autonomous system for identifying different types of roadway infrastructure. A classifier is used to divide the components into subgroups for further examination once they have been extracted using a Deep Belief Network. To complement the success of the K-Nearest Neighbor (k-NN), SVMs were also used.

Different Applications in Smart Transportation

We explore and detail the Smart Transportation problems they solve in this section. We'll go through six major Smart Transportation problems that have been addressed with the help of Internet of Things technologies and machine learning algorithms. Table 2 details whether or not an ML strategy was used in each study across the six previously listed areas.

The ML-supported approaches have been thoroughly addressed in the preceding paragraphs. In order to prevent duplication, we will only mention these methods in the appropriate category and go into further detail about the non-ML alternatives.

Optimization of Route

Finding the least crowded path to a specific location is one use of route optimization. Getting people where they need to go faster and with fewer emissions is a double win when it comes to traffic congestion (Lidkea et al., 2019). IoT-based techniques to route optimization have been actively studied in the academic community.

Table 1. ML strategy used

No	ITS Application	References-ML	References-No ML
1	Route Optimization-Navigation	(Al-Fuqaha et al., 2015; Devi, 2017; Dogra & Kaur, 2022; Fusco et al., 2015; Hou et al., 2015; Simon, 2015; Yisheng et al., 2014)	(Barth, 2009; Chang et al., 2013; Distefano et al., 2017; Fan et al., 2017; Lidkea et al., 2019; Tafidis et al., 2017)
2	Parking	(Acharya et al., 2018; Almeida et al., 2015; Wu et al., 2007)	(Araujo et al., 2017; Aydin et al., 2017; Gupta et al., 2017; Rizvi et al., 2018; Saarika et al., 2017; Shi et al., 2017)
3	Lights		(Jia et al., 2018; Kokilavani & Malathi, 2017; Tripathy et al., 2017)
4	Accident Detection	(Ba, 2015; Bokaba et al., 2022; Ghosh et al., 2017; Kwon et al., 2018; Ozbayoglu et al., 2016; Ryder & Wortmann, 2017; Wang et al., 2017; Zantalis et al., 2019)	(Celesti et al., 2018)
5	Road Anomalies	(Allouch et al., 2017; Gopalakrishnan, 2018; Mamun, 2017; Nguyen et al., 2019; Soultana et al., 2020)	
6	Infrastructure		(Chowdhury et al., 2018; Geetha & Cicilia, 2017; Quadri et al., 2022)

According to Al-Fuqaha et al. (2015), a V2V connection and an MDP algorithm were employed for group routing in order to reduce congestion. When optimizing the traffic network configuration, using k-Means and DBN together is favored in Dogra and Kaur (2022). Authors in Fusco et al. (2015) handled short-term traffic forecasting, and there are a variety of methods to choose from, including the BN-SARIMA, FF-NN, and NARX models. Authors in Hou et al. (2015) compared the performance of four ML methods: RF, baseline predictor, regression tree, and an FF-NN for short-term and long-term traffic forecasts. There's another method used in Simon (2015) to estimate total journey time: an FF-NN trained using BP. The authors in Devi (2017) compared the Logistic Regression with SVM, a decision tree, an RF, and an MLP technique to forecast traffic congestion. Finally, Yisheng et al. (2014) uses a Stacked Auto Encoder technique to produce traffic flow forecasts based on huge data.

A swarm intelligence method for route planning is used in Distefano et al. (2017) to investigate the potential of Mobile Crowd-Sensing for Intelligent Transportation Systems. They use an algorithm called Ant Colony Optimization that uses crowd-sensing (MoCSACO). Users will communicate with one other and utilize the information they get to choose less crowded pathways, just how ants follow pheromone patterns while hunting for food. IoT technology may be used to help route optimization in a novel way, according to Lidkea et al. (2019). SERSUs (Scalable Enhanced Road Side Units) work in conjunction with an MCC (MCC). There are a variety of sensors and components in the SERSU that allow it to keep tabs on things like traffic and pollution levels, as well as communicate data back to the MCC over the 4G network. Through data analysis, the MCC modifies speed restrictions and suggests other routes to SERSU users based on factors such as traffic, weather, and pollution levels. Congestion on the roads would ease, and accidents brought on by bad weather would be avoided.

Improved route planning using VANETs is shown in Chang et al. (2013). The writers devise a mobile navigation software that takes into account current traffic conditions and recommends the most efficient path to take based on time saved or fuel saved. Google Maps traffic data is also acquired for routes where VANET data is unavailable. Users are given an option that takes into account traffic conditions on both networks. The authors of Tafidis et al. (2017) use crowdsourced information and Google's 'popular times' function to investigate whether or not traffic congestion and fuel emissions are related. For this research, we employ GNSS data loggers installed in vehicles and cameras placed along certain roadways to collect traffic data. Emissions are predicted using the VSP model and Google Maps' top-performing time series data. Results show a correlation between crowd-sourced data on "popular times" and emission levels; nevertheless, further data calibration is required, as is an adaptive learning system to evaluate future circumstances. When it comes to creating innovative new goods and services, Google was one of the first corporations to fully leverage the power of crowd sourcing.

You can download Google Maps for free and use it on any current mobile device. GPS, accelerometer, and gyroscope sensors are built into smart phones and other mobile devices. To help commuters navigate their way across the city, Google introduced a new service for 2009 (Barth, 2009).

Finally, in Fan et al. (2017), crowd sourcing route planning is used for the last mile to a destination. Using a basic technique like shortest path or shortest time often results in an inaccurate final mile, according to the authors. A more precise guidance would be provided by locals who could discuss their driving habits around various places, which would help with the last portion of the route A smart phone application (CrowdNavi) is used in the study, which makes use of crowd sourcing to gather data and provide recommendations for the final mile of a journey. Identifying the last portion of the program is an essential feature. Google Maps and crowd data are used in the first section, and landmark scoring is used in the last section to compute crowd density.

Smart Parking

In order to keep track of the parking lot's availability, parking applications are built, which include reservation choices for users, as well as parking detection and warning systems. Several Internet of Things (IoT) sensors have been employed to detect and transmit information on the presence of a vehicle in a parking area. Image data may also be used to discover free parking spaces by applying ML algorithms to the data. Data from smart parking lot cameras is used by the researchers in Acharya et al. (2018) to identify free parking spaces. SVM and MRF algorithms are used to analyze parking lot photos in Wu et al. (2007). Finally, Almeida et al. (2015) creates the PKLot dataset, which is then put to the test with an SVM algorithm.

In Saarika et al. (2017), the authors developed a smart parking system that included an IoT-enabled parking lot and a smart signboard to communicate relevant information. The parking lot will collect data on available parking spots through ultrasonic sensors and a WiFi module, and then transmit that information to a remote server. You may now find out if there are any open parking spots by using either the digital sign or a smartphone app. The major purpose of the signboard's informative display is to provide important data such as parking availability, weather, and driving distances to specified locations.

The authors of claim that an ultrasonic sensor installed in each parking spot indicates whether or not it is currently occupied (Gupta et al., 2017). The sensor gathers data through Bluetooth and transmits it to a cloud server microcontroller i.e. NODMCU ESP8266. Communication is achieved using the MQTT protocol. The ThingSpeak Internet of Things platform hosted on a cloud server offers management and monitoring tools for the service's users. Customers may download an Android app that facilitates parking spot reservations and payment automation.

In Aydin et al. (2017), the authors propose a modular smart parking system composed of both physical and digital components. The equipment employs magnetic sensors to identify the parked automobiles, and a gateway device on the roadside collects and transmits the information to a server somewhere. The app's primary feature is a free parking lot locator map for its users. To do this, a genetic algorithm is used to pinpoint the nearest open time slot to the user's present position. Our concept of ML excludes genetic algorithms since their core functionality is optimization. In Shi et al. (2017), we get a detailed explanation of a smart parking application. The system is comprised of both hardware, such as sensors and microcontrollers embedded in parking spots, and software, such as a cloud server, mobile app, and payment processor. Geomagnetic vehicle detectors in parking lots fitted with a BC95-B5 NB-IoT module scan for cars and report their locations to a central database.

Another method of intelligent parking (ASPIRE) is presented in Rizvi et al. (2018) with the Agent-Oriented Smart Parking Recommendation System. Through communication with a "Local Agent," users of the ASPIRE parking reservation system can specify details about their parking needs, such as the maximum amount of time they can spend walking to their destination and the area in which they would want to park. A cloud-based software agent will prioritize parking options and generate a prioritized list. The Local Agent will get in touch with the consumer to let them choose their preferred parking location. The parking recommendation system uses the Analysis Hierarchy Process (AHP) to evaluate complex choices. RFID scanners are set at the parking lot's entrance in order to track and record the vehicles that enter and leave the lot. Vehicles should have RFID tags installed in order to simplify identification.

Over 96% reliability was discovered in an analysis of smart parking systems (Araujo et al., 2017). The ultrasonic sensors in the system are powered by an ESP8266 controller with built-in WiFi. A REST API is used for the data exchange between parking sensors and a private cloud server. The FIWARE IoT platform's Orion Broker is in charge of managing sensor registration and availability. Mobile-friendly interfaces are built on top of the existing application layer.

Smart Street Lights

We consider SSL to include smart street lighting, which is a critical component of any smart city. Smart lights have the potential to reduce energy consumption and offer dynamic functionality and control. The authors of Jia et al. (2018) built an IoT-based SSL solution. The components of a smart street light include a light sensor, an infrared sensor, a global positioning system, and a wireless communication module. As a consequence, the lights are able to recognize crowded areas and dynamically alter their light output to ensure the safety of pedestrians while reducing energy consumption in high-traffic areas. The GPS can let a centralized system track the lights and respond more quickly to a broken lamp's maintenance needs. The NB-IoT network is used for the SSL and management system's two-way communication. Fog nodes, the backbone of the system, regularly check in on the status of the lights in a network. SSLs not only allow for automated processes, but also allow for remote management using an already existing administration platform. A similar but less complicated approach to smart lighting is presented in Kokilavani and Malathi (2017). In this approach, a microcontroller in the form of a Raspberry Pi is used to link the lamp's light sensor, infrared sensor, and infrared light emitting diode together. The sun's rising and setting will be detected by the light sensors, which will then trigger on/off signals to be sent to the light fixture. In addition, vehicles and people may be detected by the lights, and the lighting adjusted accordingly to save power use. Finally, in Tripathy et al. (2017), the authors propose a smart lighting system in which each lamp post acts as a WiFi hotspot, transmitting collected data to a centralized website. There will be significant energy savings since the lights will turn on/off or dim based on their proximity to other objects in the room. In order to safeguard citizens during emergencies, assess current environmental conditions, and broaden the utility of a regular lamp post, they will be equipped with cameras and environmental monitoring sensors.

Prevention/ Detection of Accident

Accident detection and prevention is essential in any city or smart transport zone because it has the potential to save lives through proactive measures. Drivers who are able to concentrate on the road ahead are less likely to cause accidents. The driver can be given ample time to react to a potentially dangerous situation thanks to the assistance of an accident-avoidance system. Accident detection can help reduce the frequency and severity of accidents and traffic bottlenecks by pinpointing accident hotspots and actual occurrences in the real-time traffic system. The application of ML to the problem of predicting and advising drivers on how to avoid road accidents has shown to be successful.

The authors of Zantalis et al. (2019) created a system for cooperative vehicle perception that use a CHMM approach to ensure that information is communicated among cars in a timely way in order to avert accidents. Ozbayoglu et al. (2016) analyzes data from road sensors using an FF-NN, a Regression Tree, and the k-NN algorithms to identify real-time autonomous accidents. V2V communication, in conjunction with the usage of an RF technique as opposed to an SVM and an ANN, is employed for road accident detection (Bokaba et al., 2022). Kwon et al. (2018) employs an innovative way to identify things in the blind spot of smart cars by employing an FCN algorithm. Because it can aid with multiple item recognition from picture data, the DRAM approach established in Ba (2015) can also be employed for road accident detection. In the study Ghosh et al. (2017), the drivers' awareness is monitored using picture data processed by AdaBoost in order to avoid potential accidents. In Ryder and Wortmann (2017), an Inception Neural Network is used to detect accident prone locations. Finally, Wang et al. (2017)'s effort to recognize street components may aid in accident prevention. The study used a DBN in conjunction with a k-NN or SVM classifier.

The authors of the research (Celesti et al., 2018) propose using an Internet of Things cloud platform to visualize traffic and provide advance warnings of sudden slowdowns that might lead to accidents. The established arrangement will supply not just the usual suspects like Infrastructure as a Service (IaaS) and Platform as a Service (PaaS) and Software as a Service (SaaS), but also a novel approach called Internet of Things as a Service (IoTaaS). Devices put in volunteer vehicles collect GPS data and upload it to the cloud through a 4G network. Implementation success is heavily dependent on the speed with which the system can react, and the proposed methods can send an alarm over a distance of 1 km in around 120 ms.

Road Abnormalities

Smart transportation relies heavily on the detection of road irregularities because of the direct impact road conditions have on so many other aspects of transportation. A road anomaly detection system's principal role is to detect and alert drivers about irregularities in the road. Damage to vehicles, mishaps, and delays are all possible results of subpar road quality. Several ML techniques are well adapted to the task of spotting road irregularities, therefore that's the direction this discussion takes as well. In Allouch et al. (2017), accelerometer data from mobile smart phones is used using an FF-NN to identify potholes. Accelerometer data are also employed in Mamun (2017), which is grouped by the K-Means technique to discern between normal and aberrant roads. Authors in Nguyen et al. (2019) employ a similar strategy to discover road abnormalities, and the data in this study is likewise clustered using the k-Means method. Finally, in Soultana et al. (2020), the authors compare the approaches k-NN, RF, and SVM for detecting road irregularities.

In Gopalakrishnan (2018), the author analyses deep learning methods for detecting pavement distresses. In addition, we investigate the future prospects of deep learning frameworks for traffic anomaly detection. This article summarizes 12 recent studies on pavement degradation detection using convolutional neural network (CNN) and deep convolutional neural network (DCNN) methods. In conclusion, the author maintains that convolutional neural networks (CNNs) are superior to other methods for classifying pavement images.

Smart Transportation Infrastructure

The advent of IoT technology has been helpful to modern transportation in numerous ways. It has spawned not just novel uses, such as improved transportation, but also fresh perspectives. The potential of Intelligent Transportation Systems may be considerably increased by modifying the underlying infrastructure.

In Chowdhury et al. (2018), the authors presented a novel method of communication. Based on the Machine-to-Machine (M2M) communication paradigm popularized by the Internet of Things (IoT), the authors suggest and simulate a V2V communication architecture. With the use of GPS, vehicles in the proposed framework will be able to determine their location, communicate with one another about their speed and whereabouts, and upload this information to a central server. By notifying vehicles behind you of a rapid change in speed, accidents can be avoided, and traffic congestion can be communicated to other vehicles for better guiding services.

In Geetha and Cicilia (2017), the authors suggest a hardware/software combination for bus fleet monitoring and customer service enhancement. Buses are identified with RFID tags, passenger counts are recorded with IR sensors, and real-time whereabouts are monitored with GPS. With the help of a TI CC3200 microcontroller that has a built-in WiFi module, all of the collected information is sent to the cloud. At each stop, an LCD connected to a TI CC3200 module shows passengers the relevant data. The data is also accessible to shoppers via a dedicated mobile app.

For intelligent transportation applications, social network theory is combined with IoT concepts to develop the Social Internet of Vehicles (SIoV) idea. A multi-tiered Vehicular Social Network Protocol (VSNP) is proposed by the authors of Quadri et al. (2022) to ease communication bottlenecks in SIOV. The protocol spans the medium access control (MAC), physical, and network layers to increase data transfer rates. For ring-based networks, the MAC layer divides the available round-robin intervals. Wireless Sensor Network nodes make up the physical layer, while the network layer allows for communication between the outer rings and a central hub. The suggested protocol outperforms the current protocol (MERLIN) in MATLAB simulations.

CONCLUSION

There has been talk about how machine learning and IoT may be used in smart transportation applications. To demonstrate how well-suited smart transport applications are to ML exploitation, this study focused on the large array of ML approaches that have been suggested and validated for usage in smart transport applications. However, a significantly lesser ML coverage is discovered for smart lighting systems and parking applications given the current IoT and ML applications and infrastructure. As a result, from the perspective of machine learning, there will likely be a future need for further coverage in these domains. The most well-liked IoT approaches for ITS application categories have shown to be parking, route optimization, and accident detection/prevention. This analysis found several common themes of interest based on the difficulties addressed by smart transportation solutions. Some examples are reducing pollution, saving money on petrol, making transportation safer, and cutting down on commute times. It also became evident how much progress has been done in the sector of smart transport thanks to IoT and ML, with even more expansion expected in the coming years. ML has the potential to generate several valuable applications in response to the increasing variety and volume of data generated by the proliferation of IoT devices.

REFERENCES

Acharya, D., Yan, W., & Khoshelham, K. (2018). *Real-time image-based parking occupancy detection using deep learning.* Research Gate.

Aha, D. W., Kibler, D., & Albert, M. K. (1991). Instance-based learning algorithms. *Machine Learning, 6*(1), 37–66. doi:10.1007/BF00153759

Al-Fuqaha, A., Guizani, M., Mohammadi, M., Aledhari, M., & Ayyash, M. (2015). Internet of Things: A Survey on Enabling Technologies, Protocols and Applications. IEEE Communications Surveys &amp Tutorials. 17. *IEEE Communications Surveys and Tutorials, 2015*(4), 2347–2376. doi:10.1109/COMST.2015.2444095

Allouch, A., Koubaa, A., Abbes, T., & Ammar, A. (2017). *RoadSense: Smartphone Application to Estimate Road Conditions Using Accelerometer and Gyroscope.* IEEE Sensors Journal. doi:10.1109/JSEN.2017.2702739

Almeida, P. R. D., Oliveira, L. S., Britto, A. S., Silva, E. J., & Koerich, A. L. (2015). PKLot—A robust dataset for parking lot classification. *Expert Systems with Applications, 42*(11), 4937–4949. doi:10.1016/j.eswa.2015.02.009

Araujo, A., Kalebe, R., Girao, G., Filho, I., Goncalves, K., & Neto, B. (2017). Reliability analysis of an IoT-based smart parking application for smart cities. *Proceedings of the 2017 IEEE International Conference on Big Data (Big Data).* 10.1109/BigData.2017.8258426

Aydin, I., Karakose, M., & Karakose, E. (2017). A navigation and reservation based smart parking platform using genetic optimization for smart cities. *Proceedings of the 2017 5th International Istanbul Smart Grid and Cities Congress and Fair (ICSG).* 10.1109/SGCF.2017.7947615

Ba, J. (2015). *Multiple Object Recognition with Visual Attention.* CoRR.

Barth, D. (2009). *The Bright Side of Sitting in Traffic: Crowdsourcing Road Congestion Data.* BlogSpot. https://googleblog.blogspot.com/2009/08/bright-side-of-sitting-in-traffic.html

Behrisch, M., Bieker, L., Erdmann, J., & Krajzewicz, D. (2011). SUMO–simulation of urban mobility: An overview. *Proceedings of the SIMUL 2011, The Third International Conference on Advances in System Simulation.*

Bokaba, T., Doorsamy, W., & Paul, B. (2022). Comparative Study of Machine Learning Classifiers for Modelling Road Traffic Accidents. *Applied Sciences (Basel, Switzerland), 12*(2), 828. doi:10.3390/app12020828

Celesti, A., Fazio, M., Galán, F., Glikson, A., Mauwa, H., Bagula, A., Celesti, F., & Villari, M. (2019). How to Develop IoT Cloud e-Health Systems Based on FIWARE: A Lesson Learnt. *Journal of Sensor and Actuator Networks.*, *8*(1), 7. doi:10.3390/jsan8010007

Celesti, A., Galletta, A., Carnevale, L., Fazio, M., Lay-Ekuakille, A., & Villari, M. (2018). Lay-Ekuakille, A.; Villari, M. An IoT Cloud System for Traffic Monitoring and Vehicular Accidents Prevention Based on Mobile Sensor Data Processing. *IEEE Sensors Journal*, *18*(12), 4795–4802. doi:10.1109/JSEN.2017.2777786

Chang, I. C., Tai, H. T., Yeh, F. H., Hsieh, D. L., & Chang, S. H. A. (2013). VANET-Based A* Route Planning Algorithm for Travelling Time- and Energy-Efficient GPS Navigation App. *International Journal of Distributed Sensor Networks*, *9*(7), 794521. doi:10.1155/2013/794521

Chowdhury, D. N., Agarwal, N., Laha, A. B., & Mukherjee, A. (2018). A Vehicle-to-Vehicle Communication System Using Iot Approach. *Proceedings of the 2018 IEEE Second International Conference on Electronics, Communication and Aerospace Technology (ICECA)*. 10.1109/ICECA.2018.8474909

Daniels, D. J. (2005). *Ground penetrating radar*. Encyclopedia RF Microw. Eng.

Devi, S. (2017). *Machine Learning based traffic congestion prediction in a IoT based Smart City*. Academic Press.

Distefano, S., Merlino, G., Puliafito, A., Cerotti, D., & Dautov, R. (2017). Crowdsourcing and Stigmergic Approaches for (Swarm) Intelligent Transportation Systems. *Proceedings of the International Conference on Human Centered Computing (HCC 2017)*.

Dogra, A., & Kaur, J. (2022). Moving towards smart transportation with machine learning and Internet of Things (IoT): A review. *Journal of Smart Environments and Green Computing.*, *2*. doi:10.20517/jsegc.2021.09

El Naqa, I., & Murphy, M. J. (2015). What is machine learning? In *Machine Learning in Radiation Oncology* (pp. 3–11). Springer. doi:10.1007/978-3-319-18305-3_1

Fan, X., Liu, J., Wang, Z., Jiang, Y., & Liu, X. (2017). Crowdsourced Road Navigation: Concept, Design, and Implementation. *IEEE Communications Magazine*, *55*(6), 126–128. doi:10.1109/MCOM.2017.1600738

Friedman, N., Geiger, D., & Goldszmidt, M. (1997). Bayesian network classifiers. *Machine Learning*, *29*(2/3), 131–137. doi:10.1023/A:1007465528199

Fusco, G., Colombaroni, C., Comelli, L., & Isaenko, N. (2015). *Short-term traffic predictions on large urban traffic networks: Applications of network-based machine learning models and dynamic traffic assignment models.* IEEE. . doi:10.1109/MTITS.2015.7223242

Geetha, S., & Cicilia, D. (2017). IoT enabled intelligent bus transportation system. *Proceedings of the 2017 2nd International Conference on Communication and Electronics Systems (ICCES).*

Ghosh, A., Chatterjee, T., Samanta, S., Aich, J., & Roy, S. (2017). Distracted Driving: A Novel Approach towards Accident Prevention. *Adv. Comput. Sci. Technol., 10,* 2693–2705.

GopalakrishnanK. (2018). Deep Learning in Pavement Image Analysis and Automated Distress Detection: A Review. doi:10.13140/RG.2.2.35354.54728

Gower, J., & Ross, G. (1998). Non-probabilistic Classification. In *Advances in Data Science and Classification. Studies in Classification, Data Analysis, and Knowledge Organization* (pp. 21–28). Springer. doi:10.1007/978-3-642-72253-0_3

Gupta, A., Kulkarni, S., Jathar, V., Sharma, V., & Jain, N. (2017). Smart Car Parking Management System Using IoT. *Am. J. Sci. Eng. Technol., 2,* 112.

Hou, Y., Edara, P., & Sun, C. (2015). Traffic Flow Forecasting for Urban Work Zones. Intelligent Transportation Systems. *IEEE Transactions on Intelligent Transportation Systems, 16*(4), 1761–1770. doi:10.1109/TITS.2014.2371993

Ibrahim, A. T. H., Chang, V., Anuar, N. B., Adewole, K., Yaqoob, I., Gani, A., Ahmed, E., & Chiroma, H. (2016). The role of big data in smart city. *International Journal of Information Management, 36*(5), 748-758. doi:10.1016/j.ijinfomgt.2016.05.002

Jain, A. K. (2010). Data clustering: 50 years beyond K-means. *Pattern Recognition Letters, 31*(8), 651–666. doi:10.1016/j.patrec.2009.09.011

Jain, A. K., Murty, M. N., & Flynn, P. J. (1999). Data clustering: A review. *ACM Computing Surveys, 31*(3), 264–323. doi:10.1145/331499.331504

Jia, G., Han, G., Li, A., & Du, J. (2018). SSL: Smart Street Lamp Based on Fog Computing for Smarter Cities. *IEEE Transactions on Industrial Informatics, 14*(11), 4995–5004. doi:10.1109/TII.2018.2857918

Kanoh, H. (2005). Short-term traffic prediction using fuzzy c-means and cellular automata in a wide-area road network. *Proceedings. 2005 IEEE Intelligent Transportation Systems.* . doi:10.1109/ITSC.2005.1520184

KingmaD. P.BaJ. (2014). Adam: A method for stochastic optimization. *arXiv:1412.6980.*

Kokilavani, M., & Malathi, A. (2017). Smart street lighting system using IoT. *Int. J. Adv. Res. Appl. Sci. Technol., 3*, 8–11.

Krizhevsky, A., Sutskever, I., & Hinton, G. E. (2012). Imagenet classification with deep convolutional neural networks. *Proceedings of the Advances in Neural Information Processing Systems (NIPS 2012).*

Kubat, M. (2017). *An introduction to machine learning.* Springer.

Kwon, D., Park, S., Baek, S., Malaiya, R. K., Yoon, G., & Ryu, J. T. (2018). A study on development of the blind spot detection system for the IoT-based smart connected car. *2018 IEEE International Conference on Consumer Electronics (ICCE).* 10.1109/ICCE.2018.8326077

LeCun, Y., Bengio, Y., & Hinton, G. (2015). Deep learning. *Nature, 521*(7553), 436–444. doi:10.1038/nature14539 PMID:26017442

Lidkea, V., Muresan, R., Al-Dweik, A., & Zhou, S. (2019). *Improving the Security of Cloud-Based Intelligent Transportation Systems.* Advance online publication. doi:10.1109/CCECE.2019.8861723

Lienhart, R., & Maydt, J. (2002). An extended set of haar-like features for rapid object detection. *Proceedings of the International Conference on Image Processing.* 10.1109/ICIP.2002.1038171

Liu, G., Bao, H., & Han, B. (2018). A Stacked Autoencoder-Based Deep Neural Network for Achieving Gearbox Fault Diagnosis. *Mathematical Problems in Engineering, 2018*, 5105709. doi:10.1155/2018/5105709

Madden, S. (2012). From Databases to Big Data. *IEEE Internet Computing.* . doi:10.1109/MIC.2012.50

Mamun, M. A. A. (2017). An intelligent smartphone based approach using IoT for ensuring safe driving. In *2017 International Conference on Electrical Engineering and Computer Science (ICECOS)* (pp. 217-223). IEEE. 10.1109/ICECOS.2017.8167137

Mohammed, M., Khan, M. B., & Bashier, E. B. M. (2016). *Machine Learning: Algorithms and Applications* (1st ed.). CRC Press. doi:10.1201/9781315371658

Naik, N. (2017). Choice of effective messaging protocols for IoT systems: MQTT, CoAP, AMQP and HTTP. In *2017 IEEE International Systems Engineering Symposium (ISSE)* (pp. 12-18). IEEE. 10.1109/SysEng.2017.8088251

Nguyen, T., Wong, Y., & Lechner, B. (2019). Response-based methods to measure road surface irregularity: A state-of-the-art review. *European Transport Research Review*, *11*(1), 43. doi:10.1186/s12544-019-0380-6

Ozbayoglu, A. M., Küçükayan, G., & Dogdu, E. (2016). A real-time autonomous highway accident detection model based on big data processing and computational intelligence. In *2016 IEEE International Conference on Big Data (Big Data)*. IEEE. 10.1109/BigData.2016.7840798

Quadri, N. N., Alqahtani, H., Khan, R., Almakdi, S., Alshehri, M., & Mohammed, A. (2022). An Intelligent Traffic Surveillance System Using Integrated Wireless Sensor Network and Improved Phase Timing Optimization. *Sensors (Basel)*, *22*(9), 3333. doi:10.3390/s22093333 PMID:35591023

Rabiner, L. R. (1990). A tutorial on hidden Markov models and selected applications in speech recognition. In *Readings in Speech Recognition* (pp. 267–296). Elsevier. doi:10.1016/B978-0-08-051584-7.50027-9

Rizvi, S. R., Zehra, S., & Olariu, S. (2018). ASPIRE: An Agent-Oriented Smart Parking Recommendation System for Smart Cities. *IEEE Intelligent Transportation Systems Magazine*.

Ryder, B., & Wortmann, F. (2017). Autonomously detecting and classifying traffic accident hotspots. In *Proceedings of the 2017 ACM International Joint Conference on Pervasive and Ubiquitous Computing and Proceedings of the 2017 ACM International Symposium on Wearable Computers (UbiComp '17)*. Association for Computing Machinery. 10.1145/3123024.3123199

Saarika, P., Sandhya, K., & Sudha, T. (2017). Smart transportation system using IoT. *Proceedings of the 2017 IEEE International Conference on Smart Technologies for Smart Nation (SmartTechCon)*. 10.1109/SmartTechCon.2017.8358540

Satyanarayanan, M. (2017, January). The Emergence of Edge Computing. *Computer*, *50*(1), 30–39. doi:10.1109/MC.2017.9

Shi, J., Jin, L., Li, J., & Fang, Z. (2017). A smart parking system based on NB-IoT and third-party payment platform. *Proceedings of the 2017 17th International Symposium on Communications and Information Technologies (ISCIT)*. 10.1109/ISCIT.2017.8261235

Simon, O. (2015). Short-term Travel-time Prediction on Highway: A Review of the Data-driven Approach. *Transport Reviews, 35*.

Soultana, A., Benabbou, F., & Sael, N. (2020). *Providing Context Awareness in the Smart Car Environment: State of the Art.* Springer. . doi:10.1007/978-3-030-37629-1_59

Swan, M. (2012). Sensor mania! the internet of things, wearable computing, objective metrics, and the quantified self 2.0. *J. Sens. Actuator Netw., 1*(3), 217–253. doi:10.3390/jsan1030217

Szegedy, C., Liu, W., Jia, Y., Sermanet, P., Reed, S., Anguelov, D., Erhan, D., Vanhoucke, V., & Rabinovich, A. (2015). Going deeper with convolutions. *Proceedings of the IEEE Conference on Computer Vision and Pattern Recognition.*

Tafidis, P., Teixeira, J., Bahmankhah, B., Macedo, E., Coelho, M. C., & Bandeira, J. (2017). Exploring crowdsourcing information to predict traffic-related impacts. *Proceedings of the 2017 IEEE International Conference on Environment and Electrical Engineering and 2017 IEEE Industrial and Commercial Power Systems Europe (EEEIC/I&CPS Europe).* 10.1109/EEEIC.2017.7977595

Talari, S., Shafie-khah, M., Siano, P., Loia, V., Tommasetti, A., & Catalão, J. P. S. (2017). A Review of Smart Cities Based on the Internet of Things Concept. *Energies, 10*(4), 1–23. doi:10.3390/en10040421

Tarek, R. (2018). Fog Computing: Data Streaming Services for Mobile End-Users. *Procedia Computer Science, 134.*

Tripathy, A. K., Mishra, A. K., & Das, T. K. (2017). Smart lighting: Intelligent and weather adaptive lighting in street lights using IOT. *Proceedings of the 2017 International Conference on Intelligent Computing, Instrumentation and Control Technologies (ICICICT).* 10.1109/ICICICT1.2017.8342746

Utgoff, P. E. (1989). Incremental induction of decision trees. *Machine Learning, 4*(2), 161–186. doi:10.1023/A:1022699900025

Vangelista, L., Zanella, A., & Zorzi, M. (2015). *Long-Range IoT Technologies: The Dawn of LoRa.* FABULOUS.

Wang, J., Wang, C., Song, X., & Raghavan, V. (2017). Automatic intersection and traffic rule detection by mining motor-vehicle GPS trajectories. *Computers, Environment and Urban Systems, 64,* 19–29. doi:10.1016/j.compenvurbsys.2016.12.006

Watkins, C. J., & Dayan, P. (1992). Q-learning. *Machine Learning, 8*(3-4), 279–292. doi:10.1007/BF00992698

Werbos, P. J. (1990). Backpropagation through time: What it does and how to do it. *Proceedings of the IEEE, 78*(10), 1550–1560. doi:10.1109/5.58337

Wu, Q., Huang, C., Wang, S.-Y., Chiu, W.-C., & Chen, T. (2007). Robust parking space detection considering inter-space correlation. *Proceedings of the 2007 IEEE International Conference on Multimedia and Expo*. 10.1109/ICME.2007.4284736

Xenakis, A., Karageorgos, A., Lallas, E., Chis, A. E., & González-Vélez, H. (2019). Towards Distributed IoT/Cloud based Fault Detection and Maintenance in Industrial Automation. *Procedia Computer Science, 151*.

Yisheng, L., Duan, Y., Kang, W., & Li, Z. (2014). Traffic Flow Prediction With Big Data: A Deep Learning Approach. *IEEE Transactions on Intelligent Transportation Systems, 16*, 865–873. doi:10.1109/TITS.2014.2345663

Zantalis, F., Koulouras, G., Karabetsos, S., & Kandris, D. (2019). future internet A Review of Machine Learning and IoT in Smart Transportation. *Future Internet, 11*(4), 94. doi:10.3390/fi11040094

Zhou, Z. H. (2012). *Ensemble Methods: Foundations and Algorithms*. Chapman and Hall/CRC. doi:10.1201/b12207

Chapter 2
A Review on Application of Artificial Intelligence in Mechanical Engineering

Sambhrant Srivastava
ⓘD https://orcid.org/0000-0002-5868-1561
Rajkiya Engineering College, Azamgarh, India

Vijay Kumar
Rajkiya Engineering College, Azamgarh, India

Saurabh Kumar Singh
Rajkiya Engineering College, Azamgarh, India

Pankaj Yadav
ⓘD https://orcid.org/0000-0001-9394-4585
Rajkiya Engineering College, Azamgarh, India

Brihaspati Singh
Rajkiya Engineering College, Azamgarh, India

Amit Bhaskar
ⓘD https://orcid.org/0000-0002-6938-7114
Rajkiya Engineering College, Azamgarh, India

ABSTRACT

Advances in science and technology are making mechatronic systems more common in mechanical engineering. AI is involved in this transition. Artificial intelligence (AI) is computer software that makes decisions on its own. Simulating professionals' intelligent behaviour boosts efficiency and product quality. Artificial intelligence

DOI: 10.4018/979-8-3693-5271-7.ch002

systems have advanced since their creation. These systems are widely used in mechanical and industrial fields for image processing, intelligent perception, pattern recognition, and virtual reality. Automation and AI are common in industry and mechanics. This study examined AI in mechanical disciplines such heat transfer, production, design, and quality control. Research simulations show a variety of artificial intelligence systems that regulate mechanical manufacturing process components. ANNs, DCNN, CNN, fuzzy logic, and other AI are featured. Thus, new products and system development should be expedited. Mechanical engineering component rejections and faults may be eliminated using AI. Optimised systems can produce higher-quality, more expensive items.

INTRODUCTION

The term "artificial intelligence" (AI) refers to a newly developing technology as well as a subject of study that has been more readily available in recent years. The fundamental objective of this organisation is to investigate and advance human intelligence across a wide range of scientific and technical fields, such as engineering, psychology, cognitive science, information and system science, space science, and engineering(Huang, 2016)(Patel et al., 2021). In recent years, self-organized units that control all input parameters have been used to minimize rejections and errors in final products. This has been accomplished by continuously improving traditional methods and adding new, intricate systems of information technology network that have been analyzed and turned into new higher degree technologies. Given how cutthroat the real-time market is, it is probable that AI's future potential will manifest as a higher degree of sophisticated original thinking across a larger variety of engineering activities. This is due to the fact that real-time markets are very competitive. It is becoming more common to combine artificial intelligence (AI) with mechanical and mechatronic engineering as production gets more automated and advanced (J. Chen et al., 2019). The purpose of machine learning is to utilize enhanced data and algorithms to make accurate predictions about future events. It is not very common for information to flow backwards from the production stage to the planning stage in a normal situation; however, the information from the production stage has a significant impact on the tasks involved in planning and helps to failure rates, unscheduled downtime, and quality of production all decrease flexibility in the production process. The outcomes of this paper included AI applications in the mechanical field, such including but not limited to quality assurance and process planning, process monitoring and diagnosis, and allied fields like self-driving smart cars, unmanned aerial vehicles, and automated missiles; thermodynamics; stress analysis; mechanics; fluid mechanics; dynamic analysis and control; parameter optimization; Data and algorithms developed specifically for machine learning are used in order to produce insightful forecasts and predictions about the future. In a typical setting, the information does not typically flow backwards from the manufacturing stage to the planning stage. However, this information has a significant impact on the planning activities, which in turn reduces the number of product faults, and unexpected downtimes, and increases flexibility. This paper's findings focused on the application of artificial intelligence to the field of mechanics, specifically thermal systems, solid mechanics stress determination, fluid flow, dynamic control system, and optimization for specific parameters; control in quality for the process of planning; diagnosis of process monitoring which are used in combination for smart cars, unmanned aerial vehicle and automated missiles (Chayal & Patel, 2021). The findings of this paper were presented in the form of a paper. Here, in this review, the applications of ANN in different fields of mechanical engineering are described below.

Artificial Intelligence in Manufacturing

There are many examples of AI are:

A. **Quality Control**: Computer vision can do a much wider variety of activities in a manufacturing plant than a person can, and it can do so more quickly, correctly, and effectively. Very lately, a producer of aircraft engines has begun using computer vision technology to perform 3-D analysis of turbofan blades with an accuracy of micrometers (Belton et al., 2019). The manufacturer is able to do an analysis on each and every blade, rather than just a sample, because the technology can evaluate hundreds of blade characteristics in just 15 seconds. In addition to this benefit, the application of technology removes all likelihood of an error being caused by a human. Examination of consumer goods using automated systems might be beneficial. An automated system checks the legitimacy of labels for a manufacturer of hot sauce at a rate of one thousand labels per minute. Since the majority of these systems were developed from the ground up to fulfil a certain function, it is not possible to simply retrain them (unlike humans). Andrew has just introduced the new start-up company landing.ai, which provides inspection solutions that are more adaptable and based on machine learning.

B. **Supply Chain Optimization**: AI is capable of gathering and analyzing data from the supply chain on a fine-grained level, which enables it to manage inventory, anticipate demand, discover inefficiencies, and so on. Walmart is now conducting trials with the use of indoor drones to monitor stock levels in their facilities (Abrams, 2016). The use of machine learning to predict product demand based on local weather reveals a number of subtle tendencies that a human forecaster may have missed (for example, steaks sell better than ground beef when it's dark and windy(Neff, 2014). One such example is that steaks sell better than ground beef when it's dark and windy. It is fine for there to be some errors in the predictions made by the system so long as there is an overall improvement in its efficiency. The algorithms are unable to provide an explanation as to why these patterns exist or if they can be relied upon or are just a coincidence. On the other hand, autonomous weapons are not required to provide an explanation for why they have selected a target.

C. **Predictive equipment monitoring**: Artificial intelligence may be used to monitor industrial equipment and spot subtle changes that may suggest an impending breakdown. This monitoring may involve hundreds of networked sensors. Mueller Industries has previously detected a problem with bearings on one of its machines, which may have led to substantial downtime as a result of this system. This problem was discovered when the company discovered that another of its machines had the same problem(Crandall, 2019). It is possible that this system will migrate from preventative maintenance to predictive maintenance so that downtime and unnecessary maintenance can be reduced.

D. **Innovative forms of robotics:** Robots have been utilised in the manufacturing industry for quite some time, but they cannot be "retrained" easily, they are blind to their surroundings, and they will continue to perform the same duty regardless of what (or who) is in their path. In spite of these limitations, robots continue to find widespread application in a variety of business settings. As a result of recent developments in technology, robots now have a better chance of accurately understanding human behavior . Other researchers are looking at the idea of giving robots the ability to learn by either mimicking human movements, which would lower the costs of development or by "practising" a task until they master it (Lindley, 2022). This would allow robots to learn without the need for extensive programming. Even though the vast bulk of this work is just a proof-of-concept, technological progress is happening at a lightning-fast rate.

E. **Generative design:** Artificial intelligence is able to model how a design would operate in the real world without actually building it, and it can "evolve" changes until an optimal design is achieved. It would appear that Airbus utilized generative methodologies in order to build lighter aeroplane parts (Ravi, 2018).

F.   **Capabilities enhancement**: It's possible that humans and AI working together will be more productive than either one operating separately. While they are working, employees will be able to access information that was previously unavailable to them and visit previously inaccessible sites thanks to augmented reality (AR) (e.g., infrared imaging to see in low light). When workers wore AR glasses, they saw a 34% improvement in their productivity(Abraham & Annunziata, 2017).

G.   **Transportation:** Autonomous cars have the potential to revolutionize global transportation, but there are several technological, social, legal, and ethical challenges to be resolved (Kalra & Paddock, 2016). The employment of self-driving cars has already begun in the workplace. Tens of thousands of robots are said to be employed by Amazon in its warehouses (Shead, 2017). Long-haul trucks may have a faster time to market than self-driving consumer automobiles since interstate travel is simpler. There is a growing interest in safe, semi-autonomous trucks.

Artificial Intelligence in Thermal Engineering

It has been suggested by Cheng and colleagues that AI could be utilized to increase the effectiveness of HVAC (heating, ventilation, and air conditioning) systems. Now more than ever, automated forecasting and control, as well as predictive controls and optimization, are becoming the norm. It is anticipated that AI-assisted HVAC control will reduce overall energy consumption by a maximum of 14.4 percent and an average of 44.04 percent. According to the findings of this study, it is hypothesized that less accurate prediction tools are the root cause of lower HVAC energy savings. As shown in Figure5, utilizing AI to control HVAC systems results in an average savings of 14.02 percent of energy. The Normalize Harris Index (NHI) estimates that AI-assisted HVAC control might save anywhere from 14.4 percent to 44.04 percent on average, with huge fluctuations in the amount of energy saved. Errors of 3, 9, and 7 percentage points, respectively, are found when these findings are compared to the investigational data of 14.02 percent, 24.52 percent, and 41.0 percent (Cheng & Lee, 2019). The intelligent defect detection systems that Nasiri and his colleagues have developed rely on temperature sensors, thermal imaging, and a convolutional neural network as its primary components.

Figure 1. Heating, ventilation, and air conditioning energy saving for a full day case based on artificial intelligence assisted
(Cheng & Lee, 2019)

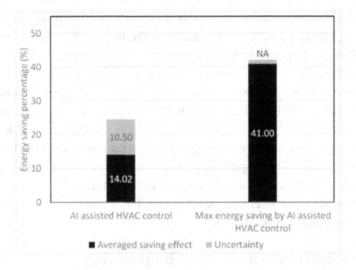

Artificial Intelligence in Engineering Design

According to Chen and colleagues' findings, in order to improve prognostics and diagnostics, it is necessary to analyse a substantial quantity of data. It is possible to achieve this goal by utilizing artificial intelligence (AI) in conjunction with various sensors. According to(S. L. Chen et al., 2008), it is anticipated that the malfunction would be identified through the utilization of vibration and electrostatic sensor data. Artificial intelligence (AI) technology was utilized throughout the design process of the bucket elevator. Even the most complicated structures could potentially be built in a relatively short length of time if this technique was utilized. The author did some research on case representation as well as fuzzy mathematics in addition to developing a new product design. The benefits of this strategy include accelerating market demand, making use of previously acquired design abilities, and reducing the amount of time spent on the design process. In a study conducted on a four-stroke, four-cylinder diesel engine by Yildirim et al., the researchers looked at the degrees of vibration, pollution, and noise. Two distinct approaches were used to introduce hydrogen into the input valve of the engine, which was driven by biodiesel derived from sunflower, canola, and maize. Both approaches were successful. In the first scenario, we have an artificial neural network, and in the second scenario, we have a support vector machine. After looking at the output and the errors, the author came to the conclusion that ANN is a superior alternative to SVM for carrying out such an analysis (Yıldırım et al., 2019). Research conducted by Sivasankari and colleagues led to the discovery of a method that can detect and prevent damage to the axles and joints of heavy-duty vehicles. It is imperative that every component of a heavy-duty vehicle undergo a comprehensive inspection, and any errors must be rectified on a consistent basis. Sensors and computer programming could be used in artificial intelligence in order to keep an eye on the nuts, bolts, and axles. It is possible to repair any damage with this technique (Abrams, 2016). According to Pratt et al findings, numerical optimization has the potential to be implemented in a diverse selection of procedures involving the design, development, and testing of jet engines(Pratt et al., 1993). The early efforts at optimization focused mostly on structural optimization projects; however, more contemporary optimization applications have a more general focus. An automated approach for the pre-designing of contemporary gas turbine engines has been developed in order to assist with optimizing the performance of compressors and turbines. The effectiveness of the component can be improved by adjusting the design parameters of the towpath while still adhering to the structural and aerodynamic restrictions. Because of a problem with the production process, a system was developed to check and compare automatically the drill hole patterns and tolerances with the related template geometries. The combination of restricting optimization techniques with penalty functions results in an interesting hybrid problem-solving procedure. An automated method for matching analytical models to engine data has been developed as a result of an endeavour to reduce the amount of acoustic data that was collected. Rapid prototypes for use in trade-off analyses have been developed through the application of parametric design approaches.

Artificial Intelligence in Product Development

Dhingra investigated the potential uses of artificial intelligence in the design and production of products, looking at areas to pick and choose parts, design something, reason, learn, perceive, sense, recognize, have intuitive thoughts, be creative, analyses, abstract, plan, and anticipate are all necessary skills. In order to reach the "ultimate destiny" of maintenance, which involves achieving the most spectacular performance possible while also having nearly no breakdowns and being able to support oneself, an intelligent framework may be required to construct the necessary tools and processes. According to the author (Dhingra, n.d.), there has been a paradigm shift in the manner in which architects and designers approach the resolution of intricate design challenges. The concepts of mechatronics and artificial intelligence technology were put forward by Huang Q, along with the investigation of the creation and composition of AI technology. Utilizing AI technology, the research is performed an investigation of the fault diagnostics of the hot forging press. The author looked into mechanical and electrical engineering as well, including the unstable system in which the electronic information system is the primary contributor to the issue. The author believes that in order to raise the level of intelligent control of the increasingly harsh competitiveness in the machinery industry, a new research hotspot that is based on fuzzy logic, neural networks, and expert systems will be developed. This will allow for a higher degree of intelligent control. The improvement of equipment fault identification through the use of an intelligent diagnostic is one of the goals that has been set by Haidong et al primary. It is able to perform in-the-moment analysis on vast amounts of data and come up with accurate diagnoses. The use of artificial neural networks and support vector machines has led to significant advancements in the area of intelligent diagnostics are now the most cutting edge and widely implemented. According to the inventor, a deep wavelet auto-encoder combined with an extreme learning machine is an innovative approach to the problem of intelligently diagnosing rolling bearing faults in rolling bearings. The suggested method is more effective than both traditional methods and standard deep learning methods (Haidong et al., 2018). This is due to the fact that it does not require the extraction of human features. According to Shaonak et al., developments in artificial intelligence (AI) are currently being utilized to enhance the design of a variety of different goods. In addition to a select number of methods, the approaches to design as well as the design systems themselves are murky. When artificial intelligence (AI) systems are integrated into a design environment, businesses are able to make better use of existing resources and increase their capabilities rather than destroying them. This allows businesses to compete more effectively. The primary goal of artificial intelligence (AI) is to improve the quality of decision-making by accelerating the flow of information and increasing the availability of knowledge and experience. We need to come up with fresh ideas and approaches as a first step in order to cope with the enormous amounts of incorrect data that we have. Second, in order to construct a versatile and global setting for product lifecycle management, it is required to combine both the technologies that are already in use and those that will be developed in the future. Human-computer interactions can be implemented in a variety of ways, each of which increases the likelihood that user requirements and data will be satisfied (Mishra & Saraswat, 2017).

Artificial Intelligence in Crash Simulation

Machine learning was utilized by (Theja & Venkateswarlu, 2022) to analyses crash simulation data. They had information from 1000 full-frontal accident simulations with different automobile designs and impact scenarios. It would have taken a lot of time and labor to understand the vast amount of simulation data. The same is true for results from robustness analysis or design space exploration.

Artificial Intelligence in Vibration Analysis

AI was utilized to analyse vibrations in a fractured beam. Initially utilized to train AI/ANN, analytical data from FE analysis on Ansys was then applied to forecast the natural frequencies of cracked beams without the aid of computer modeling and simulation. The figures 2 and 3 depict this.

Figure 2. Modal frequencies for case one

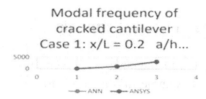

Figure 3. Modal frequencies for case two

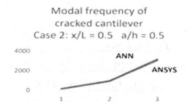

Artificial Intelligence in Daily Life

Voice commands are used to carry out tasks on Google Home. Guarding against intruders and fire, Netatmo Welcome performs the role of a guard. Kuri Home Robot (Figure 4) is an entertainment and basic housekeeping task performer.

Smart, self-driving, or autonomous vehicles keep track of the velocity, direction, and position of other vehicles and obstacles while adjusting their own position in relation to them. These actions are not affected by human error like diversion and bad judgment. Without endangering human life, smart drones use machine vision for surveillance and workplace tasks. For lighting and temperature control, use a smart thermostat. Everyday people use smartphones that have AI functions.

Figure 4. Smart home robot

Artificial Intelligence in Fault Diagnosis

The use of AI in the analysis and diagnosis of problems with mechanical equipment is increasing day by day. For example, the diagnostic tool, universal integrated neural network, is utilised in rotating machinery to detect and diagnose fan problems. The fan and motor are the two components of the rotating system. The five subsystems of the primary system are vibration, temperature, noise, oil, and performance. Dependent on the specifics of the monitoring parameters used, they are sorted into distinct categories, with the fault diagnosis and decision system serving as the brain of the entire intelligent system during the diagnosis (Huang, 2016) . For reciprocating machines, the fault diagnosis is more challenging due to the machine's complex kinematic and dynamic morphology. When it comes to applications for diagnosing diesel engine faults, any diagnostic system that uses neural networks is, by definition, a universal diagnostic system. Mechanical and performance failures are two categories of diesel engine failure. Performance problems can be identified by using a sub-neural network and performance information like as power, speed, cylinder pressure, water temperature, and others. Two sub-neural networks diagnose the mechanical issue, and using the information from oil analysis and the widely utilised vibro acoustic (VA) signal as input, a mixed neural network diagnosis method is constructed (Huang, 2016). Some typical and major issues with the hot forging process include the slider stopping beyond its limit (top dead center), stuffy cars, excessively high currents, and failure of lubrication. There are numerous causes for these failures, and rule reasoning and case reasoning can be used with the hot forging press fault diagnosis approach. The system determines failures by applying rule reasoning and case reasoning to the case library. Additionally, the closest neighbor technique is utilized to assess how closely cases match.

Figure 5. Steps in fault diagnosis by AI

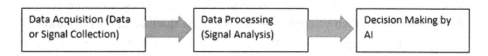

Artificial Intelligence in Mechanical Layout and Optimization

Modern mechanical systems and machines have intricate shapes. These static dwellings, which include stiffness, electricity, pressure, and other elements, give rise to intricacy in the constructions. And the homes with dynamic responses, such as pressure, displacement, speed, acceleration, frequency, and vibration, are thought to have an optimization challenge (Lindu & Zhaohan, 1996). Size, topology, and performance are the primary categories used to group optimization problems. In these circumstances, optimization techniques that are entirely dependent on mathematical programming are insufficient. At the optimum solution, the ANN can also be used to complete the optimization process. The effectiveness of AI in resolving optimization issues is illustrated (Quintana et al., 2011). AI based systems are used to optimize a variety of problems, including those involving second structures, third-dimensional structures, composite structures, vibrating systems, and acoustics (Engin & Gulez, 1999). A thermoelectricity-based problem's optimization is carried out using only coupled areas(Rao et al., 2012). The attention bodies that have experienced the simultaneous knock of thermal and mechanical fields are referred to as the coupled area. The design parameters which may be used to modify the mapping parameters in mechanical engineering can be identified through shape assessment (Szczepanik & Burczyński, 2012). In order to identify and evaluate the relationship of mapping between each of them, this method leverages the output and effort of the synthetic neural network as design parameters. It can also be applied to changing the overall structural dynamic arrangement. An intricate step in mechanical engineering is the nonlinear mapping technique of ANN used in geometric modeling. The particle surface's X, Y coordinates are provided as the input for the calculation, while the coordinate Z is provided as the output.

Artificial Intelligence in Mechanical Defect or Imperfection Analysis

Finding and gathering information that is associated with errors is the first step in producing verifiable proof. The spectra collected from the component's recurrence must be collected in order to separate the component. These errors highlight extraction two sorts of techniques can be distinguished, namely factual and model-based (Landay & Myers, 2001)(Meesad & Yen, 2000). Typically, when data sources are provided to the neuron, which then generates results based on the machine's indication and any issues it has, the process of intelligent defect recognizable proof is carried out. It is required to first evaluate the consistent sign before combining it with the item's identification condition in order to quantify the mechanical innovation of mechanical machines, recognise the remarkable destruction, and furthermore predict the approaching position. This improves the device or system's overall performance and is dependent on relative steady-state data (Council, 2018). Its main strategy is to use the most recent version of all the technology that has been discovered in earlier studies that are related to mechanical building in order to prevent errors. By looking for obvious signs of errors and using a repair investigation technique, organizations can connect mechanically based machines.

Artificial Intelligence in Wind Energy Forecasting

Today wind power harnessing is on peak and an emerging field. For predicting accurate wind velocity to determine the power generation a smart system is required, as the Global Wind Statistics 2017, released the installation capacity is almost 600 GW (Kumar et al., 2016). Demand for energy can be relieved by smart management and the use of renewable energy sources. Wind speed and wind power forecasting has been major area of study in order to achieve energy balance and make decisions about when to make power (Ummels et al., 2007). By analyzing physical, statistical, geographical correlation, and regional forecasting models, Jung et al. were able to predict wind speed and wind power with greater accuracy (Jung & Broadwater, 2014). Artificial neural network technology is used in wind energy system but not used for wind forecasting (Marugán et al., 2018). There are different parameters and basically four perspectives from which hybrid wind energy model is forecasted (Tascikaraoglu & Uzunoglu, 2014)(Xiao et al., 2015). Many researchers and scientist used different models for predicting wind and solar energy output based on four perspectives like weight based, processing, optimization, and residual error(Ren et al., 2015).

Artificial Intelligence in Refrigeration, Air Conditioning, and Heat Pump (RACHP) Systems Component

A.   Different Models are created in ANN to determine efficiency in Refrigerator compressors(Fei et al., 2016). Different inputs are created by neurons as input layer in Artificial Neural Network to predict the efficiencies like isentropic, volumetric etc. A higher order polynomial is used in hidden layers of Artificial

Neural network for determining different efficiencies of refrigerant compressors. This polynomial transfer function is proven to be best for training the model. Two Output layers of ANN are used as pure linear transfer function. As the efficiency of compressors which are provided by different manufacturers is approximately 2% and a 0.5% Standard Deviation. A different design of turbomachinery like vanes are also designed by using ANN tool (Sanaye et al., 2011). In ANN multilayers are created for feedback which is connected to input and output layer which are represented for different parameters like speed, pressure and temperature. ANOVA models are used to generate report of R, R^2 and errors which are found to be 96%, 99.8% and 3% respectively.

B. Refrigerator condenser performance are used in ANN and in similar fashion almost 12 parameters are used to predict heat transfer rate. These parameters are like tube of heat transfer area, its diameter, air flow rate, temperature etc.(Hayati et al., 2009). Adaptive neuro fuzzy interface systems are used to evaluate the errors and mean errors which are found to be approximately 9% and 3% respectively. However, Artificial Neural Network shows almost 10% of relative and 5% of mean errors. Thus, Adaptive neuro fuzzy interface are more accurate than ANN. These approaches are used to predict condensers index (Ertunc & Hosoz, 2008). But the prediction made by both the method are almost 5% accurate to experimental data.

C. A capillary tube was used to forecast the volumetric rate of refrigerant in the heat exchanger to the moderate home applications. Using MLFFN structure which focused on the back propagation learning technique only 2 neurons were added to the output layer of the MLFFN, while seven neurons were added to the input layer to monitor subcooling, temperature and different diameter (Islamoglu et al., 2005). When compared to experimental measurements, a network with a 7-7-2 design accurately predicts the temperature of the refrigerant suction line output and the refrigerant mass flow rate.

D. A comprehensive correlation of ANN-based for forecasting the refrigerant rate of mass flow(Zhang, 2005). Seven neurons made up the input layer of the network, which was constructed using dimensional analysis, and 1-D parameter made up the output layer. According to their research, networks with only one neuron in the invisible layer are capable of estimating the rate of mass flow with strong performance values (statistical). The connection between the volumetric rate of refrigerant via capillary tubes and short tube orifices and extension to the trans-critical cycle of CO_2 were produced using a modified dimensionless neural network (Yang & Zhang, 2009).

E. Cooling Systems Performance system performance parameters are predicted the using MLFFN for Cooling towers (Hosoz et al., 2007). Five neurons in their network each represent one of the inputs: dry bulb temperature, air stream relative humidity at entry, water temperature, volumetric flow rate of air and water. Outputs include cooling tower's heat rejection rate, makeup water flow rate, outlet temperatures (tower water and dry bulb) and the RH of the air stream at exit. The correlation coefficients for the network predictions and experimental values for these outputs, respectively, were 0.992, 0.981, 0.994, 0.994, and 0.975. The root mean square error was 0.78 percent, 0.09 kg/h, 0.31C, 0.31C, and 43.83W. The average relative error was found to be between 0.89 and 4.64%. Hosoz et al. (Hosoz et al., 2008) successfully applied the ANN to predict the performance parameters of an evaporative cooler, including the sensible cooling rate, DBT, RH of the leaving air, and effectiveness.

REFERENCES

Abraham, M., & Annunziata, M. (2017). Augmented reality is already improving worker performance. *Harvard Business Review*, *13*(5).

Abrams, R. (2016). Walmart looks to drones to speed distribution. *The New York Times, 2*.

Belton, K., Oslon, R., & Crandall, D. (2019). Smart Factories: Issues of Information Governance. *Manufacturing Policy Initiative*, (March), 1–68.

Chayal, N. M., & Patel, N. P. (2021). Review of Machine Learning and Data Mining Methods to Predict Different Cyberattacks. In K. Kotecha, V. Piuri, H. N. Shah, & R. Patel (Eds.), *Data Science and Intelligent Applications* (pp. 43–51). Springer Singapore. doi:10.1007/978-981-15-4474-3_5

Chen, J., Hu, P., Zhou, H., Yang, J., Xie, J., Jiang, Y., Gao, Z., & Zhang, C. (2019). Toward Intelligent Machine Tool. *Engineering (Beijing)*, *5*(4), 679–690. doi:10.1016/j.eng.2019.07.018

Chen, S. L., Craig, M., Callan, R., Powrie, H., & Wood, R. (2008). Use of artificial intelligence methods for advanced bearing health diagnostics and prognostics. *2008 IEEE Aerospace Conference*, (pp. 1–9). IEEE. 10.1109/AERO.2008.4526604

Cheng, C.-C., & Lee, D. (2019). Artificial intelligence-assisted heating ventilation and air conditioning control and the unmet demand for sensors: Part 1. Problem formulation and the hypothesis. *Sensors (Basel)*, *19*(5), 1131. doi:10.3390/s19051131 PMID:30845664

Council, G. W. E. (2018). Global wind statistics 2017. In Global Wind Energy Council Rep.

Crandall, D. J. (2019). Artificial intelligence and manufacturing. *Smart Factories: Issues of Information Governance*, 10–16.

Dhingra, M. (n.d.). Prospects Of Artificial Intelligence. *International Journal of Engineering Technology Research & Management.*, *02*, 36–38.

Engin, S. N., & Gulez, K. (1999). *A wavelet transform-artificial neural network (WT-ANN) based rotating machinery fault diagnostics methodology.* NSIP.

Ertunc, H. M., & Hosoz, M. (2008). Comparative analysis of an evaporative condenser using artificial neural network and adaptive neuro-fuzzy inference system. *International Journal of Refrigeration*, *31*(8), 1426–1436. doi:10.1016/j.ijrefrig.2008.03.007

Fei, J., Zhao, N., Shi, Y., Feng, Y., & Wang, Z. (2016). Compressor performance prediction using a novel feed-forward neural network based on Gaussian kernel function. *Advances in Mechanical Engineering*, *8*(1), 1687814016628396. doi:10.1177/1687814016628396

Haidong, S., Hongkai, J., Xingqiu, L., & Shuaipeng, W. (2018). Intelligent fault diagnosis of rolling bearing using deep wavelet auto-encoder with extreme learning machine. *Knowledge-Based Systems*, *140*, 1–14. doi:10.1016/j.knosys.2017.10.024

Hayati, M., Rezaei, A., & Seifi, M. (2009). Prediction of the heat transfer rate of a single layer wire-on-tube type heat exchanger using ANFIS. *International Journal of Refrigeration*, *32*(8), 1914–1917. doi:10.1016/j.ijrefrig.2009.05.012

Hosoz, M., Ertunc, H. M., & Bulgurcu, H. (2007). Performance prediction of a cooling tower using artificial neural network. *Energy Conversion and Management*, *48*(4), 1349–1359. doi:10.1016/j.enconman.2006.06.024

Hosoz, M., Ertunc, H. M., & Ozguc, A. F. (2008). Modelling of a direct evaporative air cooler using artificial neural network. *International Journal of Energy Research*, *32*(1), 83–89. https://doi.org/https://doi.org/10.1002/er.1336. doi:10.1002/er.1336

Huang, Q. (2016). Application of Artificial Intelligence in Mechanical Engineering BT - *Proceedings of the 2nd International Conference on Computer Engineering, Information Science & Application Technology (ICCIA 2017)* (pp. 882–887). IEEE. 10.2991/iccia-17.2017.154

Islamoglu, Y., Kurt, A., & Parmaksizoglu, C. (2005). Performance prediction for non-adiabatic capillary tube suction line heat exchanger: An artificial neural network approach. *Energy Conversion and Management*, *46*(2), 223–232. doi:10.1016/j. enconman.2004.02.015

Jung, J., & Broadwater, R. P. (2014). Current status and future advances for wind speed and power forecasting. *Renewable & Sustainable Energy Reviews*, *31*, 762–777. doi:10.1016/j.rser.2013.12.054

Kalra, N., & Paddock, S. M. (2016). Driving to safety: How many miles of driving would it take to demonstrate autonomous vehicle reliability? *Transportation Research Part A, Policy and Practice*, *94*, 182–193. doi:10.1016/j.tra.2016.09.010

Kumar, Y., Ringenberg, J., Depuru, S. S., Devabhaktuni, V. K., Lee, J. W., Nikolaidis, E., Andersen, B., & Afjeh, A. (2016). Wind energy: Trends and enabling technologies. *Renewable & Sustainable Energy Reviews*, *53*, 209–224. doi:10.1016/j. rser.2015.07.200

Landay, J. A., & Myers, B. A. (2001). Sketching interfaces: Toward more human interface design. *Computer*, *34*(3), 56–64. doi:10.1109/2.910894

Lindley, J. N. S. (2022). *Investigation into the Economic Viability of Industry 4.0 Practices in a Small Start-Up Setting: A Case Study*. The University of Texas at El Paso.

Lindu, Z., & Zhaohan, S. (1996). Combination of discrete cosine transform with neural network in fault diagnosis for rotating machinery. *Proceedings of the IEEE International Conference on Industrial Technology (ICIT'96)*, (pp. 450–454). IEEE. 10.1109/ICIT.1996.601629

Marugán, A. P., Márquez, F. P. G., Perez, J. M. P., & Ruiz-Hernández, D. (2018). A survey of artificial neural network in wind energy systems. *Applied Energy*, *228*, 1822–1836. doi:10.1016/j.apenergy.2018.07.084

Meesad, P., & Yen, G. G. (2000). Pattern classification by a neurofuzzy network: Application to vibration monitoring. *ISA Transactions*, *39*(3), 293–308. doi:10.1016/ S0019-0578(00)00027-6 PMID:11005161

Mishra, L., & Saraswat, U. (2017). Impact of Artificial Intelligence in the Mechanical Engineering. *International Journal of Mechanical and Production Engineering*, *5*(7), 9–11.

Neff, J. (2014). Cloudy with a chance of meatballs: How weather forecast predicts Walmart's sales outlook. *Advertising Age*, (October), 27.

Patel, A. R., Ramaiya, K. K., Bhatia, C. V., Shah, H. N., & Bhavsar, S. N. (2021). Artificial Intelligence: Prospect in Mechanical Engineering Field---A Review. In K. Kotecha, V. Piuri, H. N. Shah, & R. Patel (Eds.), *Data Science and Intelligent Applications* (pp. 267–282). Springer Singapore. doi:10.1007/978-981-15-4474-3_31

Pratt, T. K., Seitelman, L. H., Zampano, R. R., Murphy, C. E., & Landis, F. (1993). Optimization applications for aircraft engine design and manufacture. *Advances in Engineering Software*, *16*(2), 111–117. doi:10.1016/0965-9978(93)90056-Y

Quintana, G., Garcia-Romeu, M. L., & Ciurana, J. (2011). Surface roughness monitoring application based on artificial neural networks for ball-end milling operations. *Journal of Intelligent Manufacturing*, *22*(4), 607–617. doi:10.1007/s10845-009-0323-5

Rao, B. K. N., Pai, P. S., & Nagabhushana, T. N. (2012). Failure Diagnosis and Prognosis of Rolling - Element Bearings using Artificial Neural Networks: A Critical Overview. *Journal of Physics: Conference Series*, *364*, 12023. doi:10.1088/1742-6596/364/1/012023

Ravi, A. (2018). *What Generative Design Is and Why It's the Future of Manufacturing*. New Equipment.

Ren, Y., Suganthan, P. N., & Srikanth, N. (2015). Ensemble methods for wind and solar power forecasting—A state-of-the-art review. *Renewable & Sustainable Energy Reviews*, *50*, 82–91. doi:10.1016/j.rser.2015.04.081

Sanaye, S., Dehghandokht, M., Mohammadbeigi, H., & Bahrami, S. (2011). Modeling of rotary vane compressor applying artificial neural network. *International Journal of Refrigeration*, *34*(3), 764–772. doi:10.1016/j.ijrefrig.2010.12.007

Shead, S. (2017). Amazon now has 45,000 robots in its warehouses. *Business Insider, 3*.

Szczepanik, M., & Burczyński, T. (2012). Swarm optimization of stiffeners locations in 2-D structures. *Bulletin of the Polish Academy of Sciences. Technical Sciences*, *60*(2), 241–246. doi:10.2478/v10175-012-0032-7

Tascikaraoglu, A., & Uzunoglu, M. (2014). A review of combined approaches for prediction of short-term wind speed and power. *Renewable & Sustainable Energy Reviews*, *34*, 243–254. doi:10.1016/j.rser.2014.03.033

Theja, M. B., & Venkateswarlu, P. (2022). Artificial Intelligence and Applications in Mechanical and Materials Engineering. *NeuroQuantology : An Interdisciplinary Journal of Neuroscience and Quantum Physics*, *20*(1), 1015.

Ummels, B. C., Gibescu, M., Pelgrum, E., Kling, W. L., & Brand, A. J. (2007). Impacts of Wind Power on Thermal Generation Unit Commitment and Dispatch. *IEEE Transactions on Energy Conversion, 22*(1), 44–51. doi:10.1109/TEC.2006.889616

Xiao, L., Wang, J., Dong, Y., & Wu, J. (2015). Combined forecasting models for wind energy forecasting: A case study in China. *Renewable & Sustainable Energy Reviews, 44*, 271–288. doi:10.1016/j.rser.2014.12.012

Yang, L., & Zhang, C.-L. (2009). Modified neural network correlation of refrigerant mass flow rates through adiabatic capillary and short tubes: Extension to CO2 transcritical flow. *International Journal of Refrigeration, 32*(6), 1293–1301. doi:10.1016/j.ijrefrig.2009.03.005

Yıldırım, S., Tosun, E., Çalık, A., Uluocak, İ., & Avşar, E. (2019). Artificial intelligence techniques for the vibration, noise, and emission characteristics of a hydrogen-enriched diesel engine. *Energy Sources. Part A, Recovery, Utilization, and Environmental Effects, 41*(18), 2194–2206. doi:10.1080/15567036.2018.1550540

Zhang, C.-L. (2005). Generalized correlation of refrigerant mass flow rate through adiabatic capillary tubes using artificial neural network. *International Journal of Refrigeration, 28*(4), 506–514. doi:10.1016/j.ijrefrig.2004.11.004

Chapter 3
An Anticipatory Framework for Categorizing Nigerian Supreme Court Rulings

Sabyasachi Pramanik
(iD) https://orcid.org/0000-0002-9431-8751
Haldia Institute of Technology, India

ABSTRACT

It is important to recognize that a well-run judicial system contributes to the formation of a favorable atmosphere that fosters national growth. The efficient administration of justice is just as important to the court's efficacy as its capacity to be impartial, firm, and fair at all times. Notwithstanding these vital functions of the court, Nigeria's legal system is sometimes unsatisfactory and sluggish moving. People no longer trust the courts because of this, as most people think that justice postponed is justice denied. In recent times, machine learning methods have been used for predictive purposes in several domains. In this work, the authors used 5585 records of precedent rulings from the Supreme Court of Nigeria (SCN) between 1962 and 2022 to construct a prediction model for the categorization of judgments. Primsol Law Pavilion, an independently owned data repository, provided the data that was gathered from. Following data annotation and feature extraction, three classification methods (Decision Tree, Multi-layer Perceptron, and kNN) were used to construct the model. These techniques allowed for the identification of factors that significantly influence assessments, both from the literature and domain experts. The authors also looked at how two different feature extraction strategies, one based on correlation and the other on information, affected the models; the latter proved to be more successful in identifying pertinent characteristics. According to the study's findings, decision trees are the best machine learning algorithm for predicting how appeal cases that are submitted before the SCN would turn out.

DOI: 10.4018/979-8-3693-5271-7.ch003

INTRODUCTION

Maintaining the rule of law at all times and defending and upholding the constitution are among the judiciary's fundamental goals as the third branch of the government (Ahmad et al., 2021). Today's highly advanced and industrialized human society has produced tremendous advancements, particularly in the fields of technology and architecture (Bhilare et al., 2019). Among the most integral achievements of humanity are law and society. The development of the legal system started with the rise of human civilization. Communities bound to a certain legislature have experienced significant disruptions and anxiety as a result of the lack of openness and ignorance of the legal procedures. As data becomes more widely available, the necessity for established standards and methods becomes even more critical (Medvedeva, 2023). Many European national and international courts strive for openness by following the regulation to encourage the reuse and accessibility of public sector information and to post their records online (Marković, 2018). An exceptional chance to handle this material automatically on a broad scale is presented by digital access to a substantial body of published case law.

Computers are now machines that can learn without supervision and adapt to new inputs without needing to be reprogrammed. This is due to recent advancements in data collection, aggregation systems, algorithms, and processing power (Ashley & Brüninghaus, 2009). In the past, there have been many efforts to anticipate court judgments using statistical techniques, such as factor and linear regression analysis. In 1957, Kort made an effort to use quantitative techniques to forecast Supreme Court rulings. Probability theory and quantitative approaches were suggested by Nagel (1960) and Ulmer (1963) for the analysis of court documents. These systems, however, were noise-sensitive and did not transfer to other legal areas (Cui et al., 2022).

Machine learning algorithms' ability to forecast court decisions has gained popularity (Aletras et al., 2016). Artificial intelligence has been used to build legal decision systems that help attorneys by automatically anticipating verdicts (Kelbert et al., 2012). Big data analytics proponents contend that it will lessen human prejudice and provide the legal system a scientific, evidence-based approach (Simmons, 2018; Završnik, 2018). In order to help judges in certain instances, machine learning has been used to provide answers known as algorithmic decision predictors (Ashley, 2019). These algorithms foretell the outcome of a case, which would normally be decided by a court or judges (e.g., guilty/not guilty, plaintiff/defendant ruling) (Medvedeva et al., 2020). It is sometimes said that algorithmic decision predictors increase the consistency and predictability of judicial decision-making, which is required under the equality principle.

These arguments contend that decision predictors may help judges make decisions that are more consistent, knowledgeable, and free of prejudice (Chalkidis et al., 2019; O'Neil, 2016). Machine learning classifiers use a traditional encoding method that does not capture the overall connections between predictor variables in a machine learning-based data set, even though selecting efficient predictors and using machine learning techniques on large data sets can yield impressive results (Alghazzawi et al., 2022). The studies conducted by Bhilare et al. (2019) and Shaikh et al. (2020) emphasized the use of manually derived characteristics from the court case dataset before using a series of machine learning algorithms to construct a prediction model that was based on performance. There have been claims that this technique can unintentionally reinforce prejudice and bias that are already present in training data (Liu et al., 2018).

Numerous efforts have been made in related literatures to use machine learning-based algorithms to the creation of prediction models for the legal system, using both structured and unstructured information. Studies that took into account the usage of unstructured information, however, run the danger of making it more difficult to accurately determine the semantic link using NLP algorithms (Medvedeva et al., 2023). Because of this, using structured datasets based on characteristics taken from court cases might be a good substitute; nevertheless, questions have been raised about the accuracy of the human feature identification method (Aletras, 2016). Greater issues have arisen as a result of the steady growth in the quantity of data being saved and the use of mobile devices to access this data. This is because information is difficult for human specialists to access properly, particularly with the introduction of big data.

Because of this, we decided to use unsupervised machine learning techniques to evaluate the dependency between characteristics in order to identify features that are redundant or irrelevant, which would increase the accuracy of the prediction model. In an attempt to assist Nigerian judges in making knowledgeable decisions about related cases in the future, the effect of two feature selection algorithms on the accuracy of three classification algorithms was tested in this paper using data gathered from historical (precedent) court cases from the Supreme Court of Nigeria (SCN). In this study, we used feature selection to determine the most significant characteristics that affect how Nigerian Supreme Court rulings are categorized. Additionally, we created a classification model utilizing three distinct machine learning algorithms—decision tree, KNN, and multi-layer perceptron—to forecast court case outcomes based on data that were retrieved. Lastly, we assessed the constructed prediction models' performance.

SUPPLIES AND PROCEDURES

Nigerian Judicial Process Components

One fundamental tenet of Nigerian justice administration is judicial precedent. According to judicial precedence, issues that are similar should be resolved similarly (Ali, 2020). In circumstances when the facts are sufficiently comparable, it basically requires courts to follow decisions that have already been resolved (Ogbu, 2007). The stare decisis, or "stand by the decided," concept is used in accordance with the theory of judicial precedent. This essentially implies that lower courts must follow the rules of law established by higher courts in previous decisions.

This gives the law predictability and consistency. This concept states that a magistrate court must adopt a High Court's ruling in any case when the circumstances are comparable to those of a case that the High Court has determined. When the circumstances of a case determined by the Court of Appeal are comparable to a matter that is ongoing before a High Court, the High Court is also required to follow the Court of Appeal's judgment. When evaluating identical circumstances pertaining to both the case at hand and a matter that the Supreme Court has resolved, the Court of Appeal is required to adhere to the ruling of the Supreme Court.

A case law collection is a list of earlier decisions. It has significant weight in the Nigerian legal system and significantly influences judges' judgments. It is expensive for self-willed judges to arbitrarily depart from it since any judgment or choices these judges make might be overturned on appeal, making their process of making the decisions pointless. The Supreme Court follows its own prior rulings and will only stray from them if doing so will satisfy the essential standards of justice and fairness (Okeke, 2016).

Research Framework

Figure 1 displays a representation of the research framework that served as a guide for the investigation based on the techniques used. The processes of data identification, data collecting, feature extraction, preprocessing, and feature selection were carried out for feature identification and extraction.

Figure 1. Conceptual view of the research framework

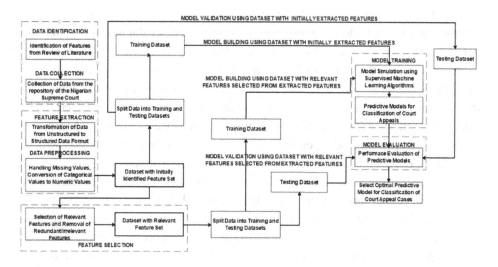

Identification of Data

The Mendeley repository has the dataset that was gathered and utilized for this work (https://data.mendeley.com/datasets/ky6zfyf669/1). The dataset is described in detail in Ngige et al. 2023. The Supreme Court of Nigeria's decisions from prior criminal and civil appeal cases decided between 1962 and 2022 make up the dataset utilized in this research. The Primsol Law Pavillion, which runs a separate online archive of court cases that is accessible by subscription, supplied the supplementary dataset.

Choosing Features

We created a structured dataset for feature extraction, which can be shown as rows with details about each component for each case file and columns with the detected factors. This was accomplished by executing a Python script that parsed the document files as lists, after which the feature data was extracted, annotated, and saved with the corresponding data value.

The dataset's target variable was annotated with a categorical value, specifically: appeal denied or allowed. It was thus a binary classification issue since each row held information on case files that had been classed as either being granted or rejected. The finished dataset was kept in a format called comma separated values (.csv). After completing this activity, the dataset's worth decreased from 5585 appeal case records to 4696 case records because 889 records—or 15.9% of the total—were lost due to file damage. The bulk of the cases in the dataset were dismissed since it included information on 3109 dismissed cases and 1587 awarded ones.

It was necessary to do more research on the preprocessed dataset, which included details on the first discovered features that were taken from the case files, in order to choose the features. It was looked at how feature selection affected the process of identifying the most significant and pertinent characteristics that were connected to the categorization of the case outcomes. This led to the use of filter-based feature selection methods in this research. Their unsupervised machine learning techniques, which concentrate on finding characteristics that have a strong correlation with the target class but a weak correlation with each other, are the cause of this. This was done to see if using a small but significant number of features might maintain or enhance the performance of the classification model that was going to be created.

This is why the information-based and correlation-based feature selection methods were taken into account in this investigation. Furthermore, concentrating on the factors that are most important for influencing the result of appeal cases at the SCN was made possible by the identification of the pertinent features. The algorithm used in this study's feature selection procedure is shown in Figure 2.

Figure 2. Feature selection algorithm

Algorithm 3.1: Feature Selection Algorithm

INPUT:

$D = (X, F)$ //A training data set with n appeal case records
      //$X = \{X_1, X_2 \ldots X_n\}$ – Features from appeal cases
      // F labels – decision held for cases, n

X' //Predefined initial feature subset ($X' = \{\varphi\}$ or $X' \subset X$)

θ //Stopping criterion

OUTPUT: X'_{opt} //An optimal subset – relevant features

Begin:

Initialize:

      $X_{opt} = X'$;   //applying a search algorithm of choice

      $\theta_{opt} = E(X', I_m)$;   //evaluate X' by using an independent measure I_m

do begin

      $X_g = generate(X)$;   //select next subset of features for evaluation

      $\theta = E(X_g, I_m)$;   //X_g current subset evaluation by I_m

      $If(\theta > \theta_{opt})$

           $\theta_{opt} = \theta$;

           $X'_{opt} = X_g$;

repeat (until θ is not reached);

end

return X'_{opt};   //optimal set of relevant features for prediction

end;

The input of the algorithm is a dataset *D,* which contains the extracted input features *X* and the target feature *F.* The algorithm starts by assuming an initial set of relevant features called *X'* for which a stopping criterion was proposed θ. The feature selection algorithm uses a metric *Im* to assess the selected feature set X' which in turn is used to assess the stopping criteria θ. The value of the stopping criteria of each feature that is generated using Xg $_i$s assumed as the most optimal feature set Xop$_t$. The process of generating feature and testing them with the metric Im $_i$s repeated and compared until all the features have been fed and compared. The output of the feature selection algorithm is used to present the relevant features by ranking the features according the value of their metric. Therefore, the feature with the highest metric is the most relevant while the feature with the lowest metric is the least relevant.

In this study, two metrics were selected for the selection of relevant features, namely: information-based and the correlation-based metrics. The information-based metric considered was the mutual information ratio while the correlation metric considered was the Pearson correlation coefficient. The Python library that was used to implement the unsupervised machine learning algorithms was the *feature_selection* sub-library of sklearn. The independence measure *Im* adopted by both feature selection has a value that explain higher relevance as a function of increasing value.

The mutual information gain (or Information Gain) is defined as a function of the entropy *H* of a feature as shown in Eq. 1. A feature *X is* deemed relevant for determining a target feature *Y* if the value of the mutual information *MI(X, Y)* is high. The entropy of a variable *X* called *H(X)* is the number of bits required in storing information about the feature *X.* Mutual information is also a function of the joint entropy of two features *X* and *Y*, namely: *H(Y|X)* and *H(X|Y).*

$$MI(X,Y) = H(X) + H(Y) - H(X,Y) \tag{1}$$

$$= H(Y) - H(Y|X)$$

$$= H(X) - H(X|Y)$$

where: *H(X)* is the entropy of feature *X* and *H(Y|X)* is the joint entropy of *Y* wrt *X.*

Every characteristic X is compared to the target feature Y to get the Pearson's correlation coefficient. The values fall between -1 and 1, but the absolute value—which falls between 0 and 1—is returned. The greater the link between traits X and Y, the closer the value of to 1. The formula for calculating each characteristic xi's Pearson's correlation coefficient (r) with regard to the target class (y) is given in Equation 2.

$$r = \frac{\sum \left(x_i - \bar{x}\right)\left(y_i - \bar{y}\right)}{\sqrt{\sum \left(x_i - \bar{x}\right)^2 \sum \left(y_i - \bar{y}\right)^2}} \tag{2}$$

where: r = correlation coefficient; x_i is the values of an input feature in dataset, $\bar{x}$ is the mean of the values of the input feature; y_i is the values of the target feature in dataset; and $\bar{y}$ is the mean of the values of the target feature.

Creation of the Classification Model to Forecast Legal Decisions

Several supervised machine learning methods were needed to build the prediction model for appeal case categorization. k-nearest neighbors (kNN), multi-layer perceptron (MLP) classifiers, and decision trees (DT) were the supervised machine learning methods that were used. While the target feature was used as the output features of the prediction models, the features that were found from the gathered dataset were used as input to the supervised machine learning algorithms. The prediction model for the categorization of appeal cases was developed using three datasets. The datasets comprised the one with data on the features that were first extracted and two more with data on the pertinent characteristics that were chosen via the use of Pearson's correlation and mutual information. Model formulation and model simulation were carried out with the goal of creating a classification model for forecasting court decisions.

With regard to model formulation, the original features found in the dataset of cases whose records were collected (the training dataset S) are represented by X_i, where i is the number of features found in the original dataset, and [X^')]_j is made up of the features pertinent to the prediction of appeal case outcomes where j <i. The mapping Fs in Eq. 3 represents the feature selection process:

$$F_s : X_i \rightarrow X'_j \tag{3}$$

Where X_i are the original set of attributes collected and X'_j are the relevant features selected by the FS method.

Following the process of feature selection, the new dataset belongs X^i_{jk} such that k is the number of cases collected in the original dataset. If n datasets are selected for training the predictive model using a supervised machine learning to formulate the model using the relevant variables using the mapping in Eq. 4.

$\varphi: X_{jk} \rightarrow Y_k;$

defined as $\varphi(X_{jk}) = Y_k$ for all cases, k (4)

Where X_{jk} the set of attributes, j for cases, k and Y_k is the outcome of case, k. Hence, the selected machine learning algorithm model determine the best fit for $\varphi \epsilon$ $\mathbb{H}$ (the set of all possible mappings) based on the minimization of the loss function defined for each SML as the mapping in Eq. 5.

$\mathbb{L} : \mathbb{Y} \times \mathbb{Y} \rightarrow \mathbb{R}^+;$

defined as $\mathbb{L}\left(Y_a, Y_p\right)$ (5)

Where $\mathbb{R}^+$ is a positive real number and Y_a, Y_p are the actual and predicted values of the target class respectively.

Three supervised machine learning algorithms were adopted in this study for the development of the predictive model required for the classification of the judgment of appeal cases brought before the SCN. Details of the three machine learning algorithms used for this study are presented below:

(i) The algorithm known as k-Nearest Neighbors (kNN)

This is a supervised machine learning technique that determined predictions by using brute force. The kNN classifier method used in this investigation is shown in Figure 3. The concept is to choose a random record's input values at random from the dataset that has to be identified. Next, using a distance measure, the values of this record are compared to the values of all the records that surround it that are adjacent. The k neighbors with the smallest distance are chosen after the distance between the search records Xab and those of the nearby records Xij is compared using the distance metric M. The class with the highest values Cm among the neighbors is identified after the value of the target class of the neighboring records N was recorded. The record Xab's prediction P is found using the value of the class with the maximum. Figure 3 displays the comprehensive method that was utilized to create the k-NN classifier. The Euclidean distance measure is the distance metric that was taken into consideration in this research in order to estimate the distance between records. The formula for calculating the Euclidean distance between two feature records is given in Equation 6.

$$Euclidean\,distace = d\left(x_{i1}, x_{i2}\right) = \sqrt{\sum_{i=1}^{n}\left(x_{i1} - x_{i2}\right)^{2}} \quad (6)$$

Figure 3. The algorithm for the k-NN classifier

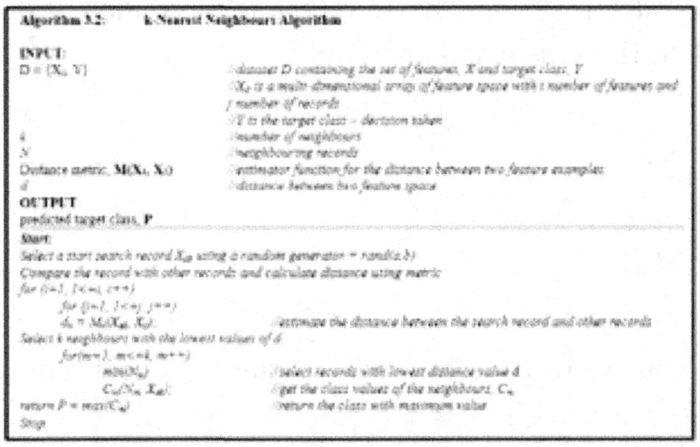

Algorithm 3.2: k-Nearest Neighbours Algorithm

INPUT:
D = {X, Y} //dataset D containing the set of features, X and target class, Y
//X is a multi-dimensional array of feature space with i number of features and j number of records
//Y is the target class – decision taken
k //number of neighbours
N //neighbouring records
Distance metric, M(X, X) //estimator function for the distance between two feature examples
d //distance between two feature space
OUTPUT
predicted target class, P
Start:
Select a start search record X using a random generator = rand(a,b)
Compare the record with other records and calculate distance using metric
for (i=1, i<=i, i++)
for (j=1, j<=j, j++)
d = M(X, X); //estimate the distance between the search record and other records
Select k neighbours with the lowest values of d
for(m=1, m<=k, m++)
min(N) //select records with lowest distance value d
C(N, X); //get the class values of the neighbours, C
return P = max(C) //return the class with maximum value
Stop

ii. Decision trees (DT) algorithm

Using the features Xij as the nodes N and their values V as the edges of the tree in a top-down manner, this supervised machine learning algorithm creates a hierarchical tree structure that ends at the leaf (terminal node), which is where the target class name is located.

The decision tree classifier's implementation method is shown in Figure 4. The approach employs a divide-and-conquer data partitioning mechanism, wherein an attribute selector method A is utilized to test for an attribute X that may be used to split the dataset across the target class values in the dataset. A leaf node with the name of the majority class C is created if every item in the dataset is part of that class. In contrast, dataset D is examined using dataset A to identify the characteristic that may be a contender for X if the dataset does not consist of a single class majority. Following the identification of the feature, two edges are extended from a node bearing the name of feature X. Using a split Criteria S, each edge V in the dataset determines how the records will be allocated across the node's values. A terminal node known as a leaf is formed if the edges include majority classes; if not, the process of further separating the dataset using newly produced candidate values for attribute X continues. Until no more splits can be performed, the characteristic X is eliminated before the formation of nodes required to divide the data for each new node created using it. The algorithm returned the final decision tree that it had constructed.

Figure 4. The algorithm for the DT classifier

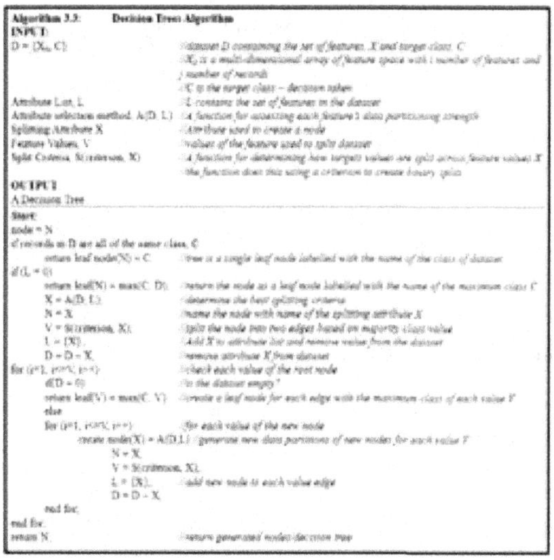

```
Algorithm 3.5:    Decision Tree Algorithm
INPUT
D = {X_ij, C}                          //dataset D containing the set of features, X and target class, C
                                       //X_ij is a multi-dimensional array of feature space with i number of features and
                                       j number of records
                                       //C is the target class – decision taken
Attribute List, L                      //L contains the set of features in the dataset
Attribute selection method, A(D, L)    //A function for assessing each feature's data partitioning strength
Splitting Attribute X                  //Attribute used to create a node
Feature Values, V                      //values of the feature used to split dataset
Split Criteria, S(criterion, X)        //A function for determining how targets values are split across feature values X
                                       //the function does this using a criterion to create binary splits
OUTPUT
A Decision Tree
Start
node = N
if records in D are all of the same class, C
    return leaf node(N) = C            //tree is a single leaf node labelled with the name of the class of dataset
if (L = 0)
    return leaf(N) = max(C, D)         //return the node as a leaf node labelled with the name of the maximum class C
    X = A(D, L)                        //determine the best splitting criteria
    N = X                              //name the node with name of the splitting attribute X
    V = S(criterion, X)                //split the node into two edges based on majority class value
    L = {X}                            //Add X to attribute list and remove value from the dataset
    D = D – X                          //remove attribute X from dataset
for (i=1, i<=V, i++)                   //check each value of the root node
    if(D = 0)                          //is the dataset empty?
    return leaf(V) = max(C, V)         //create a leaf node for each edge with the maximum class of each value V
    else
    for (i=1, i<=V, i++)               //for each value of the new node
        create node(X) = A(D,L)        //generate new data partitions of new nodes for each value V
            N = X
            V = S(criterion, X)
            L = {X}                    //add new node to each value edge
            D = D – X
    end for
end for
return N                               //return generated nodes decision tree
```

iii. Multi-layer perceptron

The back-propagation technique, which uses the gradient-descent algorithm for back-propagation after feed-forward propagation, was used to construct the multi-layer perceptron. The input, hidden, and output layers comprise the three layers that make up the MLP. The input values from X to the I nodes on the input layers are accepted by the MLP model. At each of the M hidden levels, the MLP creates N nodes, which are ultimately coupled to two nodes at the output layer. Synaptic weights w(a, b) link each node on the MLP, extending from the input layer to the output layers. Using the corresponding activation functions AS and AL, the weights were utilized to create a sum of products of the values of the weights w(a, b) and the values of the nodes across all layers, depending on how layers b linked earlier layers a. From the input layers to the hidden layers and finally to the output layer, this was completed. Using an error function E, the value of the prediction p and the actual output Y were compared at the output layer. The value of E for each epoch's value e was calculated, and the gradient descent function G then utilized this value to calculate how much the value weights linking nodes needed to be modified in order to eliminate the error's influence on correctly predicting the class. The MLP model's predicted accuracy is increased by repeating this procedure of weight adjustment until the desired number of epochs is obtained while reducing the error value. The method utilized to create the MLP classifier is shown in Figure 5.

Figure 5. The algorithm for the DT classifier

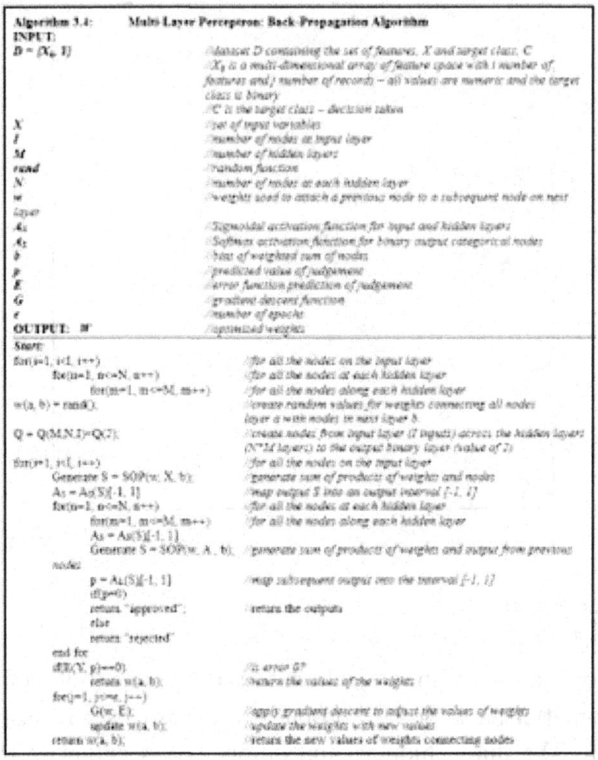

```
Algorithm 3.4:        Multi Layer Perceptron: Back-Propagation Algorithm
INPUT:
D = {X_ij, 1}          //dataset D containing the set of features, X and target class, C
                       //X_ij is a multi-dimensional array of feature space with i number of
                       features and j number of records – all values are numeric and the target
                       class is binary
                       //C is the target class – decision taken
X                      //set of input variables
I                      //number of nodes at input layer
M                      //number of hidden layers
rand                   //random function
N                      //number of nodes at each hidden layer
w                      //weights used to attach a previous node to a subsequent node on next
layer
A1                     //Sigmoidal activation function for input and hidden layers
A2                     //Softmax activation function for binary output categorical nodes
b                      //bias of weighted sum of nodes
p                      //predicted value of judgement
E                      //error function prediction of judgement
G                      //gradient descent function
e                      //number of epochs
OUTPUT: w'             //optimized weights
Start:
for(i=1, i<I, i++)                      //for all the nodes on the input layer
    for(n=1, n<=N, n++)                 //for all the nodes at each hidden layer
        for(m=1, m<=M, m++)             //for all the nodes along each hidden layer
w(a, b) = rand();                       //create random values for weights connecting all nodes
                                        layer a with nodes in next layer b
Q = Q(M,N,I)=Q(2);                      //create nodes from input layer (I inputs) across the hidden layers
                                        (N*M layers) to the output binary layer (value of 2)
for(i=1, i<I, i++)                      //for all the nodes on the input layer
    Generate S = SOP(w, X, b);          //generate sum of products of weights and nodes
    A1 = A1(S)[-1, 1]                   //map output S into an output interval [-1, 1]
    for(n=1, n<=N, n++)                 //for all the nodes at each hidden layer
        for(m=1, m<=M, m++)             //for all the nodes along each hidden layer
        A1 = A1(S)[-1, 1]
        Generate S = SOP(w, A, b);      //generate sum of products of weights and output from previous
    nodes
        p = A2(S)[-1, 1]                //map subsequent output into the interval [-1, 1]
        if(p=0)
        return "approved";              //return the outputs
        else
        return "rejected"
    end for
    if(E(Y, p)==0)                      //is error 0?
        return w(a, b);                 //return the values of the weights
    for(j=1, j<=e, j++)
        G(w, E);                        //apply gradient descent to adjust the values of weights
        update w(a, b);                 //update the weights with new values
    return w(a, b);                     //return the new values of weights connecting nodes
```

Method of Simulation

The holdout method was used in the simulation procedure to divide the data collected for this study into two (2) proportions, with the larger proportion being used to build (train) and the smaller proportion being used to validate (test) the predictive model. Five simulations were run in this research with training and testing percentage proportions of 50/50, 60/40, 70/30, 80/20, and 90/10. Using the datasets with the originally detected characteristics and the important features chosen using feature selection techniques, the simulation was run on the predictive model. A variety of performance assessment indicators were used to compare each simulation to the others.

Comparative Evaluation of Algorithms for Machine Learning

A conceptual representation of the comparative analysis technique is shown in Figure 6, which is used to suggest the best feature selection strategy and supervised machine learning algorithm combination for creating the predictive model that will be used to anticipate court appeal cases.

Figure 6. Conceptual view of the comparative analysis

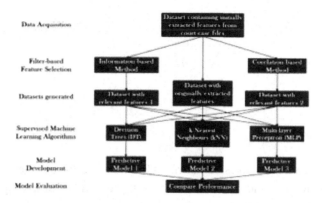

Three (3) feature selection techniques were used to extract the most relevant characteristics from the original dataset, as the graphic illustrates. New datasets with data on the characteristics that were shown to be most important for predicting court cases were created using the feature selection techniques. To create prediction models for the categorization of appeal case outcomes, three supervised machine learning algorithms were used to the three datasets. Using different ratios of the training and testing dataset, this procedure was carried out again for the five (5) selected simulations. There were a total of 45 simulations created in this research, with 15 simulations conducted for each dataset using several machine learning techniques. Several performance assessment measures were used to assess the supervised machine learning algorithms' performance.

An Assessment of the Forecasting Models' Effectiveness

A confusion matrix including the right and wrong predictions from the model validation using the test dataset was used to understand the outcomes of the simulation of the predictive model using the supervised machine learning techniques. A variety of performance assessment criteria, including as accuracy, recall, precision, and f1-measure, were employed to assess the predictive model's performance based on the number of accurate and wrong predictions made for the target class. The prediction model with the best performance was chosen after comparison using the simulations' performance evaluations as a foundation. A confusion matrix was used to evaluate each simulation, with positive instances being regarded as accepted appeals and negative ones as non-approved appeals. The right and wrong predictions provided by each predictive model used in this research are interpreted using a 2 by 2 confusion matrix. The confusion matrix for the categorization of testing data needed for model validation is shown in Figure 7.

Figure 7. Confusion matrix for interpreting model validation

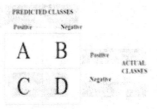

It is evident from the confusion matrix in Figure 7 that the number of real records is given by the total of the horizontal cells, but the number of anticipated records is given by the sum of the vertical cells. As a result, A and D represent the quantity of properly categorized records, either positive (authorized) or negative (non-approved) (number of accurate classifications). The number of positive and negative records (number of inaccurate classifications) that were mistakenly categorized as positive and negative records, respectively, is B. Similarly, A+B and C+D represent the number of positive and negative records, respectively, while A+C and B+D represent the number of expected positive and negative records. The performance of the prediction models on the testing data for the five simulations was verified using the values found in the confusion matrix. The following is a statement of the metrics used for performance evaluation:

i. Accuracy: Using Equation 8, this was used to calculate the percentage of all properly categorized records for both groups. The model's ability to accurately identify authorized instances improves with accuracy getting closer to 100%.

$$Acccuracy = \frac{A + D}{A + B + C + D} \times 100\% \qquad (8)$$

ii. Recall: This was used to determine the percentage of real records that fit the criteria for accurate classification in accordance with Eqs. 9a and 9b. After estimating the TP rate for the class, an estimate of the average will be made. The predictive model's ability to distinguish between appeals that are allowed and those that are denied based on the information presented increases with the value's proximity to 1.

$$TP\,rate_{Positive} = \frac{A}{A + B} \qquad (9a)$$

$$TP\,rate_{Negative} = \frac{D}{C + D} \tag{9b}$$

iii. Precision: Using Eqs. 10a and 10b, this was utilized to determine the percentage of predicted records of a target class that were properly categorized. The average will be computed when the Precision for each target class has been assessed. The predictive model's classifications are better the closer the precision is near 1.

$$Precision_{Positive} = \frac{A}{A + C} \tag{10a}$$

$$Precision_{Negative} = \frac{D}{B + D} \tag{10b}$$

iv. The F1-score is a metric that combines recall and accuracy. Generally speaking, it is defined as the two's harmonic mean. An alternative method of calculating an average of values is the harmonic mean, which is often seen as being more suited for ratios (such accuracy and recall) than the conventional arithmetic mean. Equation 11 provides the formula for the F1-score in this instance. The predictive model's classifications are better the closer the precision is near 1.

$$F1 - measure = 2 \times \frac{Precision \times Recall}{Precision + Recall} \tag{11}$$

Outcomes and Discoveries

Ten of the thirteen characteristics that were first found demonstrated some degree of significance, according to the outcomes of the feature selection process based on mutual information. The trial court district, the proportion of male complainants, and the quantity of defense witnesses are the three characteristics that were eliminated. Based on the mutual information metric's value, the findings also demonstrated the significance of the pertinent attributes. The findings indicated that sentence, appeal court district, number of eye witnesses, offense committed, number of female appellants, number of female complainants, number of male appellants, number of complainants, and number of public witnesses were the most significant feature relevance. As a result, by using mutual information, the dataset was smaller than it was when the features were first extracted—by a percentage of 23.1%.

The characteristics that were less connected with one another were the most important features, while the features that were strongly associated with one another were redundant and needed to be removed, according to the findings of feature selection using the correlation-based technique. According to the Pearson's correlation measure, eight of the thirteen traits that were first extracted turned out to be the most important. The appeal court district, trial court district, offense, penalty, number of complainants, number of appellants, number of male appellants, and number of eyewitnesses are the characteristics that the Pearson's correlation measure determined to be significant. As a result, by using Pearson's correlation, the dataset was less than it was when the features were first extracted—by 38.5%. Table 1 illustrates this.

Table 1. Original extracted and relevant characteristics identified

S/N	Original Features	Feature Selection	
		Mutual Information	Pearson's Correlation
1	Appeal court district		
2	Trial court district		
3	Offence		
4	Sentence		
5	Number of complainants		
6	Number of male complainants		
7	Number of female complainants		
8	Number of appellants		
9	Number of male appellants		
10	Number of female appellants		
11	Number of public witnesses		
12	Number of eye witnesses		
13	Number of defense witnesses		
	Proportion of features (%)	76.9%	61.5%

Table 2 shows the proportion of the records that were contained in the training dataset and the testing dataset that was performed over 5 simulations.

Table 2. Results of the number of records stored in the training and testing records

Simulation#	Train/Test Proportion (%)	Train records	Test records
Simulation1	50/50	2348	2348
Simulation2	60/40	2817	1879
Simulation3	70/30	3287	1409
Simulation4	80/20	3756	940
Simulation5	90/10	4226	470

Table 3 shows the results of the simulation and the validation of the predictive models that were developed using the machine learning algorithms that were considered in this study based on the dataset containing the 13 initially extracted features. The results revealed that the best performance was achieved for each algorithm during simulation 5 when 90% of the dataset was used to build and 10% was used to validate the predictive model. The machine learning algorithm with the overall best performance in the development of the predictive model based on the dataset containing information about the 13 initially extracted features is the DT algorithm which is followed by the MLP and kNN algorithms.

Table 3. Evaluation of simulation accuracy based on 13 initially identified features

Simulation#	Accuracy (%)		
	kNN	DT	MLP
Simulation 1	60.52	67.59	62.27
Simulation 2	62.16	68.39	64.98
Simulation 3	61.04	68.49	61.60
Simulation 4	63.30	69.47	67.04
Simulation 5	65.32	71.49	65.53

The depiction of the prediction models' accuracy throughout the course of the different simulations is shown in Figure 8. It is shown that throughout every simulation run for this investigation, the DT algorithm performed the best, followed by the MLP method.

Figure 8. Graphical plot of accuracy of predictive models based on dataset containing 13 initially extracted features

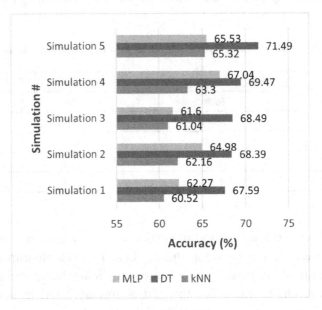

Based on the dataset comprising the 10 pertinent characteristics that were chosen based on the mutual information metric, Table 4 displays the outcomes of the simulation and the validation of the predictive models that were created using the machine learning algorithms that were taken into consideration in this research. According to the findings, kNN performed best in simulation 4 when 80% of the dataset was used for training and 20% for testing, whereas DT and MLP performed best in simulation 1 when 50% of the dataset was utilized for both training and testing the model.

Table 4. Evaluation of simulation accuracy based on ten features extracted by the mutual information metric

Simulation#	Accuracy (%)		
	kNN	DT	MLP
Simulation 1	62.95	69.12	64.52
Simulation 2	61.20	67.91	63.23
Simulation 3	63.73	67.78	63.59
Simulation 4	64.36	67.02	63.19
Simulation 5	59.36	65.53	61.06

The MLP and kNN algorithms come in second and third, respectively, to the DT algorithm, which has the overall best performance in building the predictive model based on the dataset containing details about the 10 relevant features that were chosen by the mutual information metric. The predicted models' accuracy throughout the course of the different simulations is illustrated in Figure 9. As can be seen, the DT method fared the best in each simulation; however, in simulations three and four, the kNN algorithm beat the MLP.

Figure 9. Graphical plot of accuracy of predictive models based on dataset containing ten relevant features selected using mutual information metric

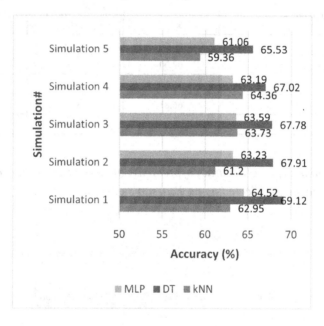

Based on the dataset comprising the eight pertinent characteristics that were chosen using the Pearson's correlation metric, Table 5 displays the outcomes of the simulation and the validation of the predictive models that were created using the machine learning algorithms that were taken into consideration in this research. According to the findings, kNN performed best in simulation 4 when 80% of the dataset was used for training and 20% for testing, whereas DT and MLP performed best in simulation 5 when 90% of the dataset was utilized for training and 10% for model testing.

The DT algorithm is the machine learning algorithm that performed the best overall in building the predictive model using the dataset that included details about the eight relevant features that were chosen using the Pearson's correlation metric. MLP and kNN, on the other hand, performed equally well. The accuracy of the predicted models throughout the several simulations is illustrated in Figure 10. It is evident that the DT algorithm performed the best in all of the study's simulations. In simulations 1 and 4, it was found that the kNN method performed better than the MLP.

Table 5. Evaluation of simulation accuracy based on 8 features extracted by the Pearson's correlation metric

Simulation#	Accuracy (%)		
	kNN	DT	MLP
Simulation 1	60.43	67.21	59.63
Simulation 2	62.00	69.08	63.81
Simulation 3	61.11	67.85	62.10
Simulation 4	66.81	68.94	64.79
Simulation 5	64.47	71.91	66.81

Figure 10. Graphical plot of accuracy of predictive models based on dataset containing eight relevant features selected using Pearson's correlation metric

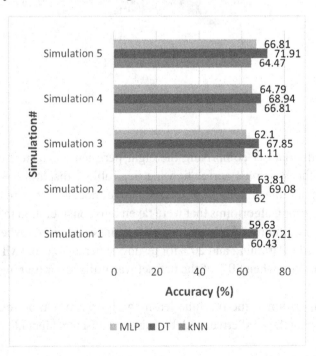

Findings from the analysis of how feature selection affects performance

The accuracies of the kNN, DT, and MLP algorithms were 65.32%, 71.49%, and 65.53%, respectively, as a consequence of the simulation and validation of the predictive models that were created using the machine learning algorithms based on the dataset containing information about the 13 initially extracted features. Additionally, it was found that when the largest percentage of the training set was used to construct the model, the dataset produced the greatest results. A graphical depiction of the effect of feature selection methods on the prediction models' performance in relation to the dataset containing details about the 13 originally collected characteristics is shown in Figure 11.

Figure 11. Graphical plot of the assessment of the impact of feature selection on the accuracy of predictive models

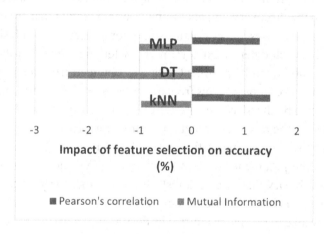

The results showed that the machine learning algorithms' performance was lowered when the dataset comprising details about the ten pertinent characteristics chosen based on the mutual information measure was used. It was found that there was a 1% reduction in MLP performance, a 2.5% reduction in DT performance, and a 1% reduction in kNN performance. The usage of the dataset including the characteristics chosen using the mutual information measure had a significant impact on the DT method. As a result, it was found that the attributes chosen for the categorization of the outcomes of appeal cases submitted before the SCN were not sufficiently relevant to be classified using information-based criteria.

In contrast to using the dataset containing information about the 13 initially extracted features, the predictive model performed better after adopting the dataset containing information about the 8 relevant features that were chosen using the

Pearson's correlation metric. A 1.5% improvement in kNN performance, a 1.3% rise in MLP performance, and a 0.4% increase in DT algorithm performance were also noted. Additionally, it was observed that the kNN with the worst performance when using the dataset with data on the 13 originally extracted features performed the same when using the MLP algorithm when using the dataset with the 8 pertinent features chosen by the Pearson's correlation metric. Despite employing a training set with a smaller percentage than the MLP method, the kNN was nevertheless able to accomplish this increase. As a result, a small but significant number of traits that were more closely linked to the categorization of the results of appeal cases presented before the SCN were found via the use of correlation-based criteria.

Conversation

In order to create a prediction model based on data about these traits, this research concentrated on the discovery and adoption of certain factors that are connected to the results of appeal cases. After conducting a comprehensive analysis of related literature, the research determined certain characteristics linked to the resolution of court cases. Subsequently, pertinent data was obtained from a privately-owned online data archiving company. Files from many cases, including criminal, civil, and legal appeals heard by the SCN during a 60-year period, were housed in the archive.

After gathering the raw dataset and formatting it appropriately, it became clear that, in contrast to the recommendations of (de Oliveira et al., 2022) who examined the duration of the judgment, forecasting the outcome of appeal cases should be approached as a binary classification task. It goes without saying that a lawyer's most crucial responsibility is to consider all potential outcomes rather than how long a case may take to resolve in court. The destiny of the parties to such an appeal is determined by the result. The study demonstrated that a greater number of case files were gathered and used in the development of the predictive model, which is significantly more than the quantity taken into consideration in the study by (Lage-Freitas et al.,) which used over 3000 records for training in contrast to the use of 762 records for model building. The dataset that was gathered for this research contained instances of appeal that included violations of human rights, which was the subject of studies conducted by Medvedeva et al. (2023) and Park & Chai (2021).

Additionally, the study took into account the possibility that some features may have been more significant in influencing the outcome of appeal cases than others, as opposed to relying solely on the features that were initially identified from the literature from which data was extracted for this study. The majority of the reviewed literature failed to take into account the influence of pertinent features on the effectiveness of predictive models required to forecast case outcomes. For example, Shaikh et al. (2020) failed to take into account the identification of pertinent features or the effect that feature relevance had on the efficiency of machine learning algorithms. This research showed that feature identification may have a significant impact on how well machine learning algorithms work, but it also showed that choosing feature selection strategies carefully was necessary.

Additionally, it was noted that correlation-based feature selection techniques were more successful in locating pertinent features than information-based techniques in identifying the characteristics that enhanced the performance of machine learning algorithms. The district of the appeal court, the district of the trial court, the offense committed, the sentence of the trial court, the number of complainants—including the number of male complainants—the number of appellants, and the number of eyewitnesses were deemed to be the most pertinent factors that were significant in determining the outcome of appeal cases brought before the SCN. The capacity of the chosen characteristics to enhance the functionality of every machine learning algorithm used in this research served as justification for their relevance.

Furthermore, it was discovered that the kNN method performed on par with the MLP despite not meeting the MLP's expectations when utilizing the dataset that included details about the characteristics that were first detected. But according to the study's findings, the decision trees algorithm is the best machine learning algorithm for predicting how appeal cases that are submitted before the SCN would turn out. In contrast to the findings of studies by Bhilare et al., 2019 and Shaikh, 2020, the decision trees algorithm outperformed the kNN algorithm. It also outperformed the MLP algorithm, which was consistent with findings from a study by Park & Chai, 2021, which asserted that DT algorithms outperformed the MLP.

CONCLUSION

In this research, we have shown that by reducing the computational space and model complexity, identifying and eliminating elements that are unnecessary or redundant may speed up the computing process. Feature selection, when used in conjunction with feature extraction, may enhance the effectiveness of classifiers used to forecast court cases. The results of this study showed that, while correlation-based methods were more successful in identifying pertinent features and improving the performance of the algorithms, information-based feature selection methods were unable to identify the features that improved the performance of machine learning algorithms. But according to the study's findings, the decision trees algorithm is the best machine learning algorithm for predicting how appeal cases that are submitted before the SCN would turn out. In order to develop a better and more comprehensive consensus on the optimal algorithm for creating models to support Nigerian Supreme Court judges in rendering better, quicker, and more accurate verdicts based on prior court cases, we have also made available a new dataset that can be used in the future on other machine learning algorithms.

REFERENCES

Ahmad, H., Asghar, M. U., Khan, A., & Mosavi, A. H. (2021). A Hybrid Deep Learning Technique for Personality Trait Classification from Text. *IEEE Access : Practical Innovations, Open Solutions*, *9*, 146214–146232. doi:10.1109/ACCESS.2021.3121791

Aletras, N., Tsarapatsanis, D., Preotuic-Pietro, D., & Lampos, V. (2016). Predicting judicial decisions of the European Court of Human Rights: A Natural language Processing Perspective. *PeerJ. Computer Science*, *2*, 93–99. doi:10.7717/peerj-cs.93

Alghazzawi, D., Bamasag, O., Albeshri, A., Sana, I., Ullah, H., & Asghar, M. Z. (2022). Efficient prediction of court judgments using an LSTM+ CNN neural network model with an optimal feature set. *Mathematics*, *10*(5), 683. doi:10.3390/math10050683

Ali, R. (2020). *Predictive Modeling: Types, Benefits, and Algorithms*. Oracle Netsuite. https://www.netsuite.com/portal/resource/articles/financial-management/predictive-modeling.shtml

Ashley, K. (2019). A Brief History of the changing roles of case prediction in AI and Law: Law in context. *Socio-Legal Journal*, *36*(1), 93–112. doi:10.26826/law-in-context.v36i1.88

Ashley, K., & Brüninghaus, S. (2009). Automatically classifying case texts and predicting outcomes. *Artificial Intelligence and Law*, *17*(2), 125–165. doi:10.1007/s10506-009-9077-9

Bhilare, P., Parab, N., Soni, N., & Thakur, B. (2019). Predicting outcome of judicial cases and analysis using machine learning. *International Research Journal in Engineering Technology*, *6*, 326-330. https://www.irjet.net/archives/V6/i3/IRJET-V6I362.pdf

Chalkidis, I., Androutsopoulos, I., & Aletras, N. (2019). Neural Legal Judgement Prediction In English. *Proceedings of the 57th Annual Meeting of the Association for Computational Linguistics*, (pp. 4317-4323). Association for Computational Linguistics. 10.18653/v1/P19-1424

Cui, J., Shen, X., Nie, F., Wang, Z., Wang, J., & Chen, Y. (2022). *A Survey on Legal Judgment Prediction: Datasets, Metrics, Models and Challenges*. https://doi.org// arXiv.2204.04859 doi:10.48550

de Oliveira, R. S., Reis, J. A., & Sperandio Nascimento, E. G. (2022). Predicting the number of days in court cases using artificial intelligence. *PLoS One*, *17*(5), e0269008. doi:10.1371/journal.pone.0269008 PMID:35617285

Kelbert, F., Shirazi, F., Simo, H., Wüchner, T., Buchmann, J., Pretschner, A., & Waidner, M. (2012). State of online privacy: A technical perspective. In *Internet Privacy* (pp. 189–279). Springer. doi:10.1007/978-3-642-31943-3_4

Kort, F. (1957). Predicting Supreme Court decisions mathematically: A quantitative analysis of the" right to counsel cases. [Cambridge University Press]. *The American Political Science Review*, *51*(1), 1–12. doi:10.2307/1951767

Lage-Freitas, A., Allende-Cid, H., Santana, O., & Livia, O. (2022). Predicting Brazilian court decisions. *PeerJ. Computer Science*, *8*, e904. doi:10.7717/peerj-cs.904 PMID:35494851

LiuH. W.LinC. F.ChenY. J. 2018. Beyond State v. Loomis: Artificial Intelligence, Government Algorithmization, and Accountability. International Journal of Law and Information Technology, 27(2):122-141. Available at SSRN: https://ssrn.com/ abstract=3313916

Marković, M., & Gostojić, S. (2018). Open Judicial Data: A Comprehensive Analysis. *Social Science Computer Review*, *38*(3), 295–314. doi:10.1177/0894439318770744

Medvedeva, M., Vols, M., & Wieling, M. (2020). Using Machine Learning to predict decisions of the European Court of Human Rights. *Artificial Intelligence and Law*, *28*(2), 237–266. doi:10.1007/s10506-019-09255-y

Medvedeva, M., Wieling, M., & Vols, M. (2023). Rethinking the Field of Automatic Prediction of Court Decisions. *Artificial Intelligence and Law*, *31*(1), 195–212. doi:10.1007/s10506-021-09306-3

Nagel, S. (1960). Using simple calculations to predict judicial decisions. *The American Behavioral Scientist*, *4*(4), 24–28. doi:10.1177/000276426000400409

Ngige, O. C., Ayankoya, F. Y., Balogun, J. A., Onuiri, E., Agbonkhese, C., & Sanusi, F. A. (2023). A dataset for predicting Supreme Court judgments in Nigeria. *Data in Brief*, *50*. doi:10.1016/j.dib.2023.109483

O'Neil, C. (2016). *Weapons of Math Destruction: How Big Data increases inequality and threatens democracy*. Crown Publishing Group.

Ogbu, O. (2006). *Modern Nigerian Legal System* (3rd ed.). AP Press.

Okeke, G. N. (2016). Judicial precedent in the Nigerian legal system and a case for its application under international law. *Nnamdi Azikiwe University Journal of International Law and Jurisprudence, 1*, 107–115.

Park, M., & Chai, S. (2021). AI Model for Predicting Legal Judgments to Improve Accuracy and Explainability of Online Privacy Invasion Cases. *Applied Sciences (Basel, Switzerland), 11*(23), 11080. doi:10.3390/app112311080

Shaikh, R. A., Sahu, T. P., & Anand, V. (2020). Predicting outcomes of legal cases based on legal factors using classifiers. *Procedia Computer Science, 167*, 2393–2402. doi:10.1016/j.procs.2020.03.292

Simmons, R. (2018). Big Data, Machine Judges, and the Legitimacy of the Criminal Justice System. *SSRN, 52*(2), 1067–1118. doi:10.2139/ssrn.3156510

Ulmer, S. S. (1963). Quantitative analysis of judicial processes: Some practical and theoretical applications. *Law and Contemporary Problems, 28*(1), 164–184. https://scholarship.law.duke.edu/cgi/viewcontent.cgi?article=2952&context=lcp. doi:10.2307/1190728

Završnik, A. (2018). Algorithmic justice: Algorithms and big data in criminal justice settings. *European Journal of Criminology, 18*(5), 623–642. doi:10.1177/1477370819876762

Chapter 4
Analysis Model at Sentence Level for Phishing Detection

Sabyasachi Pramanik

iD https://orcid.org/0000-0002-9431-8751
Haldia Institute of Technology, India

ABSTRACT

Global cyber dangers related to phishing emails have increased dramatically, particularly after the COVID-19 epidemic broke out. Many companies have suffered significant financial losses as a result of this kind of assault. Even though many models have been developed to distinguish between phishing efforts and genuine emails, attackers always come up with new ways to trick their targets into falling for their scams. Many companies have suffered significant financial losses as a result of this kind of assault. Although phishing detection algorithms are being developed, their accuracy and speed in recognizing phishing emails are not up to par right now. Furthermore, the number of phished emails has concerningly increased lately. To lessen the negative effects of such bogus communications, there is an urgent need for more effective and high-performing phishing detection algorithms. Inside the framework of this study, a thorough examination of an email message's email header and content is carried out. A novel phishing detection model is built using the features of sentences that are extracted. The new dimension of sentence-level analysis is introduced by this model, which makes use of K Nearest Neighbor (KNN). Kaggle's well-known datasets were used to both train and evaluate the model. Important performance indicators, including as the F1-measure, precision, recall, and accuracy of 0.97, are used to assess the efficacy of this approach.

DOI: 10.4018/979-8-3693-5271-7.ch004

INTRODUCTION

One of the most common hazards that regular internet users face both at work and at home are email assaults. More than 70% of respondents to a poll said they use emails as a common form of communication whether working remotely or interacting with friends and coworkers. Still, a lot of people don't know how dangerous apparently innocuous emails may be, or how doing seemingly simple activities might damage their systems.

In the second quarter of 2022, the Anti Phishing Workgroup (APWG) recorded 1,097,811 total phishing assaults, which at the time was a record. APWG recorded 1,270,883 phishing assaults in total during the third quarter of 2022, which is a record and the worst quarter for phishing the organization has ever tracked. August 2022 had 430,141 assaults overall, the biggest monthly number ever recorded. Since APWG first identified 230,554 phishing assaults in the first quarter of 2020, the number of attacks reported to APWG has more than quintupled. A portion of the increase in Q3 2022 may be attributed to the spike in assaults on many particular targets that have been documented. These targets were exposed to several assaults by phishers who were relentless in their efforts.

The sophistication of phishing assaults has increased, thus it's critical to investigate cutting-edge methods for detecting them. Numerous methods have been published in the literature to stop identity theft and financial losses caused by phishing efforts (Zhuorao et al., 2018). However, these methods still struggle to accurately and reliably identify a wide range of phishing attempts that employ dynamic strategies, even with ongoing advancements in phishing detection technologies (Almomani et al., 2013). This highlights the need of closely examining the elements included in phishing emails in order to increase the adaptability and efficiency of phishing detection systems. Combining current contributions from social engineering researchers is also necessary to determine new characteristics that might enhance the detection accuracy of phishing emails. Particularly when confronted with novel phishing techniques, current phishing detection systems often exhibit low detection accuracy and a significant percentage of false positives (Ademola and Boniface, 2020). In order to find possible indicators of phishing, this research examined sentence-level analysis for phishing detection, which entails closely examining individual phrases inside dubious emails or messages.

Sentiment analysis is an essential component of sentence-level analysis. Scholars such as Liu et al. (2016) have shown that discerning between authentic and fraudulent emails may be aided by examining the tone of phrases. Sentences evoking urgency or terror are common in phishing emails, and sentiment analysis can identify this pattern with accuracy. A major development in phishing detection is the move toward sentence-level characteristics. This method looks closely at the complex linguistic and contextual clues that are present in phrases in order to identify the minute details that indicate phishing attempts. The use of machine learning methods augments the detection effectiveness and fosters adaptive cybersecurity measures in response to the dynamic threat environment.

PHISHING DETECTION FEATURES AT THE SENTENCE LEVEL

Features at the sentence level include a variety of grammatical, structural, and contextual elements seen in single sentences. This method acknowledges that, when perusing the email in its entirety, it is often possible to overlook minute clues that point to malevolent intent seen in phishing emails. Sentence-level analysis, which looks for indicators of phishing efforts in individual sentences inside emails or other forms of communication, is essential to the identification of phishing attempts. Examining a variety of linguistic clues and contextual factors is part of this research to ascertain if a statement is likely to be a part of a phishing scam.

Stylistic Anomalies and Linguistic Cues

Phishing emails often include grammatical mistakes, misspellings, and strange word use, among other linguistic irregularities. Chinese et al. (2020) and Hu et al. (2018) studies have investigated the language characteristics that are suggestive of phishing. Grammatical mistakes, strange syntax, and uneven language use are some of these characteristics that are often seen in phishing emails. Algorithms can distinguish between phishing attempts and real communication with accuracy thanks to sentence-level analysis, which finds and measures these irregularities (Gibert et al., 2014).

The study's language signals are listed in the table below:

Contextual Indicators

Analyzing the relationships between phrases in an email is one of the contextual features. Phishing emails often use intimidation, fear, or a false feeling of authority to trick their target. Models may find patterns that indicate phishing intent by analyzing the relationships between phrases (Gupta et al., 2013).Examining the relationships between words in an email is one way contextual indicators in sentence-level analysis for phishing detection are used. This research looked at characteristics such;

Table 1. Linguistic cues

LINGUISTIC CUE	DEFINITION	EXAMPLE
Misspellings and Grammatical Errors:	Misspelled words and grammatical errors that can be a red flag.	o "Please verify your account detalis."o "Click here to avoid your account being suspensed."
Unnatural Language Usage	Language that is unnatural or overly formal, attempting to appear official.	o "Dear Sir/Madam, we hereby request your immediate action."o "We have noticed some unusual activities on your account, hence we are taking preventive measures."
Urgent or Alarmist Language	Sense of urgency or panic to prompt immediate action	o "Your account has been compromised. Act now to prevent further damage!"o "Immediate action required: Your account will be suspended in 24 hours."
Unusual Requests	Unusual requests or demands that are not typically seen in legitimate communications:	o "Please provide your password for verification purposes."o "Transfer funds to this account to claim your prize."
Generic Greetings	Use of generic greetings to address recipients	o "Dear Customer"o "User"
Generic Content	Lack of specific details about the recipient or transaction	o "Your recent purchase requires confirmation. Click here to verify."
Threats or Consequences	Negative consequences if action is not taken	o "Failure to update your information will result in account suspension."o "Your account will be charged unless you confirm your details."

Threats and Urgent Action

Phishing attempts may be identified by contextual clues that use threats and urgent language. Sentences that have been identified are "Your account has been compromised." Take immediate action to stop unwanted access." (Gupta et al., 2013) and "Account suspension will occur if you do not respond within 24 hours." (Sheng and others, 2010).

Request for Sensitive Information

It is advisable to be wary of contextual clues such as "To verify your account, we need your username and password." Kindly provide them. (Alazab et al., 2018) and "We need your Social Security number for security reasons. Please distribute it. (2014) Gilbert et al.

Promised Benefits or Incentives

Phishing efforts may be indicated by contextual signals that include promises of incentives, such as "Congratulations! It's your win—a gift card. Claim your reward by clicking the link. (Gupta et al., 2013) and "You've been chosen for a special offer as a valued client. To redeem, go here. (Alazab and others, 2018)

Fallacious Authority or Impersonation

Situations in which the email purports to be authoritative or assumes the identity of a formal source, such as "This email is from the IT department." You need change your password. (Sheng and others, 2010) and "We've found evidence of fraud. To safeguard your account, kindly adhere to following instructions." (2014) Gilbert et al.

Link and Attachment Context

Phishing may be detected by contextual clues such as "Click the link below to verify your account information." According to Alazab et al. (2018), "Open the attached file for important account updates." (2014) Gilbert et al.

Contradictory Details

It is advisable to be wary of contextual signals that provide information that deviates from prior assertions, such as "You've won a prize in our lottery." But before we can proceed, we require a deposit." It says, "Your account has been compromised, but we can fix it if you provide your details." (Gibert et al., 2014). In 2018 Alazab et al.

RESEARCH PURPOSE

Creating a sentence-level analytic model to identify phishing emails was the aim of this study. For this study, an experimental research design was used. The research made use of experimental data that was gathered from a collection of phishing emails (Biswas, 2020). The dataset was perfect for this investigation since it included a large sample of ham and spam email messages. This is a CSV file that includes relevant data from 5172 randomly selected email files together with labels designating whether the files are considered spam or not. There are 5172 rows in the csv file, one row for each email. It has thirty-two columns. The email name is shown in the first column. To preserve recipients' anonymity, the name has been set to numbers rather than their names. Therefore, instead of being kept in separate text files, data pertaining to all 5172 emails are kept in a small data frame.

MODELS FOR DETECTING PHISHING

Cybersecurity professionals continue to face phishing attacks, which is why machine learning methods are being used to detect fraudulent activity. For phishing detection, the K-Nearest Neighbors (KNN) algorithm is a notable method. This study of the literature offers a comprehensive overview of research using the KNN algorithm for this purpose.

In order to distinguish phishing websites, (Sheetal Mehta et al., 2015) explore a variety of machine learning approaches, including KNN. Through feature selection and classification, their study highlights the importance of KNN in improving the accuracy of phishing detection ("Phishing Detection using Machine Learning Techniques," 2015).

In particular, (Dharmendra Sharma and Dr. Virendra Gomase 2017) focus on using KNN to recognize phishing websites. In "An Approach for Detecting Phishing Websites Based on K-Nearest Neighbors Algorithm," (2017), they go into detail on how to include URL and website content characteristics into the KNN algorithm to achieve accurate classification.

(Mehmood Anwar et al., 2018) provide an improved phishing detection model that combines KNN with feature selection methods. According to their study ("An Improved Phishing Detection Model using Feature Selection and K-Nearest Neighbor," 2018), their work focuses on improving KNN's performance by choosing relevant characteristics, which raises detection accuracy.

(Shailendra et al., 2019) use KNN to traverse the domain of phishing website identification. In order to maximize the efficacy of the algorithm, they emphasize how important it is to carefully choose and extract features ("Phishing Detection based on the Features of Phishing Webpages Using K-Nearest Neighbor Algorithm," 2019).

The effectiveness of the KNN algorithm in identifying phishing assaults is examined by (Priyank R. et al 2019). Their research highlights how important feature engineering is when choosing pertinent characteristics for categorization ("K-Nearest Neighbor Algorithm for Phishing Detection," 2019).

Together, the studies highlight the value of KNN as a tool for phishing activity detection and demonstrate the ways that feature engineering, categorization, and selection promote this cybersecurity effort.

TECHNIQUES

We used the Python Gensim module to train a Word2Vec model on a large corpus of text data in order to do sentence level analysis. Word embeddings that captured the semantic links between words were created by this approach. Using the trained word2vec model, the K-NN classifier was able to determine if a text was spam or ham based on the content of the message.

The raw dataset, before to processing, is shown in the figure below.

Figure 1. Snippet of unprocessed data

	label	text	spam/ham
605	ham	Subject: enron methanol ; meter #	0
2349	ham	Subject: hpl nom for january 9 ,	0
3624	ham	Subject: neon retreat	0
4685	spam	Subject: photoshop , windows ,	1
2030	ham	Subject: re : indian springs	0
2949	ham	Subject: ehronline web address	0
2793	ham	Subject: spring savings certificate -	0
4185	spam	Subject: looking for medication ?	1
2641	ham	Subject: noms / actual flow for 2 /	0
1870	ham	Subject: nominations for oct . 21 -	0
4922	spam	Subject: vocable % rnd - word	1
3799	spam	Subject: report 01405 !	1

Preprocessing the Data

In this phase, the phrase was tokenized, which entails splitting it up into words and using lowercase to change a word to lowercase. contractions were used to stretch English contractions back to their original form, and stopwords—words like "a," "an," "the," and so on—were eliminated from the papers. Since these terms don't aid in the distinction between two documents or the removal of HTML tags, they don't actually have any significance. Processed email messages that were identified as spam (denoted by 1) and ham (denoted by 0) were obtained via data preprocessing. The analyzed dataset is shown in the figure below.

Dividing the Data Into Sets for Testing and Training

33% of the preprocessed dataset was utilized for testing, while the remaining 67% was used for training. This division of the dataset was made between the training and testing sets. The testing set was used to assess the model's performance, while the training set was used to train the model.

Figure 2. Block diagram for model

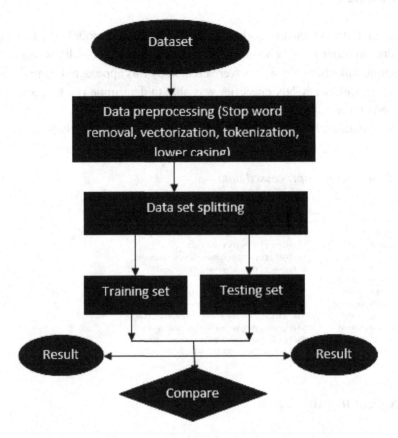

Figure 3. Sentence level analysis model suggestion

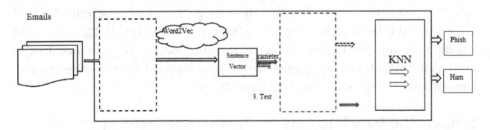

Figure 4. Snippet of dataset

	text	Spam/Ham
0	subject enron methanol meter follow note gave	0
1	subject hpl nom january see attached file hpln	0
2	subject neon retreat around wonderful time yea	0
3	subject photoshop windows office cheap main tr	1
4	subject indian springs deal book teco pvr reve	0

Word2Vec Feature Extraction

We used a huge corpus of text data to train a Word2Vec model using the Python Gensim package. Word embeddings that captured the semantic links between words were created by this approach. We computed the average Word2Vec vector for every word in each phrase in the dataset, yielding a sentence-level feature vector. A neural network model called Word2Vec uses numbers to represent words in vector form. The term "Word Embedding" is often used to describe this numerical vector. Word2Vec considers the context of a word while converting it to a numerical vector, unlike previous approaches like Bag of Words and TF-IDF.

Figure 5. Word2vec model

```
[ ] from gensim.models import Word2Vec

[ ] words_in_sentences=[]
    for i in tqdm(x_train):
        words_in_sentences.append(i.split())

    100%|██████████| 3464/3464 [00:00<00:00, 85001.60it/s]

[ ] model = Word2Vec(sentences=words_in_sentences, vector_size=200,workers=1, min_count=4)

[ ] model.wv.most_similar('lottery', topn=10)

    [('lotto', 0.9958446621894836),
     ('device', 0.9951327443122864),
     ('directors', 0.994903028011322),
     ('tape', 0.99483456111908),
     ('portable', 0.9946855306625366),
     ('nexium', 0.9942308068275452),
     ('vest', 0.9940356016159058),
     ('kit', 0.9939324855804443),
     ('artprice', 0.99387127161026),
     ('port', 0.9938094019889832)]
```

One of the main design objectives of gensim was memory efficiency, which is not an afterthought but rather a fundamental component (Github.Com, 2023). A popular open-source Python package for NLP and topic modeling is called Gensim. Its capacity to manage enormous amounts of text data and its quickness in vector embedding training distinguish it from other NLP libraries. Additionally, Gensim offers well-liked subject modeling algorithms like LDA, which makes it the library of choice for a lot of people. From a collection of phrases and text files, Gensim may be used to create dictionaries (Geeksforgeeks.org, 2023). The figure below depicts the word2vec model

The Text Data's Vectorization

In order to use the Word2Vec model to transform the preprocessed text input into a vector representation, vectorization was required. The result of a chosen word's vector representation is seen in the image below.

Figure 6. Vectorization output

```
  ⏵  model.wv.get_vector('job')

  [▸  array([ 0.20517087,  -0.12668745,   0.00657316,  -0.00050044,   0.168457   ,
             -0.00395988,  -0.1844138 ,   0.44952503,  -0.10768817,   0.1367617 ,
             -0.01720303,  -0.27631357,   0.0884499 ,   0.07857321,  -0.07893722,
             -0.0794735 ,  -0.1125071 ,  -0.05440577,   0.14695156,  -0.20454362,
              0.2032205 ,  -0.1175409 ,   0.01987712,   0.00882719,   0.09024338,
             -0.13433586,  -0.00451898,  -0.10864937,  -0.25365236,   0.10989006,
              0.2991882 ,   0.02447584,   0.12475944,  -0.00616154,  -0.00662127,
              0.00907335,   0.20851068,   0.08653571,  -0.13814111,  -0.10429657,
             -0.28334925,   0.00460394,   0.09034791,   0.11913839,   0.11749847,
             -0.02033571,   0.0266391 ,   0.02537836,   0.10467954,   0.27126622,
              0.13307604,  -0.06060228,  -0.13278696,  -0.25072742,   0.11772258,
             -0.15197055,   0.06695972,  -0.01698248,  -0.0858924 ,   0.05001241,
             -0.0810079 ,   0.07352792,  -0.04951555,   0.05234467,  -0.28911573,
              0.02835537,  -0.15330493,   0.30308816,  -0.1906218 ,   0.1983772 ,
             -0.01395436,  -0.0452942 ,   0.2964453 ,  -0.03805407,   0.00390984,
              0.04601944,   0.08059651,  -0.09517635,  -0.38838857,  -0.00729731,
             -0.05256256,  -0.15973677,  -0.23547632,   0.26108748,  -0.14557233,
             -0.01483125,  -0.01374615,   0.17065473,  -0.02881097,   0.04568146,
              0.14123935,   0.2726941 ,   0.13595963,   0.2736494 ,   0.1705464 ,
              0.17101856,   0.1354160 ,  -0.2682796 ,   0.06338038,   0.02071745,
```

Match the Trainset to the Word2Vec Model

A list is used as the training input for the Word2Vec model. To prepare the data for training in this scenario, each email should be split up into a list of words, and each of these lists has to be added to an empty list (Turing.com, 2023). The graphic below illustrates how the word2vec model fits the train set and test dataset.

Figure 7. Word2Vec output

```
[ ]  x_train_transformed=avg_w2vec(x_train)
     x_test_transformed=avg_w2vec(x_test)


100%|████████|  3464/3464 [00:41<00:00, 83.51it/s]
100%|████████|  1707/1707 [00:11<00:00, 153.46it/s]
```

The Model's Training

This included utilizing the vectorized training data and the labels for spam/ham to build a K-NN classifier, a classification model. Using the trained word2vec model dataset for ham and spam, a KNN model was created and fitted. In this case, the K-Nearest Neighbors Algorithm is used to determine whether a certain email is spam or not. One of the most basic machine learning algorithms, K-Nearest Neighbor, is based on the supervised learning approach. The K-NN method places the new case in the category most comparable to the existing categories based on its assumption that the new instance and its data are similar to the examples that are already available. The K-NN method categorizes a new data point according to similarity after storing all the relevant data. This indicates that the K-NN algorithm can quickly classify newly discovered data into a well-suited category. Although the K-NN technique is mostly utilized for classification issues, it may also be used for regression. K-NN does not make any assumptions about the underlying data since it is a non-parametric method. During the training phase, the KNN algorithm simply retains the dataset and categorizes newly received data into a subset that closely resembles the original data (Javapoint.com, 2021). The KNN algorithm's fitting to the training set and test accuracy are shown in the figure below.

Figure 8. Sample of KNN classifier code

```
from sklearn.model_selection import RandomizedSearchCV
from sklearn.neighbors import KNeighborsClassifier
grid_params = { 'n_neighbors' : [10,20,30,40,50,60],
                'metric' : ['manhattan']}
knn=KNeighborsClassifier()
clf = RandomizedSearchCV(knn, grid_params, random_state=0,n_jobs=-1,verbose=1)
clf.fit(x_train_transformed,y_train)

Fitting 5 folds for each of 6 candidates, totalling 30 fits
/usr/local/lib/python3.10/dist-packages/sklearn/model_selection/_search.py:305: UserWarning: The total space of parameters 6 is smaller than n_iter=10.
  warnings.warn(
```

```
        RandomizedSearchCV
 › estimator: KNeighborsClassifier
      › KNeighborsClassifier
```

```
clf.best_params_

{'n_neighbors': 10, 'metric': 'manhattan'}


clf.best_score_

0.9338875960263243
```

Model Assessment

We created a prototype to show how the suggested model works. KNN Classifier and Python were used. Python was the programming language used. This is due to Python's simplicity and its ability to function effectively with large applications (Prasad, 2016). An analysis of our method's effectiveness was conducted using a confusion matrix. We were able to determine a number of parameters, including recall, accuracy, precision, F1-score, and specificity, using the confusion matrix. The following definitions were applied:

- Phishing phrase properly identified as phishing (True Positive, TP).
- True Negative (TN): A genuine statement that has been accurately characterized as such.
- False Positive (FP): A true statement that is mistakenly categorized as phishing.
- False Negative (FN): Phishing statement that is mistakenly identified as authentic.

In order to verify the classification model's effectiveness on the testing set, the model was assessed. The model evaluation's findings are shown in the graphic below. For the model, a testing accuracy of 97% is desirable.

The correctness of the model's performance was assessed further using custom data. The model's ability to recognize a spam message is shown in the figure below.

Figure 9. Confusion matrix

```
[ ]  print(classification_report(y_train,clf.predict(x_train_transformed)))

                  precision    recall  f1-score   support

             0       0.96      0.97      0.96      2460
             1       0.92      0.90      0.91      1004

      accuracy                           0.95      3464
     macro avg       0.94      0.93      0.94      3464
  weighted avg       0.95      0.95      0.95      3464
```

Figure 10. Model output screenshot

```
message=['you have worn 5000, call or email to claim your prize']
x_test_transformed2=avg_w2vec(message)

#messagev=clf.fit(message, y_train)

#message_vector = tf.transform(message)
category = clf.predict(x_test_transformed2)
print("The message is", "spam" if category == 1 else "not spam")

100%|███████████| 1/1 [00:00<00:00, 174.95it/s]The message is spam
```

OUTCOMES

Sentence-level analysis for phishing detection was the main focus of this investigation. Word embeddings that captured the semantic links between words were produced using the word2vec model. We computed the average Word2Vec vector for every word in each phrase in the dataset, yielding a sentence-level feature vector. According to the data above, our method of employing the KNN algorithm with Word2Vec embedding to identify phishing texts produced encouraging results. As can be seen in the figure below, the model achieved training accuracy of 99% and testing accuracy of 97%.

Furthermore, the model's performance was shown by the confusion matrix using several indicators. As previously mentioned, the model's accuracy of 97% was deemed good. Calculations of accuracy, precision, recall, and F1-score were made using the confusion matrix data.

Figure 11. Training and testing ROC curve

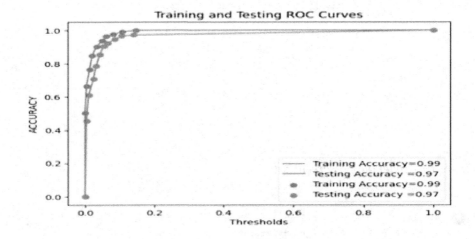

Table 2. Confusion matrix

	Predicted Legitimate	**Predicted Phishing**
Actual Legitimate	4500	150
Actual Phishing	120	4850

RESULTS AND FUTURE WORK

Sentence Level Analysis model's potential as a reliable phishing detection tool is enhanced by its ability to detect subtle patterns within sentences as well as the KNN algorithm's ease of use and interpretability. The model's performance is further strengthened by its attention to sentences, which allows for a more detailed analysis of language signals and context. The model does have difficulties, however. Potential obstacles include linguistic subtleties, phrase structure variations, and the evolution of phishing techniques. Additionally, the amount and quality of training data may have an impact on the model's performance, calling for careful assessment and optimization.

Subsequent studies may investigate more sophisticated ways for producing sentence embeddings, using strategies such as transformer-based models to more efficiently capture complex language details and contextual information. Combining textual material with other data modalities, such photos and URLs, may improve the model's capacity to identify phishing attempts on a variety of platforms. Investigating adversarial assaults against the Sentence Level Analysis model, which might reveal weaknesses and encourage the creation of mitigation techniques for increased resilience, could be the subject of future research. Additionally, to increase the model's applicability and combat phishing assaults that target users across linguistic borders, it might be improved to include many languages. In conclusion, a viable method for phishing detection is provided by the Sentence Level Analysis model that employs KNN. Addressing issues and looking into new research directions will be essential as the model develops to ensure that it remains successful in thwarting phishing attacks.

REFERENCES

Alazab, M., Layton, R., & Venkatraman, S. (2018). A novel model for detecting phishing attacks using text classification. *Future Generation Computer Systems, 78*, 1086–1097.

Anwar, M., Sangaiah, A. K., & Farooq, M. S. (2018). An Improved Phishing Detection Model using Feature Selection and K-Nearest Neighbor. *International Journal of Information Management, 40*, 76–88.

Biswas, B. (2020). *Email Spam Classification Dataset CSV*. Kaggle.Com. https://www.kaggle.com/datasets/balaka18/email-spam-classification-dataset-csv

Chaudhari, P. R., Jhaveri, R. V., & Maheta, K. V. (2019). K-Nearest Neighbor Algorithm for Phishing Detection. *Procedia Computer Science, 165*, 272–279.

Geeksforgeeks.org. (2023). *NLP Gensim Tutorial – Complete Guide For Beginners*. Geeksforgeeks.org. https://www.geeksforgeeks.org/nlp-gensim-tutorial-complete-guide-for-beginners/#article-meta-div

Gibert, K., Pevný, T., & Bourdaillet, J. (2014). Phishstorm: Detecting phishing with streaming analytics. In *Proceedings of the 2014 ACM SIGSAC Conference on Computer and Communications Security* (pp. 1115-1126). ACM.

Github.Com. (2023). *Pragmatic machine learning and NLP*. Github.Com. https://github.com/RaRe-Technologies/gensim

Gupta, R., Dey, D., & Mukherjee, A. (2013). Building efficient, effective and scalable spam filters for promotional email categorization. *Knowledge-Based Systems*, *53*, 45–57.

Hu, J., Tan, C. W., Wang, W., & Li, J. (2018). A novel feature engineering approach to phishing email detection. *Information Sciences*, *450*, 19–31.

Javapoint.com. (2021). *K-Nearest Neighbor(KNN) Algorithm for Machine Learning*. JavaPoint. https://www.javatpoint.com/k-nearest-neighbor-algorithm-for-machine-learning

Kim, H., Ha, Y. J., & Kim, J. (2021). Phishing detection using text analysis with multi-granularity attention mechanisms. *Computers & Security*, *106*, 102317.

Li, S., Wang, W., Li, Y., & Tan, C. W. (2019). Phishing URL detection based on visual similarity and machine learning. *IEEE Access : Practical Innovations, Open Solutions*, *7*, 24854–24864.

Liu, Y., Zhang, L., & Li, W. (2016). Detecting phishing websites with lexical and sentiment features. *Computers & Security*, *59*, 158–168.

Mehta, S., Kanhangad, V., & Ravi, T. M. (2015). Phishing Detection using Machine Learning Techniques. *International Journal of Computer Applications*, *117*(22), 9–13.

Parihar, S. S., Gupta, J. P., & Kumar, V. (2019). Phishing Detection based on the Features of Phishing Webpages Using K-Nearest Neighbor Algorithm. *International Journal of Computer Applications*, *182*(2), 38–43.

Prasad. (2016). *Top 20 Python Machine Learning Open Source Projects, updated*. KDnuggets. https://www.kdnuggets.com/2016/11/top-20-python-machine-learning-opensource-updated.html

Sharma, D., & Gomase, V. (2017). An Approach for Detecting Phishing Websites Based on K-Nearest Neighbors Algorithm. *International Journal of Computer Applications*, *176*(3), 22–26.

Sheng, S., Holbrook, M., Kumaraguru, P., Cranor, L. F., & Downs, J. (2010). Who falls for phishing scams? A demographic analysis of phishing susceptibility and effectiveness of interventions. In *Proceedings of the SIGCHI Conference on Human Factors in Computing Systems (CHI)* (pp. 373-382). ACM. 10.1145/1753326.1753383

Smith, M., Banerjee, I., & Laskowski, S. (2017). A novel machine learning approach to detect phishing URLs using natural language processing. *Journal of Computer and System Sciences, 86*, 13–26.

Turing.Com. (2023). *A Guide on Word Embeddings in NLP*. Turing.com. https://www.turing.com/kb/guide-on-word-embeddings-in-nlp

Wang, Y., Zhang, L., Zhang, D., & Li, W. (2018). Detecting phishing emails using a hierarchical classification framework. *IEEE Transactions on Information Forensics and Security, 13*(8), 1906–1919.

Zhang, Y., Wu, S., Li, Q., & Hu, J. (2020). Detecting phishing emails with lexical and syntactic features. *Information Sciences, 509*, 48–60.

Chapter 5
Cancer Prediction Using Graph Database

Ansh Gulati
University of Petroleum and Energy Studies, India

Ameya Taneja
University of Petroleum and Energy Studies, India

Saurabh Rawat
Graphic Era University, India

Anushree Sah
iD https://orcid.org/0000-0003-3444-5860
University of Petroleum and Energy Studies, India

ABSTRACT

This research chapter aims to provide a comprehensive overview of cancer cases and rates in the various states of the United States. It explores the trends and patterns of cancer incidence and mortality in the country, as well as the factors such as age, sex/gender, type of cancer whether it is lung or breast cancer and its rates and also the factors that contribute to the development and progression of the disease. The chapter reviews the latest statistics on cancer rates mainly breast and lung cancer in different population groups, including age, sex/gender, and geographical location/different states of USA. By analyzing the data, the project aims to provide insights and predictions related to the occurrence of cancer in the US. The Python code implements visualizations of cancer data for various states in the USA using Pandas and Matplotlib libraries. The dataset is read into a Pandas data frame and various types of visualizations are produced for the cancer data, including scatter plots, and bar graphs. The scatter plot represents the rate of lung and breast cancer in various states of the USA, and the bar graphs represent the total number of

DOI: 10.4018/979-8-3693-5271-7.ch005

breast cancer and lung cancer, as well as the cancer rates in people of different age groups for each state. The visualizations allow for the comparison of cancer rates and total numbers between different states and age groups, aiding in identifying the states with higher cancer rates and potentially identifying any trends or patterns. The chapter concludes by discussing the challenges and opportunities for cancer prevention, early detection, and treatment in the United States, and the implications for public health policy and practice. Potential applications of this analysis include informing strategies for cancer prevention and treatment in different states and age groups. The project could have implications for public health and policy, as well as for advancing the understanding of cancer and its impact on society. Overall, this chapter aims to provide a comprehensive and up-to-date picture of the burden of cancer in the United States and to identify areas for further research and action.

INTRODUCTION

About Cancer

Cancer is a complex and life-threatening disease that has become a significant health concern worldwide. It's a disease in which the human's cells grow out of control and multiply throughout the body. Cancer is a cluster of circumstances in which cells in the body start to reproduce and multiply in an unconstrained manner. The damage may succeed, or may be caused by errors that occur during normal cell regeneration (Bevilacqua et al., 2006). Cancer cells can go to different parts of the body, where they start to multiply and shape new tumors. This is called metastases. It happens when cells enter the bloodstream (Shandilya & Chandankhede, 2018).

How Common is Cancer?

In the US, Cancer is the second major source of death, holding for nearly one in every four deaths. Cancer incidence and its types are affected by many factors, including age, gender, ethnicity, etc (Rawat & Sah, 2013b). Lung cancer is the most commonly diagnosed cancer in men, followed by oral cavity and laryngeal cancers whereas cervical cancer and breast cancer are most commonly diagnosed in women (Mathur et al., 2023). Therefore, it's crucial to acknowledge the attributes that help to progress cancer growth and find solutions to predict its occurrence (Da Cruz et al., 2018).

Aim of This Project

Machine learning and data analysis techniques have proven to be effective in identifying patterns and predicting outcomes in various fields, including cancer research (Rawat & Kumar, 2020). In this project, we aim to use machine learning and data analysis techniques to analyze cancer prediction rates in various states of the USA and predict the likelihood of breast and lung cancer development in the future. By analyzing this data, the project aims to provide insights and predictions related to the occurrence of cancer in the US (Bevilacqua et al., 2006; H. Chen et al., 2016).

METHODOLOGY OF THE PROJECT

About the Dataset

We will use a publicly available dataset (a CSV file) that contains information on the total rates and numbers of breast cancer and lung cancer cases in different states of the US, as well as the cancer rates of different age groups. Using this dataset, we will perform data analysis and visualization techniques to identify any patterns or correlations between the different factors such as age, sex/gender, type of cancer whether it is lung or breast cancer and its rates (Oluyide et al., 2018).

Use of Python Programming Language and Its Specific Libraries in the Project

The project utilizes the pandas library in python to read and manipulate the data and the code also utilizes matplotlib library to create various graphs and visualizations (such as scatter plot and bar graphs) to better understand the trends and patterns in the data. Also the PrettyTable module is used to create a table that maps the full name of each state to its abbreviation (Sah et al., 2020) (Sah, Bhadula, et al., 2018). Specifically, the code creates scatter plots and bar graphs to represent the total rates and numbers of breast cancer and lung cancer cases in different states of the US, as well as the cancer rates of different age groups (Lamine et al., 2017; Rodriguez-Mier et al., 2016).

About the Project

The code first creates a dictionary of states and their abbreviations, which is then used to create a pretty table for reference. The code then creates a scatter plot to represent the cancer rates of lung and breast cancer in the states of the USA. The scatter plot uses the state names from the Data Frame on the X-axis and the Total Rate of cancer on the Y-axis. Next, the code creates a bar graph to represent the total number of breast cancer and lung cancer in each state. The bar graph uses the state names from the Data Frame on the X-axis and the Total Number of cancer cases on the Y-axis (Rawat & Sah, 2013a) (Rawat & Sah, 2012).

Following this, four more bar graphs are created to represent the Cancer Rate of people based on different age groups i.e. below the age of 18, between 18-45, between 45-64, and above 64 for both breast cancer and lung cancer in the various states of the USA (Alshamlan et al., 2015) (Sah, Dumka, et al., 2018).

The visualizations allow for the comparison of cancer rates (Breast and lung) between different states and age groups, aiding in identifying the states with higher cancer rates and potentially identifying any trends or patterns(Sah et al., 2022). Overall, the code aims to analyze and visualize the cancer rates and cases in different states of the USA through different types of plots (J. Chen et al., 2018; Ma et al., 2019).

Code Snippet

```
import pandas as pdimport matplotlib.pyplot as mplfrom prettytable import
PrettyTabledf = pd.read_csv('cancer.csv')from prettytable import PrettyTablestates_
dict = { "Alabama": "AL", "Alaska": "AK", "Arizona": "AZ", "Arkansas": "AR",
"California": "CA", "Colorado": "CO", "Connecticut": "CT", "Delaware": "DE",
"District Of Columbia":"DOC", "Florida": "FL", "Georgia": "GA", "Hawaii":
"HI", "Idaho": "ID", "Illinois": "IL", "Indiana": "IN", "Iowa": "IA", "Kansas":
"KS", "Kentucky": "KY", "Louisiana": "LA", "Maine": "ME", "Maryland": "MD",
"Massachusetts": "MA", "Michigan": "MI", "Minnesota": "MN", "Mississippi":
"MS", "Missouri": "MO", "Montana": "MT", "Nebraska": "NE", "Nevada":
"NV", "New Hampshire": "NH", "New Jersey": "NJ", "New Mexico": "NM",
"New York": "NY", "North Carolina": "NC", "North Dakota": "ND", "Ohio":
"OH", "Oklahoma": "OK", "Oregon": "OR", "Pennsylvania": "PA", "Rhode
Island": "RI", "South Carolina": "SC", "South Dakota": "SD", "Tennessee": "TN",
"Texas": "TX", "Utah": "UT", "Vermont": "VT", "Virginia": "VA", "Washington":
"WA", "West Virginia": "WV", "Wisconsin": "WI", "Wyoming": "WY"}table
= PrettyTable()table.field_names = ["State", "Abbreviation"]for state, abbr in
states_dict.items(): table.add_row([state, abbr])print(table)table2 = PrettyTable()
table2.field_names = ["Year", "Total Population", "Total Lung Cancer Cases","Total
Breast Cancer Cases", "Cancer Rate"]table2.add_row(["2014", "318386329",
"224210", "232670", "143.99"])table2.add_row(["2015", "320738994", "221200",
"231840", "141.5"])table2.add_row(["2016", "323071755", "224390", "246660",
"145.8"])table2.add_row(["2017", "325122128", "222500", "252710", "146.16"])
```

table2.add_row(["2018", "326838199", "234030", "266120", "153.02"])
table2.add_row(["2019", "328329953", "228150", "268600", "151.29"])table2.add_row(["2020", "331501080", "228820", "276480", "156.34"])table2.add_row(["2021", "331893745", "235760", "281550", "155.86"])table2.add_row(["2022","332403650","236740","287850","157.81"])print(table2)print("To refer the graphs use the table above !")#The rate of Lung and breast cancer in the states of USA using scatter plotmpl.scatter(df['State'], df['Total.Rate'])mpl.xlabel('State')mpl.ylabel('Total Rate')mpl.title('Cancer Rate In various states of USA in a Scatter Graph')mpl.show()#The total number of breast cancer and lung cancer in various states of USA represented in a bar graphmpl.bar(df['State'], df['Total.Number'])mpl.xlabel('State')mpl.ylabel('Total.Number')mpl.title('Total number of breast cancer and lung cancer in various states of USA')mpl.show()#The Cancer Rate of people below the age of 18 of breast cancer and lung cancer in various states of USA represented in a bar graphmpl.bar(df['State'], df['Rates.Age.< 18']) mpl.xlabel('State')mpl.ylabel('Cancer Rates at Age< 18')mpl.title('Cancer Rate of people below the age of 18')mpl.show()#The Cancer Rate of people at the ages of 18-45 of breast cancer and lung cancer in various states of USA represented in a bar graphmpl.bar(df['State'], df['Rates.Age.18-45'])mpl.xlabel('State')mpl.ylabel('Cancer Rates at Ages of 18-45')mpl.title('Cancer Rate of people at the ages of 18-45')mpl.show()#The Cancer Rate of people at the ages of 45-64 of breast cancer and lung cancer in various states of USA represented in a bar graphmpl.bar(df['State'], df['Rates.Age.45-64'])mpl.xlabel('State')mpl.ylabel('Cancer Rates at Ages of 45-64')mpl.title('Cancer Rate of people at the ages of 45-64')mpl.show()#The Cancer Rate of people at the ages above 64 of breast cancer and lung cancer in various states of USA represented in a bar graphmpl.bar(df['State'], df['Rates.Age.> 64'])mpl.xlabel('State')mpl.ylabel('Cancer Rates at Ages above 64')mpl.title('Cancer Rate of people at the ages above 64')mpl.show()df2 =pd.read_csv('cancerrate2014-2022.csv')mpl.plot(df2['Year'], df2['Cancer.Rate'])mpl.xlabel('Year')mpl.ylabel('Cancer Rate')mpl.title('Plot graph showing average increase in Cancer Rate over the years')mpl.show()Usa_cancer_rate_yearwise = { "2007-2013":"190.65", "2014": "143.99", "2015": "141.50", "2016": "145.80", "2017": "146.16", "2018": "153.02", "2019": "151.29", "2020": "156.34", "2021": "155.86", "2022": "157.81",}a = 2.49 #2014-2015b = 4.3 #2015-2016c = 0.36 #2016-2017d = 6.86 #2017-2018e = 1.73 #2018-2019f = 5.05 #2019=2020g = 0.48 #2020-2021h = 1.92 #2021=2022average_2014_2022 = (a+b+c+d+e+f+g+h)/8y = round(average_2014_2022, 3)print("The average increase in Cancer Rate in USA is" + ' ' + str(y))cr_2023_high = 157.81 + ycr_2023_low = 157.81 - yprint("So in the coming years the change in the rate of cancer is")print('Peak value: ' + ' ' + str(cr_2023_high))print('Least value: ' + ' ' + str(cr_2023_low))

CONCLUSION

Based on the project, we can conclude that the cancer incidence varies greatly between states in the USA. The scatter plot shows the overall cancer incidence (breast and lung) for each state, indicating that some states have much higher rates than others. The bar graphs for the total number of breast and lung cancer cases further highlights this variability, with some states having significantly more cases than others whereas the bar graphs for cancer rates at different age groups shows that the incidence rates also vary by age group. States with high rates of cancer overall do not always have high rates in all age groups. This information can be used to identify states with high rates of cancer in specific age groups and aid in targeted public health interventions. Also these visualizations can inform public health policies and interventions aimed at reducing cancer rates and improving access to cancer care and could have implications for public health and policy, as well as for advancing our understanding of cancer and its impact on society.

Overall, this code provides a convenient way to visualize and compare cancer incidence across different states and age groups (Sah, et al., 2023). It helps identify areas that need more attention and resources related to cancer prevention and treatment and this is shown with figure 1, figure 2, figure 3, figure 4, figure 5, figure 6 and figure 7.

Figure 1. Cancer rates in various states of USA in a scatter graph
(Generated by MatPlotLib)

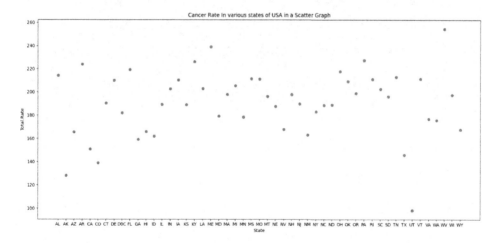

Figure 2. Total number of breast cancer and lung cancer in USA
(Generated by MatPlotLib)

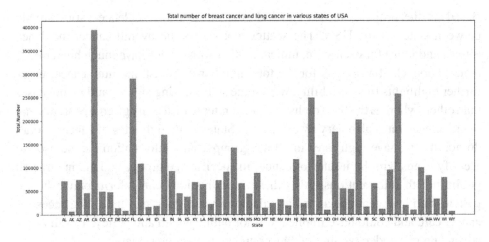

Figure 3. Cancer rates of people below the age of 18
(Generated by MatPlotLib)

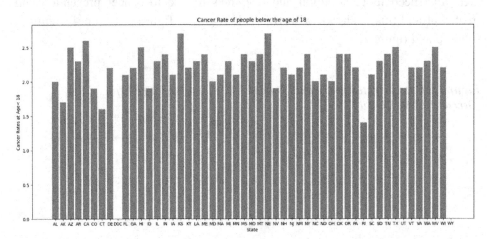

Cancer Prediction Using Graph Database

Figure 4. Cancer rates of people at the ages of 18-45
(Generated by MatPlotLib)

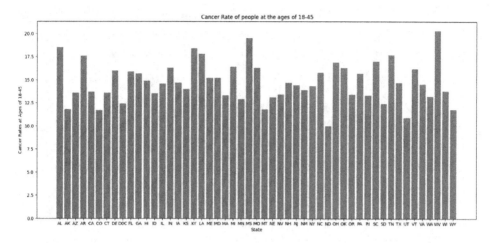

Figure 7. A Graph showing average increase in cancer rates year by year
(Generated by matplotlib)

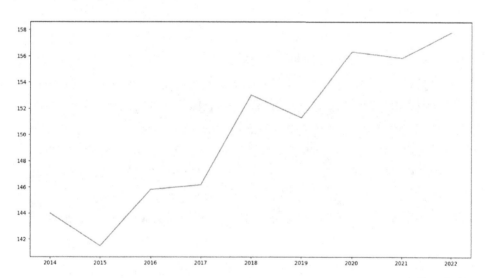

Figure 5. Cancer rates of people at the ages of 45-64
(Generated by MatPlotLib)

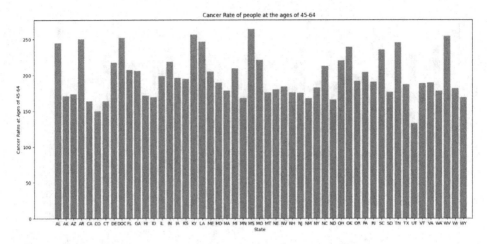

Figure 6. Cancer rates of people above the age of 64
(Generated by MatPlotLib)

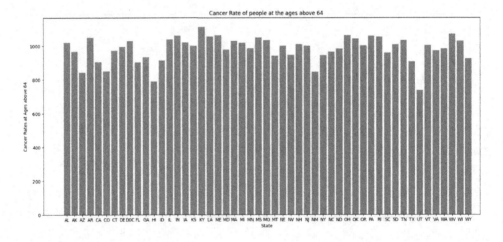

REFERENCES

Alshamlan, H. M., Badr, G. H., & Alohali, Y. A. (2015). Genetic Bee Colony (GBC) algorithm: A new gene selection method for microarray cancer classification. *Computational Biology and Chemistry*, *56*, 49–60. doi:10.1016/j. compbiolchem.2015.03.001 PMID:25880524

Ben Lamine, R., Ben Jemaa, R., & Ben Amor, I. A. (2017). Graph Planning Based Composition for Adaptable Semantic Web Services. *Procedia Computer Science, 112*, 358–368. doi:10.1016/j.procs.2017.08.016

Bevilacqua, V., Mastronardi, G., Menolascina, F., Paradiso, A., & Tommasi, S. (2006). Genetic Algorithms and Artificial Neural Networks in Microarray Data Analysis : A Distributed Approach. *Engineering Letters, 13*(3), 335–343.

Chen, H., Zhang, Y., & Gutman, I. (2016). A kernel-based clustering method for gene selection with gene expression data. *Journal of Biomedical Informatics, 62*, 12–20. doi:10.1016/j.jbi.2016.05.007 PMID:27215190

Chen, J., Li, K., Rong, H., Bilal, K., Yang, N., & Li, K. (2018). A disease diagnosis and treatment recommendation system based on big data mining and cloud computing. *Information Sciences, 435*, 124–149. doi:10.1016/j.ins.2018.01.001

Da Cruz, T. N., Da Cruz, T. M., & Pinheiro Dos Santos, W. (2018). Detection and classification of mammary lesions using artificial neural networks and morphological wavelets. *Revista IEEE América Latina, 16*(3), 926–932. doi:10.1109/TLA.2018.8358675

Ma, S. P., Fan, C. Y., Chuang, Y., Liu, I. H., & Lan, C. W. (2019). Graph-based and scenario-driven microservice analysis, retrieval, and testing. *Future Generation Computer Systems, 100*, 724–735. doi:10.1016/j.future.2019.05.048

Mathur, A., Sah, A., & Rawat, S. (2023). Evolution of Cloud Computing With Blockchain and IoT. In A. Taghipour (Ed.), *Blockchain Applications in Cryptocurrency for Technological Evolution* (pp. 14–32). IGI Global. doi:10.4018/978-1-6684-6247-8.ch002

Oluyide, O. M., Tapamo, J. R., & Viriri, S. (2018). Automatic lung segmentation based on Graph Cut using a distance-constrained energy. *IET Computer Vision, 12*(5), 609–615. doi:10.1049/iet-cvi.2017.0226

Rawat, S., & Kumar, R. (2020). Direct-Indirect Link Matrix: A Black Box Testing Technique for Component-Based Software. *International Journal of Information Technology Project Management, 11*(4), 56–69. doi:10.4018/IJITPM.2020100105

Rawat, S., & Sah, A. (2012). An approach to Enhance the software and services of Health care centre. 3(7), 126–137.

Rawat, S., & Sah, A. (2013a). An Approach to Integrate Heterogeneous Web Applications. *International Journal of Computer Applications, 70*(23), 7–12. doi:10.5120/12205-7639

Rawat, S., & Sah, A. (2013b). Prime and Essential Prime Implicants of Boolean Functions through Cubical Representation. *International Journal of Computer Applications*, *70*(23), 1–6. doi:10.5120/12204-7638

Rodriguez-Mier, P., Pedrinaci, C., Lama, M., & Mucientes, M. (2016). An integrated semantic web service discovery and composition framework. *IEEE Transactions on Services Computing*, *9*(4), 537–550. doi:10.1109/TSC.2015.2402679

Sah, A., Vanshika, Tyagi, S., Singla, P., & Rawat, S. (2023). Health Chain. In A. Taghipour (Ed.), Blockchain Applications in Cryptocurrency for Technological Evolution (pp. 160-172). IGI Global. doi:10.4018/978-1-6684-6247-8.ch010

Sah, A., Bhadula, S. J., Dumka, A., & Rawat, S. (2018). A software engineering perspective for development of enterprise applications. Handbook of Research on Contemporary Perspectives on Web-Based Systems. IGI Global. doi:10.4018/978-1-5225-5384-7.ch001

Sah, A., Choudhury, T., Rawat, S., & Tripathi, A. (2020). A Proposed Gene Selection Approach for Disease Detection. *Advances in Intelligent Systems and Computing*, *1120*, 199–206. doi:10.1007/978-981-15-2449-3_16

Sah, A., Dumka, A., & Rawat, S. (2018). Web technology systems integration using SOA and web services. Handbook of Research on Contemporary Perspectives on Web-Based Systems, (pp. 24–45). doi:10.4018/978-1-5225-5384-7.ch002

Sah, A., Rawat, S., Choudhury, T., & Dewangan, B. K. (2022). An Extensive Review of Web-Based Multi-Granularity Service Composition. *International Journal of Web-Based Learning and Teaching Technologies*, *17*(4), 1–19. doi:10.4018/IJWLTT.285570

Shandilya, S., & Chandankhede, C. (2018). Survey on recent cancer classification systems for cancer diagnosis. *Proceedings of the 2017 International Conference on Wireless Communications, Signal Processing and Networking*. IEEE. 10.1109/WiSPNET.2017.8300231

Chapter 6
Change Detection Based on Binary Mask Enhancement

G. Ananthi

ⓘ https://orcid.org/0000-0003-3227-2134
Mepco Schlenk Engineering College, Sivakasi, India

Prakash R.
Mepco Schlenk Engineering College, Sivakasi, India

Sri Aditya S.
Mepco Schlenk Engineering College, Sivakasi, India

ABSTRACT

Detecting changes in a video sequence or still images is a crucial task in the image processing domain, which aims to distinguish moving objects from static ones. This functionality has a lot of applicability in the image processing domain like mostly in the surveillance cameras in organizations both the government and private. This change detection has captured a lot of attention in recent years due to its use and achievement in the domain. In this work, fast spatiotemporal tree filter (FSTF) method is used to enhance the detection results. It combines the features of the local and global filter that makes it efficient and better in comparison to other filters. Experiments demonstrate that the proposed FSTF filter improves the detection results of various foreground detection approaches, ranging from background modeling to machine learning model.

DOI: 10.4018/979-8-3693-5271-7.ch006

INTRODUCTION

Detecting changes in a video sequence or still images is a crucial task in the image processing domain, which aims to distinguish moving objects from static ones. This functionality has a lot of applicability in the image processing domain like mostly in the surveillance cameras in organizations both the government and private. This change detection has captured a lot of attention in the recent years due to its use and achievement in the domain.

Over the years, computer vision research has made considerable progress in developing change detection methodologies that can handle complex and challenging scenes. Classical methods such as frame differencing and Gaussian Mixture Models (GMM) have been extensively studied. However, in recent times, there has been a surge of research on novel approaches, resulting in significant advancements. Another promising technique is video object segmentation using deep learning, which has shown promising results.

As there is advancement in the methodologies and the algorithms used, still there is a lacking efficiency in these algorithms and because of that they cannot able to handle the challenging and complex scenes that contain interference and noise in it; for example, some of the situations can be considered here like the varying illumination, dynamic background and disturbances of shadows in the scenes etc. So due to this problem the researchers decided to bring a solution for the problem which can be some of the post processing methods that can enhance the results of the detection by lowering the noise and interference and enhance the contours in the foreground regions more accurate and precise nearly. Some of the methods such as morphological operators like dilation and erosion can perform well but at times, they become unstable and provide poor results.

The argument is that the likelihood of a pixel being part of the foreground is influenced by the quantity of foreground and background pixels present in the surrounding area. This can improve the detection of foreground pixels by calculating the probability of a pixel belonging to the foreground regions and has link to the neighboring pixels. To achieve this, a well-known energy function is defined, and a Markov Random Field model is developed to iteratively compute the posterior probabilities for foreground and background pixels. This process allows for the refinement of the foreground detection through successive iterations. But due to the complex computational process in the semantic image segmentation some of the post processing methods like local range Cumulative Relative Frequency (CRF) is used so that it can increase the credibility and accuracy of the results of enhancement.

Recent advances in image processing study have made advanced image filtering a hot topic. It is frequently used for stereo matching, picture haze removal, and image denoising. Image filtering is the process of separating pixel data from noise and recovering the true structure of the pixels. Typically, change detection produces a coarse binary mask which can be easily improved with sophisticated image filters. An image that acts as a different version of itself can be linked to the same image which can be given to a class of cutting-edge filters while filtering. For filtering the input picture, they consider the guidance image's information to be a trustworthy reference.

As image filtering enhances the change detection results, it is simply performed by some operations in the pixel values of an image. First, the working principle of two types of image filtering i.e., local and global filter are discussed. In the local image filter, the filtering process is done by moving a small window which is a kind of mask like a square matrix that slides the image pixels and captures the fine edge details but it fails to account for the long-range dependencies between the pixels. Whereas, the global filter allows each pixel in the image to change all the pixels in the vicinity that handles the problem of rich textures in the foreground region. But still the global filter lacks the capacity for preserving the edges. Guided filter and spatial tree filter are the examples of local and global filter respectively.

The spatial tree filter considers every pixel in an image and helps to support pixels with similar colors that are far apart from each other. This makes the filtering process more efficient. Global filtering, on the other hand, can leave textured foreground areas with a consistent white color and dispersed background noise. In saliency detection (identifying the most noticeable parts of an image), the algorithm can effectively sketch the general shape of an object, like a bear, but loses some of the hairy details near the edges. When it comes to edge healing (fixing breaks or inconsistencies in an edge), local filters perform significantly better than global tree filters. Enlarged areas processed with local filters contain richer information than those processed with global filters.

Spatial tree filter performs better than the local and global filters. The motivation in this work is to design a better filter that performs enhancement in the change detection results compared to other traditional available filters. It is proposed to combine two different types of filters to detect the changes more efficiently than any other enhancement methods available. The proposed integrated filter enhances the binary change detection masks by combining the benefits of local and global filtering, and considering spatiotemporal information in image sequences. This combination consists of local image filter and spatiotemporal tree filter that improves the detection masks from the filter. The non-local image filter considers spatial coherence of the pixels in an image. But the issue is solved by implementing a filter that uses the temporal features in the frames of videos. By using the features extracted from the consecutive frames, it enhances the detection masks. The spatial tree filter simply uses the minimum spanning tree to transfer the support weights. This method of enhancement properly captures the missing foreground pixels while removing the noise and interference from the spatial and time domain of the image.

In many of the existing change detection enhancement methods or filters such as Markov Random Field that uses the calculation of the background probabilities and the foreground probabilities of each pixel in the image to improve the coarse binary masks from the change detection algorithms. But it poses a problem of the applicability of these filters or enhancement methods. But the proposed methodology is more flexible and requires a few successive frames and their detection masks from the detection algorithm to improve the current time's binary mask, so that it can be used in the accurate calculation of changes in frames. By eliminating that need for complex probability calculations, the proposed methodology simplifies the enhancement process and provides a superior result compared to others and brings an efficient result.

FILTERING METHODS

Image filters which were used in enhancing the change detection results are discussed first. Then, Fast Spatiotemporal Tree Filter which is an extension of the spatial tree filter and that operates in the spatial domain and temporal domain, is explained.

Working Principle of Change Detection Algorithms

The simple working principle behind any change detection algorithm is that the algorithms B take an input image and a reference image. Both of these images are same but of different version. To detect the changes, the reference image is compared with the input image. To improve the accuracy of detecting objects in an image, a guidance image is used during the filtering process to provide additional information about texture and smoothness. The initial binary image, which distinguishes between foreground and background with white and black pixels, may contain errors due to noise or detection limitations. By using the reference image to create a filtered detection image, the errors will be lowered and the rate of accurate detection results are enhanced. The filtered image is grayscale, with brighter pixels indicating a higher likelihood of being part of the foreground object. This process helps reduce false detection and better capture the actual object area.

Joint Bilateral Filter

The Joint Bilateral Filter (JBF) is a powerful image processing filter that can preserve edges while smoothing the image. It is an enhanced version of the Bilateral Filter that considers the distance and intensity of neighboring pixels to preserve edges. Unlike the Bilateral Filter, the JBF incorporates an additional parameter, known as a guide image, to provide additional information about the image being filtered. This guide image can be a depth map, a color image, or any other image that provides information about the scene's structure.

By including a guide image, the JBF can enhance the filtering process by utilizing additional information about the image's content. This results in a more precise and accurate filtering process, particularly in complex scenes with varied textures and colors.

The JBF can be formulated as in Equation (1).

$$f(x) = \frac{1}{w(x)} \sum_{y \in \Omega} f(y) g \left(\|x - y\| \right) h \left(\|d(x) - d(y)\| \right) \tag{1}$$

Guided Filter

The guided filter is a local filter that uses a reference image to control the filtering process. The guidance image is typically a version of the input image that contains information about the structure or edges of the image. The filter then uses this information to smooth or enhance the image while preserving these structures or edges. The guided filter can be expressed mathematically as in Equations (2) to (4).

$$q(i) = a(i).I(i) + b(i) \tag{2}$$

$$a(i) = \frac{1}{|C(i)|} \sum_{j \in C(i)} \frac{p(j).I(j)}{\sigma 2 + \epsilon} \tag{3}$$

$$b(i) = \frac{1}{|C(i)|} \sum_{j \in C(i)} \left(p(j) - a(i).I(j) \right) \tag{4}$$

Spatiotemporal Tree Filtering

Spatiotemporal tree filtering is a method used in image and video processing to remove noise or unwanted data from spatiotemporal (both spatial and temporal) data. This method involves using a spatiotemporal filter that operates on the data represented in a tree structure.

The spatiotemporal tree filtering algorithm works by first constructing a tree structure that represents the spatiotemporal data. This tree structure is typically constructed using a wavelet transform or a similar decomposition method. The nodes in the tree represent different frequency bands and different levels of detail in the data.

Once the tree structure is constructed, the spatiotemporal filter is applied to the tree by filtering the nodes at different levels of the tree. The filter used at each level of the tree depends on the properties of the data and the specific filtering task. It is represented in Equation (5).

$$Y(i, j, k) = 1/\text{sum}(w(i, j, k, i', j', k')) * \text{sum}(w(i, j, k, i', j', k') * X(i', j', k'))$$

(5)

where $Y(i, j, k)$ is the weight function that depends on the Euclidean distance between the coordinates (i, j, k) and (i', j', k') in the spatiotemporal tree on the local statistics of the data in the neighborhood of position (i, j, k).

Fast Spatiotemporal Tree Filtering

The basic idea behind fast spatiotemporal tree filtering is to use the spatiotemporal tree to perform an efficient search for points that are within the specified region of interest. The algorithm starts at the root of the tree and recursively descends through the tree, checking each node to see if it intersects with the region of interest. If the node intersects with the region of interest, the algorithm checks its children to see if they also intersect with the region of interest. This process continues until the algorithm reaches the leaf nodes of the tree, at which point it returns the set of points contained within the region of interest. It is shown in Equation (6).

$$P_r(m, n) = \exp\left(-\sum_{ei \in Em,n} \frac{ei}{\sigma}\right) = \prod_{ei \in Em,n} exp\left(-\frac{ei}{\sigma}\right)$$

(6)

Assume a straightforward scenario in which the vertices m and n on a path of the MST are linked by a vertex w; the similarity between u and v can then be represented by a multiplication of similarity.

The route between any two nodes on the MST must be distinct; otherwise, two routes connecting the same set of nodes would result in a circle, which is incompatible with the fact that the tree is already an MST.

BACKGROUND AND LITERATURE REVIEW

Chen et al. (2019) showed that the exponential growth in the number of surveillance cameras has resulted in a massive amount of unstructured data. However, detecting moving objects in the multiple frames and angles of a security system is a challenging task for current object detection methods. Therefore, this research proposed a new model that leverages the properties of sparsity and low rankness while incorporating context regularization to improve the detection accuracy of moving objects in such scenarios.

Liu et al. (2018) presented a novel approach to change detection using unsupervised deep convolutional coupling network. The proposed model used two different images acquired from optical sensors and radar on different dates as inputs. The symmetric network was composed of one convolutional layer and multiple coupling layers on each side. The images were transformed into feature space and connected to the corresponding side of the network. The network learnt the complex relationships between the features of the two images and generates a consistent feature representation. This feature representation was then used to detect changes between the two images.

Jain and Nagel (1979) suggested that the counting of events in consecutive frames of TV images is not consistent with the sample area of the first frame. As the first frame represents a stationary scene component, any subarea of the initial estimate that differs from the stationary background can be interpreted as a moving object in the image. In this algorithm, the grey values in the subarea are replaced by the stationary background, and it does not require any prior knowledge of a particular scene.

Li et al. (2013) employed a fast and effective computational scheme that can handle various real-world situations. The foreground blocks were extracted from the distribution map of the illumination variation features, and only the valid blocks were considered. This approach ensured that the foreground blocks were accurately detected and extracted, and the system showed a satisfactory performance in comparison to other state-of-the-art methods. The proposed method addressed the limitations of existing foreground detection techniques and provided a reliable solution that can be applied in various surveillance scenarios.

Barnich and Van Droogenbroeck (2011) introduced a novel approach to detect motion in videos using a combination of various techniques. The proposed method involved maintaining a history of pixel values at a particular location in the past, and comparing the current pixel value with the stored values to identify whether the pixel belongs to the background or not. The model was adaptive in nature, and utilized random values to replace the pixel values from the background model. Whenever a pixel was identified as belonging to the background, its value was propagated to the background model of its neighboring pixels, which improved the accuracy of the model and reduced false positives.

Zhou et al. (2013) developed a unified framework for object detection that eliminated the need for a separate training phase. The proposed approach was called Detecting Contiguous Outliers in the Low-Rank Representation and it aimed to solve the problem by integrating object detection and background learning into a single optimization process. The algorithm alternated between the two tasks to achieve a balanced solution. This allowed for the detection of objects without requiring any prior knowledge or training. The optimization process involved minimizing the low-rank and sparse representations simultaneously, while imposing constraints on the structure of the data.

Liu (2018) analyzed real videos where the foreground pixels were not randomly distributed but were clustered together. To tackle this issue, the author proposed a greedy pursuit-based method that considered the group properties of foreground signals in both the spatial and temporal domains. This method was referred to as spatiotemporal group sparsity recovery, which iteratively pruned data residues. To handle critical background variations, a random strategy for background dictionary learning was utilized. This framework involved using a first pass for background modeling and a second pass for foreground detection.

McHugh et al. (2009) discussed the application of background subtraction in detecting changes in image sequences, and highlighted the challenge of designing a reliable algorithm. The authors proposed a novel approach based on a foreground model using a small spatial neighborhood to enhance discrimination sensitivity. Additionally, a Markov model was applied to change the labels, improving the spatial coherence of the detection. The method described was applicable to a range of background models, and employed a probabilistic model for the background intensities. By utilizing a small spatial neighborhood in the foreground model, the proposed approach effectively addressed the challenge of discriminating between the foreground and the background.

Chen et al. (2018) discussed the use of deep learning for image segmentation, with a focus on the power of atrous convolution or convolution with unsampled filters. Atrous convolution is a useful tool for dense prediction tasks as it allows for explicit control of the feature response resolution within deep convolutional neural networks (DCNNs). To improve the localization of object boundaries, the authors proposed combining methods from DCNNs and probabilistic graphical models. The commonly used combination of max pooling and down sampling in DCNNs resulted in loss of localization accuracy, which the proposed method addressed.

He et al. (2013) presented an explicit image filter, called guided filter, which was derived from a local linear model. The filter only considered the content of a guidance image while filtering the output. This allowed the transfer of structures from the guidance image to the filtering output, which enabled new filtering applications such as guided feathering and dehazing. The authors further demonstrated that guided filter outperformed other popular filters such as bilateral filter, detail preserving filter and total variation filter in many applications. Guided filter achieved high-quality results while requiring fewer computations than other filters, making it a useful tool for various image processing applications.

Chen et al. (2014) explored the task of background modeling and subtraction using pixel-level and region-based background models. Pixel-level background models rely on Gaussian mixture models or kernel density estimation to represent the pixel value distribution. However, these models have limitations in processing individual pixel values. Additionally, the work suggested the use of optical flow estimation to track foreground pixels and integrate them with the temporal M-smoother to ensure consistent background subtraction. This approach provided a robust solution for background modeling and subtraction that can handle noise and periodic changes in pixel values.

Cheng et al. (2011) improved the salient object detection using Convolutional Neural Networks. The researchers observe that generic FCN models are not well-suited for addressing scale-space issues. This innovative approach resulted in a framework that gave feature maps in high scale in each layer of the network, which is crucial for accurately detecting and segmenting salient objects. The skip-layer connections were used to allow information to be passed from one layer to another. This approach enhanced the feature representation of the network and lead to improved performance in detecting salient objects.

MAIN FOCUS OF THE CHAPTER

Detecting changes in a video sequence or still images is a crucial task in the image processing domain, which aims to distinguish moving objects from static ones. This functionality has a lot of applicability in the image processing domain like mostly in the surveillance cameras in organizations both the government and private. This change detection has captured a lot of attention in the recent years due to its use and achievement in the domain. Change detection performance in various algorithms with various enhancement filters is computed and the best enhancement filter is identified for change detection.

PROPOSED METHODOLOGY

The local directed filtering is an effective method for edge-preserving filtering, but it is limited by its inability to consider pixel information beyond the window range. On the other hand, the global tree filtering technique takes global pixel association into account, but its edge-preserving ability is not as effective as guided filtering. However, by incorporating foreground history data through spatiotemporal tree filtering, the performance of the initial non-local tree filter can be improved. As a result, it is thought to combine the advantages of local and global filtering in order to create a new integrated filter that can generate the detection mask and be more accurate. The integrated filter is represented in Equation (7).

$$q_i(k)=w_1 \frac{\sum_{j\in I, i\in I(k)} Si(i,j) Pj}{\sum_{j\in I, i\in I(k)} Si(i,j)} + w_2 * \sum_{i,j\in I(k),(i,j)\in w} \frac{1}{|w|2} \sum_{i,j\in I(k),(i,j)\in W} \left[1 + \frac{(Ii(k)-\mu w)(Ij(k)-\mu w)}{\sigma_w^2}\right] pi(k)$$

$$(7)$$

The first part of the integrated filter employs the standard guided filter, which applies a weighted average of the pixels in the vicinity of the object to smooth the foreground image while preserving edges. The second part, which is the spatiotemporal tree filtering procedure, uses cropped guidance images of the same object at k consecutive times to construct a spatiotemporal tree. This tree captures the global pixel association information and facilitates the suppression of the noise in the foreground. The weights assigned to the two parts of the filter ensure that they complement each other, resulting in an effective filtering outcome that preserves edges and reduces noise.

The proposed change detection system includes the modules such as: foreground extraction, foreground enlargement, noise removal, filtering, binarization. These modules are described below.

(i)   Foreground extraction: Foreground extraction is a process in computer vision and image processing that aims to identify and extract the region of interest or the moving object from a video or image sequence. The goal is to identify the foreground pixels from the background pixels of the scene. The extracted foreground can be used for various applications, such as object tracking, video surveillance, action recognition, and video compression. The foreground extraction process involves several steps, including background modeling, foreground detection, and object segmentation. In the background modeling step, a statistical model of the background is created based on the input video frames. This model can be created using techniques such as median filtering, Gaussian mixture models, or kernel density estimation.

(ii)   Foreground enlargement: Foreground enlargement refers to the process of expanding or growing the boundaries of the extracted foreground region in an image or video frame. The purpose of foreground enlargement is to include more of the object or objects of interest within the extracted region, while minimizing the inclusion of background pixels. Foreground enlargement can be achieved through various methods, such as morphological operations like dilation and erosion, which manipulate the shapes and sizes of objects in an image by altering the size and shape of the structuring element.

(iii) Noise removal: Noise removal is a process of eliminating unwanted or irrelevant information from an image signal. In the context of image processing, noise is generally defined as any random variation in brightness or color information that does not correspond to the actual image content. Noise can occur due to various factors, such as low light conditions, sensor limitations, or transmission errors.

(iv)   Integrated filtering: The integrated filtering process is a way to make video images clearer and easier to understand. It has two main steps that is guided filtering and spatiotemporal tree filtering, so it combines both the features of the filter that can maximize the enhancement result of the detection result. Guided filtering removes noise from the image by using information from another part of the same image. Spatiotemporal tree filtering matches parts of the image from previous frames to create a volume of information for each moving object in the video. This helps to always filter out the background and focus on the moving objects. The final output is a clearer image of the moving object.

(v)   Binarization: Binarization is the process of converting a grayscale or color image to a binary image, where each pixel is either black or white. The main goal of binarization is to separate the foreground from the background in an image. This is typically done by setting a threshold value, where pixels below the threshold are set to black and pixels above the threshold are set to white. The threshold can be set manually or automatically based on various criteria, such as histogram analysis or adaptive thresholding techniques. Binarization is a common preprocessing step in many computer vision applications, including object recognition, document analysis, and image segmentation.

The algorithm for the Fast Spatiotemporal Tree Filter which is used in the enhancement of the coarse binary mask, for change detection is mentioned below:

```
For each foreground region fg_j do
Set item_j, and fg_list = fg_j
For each frame frame_t in the range 1, ..., j-1 do
temp_difference ← +∞, and temp_index ← 0;
For fg_i in frame_t do
If distance(center_m, center_i) < threshold && abs(feature_m -
feature_i) < temp_difference
temp_difference ← feature_i,
temp_index ← i ;
End if
End for
If temp_index > 0
Push fg_temp into fg_list ;
and Stack item_temp under item_j.
End If
End for
```

The algorithm tries to create a coherent tracking of objects over time by using a collection of foreground regions in a video and prior frame. The current foreground region is used to initialize an *item_j* and a *fg_list* for each foreground region in the current frame *j*. The algorithm attempts to locate a foreground region *fg_i* that matches the current foreground region *fg_j* in each previous frame, *frame_t* in the range of 1 to *j*-1. In order to accomplish this, it iteratively loops through each foreground region in *frame_t*, *fg_i*, and determines whether the absolute difference between their features—which is not specified in the algorithm—is less than the current minimum difference *temp_difference*.

If a foreground region *fg_i* matching *fg_j* is discovered, it is added to the list of foreground regions (*fg_list*) for *fg_j*, and *item_j* is stacked beneath *item_i* (i.e., *fg_j* is connected to the same object as *fg_i* from the prior frame). Updates are made to the associated index *temp_index* and the minimum difference *temp_difference*. The algorithm then moves on to the following foreground region in the current frame, *fg_j*, if a matching foreground region *fg_i* was discovered after looking through all of the previous frames. If not, *fg_j* is a brand-new object and is tracked independently.

EXPERIMENTAL RESULTS

In order to directly compare the proposed technique with seven other approaches, first the video sequences from the CDnet2012 dataset, which is the "traffic" dataset are tested. The selected segments are challenging; some have jittering cameras and others have symmetrical foregrounds and backgrounds.

In the experiment here the input frames are preprocessed by passing it to the foreground extraction and extracting the foreground and background pixels, then performing the foreground enlargement. The noise and artifacts from the input frames are removed using morphological operators such as erosion and dilation. Then, this noise removed frames are binarized using the preset threshold value. The obtained binary masks are given to the 4 different change detection algorithms namely, GMM, SpKmeansEM, ViBe, FgSegNet. The result from these is the coarse binary mask and their results are further enhanced by the filters.

For the different change detection algorithms, there are different parameters that affect the performance of the detection results, so the parameters need to be chosen carefully, such that they have better performance compared to others. For the assessment of best filter, f1-score metric is used. F1-score is computed as in equation (8).

$$F1 - score = \frac{2*A*B}{A + B} \tag{8}$$

Here in equation (8), *A* represents Precision and *B* represents Recall, Precision and Recall are two metrics used to evaluate the performance of an algorithm in detecting foreground objects in an image or video. Precision is the ratio of true positives (correctly detected foreground pixels) to the sum of true positives and false positives (incorrectly detected foreground pixels). Recall is the ratio of true positives to the sum of true positives and false negatives (foreground pixels missed by the algorithm). True positives are the number of pixels correctly identified as foreground, while true negatives are the number of pixels correctly identified as background. False positives are the number of pixels identified as foreground but are background, and false negatives are the number of pixels identified as background but are foreground.

Perhaps the oldest algorithm for foreground enhancement is the morphological procedure. These are the parameter configurations: $r = 4$ and $\mathcal{E} = 0.2*0.2$, that are used for guided image filtering when used independently and when used as a weighted component of our combined filtering $\sigma_s = 150$, $\sigma_r = 0.2$ and $r = 5$ are the values for the joint bilateral filter. In the new filter, the features and ability of both spatial tree filter and Fast spatiotemporal tree filter are very much similar.

Only the MO filter, JBF, GF and spatial tree filters are contrasted with the recommended technique on ViBe in order to do this. MRFs don't work well with FgSegNet because it is unable to enhance and get the foreground probability chance for every pixel in the frames. Only the suggested method, the morphological operation, the bilateral filter, the directed filter, the spatial tree filter, and the CRF for FgSegNet are contrasted.

FgSegNet is a deep learning-based change detection algorithm. It is designed to detect changes between consecutive frames in a video sequence, with the aim of detecting moving objects in dynamic scenes. FgSegNet works by first preprocessing the input frames to remove noise and enhance the features of the objects in the scene. It then uses a convolutional neural network (CNN) to classify each pixel in the current frame as either foreground or background. The CNN is trained on a dataset of labeled frames, with the goal of learning to distinguish between static background and moving foreground objects. The output of the CNN is a binary mask that highlights the regions of the image that correspond to moving objects.

One advantage of FgSegNet over other change detection algorithms is its ability to adapt to changes in lighting conditions and other environmental factors. The CNN is trained on a large dataset of frames that cover a wide range of lighting conditions and other environmental factors, which helps it to generalize well to new scenes.

The FgSegNet change detection algorithm uses an FCNN (Full Conventional Neural Network) that trains its networks with the model, the model takes input as RGB images or the frames from the video for training the FgSegNet model and for ground truth images which consists of foreground and background pixels in the image separated to identify the moving objects in the image sequences, this is used for the validation of the model, and for testing the model uses RGB image. The entire dataset is split as 80-20 split for training and testing.

For training and validation, 350 images were used. For testing the constructed model, 400 images in RGB were used. The constructed model nearly uses 10 epochs, each of batch size 8. Once the model is trained for detecting the changes, the model tests each image an iteration with a length of iteration equal to number of images in the testing data. At the same time of testing, the model predicts and converts the tested images to a binary mask list based on the threshold. The result is a binary mask list.

The FgSegNet algorithm has several advantages over traditional change detection algorithms. It can handle complex scenes with multiple moving objects and changing backgrounds. It can also adapt to changes in illumination and shadow conditions, which can be challenging for traditional algorithms. Moreover, it does not require any prior knowledge about the scene or any manual parameter tuning, making it easy to use.

The details of model training and its summary, the plot of epoch against the accuracy and loss are given in Table 1. Computational cost of the proposed method is 0.075ns.

Table 1. Model training and validation results

Training Loss	Training accuracy	Validation Loss	Validation accuracy
2.5094	0.8284	1.1710	0.9241
1.5142	0.9015	1.4055	0.8852
1.5223	0.9001	1.1559	0.9241
1.3461	0.8814	1.1066	0.9240
1.4616	0.8813	1.1286	0.9241
0.8211	0.8410	0.4576	0.8513
0.3697	0.8928	0.2767	0.9238
0.3285	0.9007	0.2829	0.9237
0.3179	0.9010	0.2636	0.9239
0.3279	0.9006	0.3051	0.9240

Therefore, the model gives us a final training accuracy of 90% and the validation accuracy of 92%, so the model can detect the changes in the images more efficiently and accurately.

The plot for Model Epoch vs accuracy and Model Epoch vs loss are shown in Figures (1) and (2) respectively. From figure (2), it is understood that when the number of epochs is increased, the loss gets decreased.

Figure 1. Model epoch vs. accuracy

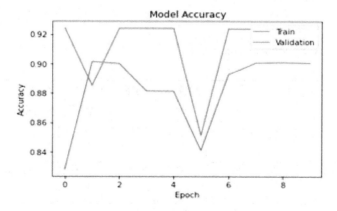

Thus, the FgSegNet change detection algorithm provides an accurate result in detecting the changes in the image sequences.

Figure 2. Model epoch vs. loss

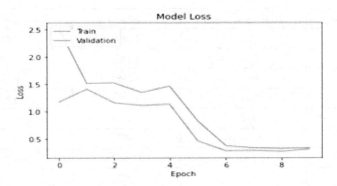

The results for each detection algorithm and the associated filters are shown in Table 2. This metric is used to assess how well changes in the image sequences can be identified. Here, the final outcome is presented as a value ranging from 0 to 1, which represents the F1-score value of each change detection algorithm against the seven enhancement filters.

In table 2, *A* denotes four different change detection algorithms and *B* represents seven different filters that were used. For all possible combination of change detection algorithm and filter, the F1-score is computed and listed in Table 2. From the table 2, it is visible that Fast Spatiotemporal Tree Filter provides the best F1-score for all the four change detection algorithms. FSTF with FgSegNet results in the best F1-Score of 97.97%. This shows the superiority of the proposed method in both qualitative and quantitative aspects.

Table 2. F-measure values of the filters

B ⟍ A	JBF	GF	MO	CRF	Li MRF	FA MRF	FSTF
GMM	0.92093	0.90631	0.89662	0.92671	0.93482	0.87242	0.93866
SpKmeansEM	0.92798	0.92488	0.95174	0.92722	0.91533	0.93706	0.96366
ViBe	0.89067	0.92812	0.91959	0.93558	0.90197	0.92882	0.95899
FgSegNet	0.93893	0.94335	0.94934	0.95649	0.93387	0.95904	0.97970

FUTURE RESEARCH DIRECTIONS

This system has used the publicly available database for change detection. To make it more customized for particular application, the self-built or custom database can be created and tested.

CONCLUSION

Numerous issues plague change detection systems, including detection noise, inaccurate foreground contours, inadequate adaptability to a wide variety of complicated scenarios, and susceptibility to scene modifications. In this chapter, an enhancement-based filter that has the capacity to enhance the detection results is proposed. The enhancement method devised can combine the features of the local and global filter that makes it efficient and better in comparison to other filters. Because of this combined feature it has the edge preserving, smoothing and accurate enhancement in the change detection results.

Experiments demonstrate that the proposed FSTF filter can improve the detection results of various foreground detection approaches, ranging from background modeling to machine learning model and train the model using CNN. Its performance can be visualized and compared quantitatively using the metrics. In future the enhancement framework will eventually be more broadly applied to a variety of applications, including multi-category semantic segmentation, stereo vision, and visual saliency detection.

REFERENCES

Barnich, O., & Van Droogenbroeck, M. (2011). ViBe: A universal background subtraction algorithm for video sequences. *IEEE Transactions on Image Processing*, *20*(6), 1709–1724. doi:10.1109/TIP.2010.2101613 PMID:21189241

Chen, B.-H., Shi, L.-F., & Ke, X. (2019). A robust moving object detection in multi-scenario big data for video surveillance. *IEEE Transactions on Circuits and Systems for Video Technology*, *29*(4), 982–995. doi:10.1109/TCSVT.2018.2828606

Chen, L.-C., Papandreou, G., Kokkinos, I., Murphy, K., & Yuille, A. L. (2018). DeepLab: Semantic image segmentation with deep convolutional nets, atrous convolution, and fully connected CRFs. *IEEE Transactions on Pattern Analysis and Machine Intelligence*, *40*(4), 834–848. doi:10.1109/TPAMI.2017.2699184 PMID:28463186

Chen, M., Yang, Q., Li, Q., Wang, G., & Yang, M. (2014). Spatiotemporal background subtraction using minimum spanning tree and optical flow. in *Proc. European Conference on Computer Vision (ECCV)*. Springer. 10.1007/978-3-319-10584-0_34

Cheng, M., Hu, X., Borji, A., Tu, Z., & Torr, P. (2011). Deeply supervised salient object detection with short connections. *IEEE Transactions on Pattern Analysis and Machine Intelligence*, *33*(2), 353–367. PMID:21193811

He, K., Sun, J., & Tang, X. (2013). Guided image filtering. *IEEE Transactions on Pattern Analysis and Machine Intelligence*, *35*(6), 1397–1409. doi:10.1109/TPAMI.2012.213 PMID:23599054

Jain, R., & Nagel, H.-H. (1979). On the analysis of accumulative difference pictures from image sequences of real-world scenes. *IEEE Transactions on Pattern Analysis and Machine Intelligence*, *2*(2), 206–214. doi:10.1109/TPAMI.1979.4766907 PMID:21868850

Li, D., Xu, L., & Goodman, E. D. (2013). Illumination-robust foreground detection in a video surveillance system. *IEEE Transactions on Circuits and Systems for Video Technology*, *23*(10), 1637–1650. doi:10.1109/TCSVT.2013.2243649

Liu, J., Gong, M., Qin, K., & Zhang, P. (2018). A deep convolutional coupling network for change detection based on heterogeneous optical and radar images. *IEEE Transactions on Neural Networks and Learning Systems*, *29*(3), 545–559. doi:10.1109/TNNLS.2016.2636227 PMID:28026789

Liu, X., Yao, J., Hong, X., Huang, X., Zhou, Z., Qi, C., & Zhao, G. (2018). Background subtraction using spatiotemporal group sparsity recovery. *IEEE Transactions on Circuits and Systems for Video Technology*, *28*(8), 1737–1751. doi:10.1109/TCSVT.2017.2697972

McHugh, J. M., Konrad, J., Saligrama, V., & Jodoin, P.-M. (2009). Foreground adaptive background subtraction. *IEEE Signal Processing Letters*, *16*(5), 390–393. doi:10.1109/LSP.2009.2016447

Zhou, X., Yang, C., & Yu, W. (2013). Moving object detection by detecting contiguous outliers in the low-rank representation. *IEEE Transactions on Pattern Analysis and Machine Intelligence*, *35*(3), 597–610. doi:10.1109/TPAMI.2012.132 PMID:22689075

Chapter 7
Computer Vision and Its Intelligence in Industry 4.0

K. G. Suma
VIT-AP, India

Preeti Patil
D.Y. Patil College of Engineering, India

Gurram Sunitha
ⓘ https://orcid.org/0000-0002-3305-8167
Mohan Babu University, India

Vijaykumar P. Mantri
MIT Academy of Engineering, India

Navnath D. Kale
MIT Academy of Engineering, India

ABSTRACT

Industry 4.0 drives automation, efficiency, and data-driven decision-making. Computer vision plays a pivotal role in Industry 4.0, driving innovation, automation, and efficiency across various domains. This book chapter explores the intersection of computer vision and Industry 4.0, highlighting the intelligence and advancements brought by computer vision in modern industrial settings. The ability of computer vision and its intelligence to extract meaningful information from visual data and understand the surrounding environment is highlighted. Insights into the advanced techniques and technologies, challenges and future directions of this rapidly evolving field are provided. Challenges and limitations are addressed with a view of handling complex industrial environments and variability. Insights into future directions, potential disruptions, and transformative effects in Industry 4.0 are provided. The chapter concludes by highlighting possibilities for future research and development to further unlock the potential of computer vision in driving advancements in industrial sectors.

DOI: 10.4018/979-8-3693-5271-7.ch007

INTRODUCTION

Computer vision (CV) has emerged as a revolutionary field that enables machines to perceive and interpret visual information like humans. It is a branch of Artificial Intelligence (AI). Its motivations lie in extracting meaningful insights from digital images and digital videos. Computer vision algorithms utilize various techniques such as image processing, pattern recognition, and machine learning to analyze and understand visual data.

Computer vision aims to replicate the remarkable capabilities of human vision. Thereby, allowing machines to recognize objects, understand scenes, and interpret visual cues. Computer vision uses the power of advanced algorithms and processing techniques to enable groundbreaking applications. Its applications span numerous industries such as healthcare, transportation, retail, manufacturing etc.

The Fourth Industrial Revolution in the commercial market is most popularly termed as Industry 4.0. It represents the ongoing digital transformation of industries. It leverages cutting-edge technologies to revolutionize the way goods are manufactured and produced (Ghobakhloo et al., 2020). It is an integration of key technologies such as Cyber-Physical Systems, Internet of Things (IoT), Cloud Computing, Artificial Intelligence, Big Data, Robotics, Augmented and Virtual Reality, Cyber Security etc (Figure 1). Industry 4.0 aims to create a highly interconnected and intelligent industrial ecosystem.

Figure 1. Key technologies of industry 4.0

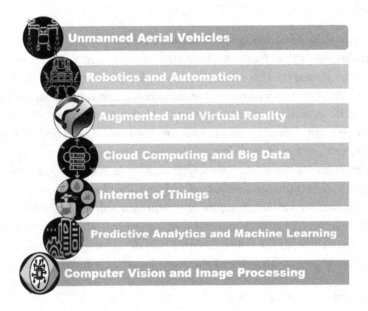

Industry 4.0 aims to optimize productivity, increase efficiency, and enhance decision-making processes by leveraging advanced technologies (Sony et al., 2020). It encompasses the digitalization and automation of manufacturing processes. Resulting in what is often referred to as "smart factories" or "digital factories". These factories are characterized by their seamless data exchange between machines, their real-time monitoring and control, and their utilization of intelligent systems to make autonomous decisions (Javaid et al., 2022).

The convergence of computer vision and Industry 4.0 has unlocked tremendous potential for transforming the industrial landscape. Computer vision enables machines to cognize the visual aspects of industrial processes. Manufacturers can enhance quality control, streamline production, improve safety measures, and achieve significant cost savings by integrating computer vision capabilities into Industry 4.0 frameworks (Dalenogare et al., 2018).

Computer vision systems can accurately inspect and analyze products, identifying anomalies with a level of precision and speed that exceeds human capabilities. This capability reduces the risk of faulty products reaching the market thereby improving customer satisfaction. Also, minimizing the costs associated with product recalls. Further, computer vision can facilitate real-time object recognition and tracking. Thereby, enabling seamless automation and optimization of manufacturing operations (Ramya et al., 2023).

In addition to enhancing traditional manufacturing processes, computer vision in Industry 4.0 opens doors to new possibilities. Computer vision-enabled Augmented Reality (AR) and Virtual Reality (VR) apps can revolutionise training procedures by enabling employees to get practical experience in virtual environments. Robotics and automation, powered by computer vision algorithms, can automate repetitive and hazardous tasks, improving workplace safety and efficiency.

Moreover, computer vision can be integrated with IoT devices and sensors to create an interconnected ecosystem. A system where visual data can be seamlessly collected, analyzed, and acted upon. This integration enables real-time decision-making, predictive maintenance, and optimized supply chain management.

The combination of computer vision and Industry 4.0 is poised to reshape traditional manufacturing practices. Thereby, unlocking unprecedented levels of productivity, flexibility, and innovation. However, with these advancements comes new challenges and considerations, such as data privacy, security, and ethical implications. It is crucial to navigate these challenges thoughtfully and responsibly as we move towards a future where intelligent machines and visual perception coexist seamlessly (Devezas et al., 2017).

The subsequent sections of this chapter, will explore the fundamentals of computer vision, its diverse applications in Industry 4.0. It presents a motivating discussion on advanced techniques, technologies, challenges, and limitations. A thorough speculation on the future directions and trends of this exciting field is also performed. Through this exploration, this chapter aims to provide highlights of the profound impact of computer vision's for Industry 4.0.

FUNDAMENTALS OF COMPUTER VISION

This section introduced the fundamentals of computer vision including discussion on image processing, image analysis, key components (Figure 2). Also, significance of machine learning for computer vision is highlighted.

Image Processing and Analysis

Image processing forms the foundation of computer vision systems. It enables the extraction and manipulation of visual information. It involves a series of techniques and algorithms to enhance, analyze, and interpret images for subsequent computer vision tasks (Siddique et al., 2023).

Figure 2. Fundamentals of computer vision

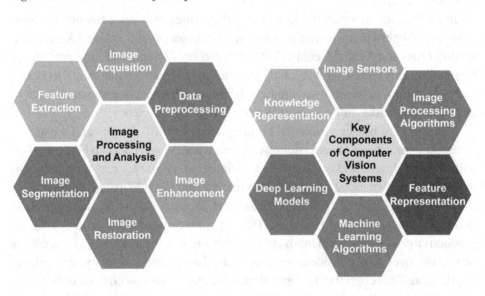

Some of the key concepts and methods in image processing are as follows.

1) Image Acquisition: It is the process of capturing images using cameras or other devices. The challenge is to acquire quality dataset which involves factors such as resolution, colour space, background, zoom, environment, sensor characteristics etc

2) Data Preprocessing: It involves enhancing and cleaning the acquired images in order to improve their quality. Thereby, increasing the efficacy of the subsequent process. It includes techniques like noise reduction, image denoising, contrast enhancement, image resizing etc.

3) Image Enhancement: Preprocessed images must be enhanced in order to improve their visual quality. Techniques like histogram equalization, contrast stretching, sharpening filters etc can be applied to enhance details and improve visibility.

4) Image Restoration: Images collected from real-world suffer degradation due to noise, blur, and environmental factors. Restoration techniques aim to reduce noise, eliminate artifacts, and restore image details. Methods such as deconvolution, image inpainting etc can be used.

5) Image Segmentation: Generally, computer vision tasks involve segmenting objects/features/regions of interest from other objects/background. It is a process of partitioning an image into meaningful regions/objects based on similarities in colour, texture, and other visual characteristics. Segmentation enables the identification and isolation of objects for further analysis. Segmentation techniques can be applied to highlight objects/features/regions of interest from other objects/background.

6) Feature Extraction: There are multitude of computer vision tasks that can be performed on images. Features most relevant to the undertaken computer vision task are to be identified, extracted and processed. Features can include edges, corners, textures, or higher-level descriptors derived from learning models.

Key Components of Computer Vision Systems

The essential components of a computer vision system work together to process visual data and extract meaningful information(Siddique et al., 2023). Understanding these components is crucial for building effective computer vision solutions. The key components are presented below.

1) Image Sensors: These are devices such as cameras, depth sensors etc that capture visual data and convert it into digital signals. These play a vital role in acquiring raw visual information for subsequent visual processing and analysis.

2) Image Processing Algorithms: These algorithms and techniques operate on the acquired images to enhance, segment, and extract relevant features. These

algorithms include image filtering, edge detection, feature extraction, and object recognition.

3) Feature Representation: Visual features are to be represented in a suitable format for analysis and comparison. Features can be represented in the form of vectors, histograms etc. They can also be represented as higher-level descriptors like deep learning embeddings etc. Thereby, enabling efficient computation and comparison.

4) Machine Learning Algorithms: These algorithms enable computer vision systems to learn patterns and models from data. Machine learning algorithms can be used for tasks such as facial expression analysis, image captioning, image classification, object detection and tracking etc. They learn from labelled/ unlabelled data to make predictions.

5) Deep Learning Models: These models utilize neural networks with multiple layers deep enough to learn hierarchical representations of visual data. A variety of deep models are widely used in computer vision tasks.

6) Knowledge Representation: Visual knowledge should be represented and organized within the computer vision system. Such representations shall facilitate reasoning and understanding of visual data. Different types of representations include structured representations, semantic graphs, ontologies etc.

7) Decision Making: The final stage of the computer vision system processes the analyzed visual information and makes predictions. Decision-making processes include rule-based models, probabilistic models, machine learning models etc.

Machine Learning in Computer Vision

Machine learning has revolutionized computer vision by enabling automated learning of features and patterns from large amounts of labelled data. These algorithms play a vital role in various computer vision tasks. Examples of computer vision tasks include facial expression analysis, image captioning, image classification, object detection and tracking, scene understanding etc (Aggarwal et al., 2022).

1) Machine Learning Algorithms: Traditional machine learning algorithms, such as gradient boosting machines, Hidden Markov Models etc have been widely used in computer vision. These algorithms learn from labelled training data to build models that can recognize and classify objects or scenes based on extracted features. They rely on handcrafted features, which are manually designed to capture relevant information from images.

2) Convolutional Neural Networks (CNNs): CNNs have become the backbone of modern computer vision systems. Especially for tasks such as image classification, object detection etc. CNN deep layers are designed to collectively

extract and process features at different levels of abstraction. CNNs can classify and localize objects within an image by leveraging their ability to learn discriminative features (Mezair et al., 2022). This capability has been instrumental in advancing areas such as autonomous driving, surveillance, medical imaging etc.

3) Recurrent Neural Networks (RNNs): RNNs are commonly used in computer vision tasks that involve sequential data. Examples include video analysis, natural language processing etc. They can capture temporal dependencies and process sequences of data. Thus, making them suitable for tasks like action recognition, video captioning, video tracking etc.

4) Transfer Learning: A learning model is pretrained on one task. Such model learns representations. Then those learned representations are used aid in solving another related task. By utilizing the knowledge gained from one task, transfer learning allows the transfer of learned features to new, related tasks. i.e., the pretrained model can be fastly trained on other related task. This significantly reduces the training time and resource requirements. Thereby, making it more feasible to apply deep learning models to various CV tasks. This is advantageous especially when the related task has limited training data.

The advancements in machine learning has revolutionized capabilities of computer vision systems. Thus, pushing them to unprecedented levels. They exhibit capacity to acquire and adapt from extensive datasets. The progress in hardware and computational resources has revealed a holistic set of opportunities for intelligent visual perception and analysis.

Figure 3. Computer vision applications for Industry 4.0
(Icons Source: https://www.flaticon.com/free-icon/)

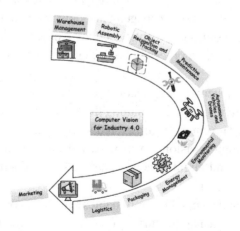

APPLICATIONS OF COMPUTER VISION IN INDUSTRY 4.0

Diverse applications of CV in Industry 4.0 include quality control and inspection processes, object recognition and tracking in manufacturing, robotics and automation, AR and VR applications, safety and security systems, supply chain optimization etc (Goundar et al., 2021). Figure 3 shows a few of the computer vision applications for Industry 4.0.

Quality Control and Inspection Processes

Computer vision systems can automatically analyze and evaluate the quality of products/components during manufacturing. Thereby, ensuring adherence to strict quality standards. By integrating computer vision into production lines, manufacturers can detect defects, anomalies, variations etc in real-time. Thus, minimizing the risk of faulty products reaching the market. This leads to improved product quality, reduced waste, and increased customer satisfaction.

Computer vision algorithms can inspect and measure product attributes such as dimensions, shape, colour, texture, surface defects etc. Computer vision systems can identify deviations from the desired specifications through analysis of visual data. Appropriate actions such as automated rejection, adjustment of production parameters etc are then triggered. Computer vision has the ability to perform precise and objective quality control. So, it can accelerate the inspection process, reduce manual labour, leading to higher production throughput.

Object Recognition and Tracking in Manufacturing

Computer vision plays a pivotal role in manufacturing environments by enabling precise object recognition and tracking. This capability has significant implications for various tasks, like inventory management, logistics, assembly line operations etc. Computer vision systems can identify and track objects, components, products etc throughout the production process by training machine learning models on vast datasets.

As inventory management application, computer vision can automatically recognize and count items. Thus eliminating the need for manual inventory checks. This leads to improved inventory accuracy, reduced stockouts, and optimized supply chain operations. Computer vision can also assist in automating assembly processes by precisely locating and aligning components. Thus, reducing human error and ensuring correct placement.

Object tracking using computer vision enables real-time monitoring and control of objects' movement within manufacturing environment. Such capability is especially valuable in scenarios where objects need to be tracked across multiple stages of production and in complex logistics operations (Zhou et al., 2022). Real-time tracking information enables efficient coordination, planning, and optimization of manufacturing processes.

Robotics and Automation

Equipping robots with vision systems will make them perceive and understand their environment. Thereby, allowing them to interact with objects, navigate complex spaces, and perform tasks with precision and efficiency.

Vision-guided robots can autonomously identify and manipulate objects which enables them to perform tasks such as pick-and-place operations, assembly, packaging etc (Ribeiro et al., 2021). Computer vision systems provide robots with the ability to recognize objects, determine their pose, orientation. This helps them to plan appropriate actions accordingly. Such a capability enhances the versatility and adaptability of robotic systems. Thereby, enabling them to effectively handle a diverse array of products and/or components within dynamic manufacturing environments.

Moreover, computer vision enables collaborative robotics, where humans and robots can work together safely. Robots can detect and track human presence by incorporating vision systems, thereby ensuring safe and efficient collaboration. Computer vision-based safety measures, such as detecting and avoiding collisions, further enhance the integration of robots into the manufacturing workflow. Thereby, improving productivity and worker safety.

AR and VR Applications

Computer vision is key technology in AR and VR applications. These applications have significant potential in Industry 4.0. AR and VR technologies merge the digital and physical worlds. Thereby, providing immersive and interactive experiences for training, maintenance, design, and visualization.

In AR applications, computer vision enables the alignment of virtual objects with the real-world environment. Computer vision systems allow virtual objects to be placed and interacted with in real-time by accurately tracking the user's position and orientation. Thus, enhancing training processes such as simulating assembly, maintenance procedures etc. AR-based guidance systems can overlay visual instructions, annotations etc onto the physical workspace. Such systems can assist workers in performing complex tasks or providing real-time information (Damiani et al. 2018).

In VR applications, computer vision enables the tracking of user movements and gestures. Thereby, allowing for natural interaction and manipulation of virtual objects. Computer vision-based hand tracking systems, body tracking systems etc provide users with a more immersive and intuitive VR experience. These technologies find applications in areas of manufacturing processes such as virtual prototyping, design reviews, virtual simulations etc.

Safety and Security Systems

Computer vision plays a crucial role in ensuring safety and security in Industry 4.0 environments. CV systems can detect potential safety hazards, security threats, risks. It enables protecting workers, assets, facilities etc by analyzing visual data.

In safety systems, computer vision can monitor and analyze the behavior of workers and equipment to identify potentially unsafe actions and situations (Gumzej 2022). For example, computer vision can detect workers in hazardous zones, detect deviations from safety protocols etc. It can react by triggering immediate alerts to the concerned authority. Computer vision can also be used to detect and respond to potential equipment malfunctions and failures, thereby preventing accidents. This will also minimize production downtime.

In terms of security, computer vision can be utilized for access control, intrusion detection, and perimeter surveillance. By analyzing video streams from surveillance cameras, computer vision systems can automatically identify unauthorized individuals, suspicious activities etc. Thus enabling timely response and preventing security breaches (Deshmukh et al., 2023). Additionally, computer vision-based facial recognition systems can enhance access control measures. Thereby, ensuring only authorized personnel can access restricted areas.

Supply Chain Optimization

CV plays a significant role in optimizing supply chain operations within Industry 4.0. CV systems leverage visual data of various aspects of supply chain. This enables real-time monitoring, analysis, and optimization. Thereby, leading to improved efficiency, cost savings, and customer satisfaction.

CV can be used for automated package identification and sorting in logistics and distribution centres. CV systems can accurately identify packages by analyzing visual features like barcodes. Such systems will ensure correct routing with minimized errors. This leads to faster processing, reduced shipment delays, improved order fulfilment (Cimini et al., 2019).

CV-based analytics provide valuable insights into customer behavior and their preferences. Visual data from retail environments, e-commerce platforms etc can be analyzed. By doing so, deeper understanding of customer interactions, product placements, shopping patterns etc can be gained. This information can be used to provide increased customer satisfaction and competitive advantage.

ADVANCED TECHNIQUES AND TECHNOLOGIES

This section discusses advanced techniques and technologies in CV for applications of Industry 4.0. The illustration of key features, applications, and limitations of each method for the application of computer vision and intelligence for development of Industry 4.0 is provided in Table 1.

Table 1. Methods, key features, applications, and limitations of computer vision for Industry 4.0

Method	Key Features	Applications	Limitations
Traditional ML Algorithms	Well-established and interpretable	Image classification, object detection	Limited capability in handling complex data
CNNs	Feature learning, hierarchical representation	Object recognition, segmentation	Requires large amounts of labeled data
Transfer Learning	Leveraging pre-trained models for new tasks	Improved performance with limited data	Dependency on source domain characteristics
Multi-Modal Fusion Techniques	Integration of information from diverse sources	Enhanced understanding in complex scenarios	Challenges in aligning modalities and features
Edge Computing	Processing data locally on edge devices	Real-time applications, reduced latency	Limited computing resources on edge devices
3D Vision and Depth Sensing	Capturing spatial information in three dimensions	Robotics, quality control in manufacturing	Hardware requirements for depth sensing
Real-time Processing	Swift analysis and decision-making	Autonomous vehicles, surveillance	Resource-intensive, may require specialized hardware
Internet of Things	Interconnected devices for data exchange	Monitoring, predictive maintenance	Security and privacy concerns, data management
Blockchain	Secure and transparent data transactions	Supply chain traceability, data integrity	Overhead in terms of computational resources
Explainable AI	Interpretable models for transparent decision-making	Regulatory compliance, ethical AI	Potential trade-off with model complexity
Bayesian Fusion	Probabilistic models for uncertainty estimation	Multi-modal fusion with uncertainty	Computationally intensive, complexity in implementation

3D Vision and Depth Sensing

3D vision and depth sensing technologies have emerged as important elements in Industry 4.0 CV systems. Traditional 2D images provide valuable information. They do not, however, have depth perception, which is necessary for interpreting spatial connections between items in the environment. CV systems can overcome this constraint by integrating 3D vision and depth sensing capabilities (Nagy et al., 2022).

Reconstruction of 3D representations of objects and settings using numerous camera views and depth sensors is possible with 3D vision methods. These models capture basic appearance of the scene. They also capture geometric properties and spatial layout. CV systems can do more complex tasks such as object localization, scene interpretation, AR applications, and so on with correct depth information.

Structured light, time-of-flight, stereo vision, and other depth sensing technologies allow for the measuring of distances to objects in a scene. These sensors collect depth information by emitting and measuring time-of-flight, light triangulation, and so on. Computer vision systems can recognise object forms, identify occlusions, and estimate object locations in three dimensions. Combining depth data with typical 2D picture data makes this possible.

Integration of 3D vision and depth sensing into computer vision systems enhances applications such as object manipulation, robot navigation, virtual reality simulations, architectural modeling etc. These advanced techniques enable more accurate and reliable analysis of the environment. Thereby, leading to improved decision-making, increased automation, and enhanced user experiences.

Multi-modal Fusion in Computer Vision Systems

Multi-modal fusion is an advanced technique in computer vision that combines information from multiple sources in various modalities. The purpose is to enhance the overall understanding of visual data. In Industry 4.0, computer vision systems often need to process diverse types of data like images, videos, depth maps, sensor data, textual information etc. Computer vision systems can capture complementary information and achieve more robust and comprehensive analysis by fusing different modalities.

Multi-modal fusion techniques can involve early/late fusion. Late fusion is the technique in which information from individual modalities is fused at a higher-level representation/decision-making stage. Early fusion is the technique in which combines data from different modalities are combined before feeding into CV system. Fusion can be performed using various methods, including attention mechanisms, hierarchical fusion, ensemble fusion etc.

Computer vision systems can leverage the strengths of each modality by integrating multiple modalities. The goal is to overcome limitations of individual data sources. For example, combining visual and textual information can enhance image understanding tasks such as image captioning, visual question answering etc. Integrating depth information with RGB images can improve object detection and tracking in challenging scenarios. Sensor data from different sources such as cameras, LiDAR, radar etc can be fused. So as t, enable robust perception for autonomous vehicles and industrial robotics.

Multi-modal fusion in computer vision systems is an active research area. With ongoing advancements in deep learning, statistical modeling, and sensor integration. Integration of multiple modalities enhances reliability, accuracy, and adaptability of computer vision systems. Thereby enabling them to handle complex real-world scenarios in Industry 4.0 applications.

Real-Time Processing and Edge Computing

Real-time processing is a critical requirement in many Industry 4.0 applications. In such systems timely decision-making and immediate responses are essential. Computer vision systems need to process visual data and extract relevant information within strict time constraints. Thus allowing for real-time control, monitoring, and feedback.

Advanced optimization techniques, parallel computing, and hardware acceleration are often employed to achieve real-time processing. Graphics Processing Units, Specialized Vision Processing Units are utilized to perform computationally intensive tasks in parallel. Thus accelerating the processing speed of computer vision algorithms.

In addition to real-time processing, edge computing has gained prominence in Industry 4.0. In such systems, data processing and analysis are performed closer to the data source. Rather than relying solely on centralized cloud-based solutions. Edge computing reduces latency, bandwidth requirements, and dependency on network connectivity; which makes it well-suited for time-critical computer vision applications (Sittón-Candanedo et al., 2020).

Capturing visual data, real-time processing can be achieved with reduced latency. Latency can be optimized by deploying computer vision algorithms at the edge, near the devices, near the sensors. This is particularly beneficial in applications where immediate action is crucial, such as autonomous vehicles, real-time monitoring systems, safety-critical environments.

Edge computing also offers advantages in terms of privacy, security, and data privacy compliance. Sensitive information can be kept within the edge devices by processing data locally. This reduces the risk of data breaches and privacy violations. It also enables compliance with data protection regulations. These regulations require certain data to remain within specific geographical boundaries.

Integration of Computer Vision With IoT Devices

Integration of computer vision with IoT devices is a significant trend in Industry 4.0. Here smart and interconnected systems play a crucial role. By combining computer vision capabilities with IoT devices, a comprehensive and intelligent perception of the physical world can be achieved. This enables advanced automation, monitoring, and decision-making processes (Zhang et al., 2022).

IoT devices, such as cameras, sensors, drones etc capture visual data from the industrial environment. These devices act as the "eyes" of the system. They provide real-time visual information that can be processed and interpreted. Computer vision algorithms can be deployed on edge devices or in the cloud. They can then analyze the visual data, extract meaningful insights. The analysis results can then trigger appropriate actions.

The integration of computer vision with IoT devices enables applications such as smart surveillance, environmental monitoring, predictive maintenance, precision agriculture etc. For example, CV algorithms can analyze video streams from smart surveillance systems to identify objects/events of interest. Thus, providing real-time alerts (Shereesha et al., 2022).

Integration of computer vision and IoT devices also facilitates the creation of large-scale visual sensor networks. These networks enable collaborative perception where multiple devices collectively capture and analyze visual data. Thereby providing a comprehensive and distributed understanding of the environment. Such networks can be utilized for crowd monitoring, traffic management, industrial process optimization etc.

Advanced techniques and technologies in computer vision are instrumental in advancing the capabilities of Industry 4.0 systems. 3D vision and depth sensing enable accurate spatial perception. While multi-modal fusion enhances the overall understanding of visual data. Real-time processing and edge computing ensure timely decision-making. Integration of computer vision with IoT devices enables intelligent perception and automation. These advancements pave path towards the creation of intelligent and autonomous systems. Thus, revolutionizing industries and propelling the advancement of Industry 4.0.

CHALLENGES AND LIMITATIONS

This section addresses the challenges and limitations in the field of computer vision for Industry 4.0. The discussion encompasses data privacy and security concerns, ethical considerations, biases and fairness issues in algorithms, and handling of complex environments and variability (Figure 4).

Data Privacy and Security Concerns

One of the significant challenges in CV applications within Industry 4.0 is handling of data privacy and security concerns. Computer vision systems rely on vast amounts of visual data. So there is a need to ensure that the collection, storage, and processing of visual data comply with privacy regulations. This is required so as to protect sensitive information.

The use of cameras and sensors in capturing visual data raises concerns about privacy invasion. Because these systems can inadvertently capture personal and sensitive information. Implementing privacy-preserving techniques is imperative to ensure protection of individuals' privacy depicted in visual data. These techniques encompass strategies like data anonymization, encryption, secure data transfer protocols etc. Privacy of individuals can be effectively safeguarded by employing such measures (Tyagi et al., 2023).

Securing the infrastructure and communication channels involved in computer vision systems is crucial to prevent unauthorized access, data breaches, and tampering. Protecting integrity and confidentiality of sensitive information includes implementing robust authentication mechanisms, access controls, and encryption protocols.

Addressing data privacy and security concerns requires a comprehensive approach, involving legal compliance, technological safeguards, and organizational policies. Industry stakeholders and policymakers must collaborate to establish guidelines and standards. They can together ensure responsible data handling practices in computer vision applications.

Figure 4. Challenges and limitations of computer vision for Industry 4.0

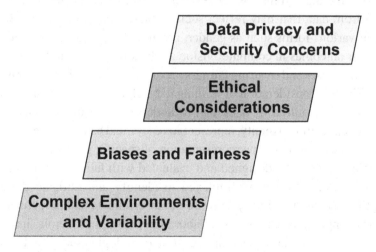

Ethical Considerations in Computer Vision Applications

The growing influence of computer vision in Industry 4.0 raises ethical considerations that need to be carefully addressed. Computer vision systems have the potential to impact individuals, communities, and society as a whole. Their deployment should be guided by ethical principles and considerations.

One ethical concern is the potential misuse of computer vision technologies. Examples are unauthorized surveillance, invasion of privacy, unethical data usage etc. Establishing well-defined guidelines and regulations is of utmost importance. They can ensure ethical and responsible deployment and utilization of computer vision systems. Such measures are essential in upholding individual rights, protecting privacy, and aligning with societal norms (Waelen et al., 2023).

Transparency and accountability are crucial ethical considerations in computer vision applications. Ensuring transparency and explainability in decision-making processes and algorithms employed by computer vision systems is of utmost importance. This allows individuals to understand the basis of decisions made by the system. It also helps identify and rectify biases.

Another ethical consideration is the potential impact on employment and workforce dynamics. Computer vision systems automate tasks traditionally performed by humans, there may be concerns. It is essential to consider the social and economic implications of deploying computer vision systems. Then develop strategies to mitigate potential negative consequences.

Addressing Biases and Fairness Issues in Algorithms

Computer vision algorithms can be susceptible to biases and fairness issues. As they learn from data that may reflect societal biases and imbalances. Biases can manifest in various forms such as gender, racial, cultural biases etc. These biases lead to unfair outcomes in computer vision applications (Nair et al., 2021).

Addressing biases and ensuring fairness in computer vision algorithms is a critical challenge. Careful consideration of training data, algorithm design, and evaluation methodologies is required. It is crucial to undertake measures to guarantee that training datasets exhibit diversity, representativeness, and balance. Thereby avoiding the underrepresentation and misrepresentation of specific groups.

Algorithms need to be designed and evaluated with fairness in mind. Fairness metrics and techniques can be employed to identify and mitigate biases. Thus ensuring that computer vision systems do not discriminate and perpetuate societal inequalities. Ongoing research and collaboration between academia, industry, and policymakers are essential to develop robust methodologies and guidelines. Biases and fairness issues in computer vision algorithms shall be addressed.

Handling Complex Environments and Variability

Computer vision algorithms often face challenges when operating in complex and dynamic environments. Real-world conditions include variations in lighting, weather, occlusions, object appearances etc. They can significantly impact the performance and reliability of computer vision systems.

Complex environments introduce variability that algorithms must handle effectively. This requires development of robust and adaptive algorithms that can generalize well across diverse scenarios. Machine learning techniques can help in learning complex patterns and improving the robustness of computer vision systems. However, collecting diverse and representative training data is crucial for achieving reliable performance. Collected data shall cover the variability of real-world conditions (Tyagi et al., 2020).

Another aspect of handling complex environments is the need for real-time adaptation and decision-making. Computer vision systems must be able to quickly adapt to changing conditions, update their models, and make accurate decisions in dynamic environments. This may involve techniques such as online learning, sensor fusion, adaptive processing etc. Responsiveness and adaptability of computer vision algorithms shall be ensured.

Despite the immense potential of CV in Industry 4.0, there exist a set of challenges and limitations that necessitate careful consideration and resolution. Data privacy and security concerns, ethical considerations, bias and fairness issues, and handling complex environments are crucial areas. This requires ongoing research, collaboration, and the development of appropriate guidelines and standards.

FUTURE DIRECTIONS AND TRENDS

This section provides insights into future directions and trends. It discusses emerging technologies and innovations, the impact of CV on workforce and job roles. It also presents potential disruptions and transformative effects if CV in Industry 4.0.

Emerging Technologies and Innovations

The field of CV is evolving rapidly. Several emerging technologies and innovations are expected to shape the future of CV for Industry 4.0.

1) Deep Learning: Deep learning has revolutionized computer vision. It enables development of highly accurate and robust algorithms. Future advancements

in deep learning architectures will continue to enhance capabilities of CV systems.

2) Generative Adversarial Networks (GANs): GANs have demonstrated significant potential in generating highly realistic images. They elevate synthesis of visual content to new levels of fidelity. They have potential to impact areas such as image editing, content creation, data augmentation etc in computer vision applications.

3) Explainable AI and Interpretable Models: As computer vision systems become more complex, the need for interpretability and explainability becomes crucial. Future research processes of computer vision algorithms will focus on developing techniques that enable the understanding and explanation of the decision-making.

4) Sensor Fusion and Multi-modal Perception: Integrating data from multiple sensors, such as cameras, LiDAR, radar etc will enable computer vision systems to achieve more robust perception of the environment. Multi-modal fusion techniques will continue to evolve towards enabling better understanding and analysis of complex scenes.

5) Edge AI and Edge Computing: Edge AI and edge computing will play a significant role in the future of computer vision with the proliferation of IoT devices. This results in reduced latency, improved responsiveness, and enhanced security measures (Sittón-Candanedo et al., 2020).

Impact of Computer Vision on Workforce and Job Roles

The widespread adoption of computer vision technologies in Industry 4.0 will inevitably have an impact on the workforce and job roles. While some tasks will be automated, computer vision also has potential to augment human capabilities, create new job opportunities, and reshape existing roles (Haeffner et al., 2018).

1) Automation and Task Offloading: Computer vision systems have capability to automate monotonous and repetitive tasks. Thereby liberating human workers to concentrate on more intricate and imaginative facets of their work. This, in turn, can result in heightened productivity, efficiency, and job satisfaction.

2) New Job Roles and Skill Requirements: Integration of computer vision in various industries will create new job roles. Examples are computer vision engineers, data analysts, AI specialists etc. These roles will require expertise in developing, deploying, and managing computer vision systems.

3) Skill Upgradation and Training: As computer vision becomes more prevalent, there will be a growing need for upskilling and retraining the workforce. It will be essential to provide training programs and educational resources to

equip individuals with necessary skills to work alongside computer vision technologies.

4) Collaborative Work Environment: Human-machine collaboration will become increasingly common in Industry 4.0. Here computer vision systems assist human workers in performing tasks. This collaboration will require effective communication, trust-building, and seamless integration of human and machine capabilities.

Potential Disruptions and Transformative Effects

Computer vision has potential to disrupt business processes, transform industries, and revolutionize the way humans interact with technology. Its impact will extend beyond specific applications and industries, influencing various sectors in Industry 4.0.

1) Enhanced Automation and Efficiency: Computer vision systems will enable advanced automation in areas such as manufacturing, logistics, quality control etc. This leads to increased productivity, accuracy, and efficiency. This will result in cost savings and improved operational performance.

2) Improved Safety and Security: Computer vision technologies can enhance safety and security systems. Thus enabling real-time monitoring, object detection, and threat identification. This will have applications in areas such as surveillance, public safety, and critical infrastructure protection.

3) Enhanced User Experiences: Integration of computer vision with AR/VR will revolutionize user experiences in various domains. From immersive gaming and entertainment to training simulations and virtual design, CV will play a crucial role in creating interactive and realistic virtual environments.

4) Personalized Services and Retail Experiences: Computer vision can enable personalized services and tailored retail experiences by analyzing customer behavior, preferences, and demographics. This will lead to targeted marketing, customized product recommendations, and enhanced customer satisfaction.

5) Healthcare and Medical Applications: Computer vision has potential to revolutionize healthcare. It enables applications such as medical imaging analysis, disease diagnosis, surgical assistance, telemedicine etc. It can improve diagnostics, treatment planning, and patient care, leading to better healthcare outcomes (Sunitha et al., 2022, Kute et al., 2022).

Future of CV for Industry 4.0 is promising and holds immense potential. Emerging technologies, such as deep learning, sensor fusion, edge computing etc will enhance the capabilities of computer vision systems. While the adoption of computer vision may impact workforce and job roles, it also presents opportunities for upskilling and creating new roles. The transformative effects of computer vision will be felt across industries, leading to improved automation, safety, user experiences, and personalized services. Embracing these future directions and trends will drive innovation and unlock new possibilities in the era of Industry 4.0.

CONCLUSION AND FUTURE DIRECTIONS

Throughout, this chapter explores the significant role of computer vision in the context of Industry 4.0. Its definition, fundamental concepts, and a myriad of applications across various industries have been explored. Insights into the advanced techniques and technologies, challenges and future directions of this rapidly evolving field are provided (Kumar et al., 2022). The chapter highlights ability of computer vision and its intelligence to extract meaningful information from visual data and understand the surrounding environment. Industry 4.0 drives automation, efficiency, and data-driven decision-making. This chapter sheds light into the concept of Industry 4.0 and its transformative impact on industries. Various applications of computer vision in Industry 4.0, including quality control and inspection processes, object recognition and tracking in manufacturing, robotics and automation, AR and VR applications, safety and security systems, supply chain optimization have been presented. These advancements enhance the accuracy, robustness, and real-time capabilities of computer vision systems.

CV plays a pivotal role in Industry 4.0, driving innovation, automation, and efficiency across various domains. As CV continues to evolve and advance, there are several areas that offer possibilities for future research and development (Leng et al., 2022).

1) Explainable and Interpretable AI: Developing techniques to explain and interpret decision-making processes of CV algorithms will be crucial for building trust and ensuring transparency in CV applications. This includes exploring methods for generating explanations, visualizing internal representations, and addressing biases/fairness issues.
2) Robustness and Generalization: Enhancing robustness and generalization capabilities of computer vision systems is essential for handling complex environments, occlusions, and variations in lighting conditions.
3) Data Privacy and Security: Research should focus on developing privacy-preserving techniques, secure data sharing frameworks, and robust authentication methods to protect sensitive visual data.

4) Ethical Considerations: Ethical considerations surrounding computer vision need to be addressed. Research should explore frameworks and guidelines to ensure ethical deployment of computer vision systems.

5) Integration with Emerging Technologies: Computer vision can leverage the integration with a range of emerging technologies, including 5G networks, edge computing, blockchain, and Internet of Things (IoT) devices, to further enhance its capabilities and applications. Exploring the synergies between these technologies will enable new opportunities and applications.

6) Human-Machine Collaboration: Investigating effective ways of integrating computer vision systems with human workers in collaborative work environments will be crucial. This includes designing intuitive user interfaces, enabling seamless interactions, and understanding the social and psychological aspects of human-machine collaboration.

In conclusion, computer vision holds tremendous potential in Industry 4.0. Future research and development should focus on addressing challenges such as data privacy, ethical considerations, robustness, and generalization. Harnessing the power of computer vision and advancing its capabilities can unlock new possibilities and shape a future where intelligent visual systems enhance productivity, efficiency, and human well-being in Industry 4.0 and beyond.

REFERENCES

Aggarwal, K., Singh, S.K., Chopra, M., Kumar, S., & Colace, F. (2022). Deep learning in robotics for strengthening industry 4.0.: opportunities, challenges and future directions. *Robotics and AI for Cybersecurity and Critical Infrastructure in Smart Cities*, 1-19.

Cimini, C., Pezzotta, G., Pinto, R., & Cavalieri, S. (2019). Industry 4.0 technologies impacts in the manufacturing and supply chain landscape: An overview. Service Orientation in Holonic and Multi-Agent Manufacturing. *Proceedings of SOHOMA, 2018*, 109–120.

Dalenogare, L. S., Benitez, G. B., Ayala, N. F., & Frank, A. G. (2018). The expected contribution of Industry 4.0 technologies for industrial performance. *International Journal of Production Economics*, *204*, 383–394. doi:10.1016/j.ijpe.2018.08.019

Damiani, L., Demartini, M., Guizzi, G., Revetria, R., & Tonelli, F. (2018). Augmented and virtual reality applications in industrial systems: A qualitative review towards the industry 4.0 era. *IFAC-PapersOnLine, 51*(11), 624–630. doi:10.1016/j.ifacol.2018.08.388

Deshmukh, A., Patil, D. S., Soni, G., & Tyagi, A. K. (2023). Cyber Security: New Realities for Industry 4.0 and Society 5.0. In Handbook of Research on Quantum Computing for Smart Environments (pp. 299-325). IGI Global.

Devezas, T., & Sarygulov, A. (2017). *Industry 4.0*. Springer. doi:10.1007/978-3-319-49604-7

Ghobakhloo, M. (2020). Industry 4.0, digitization, and opportunities for sustainability. *Journal of Cleaner Production, 252*, 119869. doi:10.1016/j.jclepro.2019.119869

Goundar, S., Avanija, J., Sunitha, G., Madhavi, K. R., & Bhushan, S. B. (Eds.). (2021). *Innovations in the industrial Internet of Things (IIoT) and smart factory*. IGI Global. doi:10.4018/978-1-7998-3375-8

Gumzej, R. (2022). Safety and Security Beyond Industry 4.0. [IJAL]. *International Journal of Applied Logistics, 12*(1), 1–10. doi:10.4018/IJAL.287556

Haeffner, M., & Panuwatwanich, K. (2018). Perceived impacts of Industry 4.0 on manufacturingg industry and its Workforce: Case of Germany. In *8th International Conference on Engineering, Project, and Product Management (EPPM 2017) Proceedings* (pp. 199-208). Springer International Publishing.

Javaid, M., Haleem, A., Singh, R. P., Rab, S., & Suman, R. (2022). Exploring impact and features of machine vision for progressive industry 4.0 culture. *Sensors International, 3*, 100132. doi:10.1016/j.sintl.2021.100132

Kumar, P., Singh, D., & Bhamu, J. (2022). Machine Vision in Industry 4.0: Applications, Challenges and Future Directions. In Machine Vision for Industry 4.0 (pp. 263-284). CRC Press.

Kute, S. S., Tyagi, A. K., & Aswathy, S. U., (2022). Industry 4.0 Challenges in e-Healthcare Applications and Emerging Technologies. *Intelligent Interactive Multimedia Systems for e-Healthcare Applications,* 265-290.

Leng, J., Sha, W., Wang, B., Zheng, P., Zhuang, C., Liu, Q., Wuest, T., Mourtzis, D., & Wang, L. (2022). Industry 5.0: Prospect and retrospect. *Journal of Manufacturing Systems, 65*, 279–295. doi:10.1016/j.jmsy.2022.09.017

Mezair, T., Djenouri, Y., Belhadi, A., Srivastava, G., & Lin, J. C. W. (2022). A sustainable deep learning framework for fault detection in 6G Industry 4.0 heterogeneous data environments. *Computer Communications, 187*, 164–171. doi:10.1016/j.comcom.2022.02.010

Nagy, M., & Lăzăroiu, G. (2022). Computer vision algorithms, remote sensing data fusion techniques, and mapping and navigation tools in the Industry 4.0-based Slovak automotive sector. *Mathematics, 10*(19), 3543. doi:10.3390/math10193543

Nair, M. M., Tyagi, A. K., & Sreenath, N. (2021). The future with industry 4.0 at the core of society 5.0: Open issues, future opportunities and challenges. In 2021 international conference on computer communication and informatics (ICCCI). IEEE.

Ramya, S., Madhubala, P., Sushmitha, E. C., Manivannan, D., & Al Firthous, A. (2023). Machine Learning and Image Processing Based Computer Vision in Industry 4.0. In Handbook of Research on Computer Vision and Image Processing in the Deep Learning Era (pp. 211-222). IGI Global.

Ribeiro, J., Lima, R., Eckhardt, T., & Paiva, S. (2021). Robotic process automation and artificial intelligence in industry 4.0–a literature review. *Procedia Computer Science, 181*, 51–58. doi:10.1016/j.procs.2021.01.104

Shereesha, M., Hemavathy, C., Teja, H., Reddy, G. M., Kumar, B. V., & Sunitha, G. (2022). *Precision Mango Farming: Using Compact Convolutional Transformer for Disease Detection*. In International Conference on Innovations in Bio-Inspired Computing and Applications (pp. 458-465). Cham: Springer Nature Switzerland.

Siddique, N., Arefin, M. S., Ahad, M. A. R., & Dewan, M. A. A. (Eds.). (2023). *Computer Vision and Image Analysis for Industry 4.0*. CRC Press. doi:10.1201/9781003256106

Sittón-Candanedo, I., Alonso, R. S., Rodríguez-González, S., García Coria, J. A., & De La Prieta, F. (2020). Edge computing architectures in industry 4.0: A general survey and comparison. In 14th International Conference on Soft Computing Models in Industrial and Environmental Applications. Springer.

Sony, M., & Naik, S. (2020). Key ingredients for evaluating Industry 4.0 readiness for organizations: A literature review. *Benchmarking, 27*(7), 2213–2232. doi:10.1108/BIJ-09-2018-0284

Sunitha, G., Arunachalam, R., Abd-Elnaby, M., Eid, M. M., & Rashed, A. N. Z. (2022). A comparative analysis of deep neural network architectures for the dynamic diagnosis of COVID-19 based on acoustic cough features. *International Journal of Imaging Systems and Technology, 32*(5), 1433–1446. doi:10.1002/ima.22749 PMID:35941929

Tyagi, A. K., Dananjayan, S., Agarwal, D., & Thariq Ahmed, H. F. (2023). Blockchain—Internet of Things Applications: Opportunities and Challenges for Industry 4.0 and Society 5.0. *Sensors (Basel), 23*(2), 947. doi:10.3390/s23020947 PMID:36679743

Tyagi, A. K., Fernandez, T. F., Mishra, S., & Kumari, S. (2020). Intelligent automation systems at the core of industry 4.0. In *International conference on intelligent systems design and applications* (pp. 1-18). Cham: Springer International Publishing.

Waelen, R. A. (2023). The ethics of computer vision: An overview in terms of power. *AI and Ethics*, 1–10. doi:10.1007/s43681-023-00272-x

Zhang, Y., Sheng, M., Liu, X., Wang, R., Lin, W., Ren, P., Wang, X., Zhao, E., & Song, W. (2022). A heterogeneous multi-modal medical data fusion framework supporting hybrid data exploration. *Health Information Science and Systems, 10*(1), 22. doi:10.1007/s13755-022-00183-x PMID:36039096

Zhou, L., Zhang, L., & Konz, N. (2022). Computer vision techniques in manufacturing. *IEEE Transactions on Systems, Man, and Cybernetics. Systems.*

Chapter 8
Detection of Pepper Plant Leaf Disease Detection Using Tom and Jerry Algorithm With MSTNet

Arunadevi Thirumalraj
https://orcid.org/0009-0003-5396-6810
K. Ramakrishnan College of Technology, Trichy, India

Rakesh Chandrashekar
New Horizon College of Engineering, India

Gunapriya B.
New Horizon College of Engineering, India

Prabhu kavin Balasubramanian
https://orcid.org/0000-0001-6939-4683
SRM Institute of Science and Technology, India

ABSTRACT

Leaf diseases have a detrimental effect on crop production quality in agriculture. In order to improve agricultural sector output, this has led to a greater emphasis on automating the detection of leaf diseases. In recent years, the process of categorising plant leaves using characteristics and machine learning has advanced. Usually, machine learning is used for supervised training of leaf classifiers using a set of data. Plant illnesses negatively impact both the amount and quality of agricultural goods by causing substantial growth and financial losses. Detecting plant diseases in big agricultural fields within a day has emerged as a critical topic of study. Three

DOI: 10.4018/979-8-3693-5271-7.ch008

processes are used in this study to forecast pepper plant diseases (PPD): picture capture, feature selection, and image classification. The Kalman filter is used to remove noise from images before processing. Feature selection becomes important because it effectively solves the issue by eliminating redundant and unnecessary data, cutting down on computation time, improving learning accuracy, and improving comprehension of the model or data. For feature selection, Tom and Jerry optimisation (TJO) is used, and for final classification, the Modified Swin Transform method (MSTNet) is used. Using TJO, MSTNet's hyperparameters are adjusted to ascertain if a leaf is contaminated. On the Plant Village Dataset, experiments are carried out with different parameter measurements. The suggested MSTNet outperforms the accuracy rates of the current models with a 99.2% classification accuracy.

INTRODUCTION

As members of the Capsicum genus, pepper plants (PP) are vulnerable to several illnesses that may negatively impact their development and productivity (Mathew, M. P., & Mahesh, T. Y. 2022). Bacterial spot, brought on by the bacterium Xanthomonas campestris, is one prevalent ailment. This disease appears on leaves as tiny, black lesions that seem to be drenched in water and are often encircled by a yellow halo (Bhagat, M., *et al.,* 2020). These patches may combine as the illness spreads, resulting in defoliation and a significant decrease in the amount and quality of fruit. Since contaminated seeds, soil, and water may transmit the highly infectious bacterial spot, early diagnosis and prevention are essential for efficient management (Karadağ, K *et al.,* 2020). Disease-resistant pepper varietals, crop rotation, and routine treatments of fungicides based on copper are among the suggested methods for managing bacterial spots in PPs.

Powdery mildew, a fungal disease caused by many species of the Erysiphales family, is another common disease that affects PPs (Jasim, M. A., & Al-Tuwaijari, J. M., 2020). Usually, powdery mildew manifests as a white, powdery material on the top parts of leaves, stems, and even fruit. Plant tissues that are impacted may undergo distortion, and early defoliation may transpire in extreme situations. In contrast to many other fungal infections, powdery mildew grows best in arid environments with high humidity, which makes it especially difficult to treat in certain regions (Baswaraju S, *et al.,* 2023). Powdery mildew may be reduced by using cultural practices such as maintaining sufficient distance between plants, allowing for enough ventilation, and avoiding overhead watering. Fungicidal treatments may also be used to stop the disease's progress and safeguard the health of PPs, particularly in the early stages of illness (Eser, S. E. R. T. 2021).

Pepper leaf infections may result in significant output losses if left untreated, which makes early diagnosis of these diseases crucial (Jana, S et al., 2020). In extreme circumstances, fungal infections like anthracnose and bacterial illnesses like bacterial spots may lead to defoliation, lower fruit quality, and even crop collapse (Lin, T. L *et al.,* 2020). PPs are susceptible to viral infections like cucumber mosaic virus, which may cause stunted growth and deformed fruit development. Beyond the immediate loss of the pepper crop, these illnesses impact farmers' livelihoods and the overall stability of the agricultural sector (Appalanaidu, M. V., & Kumaravelan, G. 2021).

Farmers or other agricultural specialists may often visually evaluate PPs as part of traditional techniques for detecting illness (Alguliyev, R., *et al.,* 2020). However, These techniques have some drawbacks as they depend on the human eye to detect minute signs, and illnesses can only be detected once they have reached more advanced phases (Zilvan, V *et al.,* 2020). Furthermore, large-scale agricultural operations make manual inspection difficult since early discovery is essential to prevent widespread contamination. Therefore, effective and precise automated systems are necessary to identify pepper leaf disease (Guan, X. 2021).

Deep learning (DL), a type of artificial intelligence, has proven to be highly helpful in agriculture for disease detection and crop monitoring. Convolutional neural networks (CNNs), in particular, are DL algorithms skilled at deciphering complicated patterns from big, complex data sets like photographs that may be invisible to the human eye (Vishnoi, V et al., 2021). DL models may be trained on large datasets of photos capturing different phases and symptoms of illnesses in the context of pepper leaf disease identification. DL plays a crucial role in pepper leaf disease identification by improving and automating the detection process. Researchers and farmers may create computer vision systems that can precisely spot early indications of illnesses by analyzing photos of PPs and using DL algorithms (Appalanaidu, M. V., & Kumaravelan, G. 2021).

Motivation

The desire to provide a reliable and effective approach for forecasting pepper leaf illnesses via the initiative is being driven by the use of feature selection, machine learning, and advanced image processing techniques. Through the automation of the detection process and the utilisation of cutting-edge methods such as the Modified Swin Transform (ST) technique for final classification, TJO for feature selection, and the Kalman filter for image preprocessing, the research aims to enhance the overall yield and economic results in agriculture while tackling the difficulties related to large-scale crop field monitoring.

Main Contributions

Innovative Kalman Filter-Based Image Preprocessing: This study presents the use of Kalman filters for image preprocessing in the context of forecasting diseases of pepper leaves. by successfully eliminating noise from images in the first phases of the procedure.

Effective Feature Selection via TJO: Using TJO for feature selection streamlines the learning model by removing duplicate and unnecessary data, which is a major contribution.

MSTNet classification: For the final picture classification, the study presents MSTNet, which provides an innovative and efficient method for differentiating between pepper leaves that are healthy and those that are sick. Experiments on the Plant Village Dataset show that further optimising MSTNet's performance via the use of TJO to tune hyperparameters leads to better classification rates when compared to other approaches.

RELATED WORKS

To develop a completely connected layer of pepper sickness classification model, (Bezabih, Y. A., et al., 2023) created a concatenated neural network by fusing the features of the resulting AlexNet and VGG16 networks. Phases include gathering datasets, preparing images, segmenting, extracting features, reducing noise, and classifying were used to develop the concatenated CNN model. The final evaluation yielded values for the concatenated CNN model that were 97.29% for validation, 100% for training classification, and 95.82% for testing effectiveness. The total research findings show that the concatenation model can correctly recognise fruit and pepper leaf diseases from digital pictures of peppers.

A five-layered CNN model was presented in the paper of (Mustafa, H., *et al.,* 2023) for the automated diagnosis of plant disease using leaf photos. The goal of creating 20,000 augmented photos was to improve CNN model training. Based on test findings, the optimised CNN model was able to identify 99.99% accuracy in determining whether a pepper bell plant's leaf was bacterial or healthy. The reliable results demonstrated that the enhanced-CNN model could identify diseases in a real-world agricultural setting and serve as an early warning system.

Three processes made up the (Bhagat, M., et al., 2022) technique: picture pre-processing, classification, and feature extraction. Three characteristics were considered for feature extraction: fused LBP & VGG-16 qualities, local binary pattern (LBP) characteristics, and visual geometry group network (VGG-16) properties. A comparison was made between the accuracy of the classifications produced by the proposed model and the accuracy reported by several researchers in their publications. With the pepper bell dataset containing LBP feature, VGG-16 feature, and LBP + VGG-16 fused characteristic, the RF classifier's accuracy was 78.11%, 92.28%, and 99.75%, respectively. Farmers may be able to promptly identify the beginning of plant diseases and take preventive action to lessen their effects with the use of the suggested method. The study's objective was to create a method that would enable bell PPs to be diagnosed with bacterial spot illness based only on farm photos.

The primary objective of (Khalid, et al., 2023) intended to use sophisticated convolutional neural networks to identify plant diseases in leaves in real time. Due to farmers depended on manual detection methods and were unaware of leaf diseases, their output declined as the infections spread. But since the infrastructure was lacking in many areas of the globe, fast identification proved difficult. With advancements in deep learning-based computer vision and a global increase in smartphone use, mobile devices may now be used for illness detection. To conduct this experiment, a dataset including images of both damaged and healthy money plant leaves was created. Hundreds of images have to be taken in a controlled setting using an exact dimensions dataset that was made accessible to the public. Training a deep model to distinguish between healthy and unhealthy leaves was the next step. The whole picture could be seen in a single scan, and even the tiniest illness patches could be quickly and precisely identified thanks to the trained YOLOv5 model. Farmers benefited from the study's results since they made it possible for them to quickly detect ill leaves and adopt the required safety measures to prevent the illness from spreading. The main goal was to identify the best hyperparameters for identifying healthy and ill leaf sections in both public and private datasets. 93% accuracy on the test set was attained by the trained YOLOv5 model.

Leaf disease was examined in the research by (Bothra, et al., 2023) using the Jupyter tool and a Python script. Farmers have turned to potentially hazardous pesticide spraying to solve problems including soil erosion, decreased fertility, climate change, and the difficulty of identifying ailments on leaf surfaces. Thus, early detection of sickness became crucial for anticipating and suggesting preventative measures. This showed farmers that the software's accuracy rate for diagnosing illnesses was 95.80%. In the assessment portion, the system's capacity to recommend pesticides and prevent leaf diseases was assessed.

Plant disease detection was studied by (Ojo, M. O., and Zahid, A. et al., 2023) to ascertain the impacts of various preprocessing techniques, strategies for class imbalance, and DL classifier phases. The goal of the research was to determine if improving data preparation and addressing Inconsistent data within the plant disease process could lead to a substantial improvement in DL classifier performance. The evaluation's findings showed that generative adversarial network (GAN) resampling, contrast-limited adaptive histogram equalisation (CLAHE), and picture sharpening were the most effective preprocessing and resampling methods. supplied to a ResNet-50 DL classifier produced a 97.62% average F1-score and a 97.69% average classification accuracy.

A better method for identifying infections and illnesses in plants, called GreenViT, was presented by (Parez, et al., 2023) and was based on Vision Transformers (ViTs). They separated the input picture into smaller blocks or patches, much like word embedding, and then fed it to the ViT piecemeal. Their method used the advantages of ViTs to get around the drawbacks of CNN-based models. Trials were carried out with extensively used reference datasets to assess the effectiveness of the suggested GreenViT.

Research Gaps

There are still a lot of research gaps that require attention despite the advancements achieved in the use of different approaches for PPD identification. First off, even though some studies have shown good classification accuracy, more thorough validation in actual agricultural contexts is required to evaluate the practical usefulness and resilience of these models. Many of the works that are now available concentrate on certain illnesses, such bacterial spot, but a comprehensive strategy that covers a wider range of PPD is necessary for a more flexible diagnostic instrument. Furthermore, the influence of environmental elements on model performance such as different lighting conditions and plant development stages has not received much attention. Furthermore, not enough research has been done on how well the suggested models scale and adapt to various datasets and geographic areas. Filling in these research voids will help provide more dependable and broadly used methods for agricultural practises to identify PPD.

PROPOSED METHODOLOGY

The proposed work flow is illustrated in figure 1 with respect to all the techniques used in this work. A three-step method is used in the study effort to forecast pepper leaf disease. First, the Kalman filter is used for image preprocessing in order to remove noise. Second, to improve learning accuracy and shorten calculation time, TJO is used for feature selection. Lastly, TJO is utilised to optimise hyperparameters when the MSTNet is applied for image classification. Image capture, Kalman filtering, TJO-based feature selection, and MSTNet-based classification are all shown in the block diagram. The technique evaluates multiple performance metrics via experiments on the Plant Village Dataset with the objective of improving classification rates in comparison to current methods.

Figure 1. Block diagram

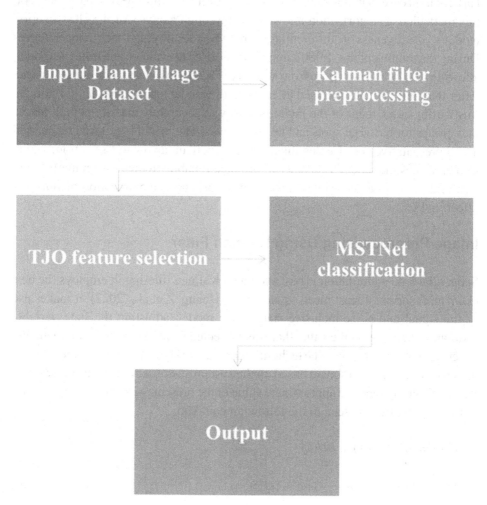

Dataset Description

The Pepper Leaf Disease dataset, a subset of the larger Plant Village dataset created especially for examining PPD, issued in this study. The Pepper Leaf Disease dataset is a large collection of 54,306 samples that include 26 different kinds of photos of sick leaves linked to 14 different plant species. A subset of 2,475 samples from this dataset are exclusive to PPs, which allows for an accurate representation of the variety of both healthy and damaged leaves. 997 samples of PPs fall into the healthy group, which serves as a benchmark for comparison. In the meanwhile, 1,478 samples fall under the category of bacterial spots, indicating a notable emphasis on a particular disease that affects PPs. With a focus on detecting cases of bacterial spot, this meticulous categorization allows for a thorough analysis of the classification model's effectiveness in differentiating between healthy and sick pepper leaves During the training phase, 1,980 samples are utilised to evaluate and train the model, allowing the algorithm to learn from a variety of scenarios and become more generic. After that, 495 samples are used to evaluate the model's performance, providing a trustworthy assessment of the model's ability to accurately classify pepper leaves into groups for bacterial spots and healthy leaves. The model is exposed to a varied and representative set of cases thanks to the meticulous dataset selection, which also enhances the model's capacity to produce reliable predictions on unobserved data and offers crucial insights into the diagnosis and categorization of illnesses affecting PPs.

Image Preprocessing Using Kalman Filter

Sequential data assimilation is best shown by Kalman filtering, it employs the best estimate criterion of least mean square error (Huang, Z et al., (2022). It makes use of the signal and noise-inclusive state space model, adjusting the state variable estimate depending on the value that was projected from the previous moment and the current observed value. The technique generates a signal estimate that minimises the inaccuracy in mean square based on the system and observed equations created, iteratively computing the approximate value of the present moment. The correlation in the Kalman filter is seen in the following equation:

$$X(k| k-1)= AX(k| k-1) + BU(k) \tag{1}$$

$$P\left(k\# \ k - 1\right) = AP\left(k\# \ k - 1\right)A' + Q \tag{2}$$

$$X\left(k\# \ k\right) = X\left(k\# \ k - 1\right) + Kg\left(k\right)\left(Z\left(k\right) - HX\left(kk - 1\right)\right) \tag{3}$$

$$Kg\left(k\right) = P\left(k\# \ k - 1\right)H' / \left(HP\left(k\# \ k - 1\right)H' + R\right) \tag{4}$$

$$P(k|k)= (1-Kg(k)H)P(k| k-1) \tag{5}$$

The update equation for the system state model is represented by equation (5), where P stands for the system covariance and X(k) for the expected system value. The present state is optimally estimated using the observed value Z(k) and the expected value. In this case, Kg(k) represents the Kalman gain, and effective signal estimation requires finishing the recursive process and providing simultaneous updates to the covariance of the current state. Equation (10) makes it clear that the estimated value $X(k|k)$ of the Kalman filter is influenced by the observed value Z(k), with the degree of this effect indicated by Kg(k). Noise in the present signal causes the gain to gradually decrease, which affects the Kalman filter estimation's accuracy.

Kalman filtering is not typically used for feature extraction from images. It's used for state estimation in systems where observations are corrupted by noise. So, applying Kalman filtering to an image might not result in the extraction of features in the traditional sense. Instead, it might be used for tasks like tracking objects in videos or estimating the motion of a camera. Without specific information about the TJO algorithm, it's difficult to determine its effect on feature reduction or extraction. However, if the TJO algorithm is designed to reduce features in an image, it might perform tasks like noise reduction, image denoising, or dimensionality reduction.

TJO Feature Selection

TJO uses pre-processed photos of PPs in order to select features. This section provides the mathematical model for the TJO and describes its theory for application in solving different kinds of issues (Sankar, K et al., 2023).

TJO is a population-based algorithm that takes its cues from the instinctive actions of a mouse running for cover and a cat attacking it. In this technique, search agents are divided into two groups: mice and cats. The agents roam randomly around the issue search area. The population members are updated by the algorithm in two stages. It depicts Tom's approach to Jerry at first, and then it models Jerry's flight to safe havens in order to save its life.

Every member of the population represents a potential solution to the issue from a mathematical standpoint. In essence, a population member uses its location in the search space to provide values for the issue variables. As a result, every member is a vector that determines the values of the issue variables. Equation (6) defines the population of the algorithm using a matrix known as the population matrix.

$$X = \begin{bmatrix} X_1 \\ \vdots \\ X_i \\ \vdots \\ X_N \end{bmatrix}_{N \times m} = \begin{bmatrix} x_{1,1} & \cdots & x_{1,d} & \cdots & x_{1,m} \\ \vdots & \ddots & \vdots & \ddots & \vdots \\ x_{i,1} & \cdots & x_{i,d} & \cdots & x_{i,m} \\ \vdots & \ddots & \vdots & \ddots & \vdots \\ x_{N,1} & \cdots & x_{N,d} & \cdots & x_{N,m} \end{bmatrix}_{N \times m} \quad (6)$$

The population matrix of TJO, represented by the symbol X in equation (7), is made up of elements X_i, each of which symbolises the ith search agent. $x_{i,d}$ shows the value that was assigned to the dth problem variable that the ith search agent had found. The population size and the number of problem variables are indicated by the parameters N and m, respectively. As previously stated, each member of the population offers recommended values for the problem variables. Equation (7) illustrates the vector of objective function values that are produced as a consequence of each member producing a distinct value for the objective function.

$$F = \begin{bmatrix} F_1 \\ \vdots \\ F_i \\ \vdots \\ F_N \end{bmatrix}_{N \times m} \qquad (7)$$

The vector of objective function values is represented by the letter F in Equation (9), where the ith search agent's objective function value is represented by each member F_i. Next, the population members are arranged in order of objective function value, beginning with the most valuable member who is also the best, and moving all the way up to the worst member having the highest value. The values of the goal function and the sorted population matrix may be obtained by using Equations (8) and (9).

$$X^s = \begin{bmatrix} X_1^S \\ \vdots \\ X_i^S \\ \vdots \\ X_N^S \end{bmatrix}_{N \times m} = \begin{bmatrix} x_{1,1}^s & \cdots & x_{1,d}^s & \cdots & x_{1,m}^s \\ \vdots & \ddots & \vdots & \ddots & \vdots \\ x_{i,1}^s & \cdots & x_{i,d}^s & \cdots & x_{1,m}^s \\ \vdots & \ddots & \vdots & \ddots & \vdots \\ x_{N,1}^s & \cdots & x_{N,d}^s & \cdots & x_{N,m}^s \end{bmatrix}_{N \times m} \qquad (8)$$

$$F^S = \begin{bmatrix} F_1^S & \min(F) \\ \vdots & \vdots \\ F_N^S & \max(F) \end{bmatrix}_{N \times 1} \qquad (9)$$

The sorted population matrix, represented by X^s in Equation (10), is arranged in accordance with the values of the goal function, with X_i^S standing in for each ith component. F^S represents the associated sorted vector of values for the objective function. The amount of the dth problem variables in the sorting populations matrix as decided by the ith search agent, is denoted by the phrase $x_{i,d}^s$.

There are two categories in the population matrix of the proposed TJO: mice and cats. According to TJO, half of the population members in the mouse population have greater values for the goal function than the members in the cat population. Using this technique, the populations of mice and cats are calculated in equations (10) and (11).

$$
M = \begin{bmatrix} M_1 = X_1^S \\ \vdots \\ M_i = X_i^S \\ \vdots \\ M_{Nm} = X_{Nm}^S \end{bmatrix}_{Nm \times m} = \begin{bmatrix} x_{1,1}^s & \cdots & x_{1,d}^s & \cdots & x_{1,m}^s \\ \vdots & \ddots & \vdots & \ddots & \vdots \\ x_{i,1}^s & \cdots & x_{i,d}^s & \cdots & x_{1,m}^s \\ \vdots & \ddots & \vdots & \ddots & \vdots \\ x_{Nm,1}^s & \cdots & x_{Nm,d}^s & \cdots & x_{Nm,m}^s \end{bmatrix}_{Nm \times m}
\tag{10}
$$

$$
C = \begin{bmatrix} C_1 = X_{Nm+1}^S \\ \vdots \\ C_i = X_{Nm+j}^S \\ \vdots \\ C_{Nc} = X_{Nm+Nc}^S \end{bmatrix}_{Nc \times m} = \begin{bmatrix} x_{Nm+1,1}^s & \cdots & x_{Nm+1,d}^s & \cdots & x_{Nm+1,m}^s \\ \vdots & \ddots & \vdots & \ddots & \vdots \\ x_{Nm+j,1}^s & \cdots & x_{Nm+i,d}^s & \cdots & x_{Nm+1,m}^s \\ \vdots & \ddots & \vdots & \ddots & \vdots \\ x_{Nm+Nc,1}^s & \cdots & x_{Nm+Nm,d}^s & \cdots & x_{Nm+Nm,m}^s \end{bmatrix}_{Nc \times m}
$$

$$\tag{11}$$

In this case, Mouse population matrix M is represented by the number of mice (Nm), and M_i is the jth mouse. In a similar vein, there are Nc cats in total, C_j is the ith cat, and C represents the cat population matrix.

The first step is to forecast the change in the cats' whereabouts based on their innate behaviour and approach to mice in order to adjust the search parameters. This update phase in the proposed TJO is mathematically described by equations (12) through (14).

$$
C_j^{new} : c_{j,d}^{new} = c_{j,d} + r \times \left(m_{k,d} - I \times c_{j,d} \right) \& \ j = 1:Nc, \ d = 1:m, k \in 1:Nm
\tag{12}
$$

$$
I = \text{round}(1 + \text{rand})
\tag{13}
$$

$$C_j = \begin{cases} C_j^{new}, |\ F_j^{c,new} < F_j^c \\ \quad C_j, |\ else \end{cases} \tag{14}$$

In this case, $c_{j,d}^{new}$ represents the dth problem variable's new value that the jth cat got, and C_j^{new} indicates the updated status of the jth cat. The variable r specifies a random number within the interval [0, 1]. Furthermore, $m_{k,d}$ symbolises the dimension of dth of the kth mouse, and $F_j^{c,new}$ represents the value of the objective function according to the most recent status of the jth cat. The suggested TJO's second phase mimics mice looking for safe havens to retreat to. Each mouse, according to TJO, chooses a haven at random and moves towards these havens in quest of protection. These havens' placements inside the search space are generated at random and are based on different algorithm components. Equations (15) through (17) provide a numerical description of this phase, which involves updating Jerry's position.

$$H_i : h_{i,d} = x_{l,d} \text{ and } i=1{:}N_m, \ d=1{:}m, \ l \in 1{:}N \tag{15}$$

$$M_i^{new} : m_{i,d}^{new} = m_{i,d} + r \times \left(h_{i,d} - I \times m_{i,d} \right) \times sign \left(F_i^m - F_i^H \right) \ \& \ i = 1 : N_{m,} \ d = 1 : m \tag{16}$$

$$M_i = \begin{cases} M_i^{new}, |\ F_i^{m,new} < F_i^m \\ \quad M_i, |\ else \end{cases} \tag{17}$$

Here, the ith mouse's haven is represented by H_i, and the objective function value linked to the selected haven is denoted by F_i^H. M_i^{new} represents the ith Tom's updated status, and $F_i^{m,new}$ represents the value of its objective function.

After every individual in the population of the algorithm has been updated, the algorithm moves on to the next iteration. Equations (10) through (17) establish the termination condition, and iterations continue until it is satisfied. Optimisation algorithms may terminate when they reach a predefined number of iterations, when an acceptable error between solutions identified in subsequent iterations is specified, or when a certain length of time is reached. When the iterations are finished and the algorithm is completely applied to the optimisation issue, TJO produces the best features for classification.

MSTNet Classification

Model Description

The research using the ST was carried out to help with the early identification of illnesses affecting PPs. The three stages of the ST framework are downstream operations, attention blocking, and image processing are shown in Figure 2.

Figure 2. Both before and after the mask is sliced: (a) Slice the mask; (b) following mask slicing

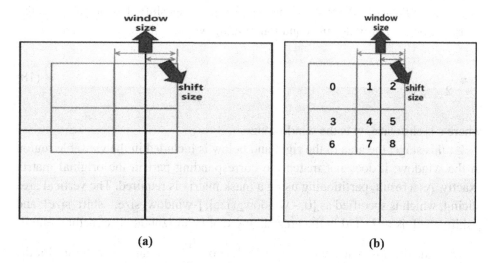

(a)   (b)

The transformer, which processes natural language sequences, comes originally from NLP. It started using patching techniques including masking, patch merging, and patch embedding.

Patch Embedding

RGB maps are converted into patch blocks that do not overlap via the patch partition algorithm. Each patch has a 4×4 size, which is multiplied by the corresponding RGB channels to obtain 4×4×3=48.

After processing, the patches are projected to the necessary dimensions to create a feature matrix.

Patch Merging

Concatenation of the four feature matrices occurs when the feature matrix obtained in the preceding phase is divided into two-by-two size frames and the appropriate location of each window is merged.

Mask

The window will only perform self-attention (SA) on the continuous portion due to the way the mask is constructed following an additional shift of the Shifted Window-Multi-Head SA (SW-MSA). Slices of the mask are visible. The original window can be located in the top-left corner of the matrix after being shifted to the bottom right.

Equation (18) provides the equation relating window size and shift size.

$$s = \frac{w}{2} \tag{18}$$

where s is shift size, w is the window size.

At this stage, the area to the right and below is included in the viewable region in the window; it does not match the corresponding part in the original matrix exactly. As a result, partitioning using a mask matrix is required. The vertical area slicing, which is specified as [0, - window_size], [-window_size, - shift_size], and [-shift_size], is reflected in the area slicing that is horizontal. The method entails splitting the window's size into uniform halves of $\frac{H}{w}$ rows and $\frac{H}{w}$ columns for the window partition-based labelled mask matrix (achieved by the window_partition function). Next, the dimension of numerical representation is merged with the dimension of batch size. This classification makes it easier to divide the initial matrix mask within more compact windows, which are measured in window units once the mask is sliced.

Figure 3. ST model

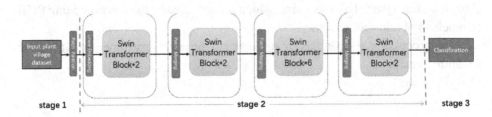

Figure 3 displays an illustration of the ST model.

Algorithm Design

First and Second Stages

The completion of the picture processing is the first step, which converts the PP picture's RGB representation into a collection of non-intersecting areas using a pattern seen in various transformer designs. In the ST configuration (Liu, Z et al., 2021), every patch has a dimension of 4 by 4. Each patch has 4x4x3 dimensions because RGB three-channel values are present in every pixel. These patches are then sent through a linear embedding layer to create a C-dimensional feature matrix.

The ST block is used in the second stage. Similar to other CNN algorithms, the ST captures deep qualities by stacking many blocks. Four repeated attention blocks are used in this study to transmit visual qualities. The input feature is first linearly embedded into C dimensions before the processed patches are projected onto the assigned region. In the ST block, there is a SW-MSA and two MLP levels. There exists a residual link that follows the layer normalisation (LN) layer in front of each MSA module and multilayer perceptron (MLP).

The next step is Patch Merging, which involves sewing patches together that are within the same 2x2 range. Consequently, we obtain a H/8×W/8 patch block count and a 4C feature size. Similar to step 1, linear embedding is used to compress the 4C, and the resultant 2C is fed through the ST block. The layered representation that these building blocks collectively produce has a feature mapping resolution that is similar to that of a standard convolutional network (Chen, Z et al., 2022).

1. SA in Non-Overlapped Windows (NOW)

For numerous vision applications that require sizable token sets for representation or dense prediction of high-resolution images, global computing appears to be suboptimal. This is because a number of tokens involved in it is quadratic in complexity. Rather, more effective modelling is possible when SA is exercised within a local window. Every picture is regularly divided into NOW Assuming M×M patches for every window, the computational complexity of the global MSA module and windows based on hardware patches images.

$$\Omega(MSA)= 4hwC^2 + 2(hw)^2C \tag{19}$$

$$\Omega(W\!-\!MSA)= 4hwC^2 + 2M^2hwC \tag{20}$$

The latter, whose linear path is set to 7 when M is constant, is a function of the square of the former patches *hw*. Window-based SA may be scaled, but global SA computing usually requires a large amount of hardware, which makes it expensive.

2. Modified Window Segmentation in Sequential Segments

Considering the constraints imposed by NOW not exchanging information, cross-window connections become essential. This method switches between Two successive ST blocks including W-MSA and SW-MSA. By connecting neighboring NOW in the higher layer, the shifted window division approach increases the perceived field of view.

The ST blocks are calculated using the shifted structure as follows.

$$\hat{z}^l = W - MSA\left(\text{LN}\left(z^{l-1}\right)\right) + z^{l-1},$$
$$z^l = \text{MLP}\left(\text{LN}\left(\hat{z}^l\right)\right) + \hat{z}^l,$$
$$\hat{z}^{l+1} = SW - MSA\left(\text{LN}\left(z^l\right)\right) + z^l, \tag{21}$$
$$z^{l+1} = \text{MLP}\left(\text{LN}\left(\hat{z}^{l+1}\right)\right) + \hat{z}^{l+1},$$

where $\hat{z}^l$ and z^l indicate, respectively, the output properties of the MLP modules for block and the (S)W-MSA module; Window-based multi head SA algorithms W-MSA and SW-MSA, respectively, use shifted and standard window partitioning configurations.

3. Multi head SA

A multi-head attention mechanism is used to transfer information from Transformer to vision. This is the exact combination.

$$\text{Attention}\left(Q, K, V\right) = \text{softmax}\left(\frac{QK^T}{\sqrt{d}} + B\right)V\left(Q, K, V \in R^{M^{2+d}}\right) \tag{22}$$

In this instance, As with the Transformer's position embedding, the relative position parameter, denoted by B, is introduced in a comparable way. The dimension size associated with each head is represented by the variable d, which is used to balance the size of QK^T and the computation of B.Q, K, and V. The matching query, key, and value values for incoming window information are retrieved after a linear layer.

B. Third Stage

The use of a ST for feature extraction is described in the preceding section. In the end, the categorization job was completed by using the ST (Zhang, L et al., 2021). Classification is a downstream job in the phase three. The quantity of classifications determines the output dimension; in its trials, there were two categories: healthy and diseased. The output is then subjected to a softmax operation in order to get the final classification probability.

Architecture Variants

The research kept The computational complexity and model size of the ST basic model, Swin-B, similar to ViT-B/DeiT-B. The experimental setup has limitations, therefore only a portion of the Swin-T or Swin-S models were employed for training. Models having computational complexity 0.25, 0.5, and twice that of the basic model, respectively, are represented by Swin-T and Swin-S. Interestingly, Swin-T and Swin-S show complications comparable to ResNet-101 and ResNet-50 (DeiT-S), respectively. M=7 is the window size that is used by default.

For every test, each head's query dimension is d=32, and each MLP's expansion layer is set to =4. For these model versions, the architectural hyperparameters are specified appropriately.

- Swin-T has the following layer configuration: {2, 2, 6, 2}, with a channel size (C) of 96.
- In addition, Swin-S has a channel size (C) of 96 and layer numbers that are organized as {2, 2, 18, 2}.
- Regarding Swin-B, the layer numbers are {2, 2, 18, 2}, and the channel size (C) is 128.where C the initial stage's hidden layers' channel number.

Loss Function

The following is the classifying mission's loss function:

$$L = \frac{1}{N}\sum_i L_i = -\frac{1}{N}\sum_i \sum_{c=1}^{M} y_{ic} \log\left(p_{ic}\right) \tag{23}$$

In this case, y_{ic} is a symbolic function that accepts values of 0 or 1, and M stands for the number of categories. It takes the value 1 if sample I's true category is 2, and the value 0 otherwise. The likelihood that the sample I was observed belongs to category 2 is predicted is indicated by the variable p_{ij}. TJO is used to adjust the hyperparameters and is also used for feature selection.

RESULTS AND DISCUSSIONS

Experimental Setup

Extensive tests are conducted using verifying the effectiveness using the Plant Village database of the suggested strategy. The MSTNet is trained on a Windows 10 PC with an Intel Core i7 processor, 32GB of RAM, and a GeForce GTX 2060 GPU. Python 3.5 is used for the implementation, which makes use of the Keras framework.

Performance Metrics

The ratio of accurate predictions to total predictions is called accuracy (ACC), and it is used to assess the classification model:

$$Accuracy = \frac{TP + TN}{TP + FP + TN + FN} \tag{24}$$

Positive predictive value, or precision (PR), is the ratio of correctly classified cases that are positive to all positive instances.

$$Precision = \frac{TP}{TP + FP} \tag{25}$$

The total amount of positive instances divided by correctly detected positive cases is known as recall (RC). It is also known as true positive rate or sensitivity at times.

$$Recall = \frac{TP}{TP + FP} \tag{26}$$

The F1-score (F1) is a single metric that combines recall and precision:

$$F1 = \frac{Precision * Recall}{Precision + Recall} \tag{27}$$

Table 1 defines the confusion matrix of PPD.

Table 1. Confusion Matrix

Actual/Predicted	Predicted Healthy	Predicted Disease
Healthy	TN	FP
Disease	FN	TP

The classification ACC (%) of many models is shown in the table 2 both before and after feature selection. Along with a suggested MSTNet model, popular architectures including VGGNet, AlexNet, MobileNet, and ResNet are among the models examined. TJO is a unique optimisation approach that was used in the feature selection process.

Table 2. ACC comparison with respect to feature selection

Models	Before Feature Selection (%)	After Feature Selection (%)
VGGNet	92.32	96.18
AlexNet	93.21	96.57
MobileNet	93.84	96.95
ResNet	92.93	97.27
Proposed MSTNet model	94.68	99.20

From table 2 and figure 4 after feature selection, significant increases were shown in the effectiveness of the suggested MSTNet model in addition to the VGGNet, AlexNet, MobileNet, ResNet models. The models' ACC before feature selection ranged from 92.32% for VGGNet, 93.21% for AlexNet, 93.84% for MobileNet, 92.93% for ResNet, and 94.68% for the suggested MSTNet model. On the other hand, all models showed a constant improvement in performance after the use of feature selection approaches. There was an increase in ResNet to 97.27%, MobileNet to 96.95%, AlexNet to 96.57%, and VGGNet to 96.18%. After feature selection, the suggested MSTNet model significantly improved and achieved an outstanding ACC of 99.20%. These results highlight the effectiveness of feature selection in enhancing and optimising proposed models' performance, with the MSTNet model showing especially encouraging outcomes within the study's framework.

Figure 4. Cross validation analysis of TJO

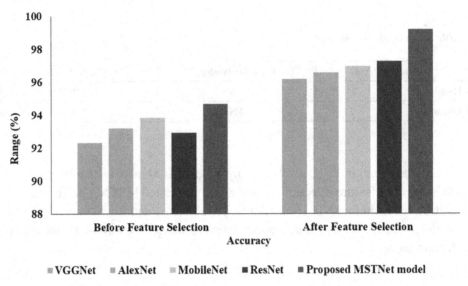

■ VGGNet　■ AlexNet　▧ MobileNet　■ ResNet　■ Proposed MSTNet model

Table 3. Cross-Validation results with feature selection

Fold	ACC (%)	PR (%)	RC (%)	F1 (%)
Fold 1	98.92	98.86	98.83	98.85
Fold 2	99.17	98.97	98.92	98.86
Fold 3	98.91	98.94	98.98	98.97
Fold 4	98.93	99.13	99.15	99.14
Fold 5	99.20	99.19	99.18	99.18

From table 3 and figure 5, five folds of evaluation were performed on a feature selection model, and the results showed consistently good metrics for ACC and PR. With PR, RC, and F1 scores of 98.86%, 98.83%, and 98.85%, respectively, the model's ACC in Fold 1 was 98.92%. Even more accurate, Fold 2's score of 99.17% was matched by scores of 98.97%, 98.92%, and 98.86% for PR, RC, and F1. Likewise, Fold 3 saw the model exhibit strong performance, producing an ACC of 98.91% along with corresponding PR, RC, and F1 scores of 98.94%, 98.98%, and 98.97%. With ACC of 98.93%, PR, RC, and F1 scores of 99.13%, 99.15%, and 99.14%, respectively, Fold 4 maintained the high level. The model performed best on the 5th fold, which had an ACC of 99.20%, and scores of 99.19%, 99.18%, and 99.18% for PR, RC, and F1. Together, these findings demonstrate the model's reliable and excellent feature selection performance throughout a range of folds.

Figure 5. Cross-Validation results with TJO

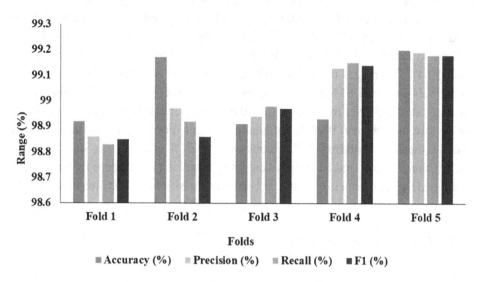

Table 4. Classification analysis of various models

Models	Class	ACC (%)	PR (%)	RC (%)	F1 (%)
VGGNet	Healthy	93.51	93.32	93.43	93.24
	Disease	94.43	94.24	94.34	94.16
AlexNet	Healthy	94.52	93.72	94.15	94.22
	Disease	94.94	93.97	93.93	94.43
MobileNet	Healthy	94.85	93.66	94.31	93.84
	Disease	94.92	94.25	94.62	94.75
ResNet	Healthy	95.31	94.43	95.24	94.16
	Disease	95.64	94.82	94.81	95.37
Proposed MSTNet model	Healthy	98.92	98.71	98.57	98.62
	Disease	99.20	99.19	98.93	99.18

From table 4 and figure 6, four performance metrics were noted when different models for an image classification of PPD were evaluated. In addition to PR values of 93.32% and 94.24%, RC rates of 93.43% and 94.34%, and F1 scores of 93.24% and 94.16%, the VGGNet model demonstrated an ACC of 93.51% for healthy pictures and 94.43% for disease images. A similar 94.52% ACC for healthy images and 94.94% ACC for disease images was shown by the AlexNet model, which also showed matching PR values of 93.72% and 93.97%, RC rates of 94.15% and 93.93%, and F1 scores of 94.22% and 94.43%. Using PR rates of 93.66% and 94.25%, RC rates of 94.31% and 94.62%, and F1 scores of 93.84% and 94.75%, the MobileNet model produced an ACC of 94.85% for healthy images and 94.92% for disease images. In addition, the ACC of the ResNet model was 95.31% for pictures of healthy and 95.64% for images of disease. PR values were 94.43% and 94.82%, RC rates were 95.24% and 94.81%, and F1 scores were 94.16% and 95.37%. Impressively, the suggested MSTNet model beat the other models, achieving an ACC of 99.20% for disease pictures and 98.92% for healthy images. For the pictures of health and disease, the corresponding ACC values were 98.71% and 99.19%, RC rates were 98.57% and 98.93%, and F1 scores were 98.62% and 99.18%. These findings imply that the MSTNet model is effective at correctly classification pictures used in PPD.

Figure 6. Classification analysis

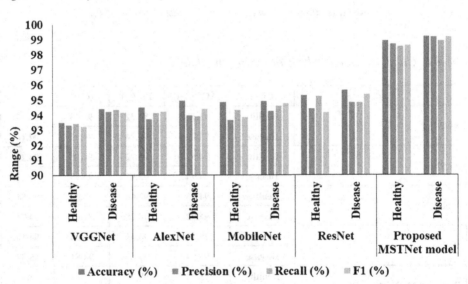

CONCLUSION

This study offers a thorough three-step procedure that includes feature selection, image classification, and image preprocessing for the purpose of forecasting pepper leaf illnesses. The suggested method makes use of cutting-edge methods to improve the precision of disease diagnostics in PP. Taking pictures and using the Kalman filter for preprocessing are the initial steps. By successfully eliminating noise from the photos, this method guarantees that the analysis that follows is based on accurate and pertinent information. Since noise reduction reduces interference from unrelated data and increases system resilience overall, it is essential for effective illness prediction. A crucial component of machine learning models, feature selection is the subject of the second stage. The study shows a calculated method to expedite learning by using TJO for feature selection. TJO helps provide more interpreted models, quicker computation times, and improved learning accuracy by methodically eliminating redundant and superfluous data. This stage is critical to enhancing the learning model's effectiveness and enabling a more comprehensive comprehension of the underlying data patterns. The last phase uses MSTNet technology for image classification. Because of MSTNet's superior ability to handle intricate patterns and correlations in data, it is used. In this stage, TJO is cleverly used once again to adjust MSTNet's hyperparameters, maximising its effectiveness for the particular purpose of classifying pepper leaf diseases. The use of TJO in feature selection and hyperparameter tweaking demonstrates the adaptability and efficiency of this technique in improving the predictive model's overall performance. The suggested technique is validated by the tests done using the Plant Village Dataset. The results validate the effectiveness of the selected strategy by showing significant gains in classification rates over current approaches. The results of this study point to a potential new direction for precise and effective diagnosis of PPD: the combination of Kalman filtering, TJO-based feature selection, and MSATNet-based image classification. When compared to other models currently in use, the suggested MSTNet model attained an accuracy of 99.2%. Regarding to future research, it may be possible to expand and modify the dataset even further to strengthen the model's resilience and make it more capable of handling a range of environmental factors and illness presentations.

REFERENCES

Alguliyev, R., Imamverdiyev, Y., Sukhostat, L., & Bayramov, R. (2021). Plant disease detection based on a deep model. *Soft Computing*, *25*(21), 13229–13242. doi:10.1007/s00500-021-06176-4

Appalanaidu, M. V., & Kumaravelan, G. (2021). Plant leaf disease detection and classification using machine learning approaches: a review. *Innovations in Computer Science and Engineering: Proceedings of 8th ICICSE*, (pp. 515-525). Research Gate.

Appalanaidu, M. V., & Kumaravelan, G. (2021). Plant leaf disease detection and classification using machine learning approaches: a review. *Innovations in Computer Science and Engineering: Proceedings of 8th ICICSE*, (pp. 515-525). Springer.

Baswaraju, S., Maheswari, V. U., Chennam, K. K., Thirumalraj, A., Kantipudi, M. P., & Aluvalu, R. (2023, December). Future food production prediction using AROA based hybrid deep learning model in agri-sector. *Human-Centric Intelligent Systems.*, *3*(4), 521–536. doi:10.1007/s44230-023-00046-y

Bezabih, Y. A., Salau, A. O., Abuhayi, B. M., Mussa, A. A., & Ayalew, A. M. (2023). CPD-CCNN: Classification of pepper disease using a concatenation of convolutional neural network models. *Scientific Reports*, *13*(1), 15581. doi:10.1038/s41598-023-42843-2 PMID:37731029

Bhagat, M., Kumar, D., & Kumar, S. (2023). Bell pepper leaf disease classification with LBP and VGG-16 based fused features and RF classifier. *International Journal of Information Technology : an Official Journal of Bharati Vidyapeeth's Institute of Computer Applications and Management*, *15*(1), 465–475. doi:10.1007/s41870-022-01136-z

Bhagat, M., Kumar, D., Mahmood, R., Pati, B., & Kumar, M. (2020, February). Bell pepper leaf disease classification using CNN. In *2nd international conference on data, engineering and applications (IDEA)* (pp. 1-5). IEEE. 10.1109/IDEA49133.2020.9170728

Chen, Z., Silvestri, F., Tolomei, G., Wang, J., Zhu, H., & Ahn, H. (2022). Explain the Explainer: Interpreting Model-Agnostic Counterfactual Explanations of a Deep Reinforcement Learning Agent. *IEEE Transactions on Artificial Intelligence.*

Eser, S. E. R. T. (2021). A deep learning based approach for the detection of diseases in pepper and potato leaves. *Anadolu Tarım Bilimleri Dergisi*, *36*(2), 167–178.

Guan, X. (2021, April). A novel method of plant leaf disease detection based on deep learning and convolutional neural network. In *2021 6th international conference on intelligent computing and signal processing (ICSP)* (pp. 816-819). IEEE. 10.1109/ICSP51882.2021.9408806

Huang, Z., Zeng, X., Wang, D., & Fang, S. (2022). Noise Reduction Method of Nanopore Based on Wavelet and Kalman Filter. *Applied Sciences (Basel, Switzerland)*, *12*(19), 9517. doi:10.3390/app12199517

Jana, S., Begum, A. R., & Selvaganesan, S. (2020). Design and analysis of pepper leaf disease detection using deep belief network. *European Journal of Molecular and Clinical Medicine*, *7*(9), 1724–1731.

Jasim, M. A., & Al-Tuwaijari, J. M. (2020, April). Plant leaf diseases detection and classification using image processing and deep learning techniques. In *2020 International Conference on Computer Science and Software Engineering (CSASE)* (pp. 259-265). IEEE. 10.1109/CSASE48920.2020.9142097

Karadağ, K., Tenekeci, M. E., Taşaltın, R., & Bilgili, A. (2020). Detection of pepper fusarium disease using machine learning algorithms based on spectral reflectance. *Sustainable Computing : Informatics and Systems, 28,* 100299. doi:10.1016/j.suscom.2019.01.001

Khalid, M., Sarfraz, M. S., Iqbal, U., Aftab, M. U., Niedbała, G., & Rauf, H. T. (2023). Real-Time Plant Health Detection Using Deep Convolutional Neural Networks. *Agriculture, 13*(2), 510. doi:10.3390/agriculture13020510

Lin, T. L., Chang, H. Y., & Chen, K. H. (2020). The pest and disease identification in the growth of sweet peppers using faster R-CNN and mask R-CNN. *Journal of Internet Technology, 21*(2), 605–614.

Liu, Z., Lin, Y., Cao, Y., Hu, H., Wei, Y., Zhang, Z., Lin, S., & Guo, B. (2021). *Swin transformer: Hierarchical vision transformer using shifted windows.* In *Proceedings of the IEEE/CVF International Conference on Computer Vision*, Montreal, QC, Canada. 10.1109/ICCV48922.2021.00986

Mathew, M. P., & Mahesh, T. Y. (2022). Leaf-based disease detection in bell pepper plant using YOLO v5. *Signal, Image and Video Processing, 16*(3), 1–7. doi:10.1007/s11760-021-02024-y

Mustafa, H., Umer, M., Hafeez, U., Hameed, A., Sohaib, A., Ullah, S., & Madni, H. A. (2023). Pepper bell leaf disease detection and classification using optimized convolutional neural network. *Multimedia Tools and Applications, 82*(8), 12065–12080. doi:10.1007/s11042-022-13737-8

Ojo, M. O., & Zahid, A. (2023). Improving Deep Learning Classifiers Performance via Preprocessing and Class Imbalance Approaches in a Plant Disease Detection Pipeline. *Agronomy (Basel), 13*(3), 887. doi:10.3390/agronomy13030887

Parez, S., Dilshad, N., Alghamdi, N. S., Alanazi, T. M., & Lee, J. W. (2023). Visual intelligence in precision agriculture: Exploring plant disease detection via efficient vision transformers. *Sensors (Basel), 23*(15), 6949. doi:10.3390/s23156949 PMID:37571732

Poornima, S., Kavitha, S., Mohanavalli, S., & Sripriya, N. (2019, April). Detection and classification of diseases in plants using image processing and machine learning techniques. In AIP conference proceedings (Vol. 2095, No. 1). AIP Publishing. doi:10.1063/1.5097529

Sankar, K., Krishnan, V. G., Saradhi, M. V., Priya, K. H., & Vijayaraja, V. (2023). Tom and Jerry Based Multi-path Routing with Optimal K-medoids for choosing Best Cluster head in MANET. *International Journal of Communication Networks and Information Security*, *15*(1), 59–65.

Vishnoi, V. K., Kumar, K., & Kumar, B. (2021). Plant disease detection using computational intelligence and image processing. *Journal of Plant Diseases and Protection*, *128*(1), 19–53. doi:10.1007/s41348-020-00368-0

Zhang, L., Sun, L., Li, W., Zhang, J., Cai, W., Cheng, C., & Ning, X. (2021). A joint Bayesian framework based on partial least squares discriminant analysis for finger vein recognition. *IEEE Sensors Journal*, *22*(1), 785–794. doi:10.1109/JSEN.2021.3130951

Zilvan, V., Ramdan, A., Suryawati, E., Kusumo, R. B. S., Krisnandi, D., & Pardede, H. F. (2019, October). Denoising convolutional variational autoencoders-based feature learning for automatic detection of plant diseases. In *2019 3rd International Conference on Informatics and Computational Sciences (ICICoS)* (pp. 1-6). IEEE. 10.1109/ICICoS48119.2019.8982494

Chapter 9

Fractional Order Epidemiological Model of Fake Information Mitigation in OSNs With PINN, TFC, and ELM

Vineet Srivastava
Rajkiya Engineering College, Azamgarh, India

Pramod Kumar Srivastava
Rajkiya Engineering College, Azamgarh, India

Ashok Kumar Yadav
(iD) https://orcid.org/0000-0002-7822-5870
Rajkiya Engineering College, Azamgarh, India

ABSTRACT

Online social networks (OSNs) have emerged as the most convenient platforms for transmitting and communicating media, including news and electronic content. It is imperative to develop technology that can mitigate the spread of fake information/ rumors, which badly harm society. This chapter employs an epidemic approach to develop a model for controlling and examining the dissemination of fake information on OSNs. The model is designed in the form of a system of fractional differential equations, exploring the real-world effects of misinformation propagation in OSNs with memory effect. It incorporates the concept of physics-informed neural networks with approximation based on the theory of functional connection and extreme learning machines. The proposed model elucidates the impact of various measures for correcting misinformation and shows how misinformation spreads across different groups. The validity of the suggested OSN model is confirmed through extensive computational analysis and investigation.

DOI: 10.4018/979-8-3693-5271-7.ch009

INTRODUCTION

The advancement of internet technology has resulted in people receiving information more quickly in these days. Additionally, the methods of obtaining information have become more varied, with social media platforms like Twitter, WhatsApp, Instagram, Facebook, Google etc. becoming indispensable for the exchange of information (Wen et al., 2013). Nowadays, many users are interacted through online social networks (OSNs) and share their required information as well as personal information via data transfer at a low cost. However, data shared on OSN platforms may contain fake information that has an impact on people's social life (Lebensztayn et al., 2011). Take COVID-19, for example, where the spread of false information about the Corona virus has made many individuals question any information they read about the infection on social media (Li et al., 2020). Recent false rumors of a COVID-19 treatment have been spreading on Facebook (Legon & Alsalman, 2020). People from all around the world have perished as a result of this sort of disinformation. In a similar way, Sommariva et al. (2018) examined how individuals are affected by incorrect information with regard to a well-known case study of the Zika virus. The writers found that bogus news frequently reaches a large audience on OSNs and spreads swiftly. One of the main issues with OSNs is verification, which involves the quantity of messages delivered and received as well as their legitimacy. A portion of the messages are spread through various social media platforms. Social media might have a disastrous effect on social harmony and peace. These messages, which are now called fake news, have the potential to be fatal. These messages are basically false information or rumors that are spread in a variety of ways (Sommariva et al., 2018), either maliciously or for amusement. Such information may cause unwarranted panic in the public and economic losses for governments (Banerjee, 1993; Dietz, 1967), as is now the case with COVID-19 spikes (Daley & Kendall, 1965). This might be attributed to the fact that OSN-related information spreads quickly and can instantly go worldwide (Dubey et al., 2020; Ren et al., 2017). On many occasions, the spread of false information over online social networks (OSNs) has had detrimental effects on society. On April 23, 2013, news propagate, two bombs detonated in the White House, injuring the US president and resulting $10 billion loss in economy (Wang et al., 2018). Another example comes from India, when a rumor on OSN stated that Sonam Gupta was disloyal. The personal life of a unknown girl named Sonam Gupta was touched as a result of this remark on social media. In a civilized society, such remarks should not be tolerated. This is a form of public humiliation for OSNs that, even if inadvertent, can have harmful repercussions. Dagher (2019) proposed a technique for blocking assaults on victims on Twitter to address these concerns. Basak et al. (2019) looked at the topic of rumor detection in microblogs. The researchers suggested a technique for detecting rumourmongers in microblogs.

Their plan is based on consumers' secret behavior. It reported incorrectly that the first patient treated with the vaccine had passed away, which had an impact on the COVID-19 medicine immunization research in the United Kingdom (Liang et al., 2015). According to references (Shu et al., 2019; Wu et al., 2013), rumors have a big impact on society. These facts increase people's vulnerability to becoming easy targets and increase their susceptibility to misleading information-related fear and sadness. Furthermore, they render terrible decisions based only on false information.

There are several mathematical models that examine the dynamics of the propogation of false information via online social media by employing the epidemic modeling technique. The vast scope and significance of social networks have made the identification of rumors and fake news a potentially important area of study. As a result, more varied mathematical models of rumour transmission are encouraged (Cannarella & Spechler, 2014; Shrivastava et al., 2020).

In recent years, epidemic modeling has gained popularity. Because of its generality and effectiveness, the SIR model (Kermack & McKendrick, 1927) is commonly employed. The susceptible (S), infected (I), and recovered (R) classes are used in the SIR model. This model helps decision-makers solve problems when an epidemic occurs by clarifying the dynamics of epidemics on networks. According to the SIR model, all nodes in the networks are homogeneous, have the same probability and connection as other nodes, and may connect to any other node through a link. Alternatively, the present study suggests that a community is a network of social connections (Girvan & Newman, 2002; Newman, 2013), whereby nodes have more connections within a cluster than outside of it, and nodes have rare connections.

In the simplest SIR models, the linear forces of infection are utilized, and they have certain limitations under normal conditions (Liu et al., 1986). Natural category formation and nonlinear processes of infection are taken into account in the new SIR models (Wang, 2006). Unfortunately, one of the main issues with the system is that the spread of malware was not detected early on. Zhang et al. (2015) provided an overview of the principles and applications of epidemic modeling. A policy to stop an epidemic from spreading over a population is made using epidemic modeling. To avoid epidemic disease outbreaks, several techniques may be used with the aid of epidemic modelling (Cheng et al., 2013). In the instance of COVID-19, Li et al. (2020) employed social distancing, lockdown, and quarantine techniques to fight the infection. In addition, the authors proposed an epidemic model for preventing rumor transmission on social media. The authors talked about an inherited SIR model that had three groups: spreaders, ignorants, and stiflers. The impact of rumor propagation on social media is studied. They have revealed the processes for removing rumors (a "virus of the mind").

The mechanism of rumor spreading in OSNs was examined by Cheng et al. (2013). In their research, the writers applied the idea of epidemic modeling. In addition, they proposed that OSNs fell into the three categories that were previously discussed in the model that was provided. They also defined infection as the strength of connections function across nodes and added the probability of infection—that is, the rate at which a certain piece of information spreads—as a variable in their model. The writers looked at how rumors spread on the social networking site Blog Catalog. Weak relationships were also talked about, namely the inability to disseminate stories quickly and widely. Researchers Nekovee et al. (2007) investigated the mechanics of rumor propagation in intricate social networks. The researchers examined the propagation of rumors in random graphs, scale-free networks, and uncorrelated scale-free networks, among other network topologies.

A SIRS model (Cannarella & Spechler, 2014; Wu et al., 2013) is used for OSN recovery rate and demographic linkage. This notion addresses the comings and goings of group members. People may join and exit an online community for a number of reasons. It might be the result of a decline in interest or a number of other things. While some new members join the community with the purpose of contributing positively, others join with the intention of spreading false information across the network. OSNs are the subject of extensive research, which includes exposure assessments, behavior detection, and the analysis of risky behaviors. The criminal group's use of these OSNs portals is likewise quickly expanding. These users want to spread false information so that it creates hazardous and harmful circumstances all over the world. Such communications have an impact and make people afraid. There is a fresh cause for concern as social networks become more and more integrated into people's daily lives. On social media, information spreads quite quickly. It is rather challenging to stop and get rid of unreliable information. Thus, it is necessary to design models that can manage rumors and to stop undesirable events in the actual world in order to safeguard the OSN from this kind of behavior. For recognizing and managing false information in OSN, a SVIR model is given, which is based on epidemic modeling of viral transmission in populations (Bjørnstad et al., 2020; Soltanolkottabi et al., 2019). This model has two layers of control mechanisms to keep rumors in the social network under control, and it is based on many types of classes. This approach believes that all users are vulnerable, which means that anybody might become a victim of disinformation or an untrustworthy message. Users are first authenticated using a validated class for security reasons. As a result, before approving any user's request, the user authentication technique is used, and the message dependability of this user is assessed in order to reduce fraudulent user activity on the OSN. It is crucial to create systems that may effectively prevent the dissemination of incorrect information or rumours that could potentially cause harm to society. They devised a model utilising the epidemic technique to analyse and regulate the spread of false information in online social networks (OSN). The suggested model demonstrates the effects of various strategies to dispel disinformation and how misinformation spreads across distinct populations.

Users that experience any kind of verification failure are considered rumor spreaders, capable of spreading unconfirmed messages over the social network. Mechanisms for eliminating and/or blocking rumors and/or dangerous users on the OSNs are therefore put into place. The suggested model aims to track the availability of misinformation, fake news, and spreaders in open social networks (OSNs) and to implement an appropriate corrective mechanism to stop or remove these kinds of disinformation and spreaders. The summary of our contributions are:

1. Design a model mathematically to track spreaders and false information in OSNs in order to prevent the spread of rumours.
2. Explore the impact of a checked status on an OSN's responsiveness and its application in preventing the spread of false messages in OSNs;
3. Investigate the impact of a recovered state (stopping, blocking, deleting, or leaving the group) on fake news and the spreader in OSNs.
4. All above will controlled by newly developed technique PINNs, The Theory of functional connection along with Extreme Learning Machine (Sivalingam,, 2023; Sivalingam & Pushpendra Kumar, 2023). In short, we can say that the controlled over false information spread/ rumours by newly developed neural network techniques.
5. In this work we employ an epidemic approach to develop a model for examining and controlling the dissemination of fake information in online social networks (OSNs). The model is utilize the concept of non singular fractional operator i.e. ABC operator for the memory effects (Atangana & Koca, 2016; Saeesian et al., 2017) of rumours.

The article comprises seven sections, with Section 2 providing concise discussions on fundamental definitions, physics-informed neural networks, the theory of functional connection, and extreme learning machines. Section 3 gives the solution methodology of ABC fractional derivative operated equation by PINN method using theory of functional connection with extreme learning machines. Section 4 outlines the model formulation for online social networks. The subsequent section, Section 5, delves into the exploration of numerical solutions and their analysis. Simulations and results analysis are then presented in Section 6. Finally, Section 7 addresses the conclusion of the article and outlines directions for future work.

LEARNING STRATEGY AND NEURAL NETWORK

In the current section we discuss the structure of Physics Informed Neural Network, Functional Connection theory and Extreme learning machines (Sivalingam,, 2023; Sivalingam & Pushpendra Kumar, 2023).

Physics Informed Neural Network

To examine following given initial value problem:

$$\frac{du}{dt} = f(u,t), u(0) = u_0.$$

(2.1)

Let us consider a neural network for input $t \in \mathbb{R}^m$ including the hidden layer, having n neurons and an output

$$n_t = \sum_{i=1}^{n} w_{2i} \rho(w_{1i} t_j + b_i), j = 1, 2, 3, \ldots, m$$

(2.2)

Where $w_{1i} \in \mathbb{R}^n$ and $\rho(.)$ is activation function while $b_i \in \mathbb{R}^n$ is the bais and $w_{2i} \in \mathbb{R}^n$

The solution to equation (2.1) using the PINN approach involves approximating the solution of the differential equations u_T as the output n_x of the neural network. The objective or loss function incorporates the physics of the problem, accounting for the specified initial conditions or boundary conditions. This is expressed in the following manner:

$$L_{ode} = \sum_{i=1}^{m} \left[\frac{du_T}{dt} - f(u_T, t_i) \right]^2,$$

(2.3)

$$L_{ic} = \sum_{i=1}^{m} \left[u_T(0) - u_0 \right]^2,$$

(2.4)

$$L_{ode} = L_{ode} + L_{ic}$$

(2.5)

The IVP is transformed into an unconstrained optimization problem by this loss function, which may then be reduced by any suitable heuristic or metaheuristic optimization technique to get the neural network's parameters, which can be used to estimate the differential equation's solution.

Functional Connection Theory

Definition 2.6. A function u(t) including n constraints can be described using the functional connections theory in the following way by utilizing the idea given (Sivalingam & Pushpendra Kumar, 2023):

$$u(t, g(t)) = g(t) + \eta p(t),$$

where $t \in [t_0, T]$, $g(t)$ with $g(t_0) \neq \infty$ is the freely selected function, p(t) is any basis function, and both functions satisfy the linear independence condition. The parameter η is specified as follows, when $p(t) = 1$,

$$\eta = u(0) - g(0).$$

So, the final constrained expression will be

$$u(t) = g(t) + (u(0) - g(0)) \tag{2.6}$$

This clearly demonstrates how the constrained expression overcomes the classical PINN limitation and satisfies the initial conditions.

Extreme Learning Machines

It is quite expensive to train a whole neural network. We may use the Huang et al. (2004) technique to train the parameters in order to lessen this. The objective of ELM is to determine the optimal weights between the hidden layers and output layers in order to minimize the loss function. Initially, the weights and bais between the input layer and hidden layers are randomly fixed. In terms of math, take into consideration the general neural network model (3) with the input $t \in \mathbb{R}^m$, one hidden layer with n neurons, and one output u as follows:

$$u \approx n_t = \sum_{i=1}^{n} w_{2i} \rho(w_{1i} t_j + b_i), j = 1, 2, 3, \ldots, m \tag{2.7}$$

Where $w_{1i} \in \mathbb{R}^n$ is the weight between the input layer and hidden layer, $\rho(.)$- the activation function used, $b_i \in \mathbb{R}^n$ - the bais, and $w_{2i} \in \mathbb{R}^n$ is the weight between hidden layer and output layer.

For ELM – based training, $b_i \in \mathbb{R}^n$ is the only parameter to be optimized. Using this, we can simulate the general loss function as

$$L = \left[u - \sum_{i=1}^{n} w_{2i} \rho(w_{1i} t_j + b_i) \right]^2 \tag{2.8}$$

The neural network may be trained using this loss function. The weight w_{2i} is often obtained via the Moore-Penrose inverse in the ELM process. However, in our process, we only use the notion of training the network to determine the weights in the neural network's output layer by taking into account the bias and weight between the input layer and the hidden layer, which can originate from a continuous probability distribution (here take uniform distribution). We then use a metaheuristic algorithm to learn the network.

SOLUTION BY PINN METHOD USING THEORY OF FUNCTIONAL CONNECTION WITH EXTREME LEARNING MACHINES

The Approximation Technique of Atangana-Baleanu Fractional Order Derivative in Caputo Sense (ABC Fractional Derivative)

This section describes how the neural network builds the loss function using approximation approaches. In order to do this, we approximate the Atangana-Baleanu fractional integral in the Caputo sense (ABC) using the fractional Adams Bashforth approach (Sabri, 2020). We extend the discretization to the generalized fractional derivative of ABC type using this method. The primary motivation behind this discretization is to lower the neural network's training computational complexity. Now, let's look at the issue with ABC fractional derivatives operator:

$$^{ABC}_{0}D^{\alpha}_{t} s(t) = b - as \tag{3.1}$$

Can be transformed into an integral equation as given below

$$s(t) = s(0) + \frac{(1-\alpha)}{B(\alpha)}\{b - as\} + \frac{\alpha}{B(\alpha)\Gamma(\alpha)}\int_0^t (t-l)^{\alpha-1}\{b - as\}\, dl \qquad (3.2)$$

Now, divide the interval [0, t] into k points $t_1, t_2, \ldots, t_k$ and the equation becomes

$$s(t_{k+1}) = s(t_0) + \frac{(1-\alpha)}{B(\alpha)} H_1(t_k)$$

$$+ \frac{\alpha}{B(\alpha)\Gamma(\alpha)} \sum_{j=0}^{j=k} \int_{t_j}^{t_{j+1}} (t_{k+1} - l)^{\alpha-1} \left(\frac{H_1(t_j)}{h}(l - t_{j-1}) - \frac{H_1(t_{j-1})}{h}(l - t_j) \right) dl$$

$$(3.3)$$

Where $H_1(t_k) = b - as(t_k)$, h is unit length of time interval i.e. $t_j = jh, j = 0, 1, 2, \ldots, n$

Solution Methodology

Loss Function

After approximation of fractional order derivative, we can make the loss function for the fractional order differential equation. The loss function at the input value $t_j \in (t_1, t_2, \ldots, t_n)$ will be:

$$L_k = \left[s(t_{k+1}) - s(t_0) - \frac{(1-\alpha)}{B(\alpha)} H_1(t_k) - \frac{\alpha}{B(\alpha)\Gamma(\alpha)} \right.$$

$$\left. \sum_{j=0}^{j=k} \int_{t_j}^{t_{j+1}} (t_{k+1} - l)^{\alpha-1} \left(\frac{H_1(t_j)}{h}(l - t_{j-1}) - \frac{H_1(t_{j-1})}{h}(l - t_j) \right) dl \right]^2 \qquad (3.4)$$

Constrained Expression

Now, as stated in the Definition, we build the constrained expression (CE) for the neural network using functional connection theory based interpolation. The CE for the function s(t) is built as follows.:

$$s_{CE}(t, g(t)) = g(t) + (s(0) - g(0)) \qquad (3.5)$$

We assume the free function $g(t)$

Consider the neural network described by equation (3.5), consisting of 10 neurons, one hidden layer, and reference function to be 1. A sigmoid function provided by is the activation function utilized in the neural network.

$$\rho(t) = \frac{1}{1+e^{-t}} \tag{3.6}$$

Now, add the output of the neural network to the loss function to get the loss at t_k, which is provided below.

$$L_k = \left[S_{CE}(t_{k+1}) - s(t_0) - \frac{(1-\alpha)}{B(\alpha)} H_{CE1}(t_k) - \frac{\alpha}{B(\alpha)\Gamma(\alpha)} \right.$$
$$\left. \sum_{j=0}^{j=k} \int_{t_j}^{t_{j+1}} (t_{k+1}-l)^{\alpha-1} \left(\frac{H_{CE1}(t_j)}{h}(l-t_{j-1}) - \frac{H_{CE1}(t_{j-1})}{h}(l-t_j) \right) dl \right]^2 \tag{3.7}$$

Currently, the neural network-related total loss of the equation is provided by

$$L = \sum_{k=1}^{n} \left[S_{CE}(t_{k+1}) - s(t_0) - \frac{(1-\alpha)}{B(\alpha)} H_{CE1}(t_k) - \frac{\alpha}{B(\alpha)\Gamma(\alpha)} \right.$$
$$\left. \sum_{j=0}^{j=k} \int_{t_j}^{t_{j+1}} (t_{k+1}-l)^{\alpha-1} \left(\frac{H_{CE1}(t_j)}{h}(l-t_{j-1}) - \frac{H_{CE1}(t_{j-1})}{h}(l-t_j) \right) dl \right]^2$$

Next, as described in Sivalingam (2023), we use extreme learning machines to train the neural network with this loss function in order to find the differential equation's solution. The Moore-Penrose inverse method for linear sets of equations is implemented with Matlab's pinv command. The nonlinear least square method is applied to nonlinear equations using Matlab's lsqnonlin command. It is evident that this strategy works best when $0 < \alpha < 1$. This method is ineffective for the integer order case.

MODELLING OF THE PROBLEM

The defence mechanism is needed to protect OSN from fake information/ rumours. To this end, the non-singular fractional order seivr (Susceptible-Exposed-Infectious-Vaccinated-Recovered) model of epidemic approach is proposed. This modelling aid in the study of the dynamics of rumours propagation in OSN, and its formulation is shown in Figure 1. Two categories of infectious states of the users are taken into consideration in the model: Infectious state and Exposed state. The false information may propagate in OSN alongwith regular/important information through the neighbouring active mode users.

Figure 1. Modelling aid in the study of the dynamics of rumours propagation in OSN

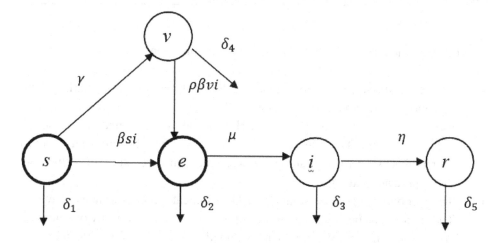

The different states of the proposed model is as follows:

Susceptible State (s): All users may not infected but they may responsible to spread the rumours unknowingly, such users can referred as in susceptible state.

Exposed State (e): In this state the user may contains the false information/ rumours but non-infectious.

Infectious State (i): Infected users have the potential to infect other.

Vaccinated State (v): In this state the users that are got filtered from fake information or Vaccinated due to antivirus software.

Recovered State (r): Those users, who are previously infected but free from infection now, are belonging to this state.

Table 1. Parameter are used in model

S. No.	Parameters	Interpretation
1	b	Susceptible entry rate
2	Υ	Vaccination rate
3	ρ	Effectiveness of vaccination rate
4	μ	Exposed rate when user change to infectious user
5	η	Rate of recovery infectious user
6	$\delta1$	rate of quit of susceptible user
7	$\delta2$	rate of quit of exposed user
8	$\delta3$	rate of quit of infectious user
9	$\delta4$	rate of quit of vaccinated user
10	$\delta5$	rate of quit of recovered user

To design the model we made the following assumptions:

- At the beginning, all users are in the Susceptible state (s), making them susceptible to spread the rumours. Susceptible users become exposed users when rumours infiltrate them. Half of the fake information ran on the vulnerable users. The rate at which a vulnerable user becomes an exposed user is β. Owing to regular operations, a certain percentage of vulnerable users quite at a rate of $\delta1$

- The user become exposed status (e) in OSN indicates inappropriate behaviour. The rumour has been placed on the exposed user and is partially operational. As a result, promptly implement a remedial step on vulnerable nodes to prevent spreading false information further in OSN. If not, these users spread at a rate of μ and become infectious. Due to rumour assault, a portion of the exposed class of users may quit at rate $\delta2$

- An OSN user node is compromised by false information, which then starts to do bad things on the network. Infected users (i) begin to disseminate rumours among nearby users and raise their own disturbances. The compromised users are only contagious and not harmful; at the same time, malevolent programmes may choose to stop targeting them. A portion of the infected users quit at a rate of $\delta3$ due to false information.

- Vaccinated state (v) users in OSN are not only immune against the attack of false information but, they have high level energy, also. Due to this users of OSN transferred in recovered state from infectious state. Some of this class of users become inactive or can quit with $\delta4$ rate of mortality.

- In addition to being resistant to rumours/fake information, users in the recovered state (R) of OSN also have a high level consciousness. A portion of the recovered users class quits at a rate of $\delta 5$
- Susceptible users are joining in OSN with the rate of b.

All users in any OSN at any time t can be classified in five states, these are named as Susceptible State s(t); Vaccinated v (t); Exposed State e(t)); Infectious State i(t); Recovered State r(t).

Let N(t) be the number of total users in OSN.

Therefore, we can write as the following equation N(t)= s(t)+e(t)+i(t)+v(t)+r(t), for any time $t \geq 0$. To analysis the propagation of fake information or rumor and to discuss the transfer of users in between different states, we presented it by the following set of differential equation. The model taken as:

$$\frac{ds}{dt} = b - \beta si - (\delta_1 + \gamma) s$$

$$\frac{de}{dt} = \beta si + \rho \beta vi - (\delta_2 + \mu) e$$

$$\frac{di}{dt} = \mu e - (\delta_3 + \eta) i \tag{4.1}$$

$$\frac{dv}{dt} = \gamma s - \rho \beta vi - \delta_4 v$$

$$\frac{dr}{dt} = \eta i - \delta_5 r$$

Let the initial conditions (ICs) for all above five states:

$$s(0) = s_0, e(0) = e_0, i(0) = i_0, v(0) = v_0, r(0) = r_0, \tag{4.2}$$

where s_0, e_0, i_0, v_0 and r_0 are nonnegative real numbers. It is necessary for the model to be dimensionally consistent model.

To address the issue of memory effect, our objective is to transform the aforementioned model (4.1) into a fractional order problem. To achieve this, we convert the model (4.1) to its equivalent integral form

$$s(t) = s_0 + \int_0^t \left[b - \beta s(p)i(p) - (\delta_1 + \gamma)s(p) \right] dp$$

$$e(t) = e_0 + \int_0^t \left[\beta s(p)i(p) + \rho\beta v(p)i(p) - (\delta_2 + \mu)e(p) \right] dp$$

$$i(t) = i_0 + \int_0^t \left[\mu e(p) - (\delta_3 + \eta)i(p) \right] dp \qquad (4.3)$$

$$v(t) = v_0 + \int_0^t \left[\gamma s(p) - \rho\beta v(p)i(p) - \delta_4 v(p) \right] dp$$

$$r(t) = r_0 + \int_0^t \left[\eta i(p) - \delta_5 r(p) \right] dp$$

To incorporate the impact of memory effect (Saeesian et al., 2017), we express equation (4.3) using time-dependent integrals:

$$s(t) = s_0 + \int_0^t \varphi(t,p) \left[b - \beta s(p)i(p) - (\delta_1 + \gamma)s(p) \right] dp$$

$$e(t) = e_0 + \int_0^t \varphi(t,p) \left[\beta s(p)i(p) + \rho\beta v(p)i(p) - (\delta_2 + \mu)e(p) \right] dp$$

$$i(t) = i_0 + \int_0^t \varphi(t,p) \left[\mu e(p) - (\delta_3 + \eta)i(p) \right] dp \qquad (4.4)$$

$$v(t) = v_0 + \int_0^t \varphi(t,p) \left[\gamma s(p) - \rho \beta v(p) i(p) - \delta_4 v(p) \right] dp$$

$$r(t) = r_0 + \int_0^t \varphi(t,p) \left[\eta i(p) - \delta_5 r(p) \right] dp$$

here $\varphi(t,p)$ serves as a time-dependent kernel with memory, analogous to how the delta function $\delta(t,p)$ functions in the classical Markov process. The selection of $\varphi(t,p)$ can be a power-law correlation function, which allows for the inclusion of a long-term memory effect that influences the system's development. Therefore, we may consider the non-local and non-singular kernel (Atangana & Koca, 2016) as:

$$\varphi(t,p) = \frac{B(\alpha)}{1-\alpha} E_\alpha \left(-\frac{\alpha (t-x)^{\alpha-1}}{1-\alpha} \right), \alpha \in (0,1].$$

Using this value of $\varphi(t,p)$ in equation (4.4), we get:

$$s(t) - s_0 = {}^{ABC}_0 D_t^{-\alpha} \left[b - \beta si - (\delta_1 + \gamma) s \right]$$

$$e(t) - e_0 = {}^{ABC}_0 D_t^{-\alpha} \left[\beta si + \rho \beta vi - (\delta_2 + \mu) e \right]$$

$$i(t) - i_0 = {}^{ABC}_0 D_t^{-\alpha} \left[\mu e - (\delta_3 + \eta) i \right] \qquad (4.5)$$

$$v(t) - v_0 = {}^{ABC}_0 D_t^{-\alpha} \left[\gamma s - \rho \beta vi - \delta_4 v \right]$$

$$r(t) - r_0 = {}^{ABC}_0 D_t^{-\alpha} \left[\eta i - \delta_5 r \right]$$

By applying the ABC fractional order derivative of order α to both sides of each equation in (4.5), we obtain our fractional order model:

We can write

$${}^{ABC}_0 D_t^\alpha s(t) = b - \beta si - (\delta_1 + \gamma) s$$

$${}^{ABC}_{0}D^{\alpha}_t e(t) = \beta si + \rho\beta vi - (\delta_2 + \mu) e$$

$${}^{ABC}_{0}D^{\alpha}_t i(t) = \mu e - (\delta_3 + \eta) i \tag{4.6}$$

$${}^{ABC}_{0}D^{\alpha}_t v(t) = \gamma s - \rho\beta vi - \delta_4 v$$

$${}^{ABC}_{0}D^{\alpha}_t r(t) = \eta i - \delta_5 r$$

It is assumed that both sides of all the equations in (4.6) have the same dimensions. Henceforth, our undivided focus will be solely on this specific model (4.6).

Fractional derivatives are highly efficient in capturing the memory effect when simulating the dynamics of OSNs. The pace at which the memory kernel $\varphi(t,p)$ decays is contingent upon the value of α. A lower value of α correlates to time-correlation functions that decay more slowly. The order α can be represented as a measure of the memory of the system, as shown in references (Atangana & Gómez-Aguilar, 2018; Toufik & Atangana, 2017).

NUMERICAL SOLUTION OF THE PROPOSED MODEL AND ANALYSIS

By utilising the fundamental theorem of fractional calculus (Sabri, 2020; Toufik & Atangana, 2017), the equation (4.6) may be converted into a fractional order integral equation:

$$s_n(t) = s_n(0) + \frac{(1-\alpha)}{B(\alpha)}\left\{b - \beta s_n i_n - (\delta_1 + \gamma) s_n\right\}$$

$$+ \frac{\alpha}{B(\alpha)\text{``}(\alpha)}\int_0^t (t-l)^{\alpha-1}\left\{b - \beta s_n i_n - (\delta_1 + \gamma) s_n\right\} dl$$

$$e_n(t) = e_n(0) + \frac{(1-\alpha)}{B(\alpha)}\left\{\beta s_n i_n + \rho\beta v_n i_n - \mu e_n - \delta e_n\right\}$$

$$+ \frac{\alpha}{B(\alpha)\text{``}(\alpha)}\int_0^t (t-l)^{\alpha-1}\left\{\beta s_n i_n + \rho\beta v_n i_n - \mu e_n - \delta_2 e_n\right\} dl$$

$$i_n(t) = i_n(0) + \frac{(1-\alpha)}{B(\alpha)}\{\mu e_n - (\delta_3 + \eta)i_n\} + \frac{\alpha}{B(\alpha)^{\alpha}(\alpha)}\int_0^t (t-l)^{\alpha-1}\{\mu e_n - (\delta_3 + \eta)i_n\}dl$$

$$(5.1)$$

$$v_n(t) = v_n(0) + \frac{(1-\alpha)}{B(\alpha)}\{\gamma s_n - \rho\beta v_n i_n - \delta_4 v_n\}$$

$$+ \frac{\alpha}{B(\alpha)^{\alpha}(\alpha)}\int_0^t (t-l)^{\alpha-1}\{\gamma s_n - \rho\beta v_n i_n - \delta_4 v_n\}dl$$

$$r_n(t) = r_n(0) + \frac{(1-\alpha)}{B(\alpha)}\{\eta i_n - \delta_5 r_n\} + \frac{\alpha}{B(\alpha)^{\alpha}(\alpha)}\int_0^t (t-l)^{\alpha-1}\{\eta i_n - \delta_5 r_n\}dl$$

Let us assume (For the sake of convenience):

$$H_{n,1}(t) = b - \beta s_n(t)i_n(t) - (\delta_1 + \gamma)s_n(t)$$

$$H_{n,2}(t) = \beta s_n(t)i_n(t) + \rho\beta v_n(t)i_n(t) - \mu e_n(t) - \delta e_n(t) \qquad (5.2)$$

$$H_{n,3}(t) = \mu e_n(t) - (\delta_3 + \eta)i_n(t)$$

$$H_{n,4}(t) = \gamma s_n - \rho\beta v_n(t)i_n(t) - \delta_4 v_n(t)$$

$$H_{n,5}(t) = \eta i_n(t) - \delta_5 r_n(t)$$

The expressions $H_{n,1}(t)$, $H_{n,2}(t)$, $H_{n,3}(t)$, $H_{n,4}(t)$, and $H_{n,5}(t)$, will satisfies the Lipschitz condition if and only if $s_n(t)$, $e_n(t)$, $i_n(t)$, $v_n(t)$ and $r_n(t)$ all have an upper bound (Owolabi & Atangana, 2019). Let $S_n(t)$ and $s_m(t)$ be two functions, then we get

$$H_{n,1}(t) - H_{m,1}(t)$$

$$= -\beta(s_n - s_m)I_n - (\delta_1 + \gamma)(s_n - s_m)$$

$$= -(\beta I_n + (\delta_1 + \gamma))(s_n - s_m)$$

$$\leq -\left(\beta I_n + \left(\delta_1 + \gamma\right)\right)\left(s_n - s_m\right)$$

$$\leq \varepsilon_1 \left(s_n - s_m\right) \tag{5.3}$$

Where $\varepsilon_1 = -\left(\beta max_{t\in[0,t_s]} i_n\left(t\right) + \left(\delta_1 + \gamma\right)\right)$.

Hence, we have

$$H_{n,1}\left(t\right) - H_{m,1}\left(t\right) \leq \varepsilon_1 \left(s_n - s_m\right) \tag{5.4}$$

Similarly, we can obtain

$$H_{n,2}\left(t\right) - H_{m,2}\left(t\right) \leq \varepsilon_2 \left(e_n - e_m\right)$$

$$H_{n,3}\left(t\right) - H_{m,3}\left(t\right) \leq \varepsilon_3 \left(i_n - i_m\right)$$

$$H_{n,4}\left(t\right) - H_{m,4}\left(t\right) \leq \varepsilon_4 \left(v_n - v_m\right) \tag{5.5}$$

$$H_{n,5}\left(t\right) - H_{m,5}\left(t\right) \leq \varepsilon_5 \left(r_n - r_m\right)$$

Thus, all the functions $H_{n,1}(t), H_{n,2}(t), H_{n,3}(t), H_{n,4}(t)$, and $H_{n,5}(t)$ satisfies Lipschitz condition, where $\varepsilon_1, \varepsilon_2, \varepsilon_3, \varepsilon_4$, and ε_5 are the related Lipschitz constant respectively. Then, applying equation (5.2) in equation (5.1) we have:

$$s_n\left(t\right) = s_n\left(0\right) + \frac{\left(1-\alpha\right)}{B\left(\alpha\right)} H_{n,1}\left(t\right) + \frac{\alpha}{B\left(\alpha\right)\Gamma\left(\alpha\right)} \int_0^t \left(t-l\right)^{\alpha-1} H_{n,1}\left(l\right) dl$$

$$e_n\left(t\right) = e_n\left(0\right) + \frac{\left(1-\alpha\right)}{B\left(\alpha\right)} H_{n,2}\left(t\right) + \frac{\alpha}{B\left(\alpha\right)\Gamma\left(\alpha\right)} \int_0^t \left(t-l\right)^{\alpha-1} H_{n,2}\left(l\right) dl \tag{5.6}$$

$$i_n\left(t\right) = i_n\left(0\right) + \frac{\left(1-\alpha\right)}{B\left(\alpha\right)} H_{n,3}\left(t\right) + \frac{\alpha}{B\left(\alpha\right)\Gamma\left(\alpha\right)} \int_0^t \left(t-l\right)^{\alpha-1} H_{n,3}\left(l\right) dl$$

$$v_n(t) = v_n(0) + \frac{(1-\alpha)}{B(\alpha)} H_{n,4}(t) + \frac{\alpha}{B(\alpha)\Gamma(\alpha)} \int_0^t (t-l)^{\alpha-1} H_{n,4}(l)\,dl$$

$$r_n(t) = r_n(0) + \frac{(1-\alpha)}{B(\alpha)} H_{n,5}(t) + \frac{\alpha}{B(\alpha)\Gamma(\alpha)} \int_0^t (t-l)^{\alpha-1} H_{n,5}(l)\,dl$$

Obtaining an iterative scheme, at given point $t=t_{k+1}$, for $k=0,1,2,\ldots$ the above equation is rewritten as:

$$s_n(t_{k+1}) = s_n(0) + \frac{(1-\alpha)}{B(\alpha)} H_{n,1}(t_k) + \frac{\alpha}{B(\alpha)\Gamma(\alpha)} \sum_{j=0}^{j=k} \int_{t_j}^{t_{j+1}} (t_{k+1}-l)^{\alpha-1} H_{n,1}(l)\,dl$$

$$e_n(t_{k+1}) = e_n(0) + \frac{(1-\alpha)}{B(\alpha)} H_{n,2}(t_k) + \frac{\alpha}{B(\alpha)\Gamma(\alpha)} \sum_{j=0}^{j=k} \int_{t_j}^{t_{j+1}} (t_{k+1}-l)^{\alpha-1} H_{n,2}(l)\,dl$$

$$(5.7)$$

$$i_n(t_{k+1}) = i_n(0) + \frac{(1-\alpha)}{B(\alpha)} H_{n,3}(t_k) + \frac{\alpha}{B(\alpha)\Gamma(\alpha)} \sum_{j=0}^{j=k} \int_{t_j}^{t_{j+1}} (t_{k+1}-l)^{\alpha-1} H_{n,3}(l)\,dl$$

$$v_n(t_{k+1}) = v_n(0) + \frac{(1-\alpha)}{B(\alpha)} H_{n,4}(t_k) + \frac{\alpha}{B(\alpha)\Gamma(\alpha)} \sum_{j=0}^{j=k} \int_{t_j}^{t_{j+1}} (t_{k+1}-l)^{\alpha-1} H_{n,4}(l)\,dl$$

$$r_n(t_{k+1}) = r_n(0) + \frac{(1-\alpha)}{B(\alpha)} H_{n,5}(t_k) + \frac{\alpha}{B(\alpha)\Gamma(\alpha)} \sum_{j=0}^{j=k} \int_{t_j}^{t_{j+1}} (t_{k+1}-l)^{\alpha-1} H_{n,5}(l)\,dl$$

Within the interval $[t_j, t_{j+1}]$, we can utilize the two points interpolation for approximate the functions $H_{n,1}(t)$, $H_{n,2}(t)$, $H_{n,3}(t)$, $H_{n,4}(t)$, and $H_{n,5}(t)$ inside the above integral.

$$H_{n,1}(l) \cong \frac{H_{n,1}(t_j)}{h}(l-t_{j-1}) - \frac{H_{n,1}(t_{j-1})}{h}(l-t_j)$$

$$H_{n,2}(l) \cong \frac{H_{n,2}(t_j)}{h}(l-t_{j-1}) - \frac{H_{n,2}(t_{j-1})}{h}(l-t_j) \quad (5.8)$$

$$H_{n,3}(l) \cong \frac{H_{n,3}(t_j)}{h}(l-t_{j-1}) - \frac{H_{n,3}(t_{j-1})}{h}(l-t_j)$$

$$H_{n,4}(l) \cong \frac{H_{n,4}(t_j)}{h}(l-t_{j-1}) - \frac{H_{n,4}(t_{j-1})}{h}(l-t_j)$$

$$H_{n,5}(l) \cong \frac{H_{n,5}(t_j)}{h}(l-t_{j-1}) - \frac{H_{n,5}(t_{j-1})}{h}(l-t_j)$$

Using equation (5.7) in (5.8) which gives:

$$s_n(t_{k+1}) = s_n(0) + \frac{(1-\alpha)}{B(\alpha)} H_{n,1}(t_k)$$

$$+ \frac{\alpha}{B(\alpha)\Gamma(\alpha)} \sum_{j=0}^{j=k} \int_{t_j}^{t_{j+1}} (t_{k+1}-l)^{\alpha-1} \left(\frac{H_{n,1}(t_j)}{h}(l-t_{j-1}) - \frac{H_{n,1}(t_{j-1})}{h}(l-t_j) \right) dl$$

$$e_n(t_{k+1}) = e_n(0) + \frac{(1-\alpha)}{B(\alpha)} H_{n,2}(t_k)$$

$$+ \frac{\alpha}{B(\alpha)\Gamma(\alpha)} \sum_{j=0}^{j=k} \int_{t_j}^{t_{j+1}} (t_{k+1}-l)^{\alpha-1} \left(\frac{H_{n,2}(t_j)}{h}(l-t_{j-1}) - \frac{H_{n,2}(t_{j-1})}{h}(l-t_j) \right) dl$$

$$i_n(t_{k+1}) = i_n(0) + \frac{(1-\alpha)}{B(\alpha)} H_{n,3}(t_k)$$

$$+ \frac{\alpha}{B(\alpha)\Gamma(\alpha)} \sum_{j=0}^{j=k} \int_{t_j}^{t_{j+1}} (t_{k+1}-l)^{\alpha-1} \left(\frac{H_{n,3}(t_j)}{h}(l-t_{j-1}) - \frac{H_{n,3}(t_{j-1})}{h}(l-t_j) \right) dl$$

$$v_n(t_{k+1}) = v_n(0) + \frac{(1-\alpha)}{B(\alpha)} H_{n,4}(t_k)$$

$$+ \frac{\alpha}{B(\alpha)\Gamma(\alpha)} \sum_{j=0}^{j=k} \int_{t_j}^{t_{j+1}} (t_{k+1}-l)^{\alpha-1} \left(\frac{H_{n,4}(t_j)}{h}(l-t_{j-1}) - \frac{H_{n,4}(t_{j-1})}{h}(l-t_j) \right) dl$$

$$r_n(t_{k+1}) = r_n(0) + \frac{(1-\alpha)}{B(\alpha)} H_{n,5}(t_k)$$

$$+ \frac{\alpha}{B(\alpha)\Gamma(\alpha)} \sum_{j=0}^{j=k} \int_{t_j}^{t_{j+1}} (t_{k+1}-l)^{\alpha-1} \left(\frac{H_{n,5}(t_j)}{h}(l-t_{j-1}) - \frac{H_{n,5}(t_{j-1})}{h}(l-t_j) \right) dl$$

After simplification we get:

$$s_n(t_{k+1}) = s_n(0) + \frac{(1-\alpha)}{B(\alpha)} H_{n,1}(t_k) + \frac{\alpha}{B(\alpha)\Gamma(\alpha)} \sum_{j=0}^{j=k} \left(\frac{H_{n,1}(t_j)}{h} I_{j-1}^{\alpha} - \frac{H_{n,1}(t_{j-1})}{h} I_j^{\alpha} \right)$$

$$e_n(t_{k+1}) = e_n(0) + \frac{(1-\alpha)}{B(\alpha)} H_{n,2}(t_k) + \frac{\alpha}{B(\alpha)\Gamma(\alpha)} \sum_{j=0}^{j=k} \left(\frac{H_{n,2}(t_j)}{h} I_{j-1}^{\alpha} - \frac{H_{n,2}(t_{j-1})}{h} I_j^{\alpha} \right)$$

$$(5.9)$$

$$i_n(t_{k+1}) = i_n(0) + \frac{(1-\alpha)}{B(\alpha)} H_{n,3}(t_k) + \frac{\alpha}{B(\alpha)\Gamma(\alpha)} \sum_{j=0}^{j=k} \left(\frac{H_{n,3}(t_j)}{h} I_{j-1}^{\alpha} - \frac{H_{n,3}(t_{j-1})}{h} I_j^{\alpha} \right)$$

$$v_n(t_{k+1}) = v_n(0) + \frac{(1-\alpha)}{B(\alpha)} H_{n,4}(t_k) + \frac{\alpha}{B(\alpha)\Gamma(\alpha)} \sum_{j=0}^{j=k} \left(\frac{H_{n,4}(t_j)}{h} I_{j-1}^\alpha - \frac{H_{n,4}(t_{j-1})}{h} I_j^\alpha \right)$$

$$r_n(t_{k+1}) = r_n(0) + \frac{(1-\alpha)}{B(\alpha)} H_{n,5}(t_k) + \frac{\alpha}{B(\alpha)\Gamma(\alpha)} \sum_{j=0}^{j=k} \left(\frac{H_{n,5}(t_j)}{h} I_{j-1}^\alpha - \frac{H_{n,5}(t_{j-1})}{h} I_j^\alpha \right)$$

Where

$$I_{j-1}^\alpha = \int_{t_j}^{t_{j+1}} (l - t_{j-1})(t_{k+1} - l)^{\alpha-1} \, dl$$

$$I_j^\alpha = \int_{t_j}^{t_{j+1}} (l - t_j)(t_{k+1} - l)^{\alpha-1} \, dl$$

On further simplification of the integrals I_{j-1}^α and I_j^α, we get

$$I_{j-1}^\alpha = -\frac{1}{\alpha} \left[(t_{j+1} - t_{j-1})(t_{k+1} - t_{j+1})^\alpha - (t_j - t_{j-1})(t_{k+1} - t_j)^\alpha \right] - \frac{1}{\alpha(\alpha+1)} \left[(t_{k+1} - t_{j+1})^{\alpha+1} - (t_{k+1} - t_{j+1})^{\alpha+1} \right]$$

$$I_j^\alpha = -\frac{1}{\alpha} \left[(t_{j+1} - t_j)(t_{k+1} - t_{j+1})^\alpha \right] - \frac{1}{\alpha(\alpha+1)} \left[(t_{k+1} - t_{j+1})^{\alpha+1} - (t_{k+1} - t_{j+1})^{\alpha+1} \right]$$

Assuming, $t_j = jh$, we can easily find that

$$I_{j-1}^\alpha = \frac{h^{\alpha+1}}{\alpha(\alpha+1)} \left[(k+1-j)^\alpha (k-j+2+\alpha) - (k-j)^\alpha (k-j+2+2\alpha) \right]$$

(5.10)

And

$$I_j^\alpha = \frac{h^{\alpha+1}}{\alpha(\alpha+1)}\left[(k+1-j)^{\alpha+1} - (k-j)^\alpha(k-j+1+\alpha)\right] \tag{5.11}$$

Utilizing the equations (5.10) and (5.11) in equation (5.9):

$$s_n(t_{k+1}) = s_n(0) + \frac{(1-\alpha)}{B(\alpha)}H_{n,1}(t_k) + \frac{\alpha}{B(\alpha)}$$

$$\sum_{j=0}^{j=k}\left(\frac{H_{n,1}(t_j)}{\Gamma(\alpha+2)}h^\alpha\left[(k+1-j)^\alpha(k-j+2+\alpha)-(k-j)^\alpha(k-j+2+2\alpha)\right]\right.$$

$$\left. -\frac{H_{n,1}(t_{j-1})}{\Gamma(\alpha+2)}h^\alpha\left[(k+1-j)^{\alpha+1}-(k-j)^\alpha(k-j+1+\alpha)\right]\right) \tag{5.12}$$

$$e_n(t_{k+1}) = e_n(0) + \frac{(1-\alpha)}{B(\alpha)}H_{n,2}(t_k) + \frac{\alpha}{B(\alpha)}$$

$$\sum_{j=0}^{j=k}\left(\frac{H_{n,2}(t_j)}{\Gamma(\alpha+2)}h^\alpha\left[(k+1-j)^\alpha(k-j+2+\alpha)-(k-j)^\alpha(k-j+2+2\alpha)\right]\right.$$

$$\left. -\frac{H_{n,2}(t_{j-1})}{\Gamma(\alpha+2)}h^\alpha\left[(k+1-j)^{\alpha+1}-(k-j)^\alpha(k-j+1+\alpha)\right]\right) \tag{5.13}$$

$$i_n(t_{k+1}) = i_n(0) + \frac{(1-\alpha)}{B(\alpha)}H_{n,3}(t_k) + \frac{\alpha}{B(\alpha)}$$

$$\sum_{j=0}^{j=k}\left(\frac{H_{n,3}(t_j)}{\Gamma(\alpha+2)}h^\alpha\left[(k+1-j)^\alpha(k-j+2+\alpha)-(k-j)^\alpha(k-j+2+2\alpha)\right]\right.$$

$$\left. -\frac{H_{n,3}(t_{j-1})}{\Gamma(\alpha+2)}h^\alpha\left[(k+1-j)^{\alpha+1}-(k-j)^\alpha(k-j+1+\alpha)\right]\right) \tag{5.14}$$

$$v_n\left(t_{k+1}\right) = v_n\left(0\right) + \frac{(1-\alpha)}{B(\alpha)} H_{n,4}\left(t_k\right) + \frac{\alpha}{B(\alpha)}$$

$$\sum_{j=0}^{j=k}\left(\frac{H_{n,4}\left(t_j\right)}{\Gamma(\alpha+2)} h^\alpha \left[\left(k+1-j\right)^\alpha\left(k-j+2+\alpha\right)-\left(k-j\right)^\alpha\left(k-j+2+2\alpha\right)\right]\right.$$

$$\left.-\frac{H_{n,4}\left(t_{j-1}\right)}{\Gamma(\alpha+2)} h^\alpha \left[\left(k+1-j\right)^{\alpha+1}-\left(k-j\right)^\alpha\left(k-j+1+\alpha\right)\right]\right)$$

$$(5.15)$$

$$r_n\left(t_{k+1}\right) = r_n\left(0\right) + \frac{(1-\alpha)}{B(\alpha)} H_{n,5}\left(t_k\right) + \frac{\alpha}{B(\alpha)}$$

$$\sum_{j=0}^{j=k}\left(\frac{H_{n,5}\left(t_j\right)}{\Gamma(\alpha+2)} h^\alpha \left[\left(k+1-j\right)^\alpha\left(k-j+2+\alpha\right)-\left(k-j\right)^\alpha\left(k-j+2+2\alpha\right)\right]\right.$$

$$\left.-\frac{H_{n,5}\left(t_{j-1}\right)}{\Gamma(\alpha+2)} h^\alpha \left[\left(k+1-j\right)^{\alpha+1}-\left(k-j\right)^\alpha\left(k-j+1+\alpha\right)\right]\right)$$

$$(5.16)$$

APPLICATION OF THE PINN METHOD WITH TFC AND ELM FOR THE SEIVR MODEL

PINNs method for the model given by system of equation (4.6) and it's approximation given by set of equations (5.12) to (5.16) subject to $s_0=998$; $e_0=1$; $i_0=0$; $v_0=1$; $r_0=0$.

The interval is discretized with a step size of 0.1. The TFC-based trail solution is constructed as

$$s_{CE}\left(t\right) = g_s\left(t\right) + \left(s(0)-g_s(0)\right)$$

$$e_{CE}\left(t\right) = g_e\left(t\right) + \left(e(0)-g_e(0)\right)$$

$$i_{CE}\left(t\right) = g_i\left(t\right) + \left(i(0)-g_i(0)\right)$$

$$v_{CE}\left(t\right) = g_v\left(t\right) + \left(v(0)-g_v(0)\right)$$

$$r_{CE}(t) = g_r(t) + (r(0) - g_r(0))$$

$$L_k^s = \left[s_{CE}(t_{k+1}) - s(t_0) - \frac{(1-\alpha)}{B(\alpha)} H_{CE1}(t_k) - \frac{\alpha}{B(\alpha)\Gamma(\alpha)} \right.$$

$$\left. \sum_{j=0}^{j=k} \int_{t_j}^{t_{j+1}} (t_{k+1} - l)^{\alpha-1} \left(\frac{H_{CE1}(t_j)}{h}(l - t_{j-1}) - \frac{H_{CE1}(t_{j-1})}{h}(l - t_j) \right) dl \right]^2$$

(3.7)

Now the complete loss of the equation with respect to the neural network is given by

$$L_s = \sum_{k=1}^{n} \left[s_{CE}(t_{k+1}) - s(t_0) - \frac{(1-\alpha)}{B(\alpha)} H_{CE1}(t_k) - \frac{\alpha}{B(\alpha)\Gamma(\alpha)} \right.$$

$$\left. \sum_{j=0}^{j=k} \int_{t_j}^{t_{j+1}} (t_{k+1} - l)^{\alpha-1} \left(\frac{H_{CE1}(t_j)}{h}(l - t_{j-1}) - \frac{H_{CE1}(t_{j-1})}{h}(l - t_j) \right) dl \right]^2$$

$$L_e = \sum_{k=1}^{n} \left[e_{CE}(t_{k+1}) - e(t_0) - \frac{(1-\alpha)}{B(\alpha)} H_{CE2}(t_k) - \frac{\alpha}{B(\alpha)\Gamma(\alpha)} \right.$$

$$\left. \sum_{j=0}^{j=k} \int_{t_j}^{t_{j+1}} (t_{k+1} - l)^{\alpha-1} \left(\frac{H_{CE2}(t_j)}{h}(l - t_{j-1}) - \frac{H_{CE2}(t_{j-1})}{h}(l - t_j) \right) dl \right]^2$$

$$L_i = \sum_{k=1}^{n} \left[i_{CE}(t_{k+1}) - i(t_0) - \frac{(1-\alpha)}{B(\alpha)} H_{CE3}(t_k) - \frac{\alpha}{B(\alpha)\Gamma(\alpha)} \right.$$

$$\left. \sum_{j=0}^{j=k} \int_{t_j}^{t_{j+1}} (t_{k+1} - l)^{\alpha-1} \left(\frac{H_{CE3}(t_j)}{h}(l - t_{j-1}) - \frac{H_{CE3}(t_{j-1})}{h}(l - t_j) \right) dl \right]^2$$

$$L_v = \sum_{k=1}^{n} \left[v_{CE}(t_{k+1}) - v(t_0) - \frac{(1-\alpha)}{B(\alpha)} H_{CE4}(t_k) - \frac{\alpha}{B(\alpha)\Gamma(\alpha)} \right.$$

$$\left. \sum_{j=0}^{j=k} \int_{t_j}^{t_{j+1}} (t_{k+1} - l)^{\alpha-1} \left(\frac{H_{CE4}(t_j)}{h}(l - t_{j-1}) - \frac{H_{CE4}(t_{j-1})}{h}(l - t_j) \right) dl \right]^2$$

$$L_r = \sum_{k=1}^{n} \left[r_{CE}(t_{k+1}) - r(t_0) - \frac{(1-\alpha)}{B(\alpha)} H_{CE5}(t_k) - \frac{\alpha}{B(\alpha)\Gamma(\alpha)} \right.$$

$$\left. \sum_{j=0}^{j=k} \int_{t_j}^{t_{j+1}} (t_{k+1} - l)^{\alpha-1} \left(\frac{H_{CE5}(t_j)}{h}(l - t_{j-1}) - \frac{H_{CE5}(t_{j-1})}{h}(l - t_j) \right) dl \right]^2$$

Figure 2. Take values of t at 0.25, 0.5, 0.75, or 1 and compare the assumed values of the machine learning model with the solutions of Susceptible State Variable (s) using the relative l² error

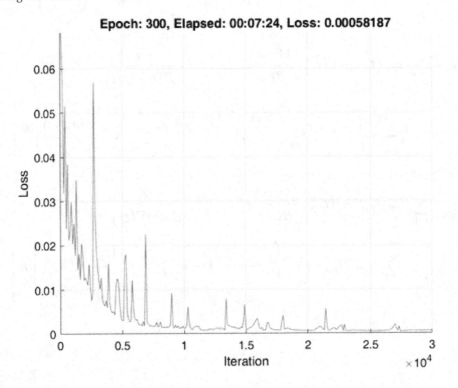

Figure 3. Take values of t at 0.25, 0.5, 0.75, or 1 and compare the assumed values of the machine learning model with the solutions of Vaccinated State Variable (v) using the relative l² error

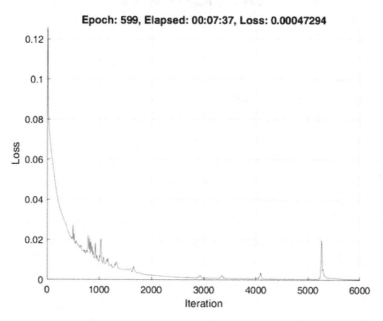

Figure 4. Take values of t at 0.25, 0.5, 0.75, or 1 and compare the assumed values of the machine learning model with the solutions of Infectious State Variable (i) using the relative l² error

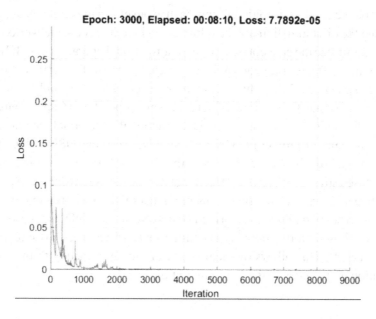

Figure 5. Variation of s, e, i, v, r against time (t) from the solution obtained by Adams-Bashforth Numerical method

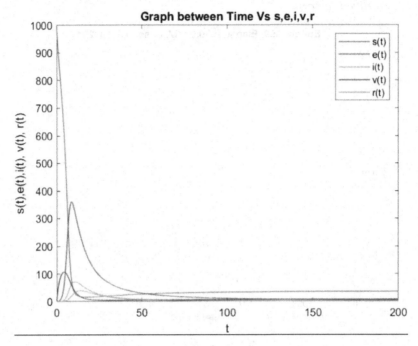

CONCLUSION

In this work, we employ an epidemic approach to develop a model for examining and controlling the dissemination of fake information in online social networks (OSNs). The model is utilize the concept of non singular fractional operator i.e. ABC operator for the memory effects (Atangana & Koca, 2016; Saeesian et al., 2017) of rumours.

In the present work, we have convincingly devised and apply a numerical scheme for Atangana-Baleanu fractional differential operator in Caputo sense (ABC fractional differential Operator). This ABC fractional differential Operator is used to model the rumour problem in Online Social Networking (OSN) which is a non linear fractional dynamical system. Note that it is the first time we used a neural network-based strategy for an ABC fractional dynamical system has been presented. In order to avoid stressful and time-consuming neural network training, the applied novel method based on Physics Informed Neural Network (PINN) uses trial solution construction based on functional connection theory and applies Extreme Learning Machine (ELM). This allows the neural network to be trained with the minimum computational resources in the least amount of time.

The loss function derived for training the Physics Informed Neural Network using fractional Adam Bashforth Numerical method. Numerical solutions, obtained by fractional Adam Bashforth Numerical method and it's stability analysis discussed in brief, the work's greatest accomplishment is the use of a Physics-Informed Neural Network to control the solution and solve the stated problem by combining Extreme Learning Machine with functional connection theory (Sivalingam, 2023; Sivalingam & Pushpendra Kumar, 2023). In short, we may state that recently developed neural network approaches have the ability to control the propagation of erroneous information and rumours.

REFERENCES

Atangana, A., & Gómez-Aguilar, J. F. (2018). Fractional derivatives with no-index law property: Application to chaos and statistics. *Chaos, Solitons, and Fractals, 114*, 516–535. doi:10.1016/j.chaos.2018.07.033

Atangana, A., & Koca, I. (2016). Chaos in a simple nonlinear system with Atangana–Baleanu derivatives with fractional order. *Chaos, Solitons, and Fractals, 89*, 447–454. doi:10.1016/j.chaos.2016.02.012

Banerjee, A. V. (1993, April). The economics of rumours. *The Review of Economic Studies, 60*(2), 309–327. doi:10.2307/2298059

Basak, R., Sural, S., Ganguly, N., & Ghosh, S. K. (2019, April). Online public shaming on Twitter: Detection, analysis, and mitigation. *IEEE Transactions on Computational Social Systems, 6*(2), 208–220. doi:10.1109/TCSS.2019.2895734

Bjørnstad, O. N., Shea, K., Krzywinski, M., & Altman, N. (2020, April). Modeling infectious epidemics. *Nature Methods, 17*(5), 455–456. doi:10.1038/s41592-020-0822-z PMID:32313223

CannarellaJ.SpechlerJ. A. (2014). Epidemiological modeling of online social network dynamics. *arXiv:1401.4208*. http://arxiv.org/abs/1401.4208

Cheng, J.-J., Liu, Y., Shen, B., & Yuan, W.-G. (2013, January). An epidemic model of rumor diffusion in online social networks. *The European Physical Journal B, 86*(1), 29. doi:10.1140/epjb/e2012-30483-5

Dagher, S. (2019). *Assad or We Burn Country: How One Family's Lust for Power Destroyed Syria*. London Back Pay Books.

Daley, D. J., & Kendall, D. G. (1965). Stochastic rumours. *IMA Journal of Applied Mathematics, 1*(1), 42–55. doi:10.1093/imamat/1.1.42

Dietz, K. (1967). Epidemics and rumours: A survey. *J. Roy. Stat. Soc.*, *130*(4), 505–528.

Dubey, S., Biswas, P., Ghosh, R., Chatterjee, S., Dubey, M. J., Chatterjee, S., Lahiri, D., & Lavie, C. J. (2020, May). Psychosocial impact of covid-19. *Diabetes & Metabolic Syndrome*, *14*(5), 779–788. doi:10.1016/j.dsx.2020.05.035 PMID:32526627

Girvan, M., & Newman, M. E. J. (2002, June). Community structure in social and biological networks. *Proceedings of the National Academy of Sciences of the United States of America*, *99*(12), 7821–7826. doi:10.1073/pnas.122653799 PMID:12060727

Huang, G.B., Zhu, Q.Y., & Siew, C.K. (2004). Extreme Learning machine: a new learning scheme of feedforward neural network. In *2004 IEEE International Joint Conference on Neural Networks* (pp. 985-990). IEEE.

Kermack, W. O., & McKendrick, A. G. (1927). A contribution to the mathematical theory of epidemics. *Proc. Roy. Soc. london. A. Containing Papers Math. Phys. Character*, *115*(772), 700–721.

Lebensztayn, E., Machado, F. P., & Rodríguez, P. M. (2011, April). On the behavior of a rumour process with random stifling. *Environmental Modelling & Software*, *26*(4), 517–522. doi:10.1016/j.envsoft.2010.10.015

Legon, A., & Alsalman, A. (2020). *How Facebook Can Flatten the Curve of the Coronavirus Infodemic*. AVAAZ. https://secure.avaaz.org/campaign/en/facebook_coronavirus_mi sinformation/

Li, L., Zhang, Q., Wang, X., Zhang, J., Wang, T., Gao, T.-L., Duan, W., Tsoi, K. K., & Wang, F.-Y. (2020, April). Characterizing the propagation of situational information in social media during COVID-19 epidemic: A case study on weibo. *IEEE Transactions on Computational Social Systems*, *7*(2), 556–562. doi:10.1109/TCSS.2020.2980007

Liang, G., He, W., Xu, C., Chen, L., & Zeng, J. (2015, September). Rumor identification in microblogging systems based on users' behavior. *IEEE Transactions on Computational Social Systems*, *2*(3), 99–108. doi:10.1109/TCSS.2016.2517458

Liu, W.-M., Levin, S. A., & Iwasa, Y. (1986, February). Influence of nonlinear incidence rates upon the behavior of SIRS epidemiological models. *Journal of Mathematical Biology*, *23*(2), 187–204. doi:10.1007/BF00276956 PMID:3958634

Nekovee, M., Moreno, Y., Bianconi, G., & Marsili, M. (2007, January). Theory of rumour spreading in complex social networks. *Physica A*, *374*(1), 457–470. doi:10.1016/j.physa.2006.07.017

Newman, M. E. J. (2013, July). Community detection and graph partitioning. *Europhysics Letters*, *103*(2), 28003. doi:10.1209/0295-5075/103/28003

Owolabi, K. M., & Atangana, A. (2019). *Numerical Methods for Fractional Differentiation* (Vol. 54). Springer Series in Computational Mathematics. doi:10.1007/978-981-15-0098-5

Ren, F., Li, S.-P., & Liu, C. (2017, March). Information spreading on mobile communication networks: A new model that incorporates human behaviors. *Physica A*, *469*, 334–341. doi:10.1016/j.physa.2016.11.027

Pratap, R. (2023). Rudra Pratap Controlling of Fake Information Dissemination in Online Social Networks: An Epidemiological Approach. *IEEE Access : Practical Innovations, Open Solutions*, *11*(April), 32229–32240.

Sabri, T. M. (2020). Study of transmission dynamics of COVID-19 mathematical model under ABC fractional order derivative. *Results in Physics*, *19*, 103507. doi:10.1016/j.rinp.2020.103507

Saeesian, M., Khalighi, M., Azimi-Tafreshi, N., Jafari, G. R., & Ausloos, M. (2017, February). Memory effects on epidemic evolution: The susceptible-infected-recovered epidemic model. *Physical Review. E*, *95*(2). PMID:28297983

Shrivastava, G., Kumar, P., Ojha, R. P., Srivastava, P. K., Mohan, S., & Srivastava, G. (2020, October). Defensive Modeling of Fake News Through Online Social Networks. *IEEE Transactions on Computational Social Systems*, *7*(5), 1159–1167. doi:10.1109/TCSS.2020.3014135

Shu, K., Bernard, H. R., & Liu, H. (2019). Studying fake news via network analysis: Detection and mitigation. Emerging Research Challenges and Opportunities in Computational Social Network Analysis and Mining. Springer.

Sivalingam, S. M. (2023). A neural networks – based numerical method for the generalized Caputo-type fractional differential equations. *Science Direct, 213*. doi:10.1016/j.matcom.2023.06.012

Sivalingam, S. M., & Pushpendra Kumar, V. (2023). Govindaraj, A novel optimization – based physics – informed neural network scheme for solving fractional differential equations. *Engineering with Computers*. doi:10.1007/s00366-023-01830-x

Soltanolkottabi, M., Ben-Arieh, D., & Wu, C.-H. (2019, April). Modeling behavioral response to vaccination using public goods game. *IEEE Transactions on Computational Social Systems*, *6*(2), 268–276. doi:10.1109/TCSS.2019.2896227 PMID:32391406

Sommariva, S., Vamos, C., Mantzarlis, A., Dào, L. U.-L., & Martinez Tyson, D. (2018, July). Spreading the (fake) news: Exploring health messages on social media and the implications for health professionals using a case study. *American Journal of Health Education, 49*(4), 246–255. doi:10.1080/19325037.2018.1473178

Toufik, M., & Atangana, A. (2017). New numerical approximation of fractional derivative with non-local and non-singular kernel: Application to chaotic models. *The European Physical Journal Plus, 132*(10), 444. doi:10.1140/epjp/i2017-11717-0

Wang, T., He, J., & Wang, X. (2018, January). An information spreading model based on online social networks. *Physica A, 490*, 488–496. doi:10.1016/j.physa.2017.08.078

Wang, W. (2006, January). Epidemic models with nonlinear infection forces. *Mathematical Biosciences and Engineering, 3*(1), 267–279. doi:10.3934/mbe.2006.3.267 PMID:20361823

Wen, S., Zhou, W., Zhang, J., Xiang, Y., Zhou, W., & Jia, W. (2013, August). Modeling propagation dynamics of social network worms. *IEEE Transactions on Parallel and Distributed Systems, 24*(8), 1633–1643. doi:10.1109/TPDS.2012.250

Wu, S., Das Sarma, A., Fabrikant, A., Lattanzi, S., & Tomkins, A. (2013). Arrival and departure dynamics in social networks. *Proc. 6th ACM Int. Conf. Web Search Data Mining (WSDM)* (pp. 233–242). ACM. 10.1145/2433396.2433425

Zhang, Z., Wang, H., Wang, C., & Fang, H. (2015, September). Modeling epidemics spreading on social contact networks. *IEEE Transactions on Emerging Topics in Computing, 3*(3), 410–419. doi:10.1109/TETC.2015.2398353 PMID:27722037

Chapter 10
Recent Trends in Pattern Recognition:
Challenges and Opportunities

Kannadhasan Suriyan

iD https://orcid.org/0000-0001-6443-9993
Study World College of Engineering, India

NAgarajan R.

iD https://orcid.org/0000-0002-4990-5869
Gnanamani College of Technology, India

ABSTRACT

Character recognition is the technique of identifying characters that have been optically processed (OCR). OCR is a method of converting a wide range of texts, PDFs, and digital pictures into an American Standard Code for Information Interchange (ASCII) or other machine-editable format in which the data may be changed or searched. Many applications, such as OCR, document categorization, data mining, and others, have demanded recent improvements in pattern recognition. Document scanners, character recognition, language recognition, security, and bank identification all rely on OCR. There are two kinds of OCR systems: online character recognition and offline character recognition. Online OCR outperforms offline OCR because characters are processed as they are written, avoiding the first step of character identification. Offline OCR is separated into two types: printed and handwritten OCR. Offline OCR is often performed by scanning typewritten or handwritten characters into a binary or grayscale picture for processing by a recognition algorithm. Scanned papers have become more valuable than typical picture files as OCR technology has advanced, converting them into text contents that computers can identify. Over the traditional process of manually retyping, OCR discovers a superior approach of automatically putting data into an electronic database. The most common issue with OCR is segmentation of linked letters or symbols. The accuracy of the OCR is proportional to the input image.

DOI: 10.4018/979-8-3693-5271-7.ch010

INTRODUCTION

Intelligent picture analysis is a fascinating topic of Artificial Intelligence study that is also critical for a number of current open research problems. Learning models to recognise pre-segmented handwritten digits is a well-researched subarea within the topic of handwritten digits recognition. It is one of the most crucial difficulties in data mining, machine learning, pattern recognition, and a variety of other artificial intelligence fields. Despite the fact that no recognition algorithm can match the level of human intellect, it has been shown to be significantly quicker, which is still appealing. Over the last decade, the main application of machine learning methods has proven efficacious in conforming decisive systems that compete with human performance and perform far better than manually written classical artificial intelligence systems used in the early days of optical character recognition technology (Brady & Brandstein, 2020; Campbell & Sturim, 2006; Gaikward, 2010; Naziya, n.d; Samudravijaya, 2010). However, not all aspects of those particular models have been examined before. A tremendous deal of effort has gone into developing effective algorithms for approximating recognition from data by researchers working in machine learning and data mining. Handwritten digit communication has its own standard in the twenty-first century, and it is utilized as a mode of dialogue and recording information to be exchanged with persons most of the time in everyday life. Because different communities may use different styles of handwriting and control to draw the same pattern of characters in their recognized script, one of the obstacles in handwritten characters identification is the diversity and distortion of handwritten character set.

One of the most difficult issues in the field of digit identification is identifying the digit from which the greatest discriminating characteristics may be retrieved. In pattern recognition, many types of region sampling approaches are employed to find such areas (Cai & Liu, 2002; Girolami & He, 2010; Kim et al., 2001; Ruiz, 2010; Vapnik, 1999). The vast variance in individual writing styles is the major source of difficulty in handwritten character identification. As a result, robust feature extraction is critical for improving a handwritten character recognition system's performance. Because of its usefulness in a variety of sectors, handwritten digit identification has attracted a lot of attention in the field of pattern recognition systems. Character recognition systems may be used as a cornerstone in the future to help create a paperless environment by scanning and processing existing paper documents (Durgesh, 2009; Kannadhasan & Suresh, 2014; Saberi et al., 2011; Santosh, 2007).

Because there may not always be crisp and completely straight lines, handwritten digit datasets are ambiguous. The basic purpose of feature extraction in digit recognition is to reduce duplication from the data and create a more effective representation of the word picture using a set of numerical properties. It deals with obtaining the majority of the important data from picture raw data. Furthermore, unlike written letters, the curves are not always smooth. Furthermore, characters may be created in a variety of sizes and orientations, but they must always be written on a guideline in an upright or straight position. As a result, by taking these restrictions into account, an effective handwriting recognition system may be constructed. It may be somewhat tedious at times to identify handwritten characters, especially because most people are unable to recognise their own written scripts. As a result, a writer's ability to write seems to be constrained in order for handwritten writings to be recognized. The software engineering module is provided first before the approach utilized to perform this study is revealed. In the field of handwritten character identification, pattern recognition and image processing play an important role. Feature extraction approaches are classified in a variety of ways, including structural feature-based approaches, statistical feature-based approaches, and global transformation approaches (Duda et al., 2020; Kannadhasan & Rajesh Baba, 2016; Watanabe, 1985). Statistical techniques are developed based on the selection of data. It makes use of data from the image's statistical distribution of pixels.

OPTICAL CHARACTER RECOGNITION

The recognition of optical characters has been studied. Perception, design division, and example order are the three main processes in example acknowledgment. With no change, clamour, determination variations, and other factors, optical character recognition (OCR) frameworks are transforming a large number of reports; either printed letters in order or manually produced into machine encoded information. Off-line and on-line character recognition are the two methods of handwriting recognition in general. Offline handwriting recognition entails the translation of text into an image, which is then converted into letter codes that may be used in computer and text-processing applications. Because various individuals have various handwriting styles, offline handwriting recognition is more challenging.

On-line character recognition, on the other hand, works with a data stream that comes from a transducer while the user is writing. A digitizing tablet that is electromagnetic or pressure sensitive is a common piece of data collection technology. When a user writes on a tablet, the pen's consecutive motions are converted into a sequence of electrical signals that the computer memorizes and analyses. Pattern recognition, artificial intelligence, machine vision, and signal processing all fall under the umbrella of Optical Character Recognition (OCR). Optical character recognition (OCR) is sometimes referred to as an off-line character recognition procedure since it scans and detects static pictures of characters. It is the non-variable mechanical or electrical conversion of pictures of handwritten characters or printed text into machine code. Pre-processing, Segmentation, Feature Extraction, Classifications, and Recognition are just a few of the stages involved in OCR. The output of one stage is the input of the next step. Preprocessing is the process of removing noise and variance from handwritten text. Offline handwriting recognition systems and pattern recognition are required in many areas where OCR is employed, including mail sorting, bank processing, document reading, and postal address identification. The process of transferring a paper-based handwritten document into an electronic version is known as digitization. Each document is made up of simply one character. The electronic conversion is achieved by scanning a document and producing an electronic representation of the original document in the form of an image file format. For digitization, we employed a variety of scanners, and the resulting digital picture was sent to the preprocessing phase. A set of actions are performed on the scanned input picture during the pre-processing phase. It improves the picture, making it segmentation-ready. The gray-level character picture is scaled to fit inside a window. We created a bitmap picture after noise reduction. The bitmap picture was then converted into a thinned version. The procedure of segmentation is the most crucial. Segmentation is achieved by separating an image's component characters.

Figure 1. Pattern recognition

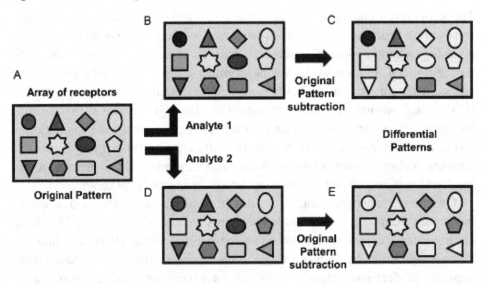

Handwritten characters are more difficult to segment into separate zones (upper, middle, and lower zone) and characters than printed texts in conventional form. This is mostly due to variations in paragraph, line, and word characters, as well as skew, slant, size, and curved. When the components of two neighboring characters are touched or overlapped, the work of segmentation becomes more complex. Because of the changed characters in the top and below zones, the issue of touching or overlapping arises often. Segmentation is a crucial step. Individual character characteristics are retrieved in this step. The performance of each character recognition system is determined on the retrieved characteristics. The extracted characteristics from the input character should allow for a one-of-a-kind categorization of the character. In order to discover the feature set for a particular character, we employed diagonal features, junction and open end points features, transition features, zoning features, directional features, parabola curve fitting–based features, and power curve fitting–based features.

In recent years, one of the most exciting and hard study topics in the realm of image processing and pattern recognition has been handwriting recognition. It makes a significant contribution to the progress of an automated process and may enhance the human-machine interface in a variety of applications. Several studies have focused on developing new strategies and methodologies that would cut processing time while increasing recognition accuracy. Off-line and on-line handwriting recognition technologies are the two main forms of handwriting recognition. The writing is normally taken optically by a scanner in off-line recognition, and the finished writing is provided as an image. However, the two-dimensional coordinates of consecutive locations are represented as a function of time in the on-line system, and the order of the writer's strokes is also provided. Due to the temporal information provided with the former, on-line approaches have been found to be better than their off-line counterparts in identifying handwritten characters. However, neural networks have been successfully deployed in off-line systems to achieve comparable high recognition accuracy levels. Off-line handwriting recognition systems are required for a variety of applications, including mail sorting, bank processing, document reading, and postal address identification is shown in figure 1. As a consequence, off-line handwriting recognition remains a hotbed of study, with researchers looking into emerging approaches to enhance recognition accuracy. Pre-processing is the initial stage in every handwriting recognition system, followed by segmentation and feature extraction.

The processes necessary to transform the input picture into a form appropriate for segmentation are referred to as pre-processing. The input picture is split into individual characters during segmentation, and each character is subsequently scaled into m x n pixels for the training network. The single most critical component in getting good recognition performance is choosing the right feature extraction approach. In the literature, many approaches of feature extraction for character recognition have been published. Template matching, Deformable templates, Unitary Image transforms, Graph description, Projection Histograms, Contour profiles, Zoning, Geometric moment invariants, Zernike Moments, Spline curve approximation, Fourier descriptors, Gradient feature, and Gabor feature are some of the most commonly used feature extraction methods. For classification and recognition tasks, an artificial neural network is utilised as the backend. Neural networks have developed as rapid and reliable methods for categorization in off-line recognition systems, allowing for high identification accuracy.

Since the 1990s, classification approaches have been used to improve handwritten character recognition. Statistical approaches based on the Bayes decision rule, Artificial Neural Networks (ANNs), Kernel Approaches, such as Support Vector Machines (SVMs), and numerous classifier combinations are among these methods.

VARIOUS SECTORS OF PATTERN RECOGNITION

Agriculture accounts for a significant share of total economic production. Researchers work with the breeding industry to discover, enhance, and breed critical features in order to meet rising demand, boost parasite and disease resistance, and minimise environmental impact (less water, less fertilizer), all while aiming for a more sustainable agriculture. If precision farming is used, these requirements may be met. According to the scientific literature on precision farming, most efforts have so far been concentrated on the development and implementation of sensor technology rather than data processing techniques specialized to agricultural measures. To put it another way, contributions to agricultural computational intelligence have mostly relied on off-the-shelf approaches found in software packages or libraries, rather than developing custom frameworks or algorithms. Pattern recognition is a multidisciplinary area that includes statistics, engineering, artificial intelligence, computer science, psychology, and physiology, among other disciplines. The area of pattern recognition is concerned with the automated detection of regularities in data using computer algorithms, as well as the application of these regularities to perform operations such as data classification.

Pattern recognition is often used for categorization or clustering, to put it simply. Humans have used analogical reasoning to solve a variety of issues for generations. When the human senses fail to perceive patterns, or when the identification process has to be automated and sped up, computer-based automated pattern recognition systems are necessary. Pattern reasoning uses the same paradigm to solve issues across several areas by examining relevant patterns. The primary idea behind pattern recognition is to elicit patterns from the research area and divide it into classes. Pattern recognition systems may be taught or untrained. Supervised learning refers to procedures that have been taught, whereas unsupervised learning refers to techniques that have not been taught. Pattern recognition solutions may be found all over the place. When choosing a pattern, a pattern recognition system should take into account the application domain. For all domains, the same pattern recognition technique cannot be used. The original input variables are often preprocessed in most practical applications to change them into a new space of variables where it is required. In the digit recognition issue, for example, the pictures of the digits are usually translated and scaled such that each digit is contained inside a fixed-size box. Because the placement and scale of all the digits are now the same, the variability within each digit class is considerably reduced, making it much simpler for a later pattern recognition algorithm to discriminate between the various classes. As an input, data from the surrounding environment is used.

The raw data is then processed to make the input usable by the pattern recognition system by either reducing noise from the data or extracting a pattern of interest from the background. The pattern's quantifiable or observable data is referred to as a feature. Feature extraction removes superfluous data and recovers the pattern's unique characteristics. The decrease of processing time in the recognition process is dependent on the elimination of unnecessary information. Data is identically processed, and pertinent characteristics are extracted. These significant characteristics come together to produce the identity of an item that has to be identified or categorised. Many feature extraction methods exist, including Fourier transform, Radon transform, Gabor Wavelets transform, Fuzzy invariant transform, principal component analysis, Semidefinite embedding, Multifactor dimensionality reduction, Multilinear subspace learning, Nonlinear dimensionality reduction, Isomap, Kernel PCA, Multilinear PCA, Latent semantic analysis, Partial least squares, Independent component analysis, Independent component analysis, Independent component analysis, Independent component analysis, Independent component analysis, Independent component analysis, Independent The goal of variable selection is to improve the predictors' prediction performance, provide quicker and more cost-effective predictors, and get a better knowledge of the underlying process that produced the data. To acquire a more discriminative or representative subset of feature vector, the list of features generated from the feature extraction stage is processed through another filtering procedure. Filtering is done without any transformations throughout this procedure, preserving the physical meaning of the original characteristics. Training data set refers to the feature vector/subset that is provided at the conclusion of this stage. We can better understand the domain by selecting features, and we can save money by limiting the number of predictors.

These feature selection features finally aid in the improvement of classification algorithm performance. This approach tries to not only accelerate the pace of dimension reduction, but also to avoid the effects of the dimensionality curse. Dimensionality reduction is not the same as feature selection. Both approaches aim to minimise the amount of attributes in a dataset, but dimensionality reduction techniques do so by inventing new combinations of attributes, while feature Selection techniques simply include and exclude existing characteristics in the data. At the top level, a feature selection methodology is divided into wrappers, filters, and embedding. Wrapper approaches score feature subsets using a prediction model. Each fresh subset is used to train a model, which is then put to the test on a control set. The score for that subset is calculated by counting the number of errors made on that hold-out set (the model's error rate). Wrapper approaches are computationally demanding since they train a new model for each subset, but they generally yield the highest performing feature set for that specific kind of model.

Figure 2. Pattern recognition processing

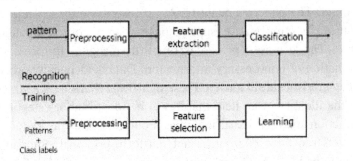

Image recognition technology is closely related to social life; it is an important branch of computer vision; neural network image recognition technology is a new type of image recognition technology developed in conjunction with modern computer technology, image processing, artificial intelligence, and pattern recognition theory]. To achieve picture recognition, first get a matching picture using an image acquisition device, resulting in a digital picture; then perform picture recognition and gather different information. The BP neural network is brought into the image recognition sector, and paired with standard digital image processing technology, a form of strong accuracy plane image identification technique is discovered in this research. Picture recognition necessitates a high processing speed and recognition accuracy, as well as real-time and fault-tolerance of the neural network in compliance with image recognition criteria. To begin, this work examines classic image recognition techniques, focusing on their limitations as well as complicated scenarios such as pictures in various states, in the process of developing an image processing algorithm for picture segmentation research and improvement. Simultaneously, based on the local minimum value of the problems present in the BP neural network, improve network efficiency, improve image recognition precision, and reduce network number of training and training time in the process of network training using the adaptive learning rate change method. The revised BP neural network technique for rotational distortion picture placement and identification will be a mix of added momentum and adaptive learning rate, effectively suppressing the network into a local minimum point and increasing the network's training pace. Finally, the optimization approach was tested by an experiment, which demonstrated its practicality and efficacy, and it was discovered that through programming, better results might be achieved.

With the evolution of technology and science, imaging has experienced certain changes. The purpose of digitising a picture is to convert it into computer memory or other types of media storage, such as a CD-ROM or hard drive. A digital image is a two-dimensional image represented by a small number of digital values known as pixels or picture components. A scanner or a video camera may be used to digitise your documents. After an image has been digitised, it may be processed using various image processing procedures. The two major responsibilities of digital image processing are improving visual information for human interpretation and processing data images for storage, representation, and transfer for autonomous machine perception. The goal of digital image processing is to identify a delegacy of intensity distribution in any picture and convert 3D pictures to 2D image values that may be used to describe and convey quantitative morphology. Many processes are used in digital image processing, such as data formatting and correction, digital augmentation for better visual interpretation, and computer-assisted target classifications and characteristics. The data must be provided and captured in a digital form that is suitable for storage on a computer disc or tape for a person to generate remote sensing imaging in a digital way. In addition, a computer system, also known as an image analysis system, with proper software and hardware to create data is required for the processing of digital images. A number of commercially available software packages have been developed expressly for remote sensing picture analysis and processing. Different approaches or approaches have been used as part of digital image processing operations. A large variety of common image processing operations are accessible in image analysis, including preprocessing, image enhancement, image transformation, and picture classification and analysis.

Preprocessing includes activities such as geometric or radiometric adjustments that are often necessary prior to the major examination of data and information extraction. Correcting the data for sensor abnormalities and unwanted sensor or ambient noise, as well as transforming the data so that it accurately represents the emitted or reflected radiation detected by the sensor, are all part of radiometric corrections. On the other hand, geometric adjustments involve correcting geometric distortions caused by sensor-earth geometry changes and rebirthing the data to real world coordinates such as longitude and latitude on the earth's surface. Picture transformations are processes that are conceptually comparable to image enhancing processes. Contrary to popular belief, picture enhancing processes are seldom used to more than one channel of data at a time. In most cases, image alterations include the coordinated processing of data from many spectral bands. To combine and transform the unique bands into new pictures that better emphasise or depict particular characteristics in the scene, arithmetic operations like as division, subtraction, addition, and multiplication are used. Band or spectral rationing, as well as principal components analysis, are two methodologies that are often used to better effectively represent information in multichannel images. To digitally categorise and identify pixels in the data, image classification and analysis processes are used. Multichannel datasets are often used for classification. Based on statistical aspects of the brightness values pixel, this approach assigns each picture and pixel to a certain theme or class. OCR's major purpose is to categorise optical patterns (which are generally included in a digital picture) that are connected to alphanumeric or other letters. Classification, segmentation, and feature extraction are all processes in the OCR process. Each step is a field in and of itself, as explained in the Matlab OCR implementation. It's a field of computer science that entails reading text from a certain paper and then translating the visuals into a format that the computer can understand. An OCR system allows a person to scan a magazine or book, input it into an electronic computer, and then edit the file in a word processor. OCR systems have a lot of potential since they allow users to harness the power of computers to retrieve printed materials. It is already in widespread usage, notably in the legal profession, where searches that used to take hours or days may now be completed in a matter of seconds.

APPLICATIONS OF NATURAL LANGUAGE PROCESSING

Character recognition is a new problem, and while there are widely available digital image processing algorithms and implementations that can detect characters from images, choosing an appropriate technique that can quickly adapt to a variety of images, whether they are very specific or complex, is critical. As a programme, MATLAB provides a comprehensive set of digital image processing tools, algorithms, and a fully integrated environment for data visualisation, analysis, and method creation. It has functions for picture analysis, enhancement, spatial transformation, and de-blurring. It also enables morphological operations like dilation, erosion, reconstruction, and others. Handwritten text is a widely utilised method in a variety of applications, and it is a technology that is now a need in the globe. Prior to the proper deployment of this technology, we were reliant on handwriting messages, which resulted in inaccuracies. It's tough to store, retrieve, and analyse physical data in a timely way. It is necessary to update the data manually, and work is required to keep the data organised properly. We have been experiencing serious data loss for a long time due to the old way of data storage.

Modern technology is a blessing, and it is causing individuals to save data on computers, which makes data storage, management, and accessibility simpler. Adopting Handwritten Text Recognition software is a good choice since it makes it simpler to save and retrieve data that was previously saved. Furthermore, it increases the data's security. Google Lens is an example of handwritten text recognition software, while OCR scanners are an example of hardware. Our project's goal is to create a model for handwritten text identification and conversion to voice for use in healthcare and personal care that can detect handwriting using deep learning ideas. We utilised Tensor Flow and OpenCV to solve our challenge since they both include pre-trained models that are immediately employed to offer accurate results when compared to other approaches. These files are kept in their own folders, and information may be taken from them. For the development of the project, we mostly employ Opensource models. The architecture of the models we utilized is based on natural language processing (NLP). Data capture, processing, querying, and visualisation are all fundamental components of this NLP architecture. This text is then transformed into a voice.

Figure 3. Applications of pattern recognition

Human intelligence distinguishes them from machines. Humans can do a variety of jobs that machines cannot do on their own. Handwritten text recognition is one of these jobs. Despite the fact that text recognition in handwritten documents has been explored as a key study field by many scholars over the last several decades, numerous automated handwritten systems have been created by various academics in the past. However, the recognition algorithm and its effectiveness are currently under investigation. Because of the wide variety of handwriting styles, state-of-the-art handwriting recognition systems typically fail to function well on a variety of handwriting samples. Handwriting recognition methods often contain many phases, including 1.preprocessing, 2.feature extraction, 3.classification, and 4.postprocessing. Feature extraction and classifier design, on the other hand, are the two most important processes in any recognition system.

Even yet, these scripts' recognition issues cannot be regarded fully resolved. In the creation of an efficient and accurate handwritten text recognition system, ANN has shown to be a lifesaver. The use of ANN in the design is one of the most common ways that computers are taught to have human-like abilities. Neural networks are based on the human brain's architecture and are especially effective for addressing problems that cannot be expressed in a sequence of straightforward stages, such as pattern recognition, object categorization, data mining, and series prediction. Pattern recognition is perhaps the most popular use of neural networks. A distinct class of target vectors is supplied to the neural network, as well as the corresponding input vectors (a vector containing pattern information). The data input might be anything from basic one-dimensional data to multi-dimensional data. Once the ANN has been taught using training data (much like the human brain), it may be used to identify patterns/classes in previously unknown data (new inputs).

The major goal of this research is to create an effective ANN-based handwritten character and number recognition system for English characters. Because handwritten characters may have a combination of case (capital and tiny letters) of English characters, this research includes 52 classes (26 for capital and 26 for tiny). The reader should be aware that we did not look at the identification of their English symbols.

Voice recognition, also known as Automatic Speech Recognition (ASR), is the act of turning a speech signal into a series of words using a computer software and an algorithm. One of the most important areas of signal processing is speech processing. The goal of the voice recognition domain is to create strategies for machine voice input. The breadth and capability of early computer systems were restricted. However, the subject of automated speech recognition has advanced as a result of the revolution in computer technology. Because of advances in computer technology, it is now possible to maintain large databases for voice recognition. Because language is the most fundamental form of communication, human computer interfaces in native languages should be expected. Speech recognition systems have only been created for a small number of languages. As a result, building voice recognizers in local languages has a lot of potential. In the realm of voice recognition, advancements in statistical modelling of speech have found extensive use. In various domains, such as automated call processing in telephone networks, data input, voice dictation, query-based updated travel information and reservations, natural language comprehension and translators, and so on, automated speech recognition has decreased human labour. In telephone networks, speech recognition technology is widely used to automate and improve operator services.

The essential building blocks of voice recognition systems, as well as technical development, are highlighted in this study. The difficulty of identifying optically processed characters is addressed by optical character recognition. Optical recognition is an offline procedure, meaning it begins after the writing or printing is finished. For the last several decades, handwritten character recognition has been a frontier field of study, and there has been a high demand for OCR on handwritten materials. Despite the fact that several research have been conducted on foreign scripts such as Chinese, Japanese, and Arabic characters, there are just a few research on handwritten character identification in Indian scripts. In the Indian situation, no comprehensive handwritten text recognition system exists, and it is challenging owing to the huge character set of Indian languages and the existence of vowel modifiers and compound characters in Indian script. Character recognition problems may be categorised using two criteria. The first is dependent on whether the text is printed or handwritten. The other is dependent on the acquisition method, which might be either online or offline.

The on-line approach of identifying handwritten text is typically thought to perform better than its off-line version. Characters are recognised in real time while using online character recognition. Since they have timing information, online systems have a greater chance of recognising characters than their offline counterparts because they can skip the first search stage of finding the character. In the case of offline character recognition, the typewritten or handwritten character is often scanned as a paper document and made accessible to the recognition system as a binary or grey scale picture. Because there is no control over the media or instrument utilised, offline character recognition is a more demanding and hard process. In the midst of the hustle and bustle of our modern "smart" lives, the creation of a smart transportation management system that gives data on vehicle counts for follow-up, analytics, and monitoring is critical. Modern traffic control systems must address vehicle tracking, identification, and management as important challenges. ALPR systems are used in a variety of traffic and security applications, including parking management, toll fee collecting, entry and border control, and the monitoring of stolen vehicles, among others. The ALPR system entails taking an image with a digital camera, pre-processing the picture to reduce noise and make it acceptable for character segmentation and identification. The licence plate of the car is the system's output, and the system may be tweaked to meet the needs of the end user.

The automation of parking security and administration at malls, universities, workplaces, and other locations is one such user request that is addressed in this article. The created technology may be utilised to detect a car entering a parking lot and/or toll booth automatically. The licence plate is derived from a photograph of the car. Once the characters have been identified, the user may utilise a graphical user interface to control the machine. The GUI displays the timestamp of the vehicle entering the premises, enabling the user to keep track of all cars that pass through. The area of pattern recognition is concerned with the automated detection of regularities in data using computer algorithms, as well as the application of these regularities to perform operations such as data classification. Its ultimate purpose is to extract patterns as efficiently as possible depending on particular parameters and to distinguish one class from the others. Pattern Recognition is used in a variety of applications is shown in figure 3. Disease classification, prediction of patient survival rates, fingerprint verification, face identification, iris discrimination, chromosomal shape discrimination, optical character identification, texture discrimination, voice recognition, and so on are some examples. The application domain should be considered while designing a pattern recognition system. It's startling and fascinating to note that artificial recognition systems, particularly those that learn from examples, are nearly entirely or only ostensibly based on a simulation of human vision and learning skills. One of the reasons is because artificial systems may be used for a variety of purposes, and they must be more reliable, as well as quicker and bigger at times, at the expense of flexibility.

Humans are pattern recognizers, not only because of our capacity to recognise patterns, but also because we are conscious of it. We can manage it, as well as explain the patterns to others and share our findings with them. Generalization is the capacity to discern the similarities of items or occurrences. The essential scientific subject of pattern recognition and how this process may be incorporated into and taught to a computer, a challenge for its algorithms, is therefore how human mind moves from observations to memory and generalisation. Machine Learning techniques may be used to achieve pattern recognition. These algorithms classify data based on previously acquired knowledge or statistical data taken from patterns and/or their representation. The capacity to discover arrangements of traits or data that produce information about a particular system or data collection is known as pattern recognition. Pattern recognition algorithms may be used in predictive analytics in data science to uncover statistically likely future movements of time series data. A pattern in a technological context could be recurring sequences of data over time that can be used to predict trends, specific configurations of features in images that identify objects, frequent combinations of words and phrases for natural language processing (NLP), or specific clusters of behaviour on a network that could indicate an attack, among an almost infinite number of other possibilities. A simple PR system is fully reliant on data, and it can generate any conclusion or model from data on its own, rapidly and correctly identifying known patterns. Preprocessing, feature extraction, and classification are the three essential components of a pattern recognition method.

For many years, pattern recognition has been a work in progress. It contains a variety of strategies that encourage the creation of multiple applications in various disciplines. Preprocessing, feature extraction, and classification are the three essential components of pattern recognition. Following the acquisition of the dataset, it is preprocessed to make it appropriate for following sub-processes. The next phase is feature extraction, which involves converting the dataset into a series of feature vectors that are meant to reflect the original data. These characteristics are employed in the classification process to categorise the data points into distinct issue types. Preprocessing's job is to separate the intriguing pattern from the background noise. It's used to bring down variances and generate more consistent results. To repair the picture from various faults, such as severe fluctuations in illumination direction and intensity, preprocessing should include some noise filtering, smoothing, and normalising. In certain applications, segmentation of the interesting pattern of a given picture from the backdrop is critical; for example, in agricultural applications, segmentation of the infected area of damaged plant photos is required. In pattern recognition, feature extraction is employed to solve the issue of high dimensionality of the input set. As a result, the input data will be converted into a feature vector, which is a reduced representation set of features. In order to complete the necessary job using this reduced representation instead of the full size input, just the necessary information from the input data should be extracted. The retrieved features should be simple to calculate, robust, rotationally invariant, and insensitive to picture distortions and changes. Then, from the input space, the ideal features subset that can produce the best accuracy outcomes should be chosen.

In pattern recognition issues, two types of features are employed. Geometric or structural traits, as well as statistical data, have a distinct physical meaning. Another kind of characteristic has no physical significance. These are referred to as mapping features. Physical characteristics have the benefit of not having to deal with unimportant aspects. The benefit of the mapping characteristics is that they make categorization simpler by establishing distinct borders between classes, but at the cost of increased computational complexity. A combinatorial search of the whole space is used in the majority of feature selection methods. Because the size of the input space is exponential in the number of features, heuristic approaches such as hill climbing must usually be used. Other approaches split the feature space into subspaces that can be readily searched. Filter and wrapper are the two most common feature selection strategies. Filters approaches choose the best features based on past knowledge without considering the bias of a subsequent induction procedure. As a result, these strategies worked regardless of the classification algorithm or error criteria. The majority of feature extraction approaches are supervised. Prior information and tagged training samples are required for these methods. Linear feature extraction and nonlinear feature extraction are the two types of supervised algorithms employed. Principal Component Analysis (PCA), Linear Discriminant Analysis (LDA), projection pursuit, and Independent Component Analysis are examples of linear feature extraction approaches (ICA). Kernel PCA, PCA network, nonlinear PCA, nonlinear auto-associative network, Multi-Dimensional Scaling (MDS), and Self-Organizing Map (SOM) are examples of nonlinear feature extraction approaches. During the classification process, the system recognises each pattern and associates it with the proper class using the characteristics gathered in the previous step. In the literature, there are two sorts of learning procedures.

CONCLUSION

Classifiers, which belong to supervised learning, include information of each pattern category as well as a criteria or metric for discriminating between them. It seeks to uncover underlying patterns in the data that may subsequently be utilized to calculate the proper output value for new data instances using unsupervised learning, in which the system parameters are altered using just the information from the input and restricted by predefined internal constraints. A face/non-face classification challenge, for example, arises when assessing if a given picture includes a face or not. Classes, also known as categories, are collections of patterns with comparable feature values based on a metric. The kind of learning utilised to create the output value in this stage is utilised to classify pattern recognition. Using certain qualities (features) collected from the previous phases, we can identify an item or a pattern in this stage. It is the process in which each feature vector's input value is assigned to one of a set of classes. In the pattern recognition process, many categorization techniques are utilised, each with its own set of skills and features.

REFERENCES

Brady, K. & Brandstein, M. (2020). *An evaluation of audio-visual person recognition on the XM2VTS corpus using the Lausanne protocol*. MIT Lincoln Laboratory.

Cai, J. & Liu, Z. (2002). Pattern recognition using markov random field models. *Pattern Recognition, 35*(3).

Campbell, W. M., & Sturim, D. E. (2006). *The MIT- LL/IBM speaker recognition system using high performance reduced complexity recognition.* MIT Lincoln Laboratory IBM.

Duda, R. O., Hart, P. E., & Stork, D. G. (2020). Unsupervised Learning and Clustering. In *Pattern classification* (2nd ed.). Wiley.

Durgesh, K. (2009). Data Classification using Support Vector Machine. *Journal of Theoretical and Applied Information Technology.*

Gaikward, S. K. (2010, November). A review on speech recognition technique. *International Journal of Computer Applications, 10*(3).

Girolami, M. & He, C. (2010). Probability density estimation from optimally condensed data samples. *Pattern Analysis and Machine Intelligence, 25*(10), 1253 – 1264.

Kannadhasan, S., & Rajesh Baba, M. (2016, December). A Novel Approach to detect Text in Various Dynamic-Color Images. In *Mathematics and its Applications.* University College of Engineering, Anna University.

Kannadhasan, S., & Suresh, R. (2014). EMD Algorithm for Robust Image Watermarking. Recent Advances in Mechanical Engineering and Interdisciplinary Developments. Advanced Materials Research.

Kim, M., Jang, D., & Yang, Y. (2001). A robust-invariant pattern recognition model using fuzzy art. *Pattern Recognition, 34*(8), 1685-1696.

Naziya, S. (n.d.). Speech Recognition System-A Review. *IOSR Journal of Computer Engineering, 18*(4).

Ruiz, L. R. (2010). *Interactive Pattern Recognition applied to Natural Language Processing.* Thesis.

Saberi, M., Azadeh, A., Nourmohammadzadeh, A., & Pazhoheshfar, P. (2011). Comparing performance and robustness of SVM and ANN for fault diagnosis in a centrifugal pump. *19th International Congress on Modelling and Simulation,* Perth, Australia.

Samudravijaya, K. (2010). *Speech and Speaker recognition tutorial*. TIFR Mumbai.

Santosh, S. (2007). Bayesian Quadratic Discriminant Analysis. *Journal of Machine Learning Research*, 8, 1277–1305.

Vapnik, V. (1999). An overview of statistical learning theory. *IEEE Transactions on Neural Networks, 10*(5).

Watanabe, S. (1985). *Pattern Recognition: Human and Mechanical*. Wiley.

Chapter 11
Review on Machine Learning as a Key Technology Enabler for Sustainable Biodiesel Production

Brihaspati Singh
National Institute of Technology, Patna, India

Anmesh Kumar Srivastava
National Institute of Technology, Patna, India

Om Prakash
National Institute of Technology, Patna, India

ABSTRACT

The increasing scarcity of fossil fuel resources has created a significant need for a clean, inexpensive, and sustainable energy source. Biodiesel, a kind of liquid biofuel, has been discovered to mitigate environmental deterioration, improve engine efficiency, and decrease the release of harmful gases. Biodiesel production and usage processes are complicated and nonlinear, requiring rapid and accurate modelling tools for design, optimisation, and monitoring. Machine learning or other forms of artificial intelligence have been found to be a superior method for modelling biodiesel production. This is due to its ability to make accurate predictions, which is inspired by the auto learning and self-improving capabilities of the brain. Uses of machine learning in biodiesel production range from quality prediction and optimisation to monitoring of process conditions and output quantification. Furthermore, the integration of AI-based solutions from Industry 4.0 with human intelligence is crucial in the context of Industry 5.0 for the biodiesel industry to increase production efficiency, guarantee economic viability, and foster sustainability. This combination facilitates the exploration of reaction mechanisms, specifically in the domain of advanced biodiesel production.

DOI: 10.4018/979-8-3693-5271-7.ch011

INTRODUCTION

In the contemporary global landscape, there has been a notable shift towards embracing environmentally sustainable practises, particularly in the realm of technology. Within this context, biofuel emerges as a pioneering force, embodying the principles and values associated with this philosophy. The prevailing circumstances of diminished fossil energy reserves and the increasing global demand for such resources have spurred a collective pursuit of novel fuel innovations. The reliance on traditional forms of energy has resulted in a significant depletion of reserves and adverse climate impacts. According to the statistical data released by the Petroleum Planning and Analysis Cell, a governmental body under the Ministry of Petroleum & Natural Gas of the Government of India, the total volume of diesel fuel sold via retail outlets in the nation from October 2020 to September 2021 amounted to 66,862 thousand metric tonnes. During the designated survey timeframe, it was observed that the transport sector constituted a significant proportion of diesel consumption, amounting to 87 percent of total retail sales. Conversely, the non-transport sector accounted for the remaining 13 percent of fuel utilisation (Bolton, 2021). According to India's National Biofuel Policy, the country's goal is to mix 5% biodiesel into its fuel supply by the year 2030 (Singh et al., 2023a). The need to find alternatives to fossil fuels has reached a critical level, since their capacity to provide global energy demands is projected to be sustainable only until the year 2030 (Jayakumar et al., 2017). Fossil-based fuels, mostly consisting of coal, oil, and gas, have served as the primary source of world energy for a period exceeding 150 years. There are valid worries over the existing state of the energy supply situation, which is deemed significantly insufficient and unsustainable in meeting the energy demands of the industrialised global world (Awogbemi & Kallon, 2023). The IEA claims that the global energy crisis brought on by the conflict between Russia and Ukraine is having a severe effect on individuals, companies, and whole economies. As a result, governments are under pressure to act quickly and have more in-depth conversations on how to increase energy security and reduce the possibility of further disruptions. By 2030, the Sustainable Development Goals (SDGs) of the United Nations, which were put into effect in 2015, called for improved energy efficiency, more access to contemporary energy services, and the use of energy derived from renewable sources. On a global scale, there has been a notable rise in zero-carbon initiatives during the span of eight years subsequent to the signing of the Paris Agreement by 196 nations (now 194). According to the STEPS analysis, it is projected that the demand for a certain resource would experience its highest point in the mid-2030s, reaching a level of 103 million barrels per day (mb/d). Subsequently, a gradual decrease in demand is anticipated, continuing until the year 2050 (IEA, 2022). Figure 1 illustrates the varying patterns of fossil and non-fossil fuel use between the years 2020 and 2050, while Figure 2 presents the changes in CO_2 emissions up to 2050. Biodiesel has been identified as a potential substitute for diesel fuel owing to its ecologically advantageous attributes and potential favourable impacts on social security (Aghbashlo, Tabatabaei, Hosseinpour, et al., 2018). Biodiesel fuel is composed of alkyl esters derived from long-chain fatty acids. These esters are generated through the transesterification process of triglycerides (TGs) utilising a light alcohol and a catalyst, which can be a base, acid, or enzyme (Aghbashlo, Tabatabaei, Rastegari, et al., 2018; Ziyai et al., 2019). Biodiesel has superior performance compared to diesel in terms of most regulated emissions released, such as CO, UHC, PM, and smoke. However, it falls short in terms of nitrogen oxides (NOx) emissions (Aghbashlo et al., 2017). The process of generating biodiesel from renewable sources involves a series of sequential procedures. These procedures include the extraction of oil, pre-treatment of the feedstock, initiation of the transesterification reaction, separation of the resulting products, recovery of unreacted alcohol, neutralisation of glycerine, washing, and ultimately, the purification of the biodiesel (Atadashi et al., 2011; Xing et al., 2021). Singh et al., (2023b) has conducted an in-depth analysis of the uncommon biodiesel feedstock in preparation for the manufacturing of biodiesel in the near future to fulfil the need for energy. Once the selection of raw materials (including feedstock, catalyst, and alcohol) and the determination of the production method and reactor have been established, the decision about process parameters becomes a crucial step that must be undertaken (Awogbemi & Kallon, 2023). This article provides an analysis of the many uses of machine learning technology in the essential stages of biodiesel making.

Machine learning (ML), commonly referred to as predictive analytics, is a field within computer science that focuses on emulating and forecasting human behaviour in order to enhance its precision. This field is often recognised as a subset of AI that enables computers to acquire knowledge from historical data and prior encounters in order to identify recurrent patterns and provide educated predictions with little human interaction (Awogbemi & Kallon, 2023; El Naqa & Murphy, 2015). ML algorithms has the capability to effectively process substantial volumes of data, discern patterns, and use this knowledge to make well-informed judgements with a high degree of precision (Wazid et al., 2022). Machine Learning (ML) is widely recognised as a significant catalyst behind the fourth industrial revolution, frequently referred to as Industry 4.0. Machine learning allows a computer system to address intricate research inquiries by means of implicit and automatic "learning" that also enhances its performance without explicit pre-programming (I. Ahmad et al., 2021). The three main categories of ML techniques are unsupervised learning, supervised learning, and reinforcement learning (China Venkaiah & Sesha Phani Deepika, 2018). Supervised learning involves the use of labelled output data in conjunction with a specified set of input data. Subsequently, the algorithm that has undergone training is used to make predictions for new datasets. Supervised learning is often used in both classification and regression scenarios. The subject topic can also be grouped as decision tree learning, association rule learning, inductive logic learning, and SVM. The algorithms that are predominantly used in various domains consist of linear regression, logistic regression, ANN, decision tree, SVM, RF, naive Bayes, and k-nearest neighbour. Unsupervised learning is a kind of machine learning that does not need the presence of labelled output (I. Ahmad et al., 2021; El Bouchefry & de Souza, 2020). Clustering is a frequently used technique in lieu of classification or regression. The classification of this concept may be expanded to include clustering, similarity and metric learning, SDL, and GA. Reinforcement learning is a kind of machine learning that does not rely on a supervisor or network trainer (POPOVIC, 2000).

Figure 1. Fossil and non-fossil energy supply by scenario, 2020-2050
(IEA, 2022)

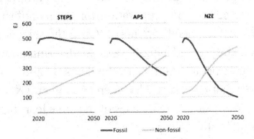

Figure 2. CO_2 emissions, 2010-2050 and temperature rise in 2100 by scenario
(IEA, 2022)

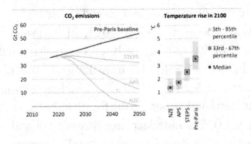

In order to effectively address the research gap and propel the progress of research in this domain, it is imperative to ascertain whether an adequate amount of research has been conducted to thoroughly examine and contextualise the implementation of machine learning (ML) technologies in the realm of biodiesel production research.

In this part, an endeavour was made to classify and evaluate the uses of machine learning technology in five essential stages of biodiesel production: soil analysis, feedstock selection, production processes, consumption patterns, and emissions monitoring (Z. Liu & Baghban, 2017). The objective of the study is to investigate the potential applications of machine learning technologies in predicting and optimising process parameters for the production of sustainable biodiesel. This aims to achieve optimum process parameters for cost-effective, quick, environmentally friendly, and sustainable biodiesel synthesis.

Applications of ML Methods in the Sustainable Biodiesel Production

In contemporary times, there has been a notable emphasis on the utilisation of data-driven ML approaches across several fields. One such topic pertains to the creation of prediction models aimed at ascertaining the fuel characteristics specific to biodiesel engines. In this article, an attempt was made to classify and evaluate the uses of machine learning technology throughout the important phases in the manufacture of biodiesel, including resource selection, optimization processes, biodiesel output, and quality monitoring.

Biodiesel Properties Determination Using ML for Improved Quality

In recent years, there has been a noticeable increase in discourse about the possible use of ML in the first step of biodiesel manufacturing, known as the feedstock phase. The most often used machine learning approaches in feedstock phase research are multiple nonlinear regression models, ANN, multiple linear regression, and statistical regression. The blend's composition, temperature, speed, and duration are typical input variables in this situation, whereas the fuel's KV, FP, OS, density, higher heating values, and cetane number are typical output variables (Xing et al., 2021). Mairizal et al. (2020) conducted an analysis on biodiesels derived from different sources including walnut oil, sunflower oil, peanut oil, rapeseed oil, hydrogenated coconut oil, hydrogenated copra oil, and beef tallow. The purpose of this analysis was to estimate the higher heating value, viscosity, flashpoint, oxidative stability, and density of these biodiesels. Multiple linear regression models were employed for this prediction. Reimann et al. (2020) have used ML approaches, including Naive Bayes, RF, and ANN, to classify micro-algae cells. The results indicated that RF exhibited superior performance compared to the other ML methods utilised in the study. The integration of the RF-based modelling approach with the microscopic features of samples has been proposed as a feasible approach to achieve a precise distinction and measurement of different species at a high resolution. Tchameni et al. (2019) has used several ANN models and non-linear regression (MNLR) techniques to predict the rheological parameters of waste vegetable oil. The results demonstrate that the ANN model outperforms the multinomial logistic regression (MNLR) technique in terms of performance. Giwa et al. (2015) used ANN as a predictive tool for determining the CN, FP, KV, and density of biodiesel on the basis of fatty acid composition of oil. According to this study's findings, the networks' average absolute deviation and prediction accuracy are as follows: The data provided includes the following percentages: CN (96.69%; 1.637%), KV (95.80%; 1.638%), FP (99.07%; 0.997%), and density (99.40%; 0.101%). Consequently, the current research shows that an ANN model can accurately forecast the fuel parameters of biodiesel. Researchers(M. I. Jahirul et al., 2021) have investigated the use of artificial intelligence-based algorithms in order to forecast certain biodiesel characteristics by analysing their chemical compositions. The experimental investigation was undertaken to provide data for training for the ANN. The findings of this research indicate that ANN may serve as a valuable tool for examining the fuel qualities based on its chemical composition. Consequently, ANN has the potential to replace the laborious and expensive experimental testing process. Jahirul et al. has conclude that ANN is a potent computational modelling technique that can find intricate connections in input-output data. In comparison to other statistical approaches, it may provide a better degree of accuracy in its prediction capabilities. As a result, ANN has developed and gained wide acceptance in a variety of fields for modelling complicated real-world situations. ANNs may be used to efficiently evaluate the complex relationship between the chemical makeup of biodiesel, fuel characteristics, and the combustion efficiency of diesel engines under a variety of operating circumstances (M. Jahirul et al., 2013). The operability of diesel fuel is determined by its cold flow characteristics (CFP), which are significantly impacted by the FA content of the feedstock. Al-Shanableh et al. (2016) used ANN methodology to forecast the cold flow property (CFP) of biodiesel based on the FA content of feedstock. This approach has the potential to minimise the need for extensive experimentation in order to develop a biodiesel product that is compatible with the prevailing climatic conditions of a certain location. The created model has shown that the cold filter plugging (CFP) properties of biodiesel were mostly impacted by the saturation or unsaturation levels of FA components, with a few exceptions. The CN has significant importance in the realm of biodiesel because to its ability to measure the rate of combustion, or more precisely, the quality of ignition. The process of experimentally measuring the CN of biodiesel is characterised by its labour-intensive nature and high cost. Nevertheless, the strong correlation between the composition of biodiesel methyl esters of fatty acids (FAMEs) and its CN presents an attractive opportunity to create cost-effective and user-friendly computerised methods for estimating biodiesel CN. Regrettably, establishing a correlation between the chemical composition of biodiesel and its CN using traditional statistical and mathematical methodologies poses significant challenges. In order to address this problem, the use of partial least squares (PLS) in conjunction with ANN has been shown and investigated as a novel methodology for accurately estimating the CN of biodiesel based on its FAMEs profile (Hosseinpour et al., 2016). Miraboutalebi et al. (2016) applied RF and ANN for CN number prediction of biodiesel. This study used RF and ANN algorithms, supported by 10-fold cross validation, to develop accurate and robust models for predicting CN. The models were constructed using experimental data from 131 distinct FAMEs obtained from various literature sources. Two distinct regression models were derived using these methodologies. In terms of accuracy, the ANN model exhibited superior performance in comparison to the RF model. Thangaraja et al. (2023) used a machine learning methodology to forecast the thermo-physical characteristics of biodiesel fuels, including density, viscosity, and specific heat, and thermal conductivity, latent heat of vaporisation, vapour pressure, and mass diffusivity in relation to temperature. A total of twenty feedstock samples were selected in order to make predictions about the thermo-physical characteristics of biodiesel. These predictions were then confirmed by comparing them to the existing experimental data, ensuring that the highest error did not exceed 14%. The proposed model presents a thorough examination of the many attributes shown by liquids and vapours, including their variations that are influenced by temperature. This model has significant potential for facilitating in-depth investigations into spray and biodiesel combustion, hence enhancing the accuracy and effectiveness of related modelling efforts. Bukkarapu & Krishnasamy (2023) found the MLR technique is inadequate for modelling the relationship between biodiesel content and characteristics due to its inability to capture nonlinear correlations, leading to limited predictive capability. The repeatability of ANN, which is widely studied as a nonlinear regression method for predicting biodiesel characteristics, is often found to be inadequate. SVM regression is a ML approach that may be used for the development of biodiesel property prediction models. One of its advantageous characteristics is its ability to effectively represent nonlinear data. Both of the nonlinear regression algorithms have strong performance in predicting the qualities of biodiesel. Specifically, the SVM approach has superior predictive capabilities compared to the ANN approach. The SVM approach yielded models that exhibited Mean Absolute Percentage Errors (MAPE) of 0.26%, 1.07%, and 1.69% for the prediction of calorific value, KV, and CN of biodiesels, respectively. Notably, these MAPE values were much lower than those obtained from the literature models. Suvarna et al. (2022) have predicted the characteristics of biodiesel and its ideal FA composition using understandable ML. In this study, predictive models using ML techniques were constructed to estimate the CN and cold filter plugging point

(CFPP). The extreme gradient boost (XGB) and RF algorithms exhibited superior performance, achieving R^2 values of 0.89 and 0.91, respectively, when evaluated on the test dataset. This investigation introduces a comprehensive ML framework that encompasses various types of analytics, such as descriptive, predictive, causal, and prescriptive, in order to forecast the properties of biodiesel based on its FA composition. Furthermore, the framework aims to determine the optimal FA composition required to ensure that the fuel properties comply with standards. Beeravalli et al. (2022) predict the density, KV, and CN of biodiesel feedstocks based on their FA compositions using ML. ML techniques provide extensive opportunities for accurately predicting certain features of biomaterials with a high degree of confidence. This study employs six distinct ML methods to forecast three fundamental characteristics of fifty diverse biodiesel feedstocks based on their respective fatty acid compositions. The issue of sparsity and anomaly within the dataset is effectively tackled via the use of well-established approaches, therefore enabling precise prediction of characteristics for every feedstock. The strong relationship between the percentage error and the coefficient of variation of a characteristic has been found, enabling scientists to establish boundaries of variability for projected values.

Biodiesel Production Using ML

The use of machine learning (ML) in the manufacture of biodiesel encompasses the implementation of ML methodologies at several phases of the biodiesel manufacturing procedure with the aim of improving efficacy, minimising expenses, and optimising the calibre of biodiesel. Machine learning (ML) has the potential to assist in the identification of optimal reaction parameters, such as pressure, temperature, and catalytic concentration, for the transesterification process. Machine learning models have the capability to forecast the biodiesel output under different reaction circumstances, hence aiding in the optimisation of the process. Biodiesel has considerable promise in its capacity to substantially assist towards enhancing the sustainability of transportation fuels. The design, optimisation, monitoring, and management of processes for biodiesel production and consumption need the use of rapid and precise modelling tools due to their intricate and nonlinear nature (Aghbashlo et al., 2021; Shelare et al., 2023). The method of biodiesel manufacturing entails the conversion of sustainable feedstocks, such as vegetable oils, animal fats, waste cooking oils, etc., into methyl ester via certain process. Machine learning (ML) has the potential to contribute significantly to the optimisation of several facets of biodiesel production, including, process optimisation, quality prediction, and other related areas (M. Jahirul et al., 2013; Xing et al., 2021).

Production Process Optimization With ML

Optimizing the biodiesel production process using machine learning involves leveraging data-driven insights to improve process efficiency, yield, and cost-effectiveness. The Bayesian optimisation algorithm-based machine learning methodologies have been used for the prediction of biodiesel generation from microalgae oil. This research explores the possible use of Bayesian optimisation algorithm (BOA) in machine learning methods, namely ANN and SVR, for the modelling of biodiesel production. The ML approach of hybrid model for biodiesel yield from microalgae oil will reduce laborious, expensive, and time-consuming laboratory trials effectively (Sultana et al., 2022). Sharma et al. (2023) have done the evaluation of ML in biodiesel production. The evaluation of the machine learning (ML) application in the context of biofuel production has shown that conventional methods for estimating data in biorefinery systems for biofuel production are challenging, time-consuming, and need significant labour. Modern ML technologies may improve energy distribution network and system decision-making and manage high-dimensional demanding scientific assignments. Data-driven probabilistic ML algorithms might cut experimental research costs and predict product yields in smart biofuel systems and networks. Sukpancharoen et al. (2023) investigated the machine learning methodologies to forecast the biodiesel output resulting from the transesterification process with different catalyst. The extreme gradient boosting methods exhibited superior predictive accuracy, achieving a coefficient of determination accuracy of about 0.98. This evaluation was conducted by using a 10-fold cross-validation technique on the input data. Jin et al. (2023) had focused on the optimisation of biodiesel production via the use of several machine learning methods. In this study, a total of 13 instances including 381 people were gathered to provide experimental data. Four ML techniques, namely KNN, SVM, RF, and AdaBoost regression, were used to estimate the biodiesel production via the transesterification reaction. The Random Forest regression model has greater suitability for reliably predicting biodiesel yield compared to three other machine learning models. This is shown by its lower root mean square error (RMSE) values for both the training dataset (2.778) and the validation dataset (5.178), as well as a higher correlation coefficient. Sumayli (2023) has examines the advancement of ML models for the optimisation of methyl ester synthesis derived from papaya oil. In this study, Gaussian Process Regression (GPR), Multilayer Perceptron (MLP), and KNN regression models were used to simulate and enhance the synthesis of Papaya oil methyl ester. Additionally, adaptive boosting was utilised for amplification purposes. Model inputs were the reaction temperature, the amount of catalyst, the processing duration, and the methanol to oil molar ratio, while the model output was the POME yield. The findings of this research demonstrate that ML approaches are strongly recommended for the prediction of biofuels production due to their ability to save costs and time. A. Ahmad et al. (2023) has applied ML techniques and GA for the purpose of forecasting and enhancing the biodiesel production yield derived from waste cooking oil. In this study three ML methodologies, including Gradient Boosting, eXtreme Gradient Boosting (XGB), and Light Gradient Boosting Machine (LGBM) regression, to forecast biodiesel output from waste cooking oil. Additionally, a GA is used to optimise the biodiesel production process. The combination of LGBM and GA has the potential to serve as a valuable instrument for strategic decision-making and optimisation in the context of high-quality biodiesel production.

Prediction of Biodiesel Yield Using ML

Machine learning plays a crucial role in enhancing the efficiency of biodiesel production via the use of predictive models that estimate the output of biodiesel based on a range of input factors. This technique offers a more effective and environmentally conscious method for the production of biodiesel, therefore supporting the continuous shift towards cleaner and renewable energy resources. In order to use machine learning techniques, researchers collect data from trials including a range of input factors and biodiesel production outputs. P. Liu & Zhang, (2023) employed ML to predict the amount of biodiesel that would be produced from palm oil during the transesterification process. In this study the most reliable and accurate model for estimating biodiesel output was determined to be the GBRT model. The results of the optimisation showed that 98.73% of the production yield could be obtained with the best working conditions (Methanol to oil ratio is 12.0, time is 45 hours, and catalyst loading is 2.0 weight percent). Corral-Bobadilla et al. (2023) analysed and examined the effects of many independent factors on the production of biodiesel from used cooking oil using an AI tool. According to the results, under optimum conditions, the transesterification method produced the most biodiesel (97.76%). Oraegbunam et al. (2023) have done modelling and optimisation of sandbox oil for biodiesel production through transesterification reaction using ANN and GA. The study shows that, optimal values found resulted in a 99.03 wt% yield of biodiesel. When compared to the Taguchi design technique, ANN-GA (ML approach) produced a higher yield. Khanna et al. (2023) have performed a study and this work employs artificial intelligence and ML algorithms to forecast biodiesel qualities and increase biodiesel output and quality. The goal of this research endeavour is to improve the sustainability and efficiency of the biodiesel manufacturing process by utilising AI and ML. Sebayang et al. (2023) have created a combined ANN-GWO optimisation method for the improvement of the production of biodiesel from rice bran oil. According to the findings of the ANN-GWO algorithm, the methyl ester yield was 98.16 weight percent at the optimal process settings of 60 percent methanol to oil, 1 weight percent catalyst concentration, and 7.76 minutes. Tang et al.,(2023) applied ML approach for optimization of biodiesel yield from algal oil. Gradient Boosting ML based approach is found to be the most broad and accurate model. The best output value of biodiesel yield using this method is 97.50 at a particular input condition. Iweka et al. (2023) have done optimization using ML for biodiesel production from watermelon seed oil. The study shows that ML produced the highest biodiesel production yield (91.7 wt%), outperforming the Central Composite Design biodiesel yield value of 91.6 wt%. Kolakoti & Satish (2023) optimized biodiesel yield by using ANN and RSM modelling tool. In this work, the use of waste chicken eggshell (WCES) as a catalyst for the production of biodiesel using waste cooking oil (WCO) was investigated. Both models achieve an excellent maximum biodiesel yield of 91%. Dharmalingam et al. (2023) has examined the ANN and RSM techniques for optimising biodiesel synthesis from mixing of waste cooking oil. For biodiesel process optimisation and yield prediction, ANN and RSM approaches are recommended. According to the experimental findings, biological catalysts impregnated with KOH generated a maximum yield of 94.7%. A. Ahmad et al. (2023) employed the machine learning techniques to optimise the process of biodiesel synthesis from waste cooking oil. The research study determined that the highest achievable biodiesel production using genetic algorithms (GA) was 98.98% (by weight). In a recent work it has been concluded that data-driven probabilistic machine learning (ML) methods have the potential to be used in intelligent biofuel systems and networks. This application has the advantage of potentially decreasing the expenses associated with experimental research, while simultaneously offering precise estimations of product yields. The researcher exhibits a comprehensive comprehension of the use of various machine learning models in the regulation and monitoring of biofuel production from waste biomass. This knowledge encompasses the areas of prediction, optimisation, and real-time monitoring (Sharma et al., 2023).

Challenges

However, in order to enhance accuracy and dependability, ML needs extensive and impartial datasets for training purposes. Acquiring such datasets may be an arduous undertaking. One further limitation associated with the implementation of ML technologies is the need of allocating sufficient time and computer resources to facilitate the learning process of the algorithms. This is crucial in order for the algorithms to acquire knowledge, comprehend information, and gain the necessary proficiency to accurately interpret the produced outputs and make dependable judgements that align with the intended objectives. ML systems generate judgements based on extensive training. However, they are still prone to mistakes, particularly in cases where there is a lack of diverse and comprehensive datasets for training purposes. These inconsistencies have the potential to initiate a cascade of errors that might require a significant amount of effort to identify and correct (Aliramezani et al., 2022; Awogbemi & Kallon, 2023). Despite the fact that several applications of machine learning models for predicting thermochemical biofuel conversion have been investigated at length, the scope of these research cannot yet be expanded to include practical implementation and plant-scale optimisation (Jeon et al., 2023). In the field of biodiesel research, in future it is essential for machine learning (ML) applications to prioritise the screening and selection of appropriate strains of microalgae oil for biodiesel production (Coşgun et al., 2023).

Future Trends Biodiesel

Industry 5.0 is the future of biodiesel industry. The concept of Industrial Revolution 5.0 entails the collaborative integration of human labour and technological instruments to enhance the efficiency of industrial production. The integration of human employees and global robots is enhancing productivity in the field of manufacturing (Majumdar et al., 2021). The concepts of circular economy, bio-economy, and green economy are further propositions within the framework of Industry 5.0, aimed at promoting sustainability in biodiesel sector (Gülseçen et al., 2019). It is expected that the implementation of Industry 5.0 would lead to a decrease in the cost of biodiesel in comparison to traditional fossil fuel sources. Hence, biodiesel exhibits the capacity to maximise its benefits, including the alleviation of fossil fuel depletion and the mitigation of greenhouse gas emissions. However, the endeavour of augmenting biodiesel manufacturing presents notable obstacles. The use of cyber-physical systems, artificial intelligence, and machine learning methodologies has been suggested and effectively utilised in the domain of advanced biodiesel manufacturing (Hansen et al., 2019). In industry 5.0, the use of third- and fourth-generation biodiesel has drawn a lot of interest as a potential solution to the drawbacks of the earlier generations (Chisti, 2018). The biodiesel industry has the potential to contribute to economic growth via the creation of employment opportunities in many sectors such as agriculture, manufacturing, and marketing. Additionally, it may play a significant role in fostering development in regional locations.

CONCLUSION

The amalgamation of ML techniques with biodiesel manufacturing processes has demonstrated immense potential to enhance efficiency, reduce resource consumption, and mitigate environmental impact. By leveraging real-time data analytics, predictive modelling, and process optimization, ML has ushered in a new era of intelligent and adaptive biodiesel production. Through the utilization of ML algorithms, biodiesel manufacturers can effectively predict feedstock characteristics, optimize reaction parameters, and improve yield rates. This not only streamlines production processes but also ensures the prudent utilization of raw materials, ultimately leading to reduced waste and energy consumption. The successful implementation of ML in biodiesel production demands access to high-quality, comprehensive data and a solid understanding of the underlying processes. In addition, the incorporation of machine learning (ML) into Industry 4.0 technologies, such as the Internet of Things (IoT), has significantly contributed to the establishment of interconnected and automated ecosystems for the production of biodiesel. The biodiesel business is actively pursuing sustainability and the reduction of carbon emissions. In this context, the interplay between machine learning (ML) and business 4.0 has emerged as a promising option. There is potential for increased utilisation of various biodiesel feedstock in the manufacturing of biodiesel, particularly in the context of industry 5.0. The global commercial viability of third- and fourth-generation biodiesel is expected to increase significantly due to advancements in technology, research, and development.

Abbreviations

Genetic Algorithms: GA
Sparse Dictionary Learning: SDL
Support Vector Machine: SVM
Random Forest: RF
Artificial Neural Networks: ANN
Artificial Intelligence: AI
Machine Learning: ML
Multilinear Regression: MLR
Cetane Number: CN
Fatty Acid Methyl Ester: FAME
Fatty Acid: FA
Support vector regression: SVR
K-nearest Neighbour: KNN
Gradient Boosting Regression Tree: GBRT
Gray Wolf Optimization: GWO
Response Surface Methodology: RSM
Carbon monoxide: CO
Unburnt hydrocarbon: UHC
Particulate matter: PM
Oxidation stability: OS

Flash point: FP
Kinematic viscosity: KV
International Environmental Agency: IEA

ACKNOWLEGMENT

The authors would like to acknowledge Center for Alternative and Renewable Energy (CARE) and Mechanical Engineering Department, Rajkiya Engineering College Azamgarh, Uttar Pradesh and Mechanical Engineering Department, National Institute of Technology Patna Bihar for the work.

REFERENCES

Aghbashlo, M., Peng, W., Tabatabaei, M., Kalogirou, S. A., Soltanian, S., Hosseinzadeh-Bandbafha, H., Mahian, O., & Lam, S. S. (2021). Machine learning technology in biodiesel research: A review. *Progress in Energy and Combustion Science, 85,* 100904. doi:10.1016/j.pecs.2021.100904

Aghbashlo, M., Tabatabaei, M., Hosseinpour, S., Rastegari, H., & Ghaziaskar, H. S. (2018). Multi-objective exergy-based optimization of continuous glycerol ketalization to synthesize solketal as a biodiesel additive in subcritical acetone. *Energy Conversion and Management, 160,* 251–261. doi:10.1016/j.enconman.2018.01.044

Aghbashlo, M., Tabatabaei, M., Khalife, E., Najafi, B., Mirsalim, S. M., Gharehghani, A., Mohammadi, P., Dadak, A., Roodbar Shojaei, T., & Khounani, Z. (2017). A novel emulsion fuel containing aqueous nano cerium oxide additive in diesel–biodiesel blends to improve diesel engines performance and reduce exhaust emissions: Part II – Exergetic analysis. *Fuel, 205,* 262–271. doi:10.1016/j.fuel.2017.05.003

Aghbashlo, M., Tabatabaei, M., Rastegari, H., Ghaziaskar, H. S., & Valijanian, E. (2018). Exergy-based optimization of a continuous reactor applied to produce value-added chemicals from glycerol through esterification with acetic acid. *Energy, 150,* 351–362. doi:10.1016/j.energy.2018.02.151

Ahmad, A., Yadav, A. K., & Singh, A. (2023). Application of machine learning and genetic algorithms to the prediction and optimization of biodiesel yield from waste cooking oil. *Korean Journal of Chemical Engineering, 40*(12), 2941–2956. doi:10.1007/s11814-023-1489-9

Ahmad, I., Sana, A., Kano, M., Cheema, I. I., Menezes, B. C., Shahzad, J., Ullah, Z., Khan, M., & Habib, A. (2021). Machine learning applications in biofuels' life cycle: Soil, feedstock, production, consumption, and emissions. *Energies, 14*(16), 5072. doi:10.3390/en14165072

Al-Shanableh, F., Evcil, A., & Savaş, M. A. (2016). Prediction of Cold Flow Properties of Biodiesel Fuel Using Artificial Neural Network. *Procedia Computer Science, 102*, 273–280. doi:10.1016/j.procs.2016.09.401

Aliramezani, M., Koch, C. R., & Shahbakhti, M. (2022). Modeling, diagnostics, optimization, and control of internal combustion engines via modern machine learning techniques: A review and future directions. *Progress in Energy and Combustion Science, 88*, 100967. doi:10.1016/j.pecs.2021.100967

Atadashi, I. M., Aroua, M. K., Aziz, A. R. A., & Sulaiman, N. M. N. (2011). Refining technologies for the purification of crude biodiesel. *Applied Energy, 88*(12), 4239–4251. doi:10.1016/j.apenergy.2011.05.029

Awogbemi, O., & Von Kallon, D. V. (2023). Application of machine learning technologies in biodiesel production process—A review. *Frontiers in Energy Research, 11*, 1122638. doi:10.3389/fenrg.2023.1122638

Beeravalli, V., Ashwath, N., Rasul, M., Khan, M., & Capareda, S. (2022). Density, Kinematic Viscosity and Cetane Number Prediction of Biofuel Feedstocks from Fatty Acid Compositions. *2022 International Conference on Futuristic Technologies (INCOFT)*, (pp. 1–6). IEEE. 10.1109/INCOFT55651.2022.10094421

Bolton, P. (2021). Petrol and diesel prices. *House of Commons Library, 04712*, 25.

Bukkarapu, K. R., & Krishnasamy, A. (2023). Biodiesel composition based machine learning approaches to predict engine fuel properties. *Journal of Automobile Engineering*. 10.1177/09544070231158240

China Venkaiah, V., & Sesha Phani Deepika, V. (2018). Computational Analysis and Understanding of Natural Languages: Principles, Methods and Applications. In *Handbook of Statistics*. North Holland. https://books.google.com/books?hl=en&lr=&id=gRJrDwAAQBAJ&oi=fnd&pg=PP1&dq=process+mining+approaches+information+security+governance&ots=LYbH5q86TS&sig=4b4o3WEnsUM9dzRagP-GQs6xI88

Chisti, Y. (2018). The saga of algal energy…. *Biotechnology Advances, 36*(5), 1553. doi:10.1016/j.biotechadv.2018.05.003

Corral-Bobadilla, M., Lostado-Lorza, R., Gómez, F.-S., Iñiguez-Macedo, S., & Fraile, C. S. (2023). A novel approach to efficient biodiesel production using waste cooking oil. *2023 8th International Conference on Smart and Sustainable Technologies (SpliTech)*, (pp. 1–4). IEEE. 10.23919/SpliTech58164.2023.10193728

Coşgun, A., Günay, M. E., & Yıldırım, R. (2023). Machine learning for algal biofuels: A critical review and perspective for the future. *Green Chemistry*, *25*(9), 3354–3373. doi:10.1039/D3GC00389B

Dharmalingam, B., Balamurugan, S., Wetwatana, U., Tongnan, V., Sekhar, C., Paramasivam, B., Cheenkachorn, K., Tawai, A., & Sriariyanun, M. (2023). Comparison of neural network and response surface methodology techniques on optimization of biodiesel production from mixed waste cooking oil using heterogeneous biocatalyst. *Fuel*, *340*, 127503. doi:10.1016/j.fuel.2023.127503

El Bouchefry, K., & de Souza, R. S. (2020). Learning in Big Data: Introduction to Machine Learning. In Knowledge Discovery in Big Data from Astronomy and Earth Observation: Astrogeoinformatics. Elsevier. doi:10.1016/B978-0-12-819154-5.00023-0

El Naqa, I., & Murphy, M. J. (2015). What Is Machine Learning? In Machine Learning in Radiation Oncology (pp. 3–11). Springer International Publishing. doi:10.1007/978-3-319-18305-3_1

Giwa, S. O., Adekomaya, S. O., Adama, K. O., & Mukaila, M. O. (2015). Prediction of selected biodiesel fuel properties using artificial neural network. *Frontiers in Energy*, *9*(4), 433–445. doi:10.1007/s11708-015-0383-5

Gülseçen, S., Reis, Z. A., Gezer, M., & Erol, Ç. (2019). Industry 4.0 from the MIS Perspective. *Industry 4.0 from the MIS Perspective*, 1–352. doi:10.3726/b15120

Hansen, S. B., Mirkouei, A., & Xian, M. (2019). Cyber-physical control and optimization for biofuel 4.0. *IISE Annual Conference and Expo 2019*. Research Gate.

Hosseinpour, S., Aghbashlo, M., Tabatabaei, M., & Khalife, E. (2016). Exact estimation of biodiesel cetane number (CN) from its fatty acid methyl esters (FAMEs) profile using partial least square (PLS) adapted by artificial neural network (ANN). *Energy Conversion and Management*, *124*, 389–398. doi:10.1016/j.enconman.2016.07.027

IEA. (2022). *World Energy Outlook 2022, Part of World Energy Outlook*. IEA. www.iea.org/t&c/%0Ahttps://www.iea.org/reports/world-energy-outlook-2022

Iweka, S. C., Falowo, O. A., Amosun, A. A., & Betiku, E. (2023). Optimization of microwave-assisted biodiesel production from watermelon seeds oil using thermally modified kwale anthill mud as base catalyst. *Heliyon, 9*(7), e17762. doi:10.1016/j.heliyon.2023.e17762 PMID:37539125

Jahirul, M., Brown, R., Senadeera, W., O'Hara, I., & Ristovski, Z. (2013). The Use of Artificial Neural Networks for Identifying Sustainable Biodiesel Feedstocks. *Energies, 6*(8), 3764–3806. doi:10.3390/en6083764

Jahirul, M. I., Rasul, M. G., Brown, R. J., Senadeera, W., Hosen, M. A., Haque, R., Saha, S. C., & Mahlia, T. M. I. (2021). Investigation of correlation between chemical composition and properties of biodiesel using principal component analysis (PCA) and artificial neural network (ANN). *Renewable Energy, 168*, 632–646. doi:10.1016/j.renene.2020.12.078

Jayakumar, S., Yusoff, M. M., Rahim, M. H. A., Maniam, G. P., & Govindan, N. (2017). The prospect of microalgal biodiesel using agro-industrial and industrial wastes in Malaysia. *Renewable & Sustainable Energy Reviews, 72*, 33–47. doi:10.1016/j.rser.2017.01.002

Jeon, P. R., Moon, J.-H., Ogunsola, N. O., Lee, S. H., Ling, J. L. J., You, S., & Park, Y.-K. (2023). Recent advances and future prospects of thermochemical biofuel conversion processes with machine learning. *Chemical Engineering Journal, 471*, 144503. doi:10.1016/j.cej.2023.144503

Jin, X., Li, S., Ye, H., Wang, J., Wu, Y., Zhang, D., Ma, H., Sun, F., Pugazhendhi, A., & Xia, C. (2023). Investigation and optimization of biodiesel production based on multiple machine learning technologies. *Fuel, 348*, 128546. doi:10.1016/j.fuel.2023.128546

Khanna, A., Lamba, B. Y., Jain, S., Bolshev, V., Budnikov, D., Panchenko, V., & Smirnov, A. (2023). Biodiesel Production from Jatropha: A Computational Approach by Means of Artificial Intelligence and Genetic Algorithm. *Sustainability (Basel), 15*(12), 9785. doi:10.3390/su15129785

Kolakoti, A., & Satish, G. (2023). Biodiesel production from low-grade oil using heterogeneous catalyst: An optimisation and ANN modelling. *Australian Journal of Mechanical Engineering, 21*(1), 316–328. doi:10.1080/14484846.2020.1842298

Liu, P., & Zhang, Y. (2023). Optimization of biodiesel production from oil using a novel green catalyst via development of a predictive model. *Arabian Journal of Chemistry, 16*(6), 104785. doi:10.1016/j.arabjc.2023.104785

Liu, Z., & Baghban, A. (2017). Application of LSSVM for biodiesel production using supercritical ethanol solvent. *Energy Sources. Part A, Recovery, Utilization, and Environmental Effects*, *39*(17), 1869–1874. doi:10.1080/15567036.2017.1380732

Mairizal, A. Q., Awad, S., Priadi, C. R., Hartono, D. M., Moersidik, S. S., Tazerout, M., & Andres, Y. (2020). Experimental study on the effects of feedstock on the properties of biodiesel using multiple linear regressions. *Renewable Energy*, *145*, 375–381. doi:10.1016/j.renene.2019.06.067

Majumdar, A., Garg, H., & Jain, R. (2021). Managing the barriers of Industry 4.0 adoption and implementation in textile and clothing industry: Interpretive structural model and triple helix framework. *Computers in Industry*, *125*, 103372. doi:10.1016/j.compind.2020.103372

Miraboutalebi, S. M., Kazemi, P., & Bahrami, P. (2016). Fatty Acid Methyl Ester (FAME) composition used for estimation of biodiesel cetane number employing random forest and artificial neural networks: A new approach. *Fuel*, *166*, 143–151. doi:10.1016/j.fuel.2015.10.118

Oraegbunam, J. C., Ishola, N. B., Sotunde, B. A., Latinwo, L. M., & Betiku, E. (2023). Sandbox oil biodiesel production modeling and optimization with neural networks and genetic algorithm. *Green Technologies and Sustainability*, *1*(1), 100007. doi:10.1016/j.grets.2022.100007

Popovic, D. (2000). Intelligent Control with Neural Networks. In Soft Computing and Intelligent Systems. doi:10.1016/B978-012646490-0/50021-4

Reimann, R., Zeng, B., Jakopec, M., Burdukiewicz, M., Petrick, I., Schierack, P., & Rödiger, S. (2020). Classification of dead and living microalgae Chlorella vulgaris by bioimage informatics and machine learning. *Algal Research*, *48*, 101908. doi:10.1016/j.algal.2020.101908

Sebayang, A. H., Kusumo, F., Milano, J., Shamsuddin, A. H., Silitonga, A. S., Ideris, F., Siswantoro, J., Veza, I., Mofijur, M., & Reen Chia, S. (2023). Optimization of biodiesel production from rice bran oil by ultrasound and infrared radiation using ANN-GWO. *Fuel*, *346*, 128404. doi:10.1016/j.fuel.2023.128404

Sharma, V., Tsai, M.-L., Chen, C.-W., Sun, P.-P., Nargotra, P., & Dong, C.-D. (2023). Advances in machine learning technology for sustainable biofuel production systems in lignocellulosic biorefineries. *The Science of the Total Environment*, *886*, 163972. doi:10.1016/j.scitotenv.2023.163972 PMID:37164089

Shelare, S. D., Belkhode, P. N., Nikam, K. C., Jathar, L. D., Shahapurkar, K., Soudagar, M. E. M., Veza, I., Khan, T. M. Y., Kalam, M. A., Nizami, A.-S., & Rehan, M. (2023). Biofuels for a sustainable future: Examining the role of nano-additives, economics, policy, internet of things, artificial intelligence and machine learning technology in biodiesel production. *Energy, 282*, 128874. doi:10.1016/j.energy.2023.128874

Singh, B., Srivastava, A. K., & Prakash, O. (2023a). Experimental analysis of biodiesel production from used cooking oil and its combustion, performance and emission analysis at different blending ratios in diesel engine. *International Journal of Renewable Energy Technology, 14*(3), 259–277. doi:10.1504/IJRET.2023.132976

Singh, B., Srivastava, A. K., & Prakash, O. (2023b). *A Comprehensive Review on Rare Biodiesel Feedstock Availability, Fatty Acid Composition, Physical Properties, Production, Engine Performance and Emission.* Process Integration and Optimization for Sustainability., doi:10.1007/s41660-023-00343-w

Sukpancharoen, S., Katongtung, T., Rattanachoung, N., & Tippayawong, N. (2023). Unlocking the potential of transesterification catalysts for biodiesel production through machine learning approach. *Bioresource Technology, 378*, 128961. doi:10.1016/j.biortech.2023.128961 PMID:36972805

Sultana, N., Hossain, S. M. Z., Abusaad, M., Alanbar, N., Senan, Y., & Razzak, S. A. (2022). Prediction of biodiesel production from microalgal oil using Bayesian optimization algorithm-based machine learning approaches. *Fuel, 309*, 122184. doi:10.1016/j.fuel.2021.122184

Sumayli, A. (2023). Development of advanced machine learning models for optimization of methyl ester biofuel production from papaya oil: Gaussian process regression (GPR), multilayer perceptron (MLP), and K-nearest neighbor (KNN) regression models. *Arabian Journal of Chemistry, 16*(7), 104833. doi:10.1016/j.arabjc.2023.104833

Suvarna, M., Jahirul, M. I., Aaron-Yeap, W. H., Augustine, C. V., Umesh, A., Rasul, M. G., Günay, M. E., Yildirim, R., & Janaun, J. (2022). Predicting biodiesel properties and its optimal fatty acid profile via explainable machine learning. *Renewable Energy, 189*, 245–258. doi:10.1016/j.renene.2022.02.124

Tang, J., Abbas, A. K., Koka, N. A., Sadoon, N., Abbas, J. K., Abdalhuseen, R. A., Abosaooda, M., Ahmed, N. M., & Abbas, A. H. (2023). Optimization of thermal biofuel production from biomass using CaO-based catalyst through different algorithm-based machine learning approaches. *Case Studies in Thermal Engineering, 50*, 103419. doi:10.1016/j.csite.2023.103419

Tchameni, A. P., Zhao, L., Ribeiro, J. X. F., & Li, T. (2019). Predicting the rheological properties of waste vegetable oil biodiesel-modified water-based mud using artificial neural network. *Geosystem Engineering*, *22*(2), 101–111. doi:10.1080/12269328. 2018.1490209

Thangaraja, J., Zigan, L., & Rajkumar, S. (2023). A machine learning framework for evaluating the biodiesel properties for accurate modeling of spray and combustion processes. *Fuel*, *334*, 126573. doi:10.1016/j.fuel.2022.126573

Wazid, M., Das, A. K., Chamola, V., & Park, Y. (2022). Uniting cyber security and machine learning: Advantages, challenges and future research. *ICT Express*, *8*(3), 313–321. doi:10.1016/j.icte.2022.04.007

Xing, Y., Zheng, Z., Sun, Y., & Agha Alikhani, M. (2021). A Review on Machine Learning Application in Biodiesel Production Studies. *International Journal of Chemical Engineering*, *2021*, 1–12. doi:10.1155/2021/2154258

Ziyai, M. R., Mehrpooya, M., Aghbashlo, M., Omid, M., Alsagri, A. S., & Tabatabaei, M. (2019). Techno-economic comparison of three biodiesel production scenarios enhanced by glycerol supercritical water reforming process. *International Journal of Hydrogen Energy*, *44*(33), 17845–17862. doi:10.1016/j.ijhydene.2019.05.017

Chapter 12
The Impact of Data Science and Participated Geographic Metadata on Improving Government Service Deliveries:
Prospects and Obstacles

Sabyasachi Pramanik
https://orcid.org/0000-0002-9431-8751
Haldia Institute of Technology, India

ABSTRACT

This chapter examined the profound influence of data science and volunteered geographic information (VGI) on the delivery of public services. Volunteered geographic information (VGI), being material created by users, has had a substantial impact on making geographic information accessible to everybody, enabling people to actively engage in the creation and management of data. The incorporation of volunteered geographic information (VGI) into government operations has introduced novel prospects for enhancing service provision in diverse sectors such as education, health, transportation, and waste management. In addition, data science has enhanced VGI by using sophisticated methodologies like artificial intelligence (AI), internet of things (IoT), big data, and blockchain, thereby transforming the whole framework of government service provision. Nevertheless, in order to effectively use VGI in public sector services, it is essential to tackle significant obstacles such as data accuracy, safeguarding, inclusiveness, technical framework, and specialized expertise. The quality of VGI data may be improved by collaborative endeavors including governments, volunteers, and academics.

DOI: 10.4018/979-8-3693-5271-7.ch012

INTRODUCTION

The integration of technology and data-driven methods has significantly revolutionized the provision of public services in recent years. The utilization of Volunteered Geographic Information (VGI) in conjunction with Data Science is a significant advancement in this domain. VGI, short for Volunteered Geographic Information, refers to location-based data that individuals willingly provide on various digital platforms, including social media, mobile applications, and crowdsourcing initiatives (Goodchild, 2007). Data science encompasses the methodologies and techniques used to derive insights and knowledge from vast databases (Brodie, 2019; Provost & Fawcett, 2013).

The use of VGI (Volunteered Geographic Information) and data science in the provision of public services has seen a substantial rise, owing to many factors. Currently, there is a significant increase in the collection and distribution of location-based data due to the widespread use of mobile devices and the availability of the Internet (Huang et al., 2021). In the present day, individuals have the ability to actively participate in the generation of spatial data, providing valuable perspectives on their requirements, choices, and encounters (Goodchild, 2007). Furthermore, conventional methods of gathering data incur significant costs and require a substantial amount of time. On the other hand, VGI offers a timely and cost-efficient alternative that allows public sector enterprises to get dependable information for decision-making processes (Ahmad et al., 2022).

The combination of Volunteered Geographic Information (VGI) with data science enables the effective analysis and interpretation of big datasets, facilitating informed and data-driven policy development (Arnaboldi & Azzone, 2020; Provost & Fawcett, 2013; Wong & C. Hinnant, 2022). Consequently, public service providers have the ability to enhance the distribution of resources, enhance the efficiency of their services, and meet the specific needs of the communities they serve. To evaluate poverty at the village level, one may integrate several data sources such as high-resolution imaging (HRI), point-of-interest (POI), OpenStreetMap (OSM), and digital surface model (DSM) data (Hu et al., 2022). In a similar vein, Ma et al. (2022) put out a method to assess the logic of the geographical distribution of public restrooms in urban functional areas. They achieved this by using POI big data and OSM. KUCUKALI et al., (2022) employed open-source geospatial data, such as OSM, to assess the ease of pedestrian access to crucial public services and facilities. In contrast, Abdulkarim et al., (2014) created a VGI application utilizing Google Street View to encourage individuals to contribute to the categorization of roof materials, thereby supporting energy efficiency initiatives.

The main purpose of this chapter is to analyze the use of donated geographic information and data science in the provision of public services. This study will examine the potential benefits and challenges of incorporating these two components in various aspects of the public domain. In order to accomplish this goal, the chapter is organized in the following manner: Section two offers a comprehensive examination of Volunteered Geographic Information (VGI), with a specific emphasis on its influence on the provision of public services. Section three explores the notion of data science and its potential to improve government services. The text examines the integration of Volunteered Geographic Information (VGI) with data science in four government sectors in section four. Section five is specifically focused on tackling the difficulties that emerge within this particular framework. Ultimately the last part functions as the closing comments of the chapter, along with providing prospective suggestions for more study.

Volunteered Geographic Information (VGI)

VGI may be defined as a kind of user-generated content that encompasses a diverse range of location-specific data, such as geotagged photographs, check-ins, reviews, and other contributions originating from a specific geographical region (Haklay, 2013; Kitchin et al., 2018). As individuals engage with their environment, they willingly collect and share these pieces of information. VGI is often generated by individuals using location-aware devices such as smartphones, where users gather geographic data in the form of text, images, or videos that are tagged with geographical information (Honarparvar et al., 2019). Subsequently, this data is disseminated via diverse online social media platforms, such as Twitter, so facilitating the establishment of Volunteered Geographic Information (VGI). OpenStreetMap (OSM) was founded in 2004 as a worldwide initiative with the goal of developing and managing an accessible and modifiable database and map of the whole globe (Grinberger et al., 2022). Regarded as a prominent illustration of Volunteered Geographic Information (VGI), it distinguishes itself via its substantial volunteer community and the huge collection of geographical data it has produced.

The core concept behind VGI is the empowerment of users to actively participate in the creation and management of geographic information, as opposed to being passive recipients of government datasets (Goodchild, 2007).Emerging digital platforms have emerged, enabling users to collectively contribute geographic information, resulting in the joint creation of digital representations and conceptualizations of nature (Calcagni et al., 2019). These systems allow users to connect with one other, working together to create and visualize geographical elements in the digital world.

In urban settings, the occurrence of catastrophic events, such as severe floods, has significant consequences that affect both the human population and vital infrastructure like road networks. These road networks are crucial for everyday living and, importantly, for emergency response systems. Volunteered Geographic

Information (VGI) has the capability to provide immediate and up-to-date data changes, allowing for swift reactions to rapidly changing conditions or occurrences. This is particularly advantageous in the context of disaster management endeavors. The geo-located information provided by affected populations during catastrophes may be very beneficial and influential (Tzavella et al., 2018).

The incorporation of Volunteered Geographic Information (VGI) has the potential to enhance the recommendation process of Recommender Systems (RS) by integrating contextual information, as suggested by Honarparvar et al. (2019). Users have the ability to contribute valuable geographical data to RS by incorporating VGI, which offers valuable insights into their preferences and interests for specific regions and areas of interest. Utilizing Volunteered Geographic Information (VGI) may improve the accuracy and relevance of location-based recommendations provided by Remote Sensing (RS). RS may use Volunteered Geographic Information (VGI) to provide suggestions for neighboring healthcare facilities, educational institutions, or social welfare agencies. Moreover, VGI has the capability to enhance the ever-changing character of recommendations by promptly incorporating alterations in user preferences and interactions with their environment (Honarparvar et al., 2019). Therefore, Volunteered Geographic Information (VGI) may enhance the customization and timeliness of recommendation systems (RS).

Land cover maps may enhance government agencies' understanding of the current land use trends in metropolitan regions. Nevertheless, it is important to evaluate these maps in order to ensure the accuracy and reliability of the data, which is crucial for urban planning and development. Volunteered Geographic Information (VGI) may be used to facilitate the land cover validation procedures (Antoniou et al., 2016; Fonte et al., 2015; Olteanu-Raimond et al., 2020). Public service companies may use validated land cover maps to precisely identify optimal locations for new infrastructure projects, neighborhoods, commercial areas, and public facilities. By promoting the systematic expansion of urban areas and optimizing resource use, this enhances the citizens' quality of life.

Advantages of Volunteered Geographic Information (VGI) in Governmental Delivery of Services

Volunteered Geographic Information (VGI) has emerged as a valuable resource for governments and public service groups. The primary advantages of Volunteered Geographic Information (VGI) in relation to public services are outlined in Figure 1 and described below.

Public Participation

Public participation in civic affairs cultivates a feeling of empowerment among individuals, as they actively contribute to the development of public services. Government organizations may get valuable insights into the genuine requirements and preferences of the community by including individuals in the process of planning, designing, and evaluating services. Volunteered Geographic Information (VGI) may function as a significant instrument for involving individuals in public services (Güiza & Stuart, 2018; Sangiambut & Sieber, 2016). By engaging in this participation, it may be ensured that services are tailored to meet the distinct requirements of residents, so enhancing overall contentment and effectiveness.

Live Data Updates

The ability of VGI to provide real-time data updates is one of its most significant benefits. Users interact with their surroundings and willingly provide location-specific data via smartphones and other devices, allowing for immediate access to the data for analysis and decision-making purposes. The real-time capability of Volunteered Geographic Information (VGI) in public services may be particularly advantageous for emergency services, traffic management, and disaster response. It allows for prompt responses and informed decision-making (Annis & Nardi, 2019; Chen et al., 2016).

Enhanced Decision-Making

Volunteered Geographic Information (VGI) offers a diverse range of geospatial data that may assist different government sectors in making more informed choices. Public service companies may get valuable information about people' preferences, needs, and obstacles related to specific locations and services via the use of VGI data. This data-driven decision-making technique enables governments to develop policies that prioritize the needs of citizens and effectively allocate resources (Dias et al., 2019; Malik & Shaikh, 2019).

Focused Service Delivery

VGI data may be used to identify regions with specific needs or inadequate public services. By examining Volunteered Geographic Information (VGI) data, governments may pinpoint neglected neighborhoods and concentrate their efforts on improving service delivery in those areas. Using Volunteered Geographic Information (VGI) to identify areas lacking enough healthcare or educational resources might expedite the development of new facilities and services (Kihumbe, 2019; Sezer et al., 2018).

Economic Efficiency

Traditional methods of gathering data may incur significant expenses and use a substantial amount of time. Conversely, VGI utilizes the collective contributions of locals, resulting in a significant reduction in data collecting costs. The affordability of gathering geospatial data has been enhanced by the availability of extensive, collaboratively generated data via VGI platforms such as OpenStreetMap (OSM) (Grinberger et al., 2022).

Revised Data

VGI datasets often exhibit more currency and dynamism in comparison to conventional government datasets. Given the continuous influx of data from people, the information is consistently up-to-date and precise. Public service companies may consistently obtain the most current information using VGI data, allowing them to promptly respond to evolving situations (Honarparvar et al., 2019).

Social sustainability refers to the capacity of a society to meet the needs of its current and future members, while promoting social well-being, justice, and equity. It involves creating and maintaining social systems and

The social sustainability of VGI activities is enhanced by considering the needs of many groups, thereby promoting inclusivity. Vulnerable and disadvantaged communities have the opportunity to voice their concerns and actively engage in the development and implementation of public services using Volunteered Geographic Information (VGI). Consequently, the creation of services that are more inclusive and equitable may be facilitated (Bittner et al., 2016; Muzaffar et al., 2017).

Data Visualization

Geo-tagged photos and videos are specific types of Volunteered Geographic Information (VGI). Visual reporting utilizes geo-tagged photographs and videos obtained by modern smartphones and cameras to provide significant on-site data. Unmanned aerial vehicles equipped with cameras may assist rescue personnel in their endeavors and enhance the assessment of destruction in catastrophic situations. Geotagged images enhance the efficiency of delivering goods and services (To et al., 2015; Tsou et al., 2017).

Strategic Planning and Efficient Execution

Public sector firms may use location data to get insights into the geographical dispersion of various services and resources. Policymakers may effectively allocate resources by using this data to guide their decisions. It aids in identifying locations with specific needs for amenities such as healthcare facilities, educational facilities, transportation infrastructure, and more (Ahmad BinTouq, 2015).

Openness and Responsibility

Governments may use Volunteered Geographic Information (VGI) as a means to demonstrate openness by providing accessible data to the general public. Data science may also contribute to enhancing data quality, validating information, and preventing data exploitation, hence enhancing accountability in government services (Georgiadou et al., 2014).

Figure 1. Benefits of VGI for government service delivery

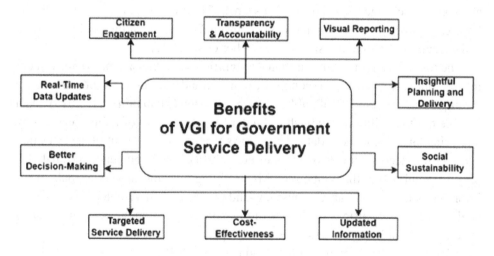

DATA SCIENCE

Data science is a multidisciplinary domain that focuses on obtaining valuable information and insights from vast and diverse data sources (Subrahmanya et al., 2022). Data analytics encompasses several techniques for managing, examining, and interpreting data, including data mining, machine learning, statistical analysis, and data visualization. These techniques are used to facilitate decision-making processes (Asamoah et al., 2020). Data science may be used to provide public services by amalgamating data from diverse sources, such as administrative borders, surveys, social media, and VGI (Volunteered Geographic Information), in order to cultivate a more profound comprehension of societal patterns and citizen requirements. Data science enables governmental entities to get valuable insights from raw data, so promoting the formulation of well-informed policies and evidence-based decision-making (Gunapati, 2011). Integrating data analytics into public services enables governments and businesses to more effectively solve issues, anticipate people' demands, and allocate resources efficiently for maximum impact (Maffei et al., 2020).

In the field of governance, the introduction of data science technologies like artificial intelligence (AI), the Internet of Things (IoT), big data and behavioral/predictive analytics, and blockchain is about to bring about a significant and revolutionary period. The use of advanced technology has the potential to completely transform the way government services are provided by incorporating data-driven innovations (Engin & Treleaven, 2019; Mikhaylov et al., 2018). They can be employed in different fields, including public health development (R & B, 2022), providing public agricultural extension services (Namyenya et al., 2022), increasing awareness about climate change (Appelgren & Jönsson, 2021), creating policy innovation labs for digital governance of education (Williamson, 2015), and aiding in the planning and execution of public transportation (Keller et al., 2022).

The field of data science has initiated a significant and transformative movement in the public sector, leading to economic expansion and offering substantial prospects for improving the standard of public service provision (Manikam et al., 2019). Data science has the ability to establish a standard for the quality of public services by analyzing large amounts of data. This allows for the enhancement of services that prioritize the needs of citizens (Manikam et al., 2019). Data intelligence and analytics play a crucial role in the public sector by enabling decision-makers to make well-informed decisions, enhance efficiency, and promote positive outcomes (Di Vaio et al., 2022). The significant influence of big data analytics on the performance and efficiency of public organizations is clearly apparent, emphasizing its potential for transformation (Rogge et al., 2017; Wahdain et al., 2019).

Auditors in the public sector may use data analytics to maintain accountability and guarantee the appropriate administration of state funds (Novita & Indrany Nanda Ayu Anissa, 2022). The use of data analytics promotes transparency and enhances financial supervision in government bodies. The advancement of data science will have a substantial impact on the future duties and responsibilities of public sector organizations in many functional areas (Gamage, 2016).

Utilizing Data Science for Government Service Delivery

Data science applications have a broad scope of usefulness in the public sector. Below, a selection of these applications is summarized in Figure 2 and shown below.

Resource Planning May Be Optimized via the Use of Predictive Analytics

Data science is widely used in the public sector for resource planning via the application of predictive analytics. Governmental entities may forecast future demand for a range of services, such as healthcare, education, and public safety, by analyzing historical data and trends. The Singaporean government use predictive analytics to strategically allocate resources and prepare for the healthcare needs of the aging population (Liming et al., 2015; Rangaswamy et al., 2021). By using this proactive approach, resources may be allocated more efficiently, resulting in enhanced service provision and decreased expenses.

Analyzing the Sentiment of Citizen Feedback

Extensive quantities of citizen comments collected via various channels, such as social media, surveys, and feedback forms, may be examined for sentiment analysis using data science techniques. By assessing the sentiment of individuals' thoughts and sentiments, governments may effectively gauge popular happiness, identify specific areas that need improvement, and promptly address public complaints (Muneeb & Chandler, 2021).

Transportation Optimization via Network Analysis

Network analysis is a crucial tool for enhancing urban transport networks by using data science approaches. Government entities may identify regions with significant traffic congestion, enhance public transportation pathways, and plan infrastructure development by examining traffic data. PTV Visum, a program developed by PTV Group, is used by the Barcelona Metropolitan Transport Authority (ATM) to conduct demand modeling and study different scenarios related to the provision of public transport services (Gomes, 2021).

Fraud Prevention via Anomaly Detection

Data science is crucial for detecting anomalies and fraudulent activities in government transactions. Government authorities have the ability to detect unusual trends and potential instances of fraud by examining financial data and transaction records. The Internal Revenue Service is using state-of-the-art technology to improve its capacity to detect tax fraud, concealed assets, money laundering, identity theft, and other types of noncompliance with greater effectiveness (Aprio, 2019; stahlesq.com, 2018).

The synergy between Volunteered Geographic Information (VGI) and Data Science is being used to enhance government services.

The combination of data science and Volunteered Geographic Information (VGI) has the capacity to greatly improve government services via a range of methods. The possible uses of VGI and data science approaches are outlined in Figure 3 and further explained below.

Figure 2. Utilizing data science for government service delivery

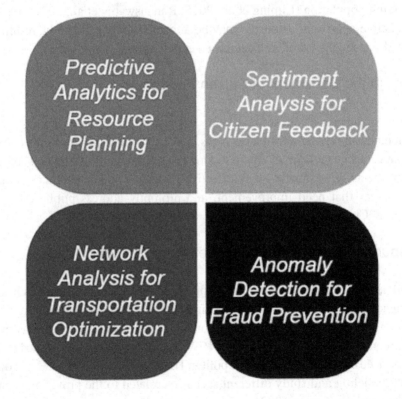

Healthcare

Monitoring and Tracking of Diseases

Volunteered Geographic Information (VGI) may be used to provide up-to-date data on symptoms and locations, enabling the monitoring and analysis of disease transmission patterns. Analyzing this data using data science methodologies enables the prediction of disease outbreaks, identification of high-risk areas, assessment of illness effect, and optimal allocation of healthcare resources. Precise cartographic representations that depict the exact locations of residences within a given area provide several benefits across multiple disciplines. Public health programs that focus on delivering services directly to households, such as indoor residual pesticide spraying for malaria treatment, are among the key areas where these maps demonstrate their usefulness. Sturrock et al., (2018) showcased the capability of ensemble machine learning methods to enhance the precision of building classification in VGI datasets. This research offers useful insights for targeted public health interventions and other uses, such as organizing fumigation campaigns. In a similar manner, Solís et al. (2018) demonstrated the use of Volunteered Geographic Information (VGI) to map building and road infrastructure in Mozambique and Kenya. This mapping was done to assist in an insecticide spray campaign that intended to reduce malaria and protect public health.

Rodriguez et al., (2021) conducted a comprehensive analysis to examine the influence of the Covid-19 pandemic on hospital services in key cities of Ecuador. They used advanced computational techniques and data from OSM to evaluate the spatial distribution and coverage of hospitals capable of treating Covid-19 patients. The study conducted by Qi et al. (2018) presented a new method for identifying and charting instances of food-borne illnesses by using Volunteered Geographic Information (VGI) datasets. Diggle (2005) emphasized the potential for corporations and governments to use data in order to enhance healthcare services for disadvantaged populations, hence guaranteeing fair and equal access to healthcare of superior quality.

Access to Healthcare and the Process of Planning for it

The use of VGI data enables the precise identification of healthcare institutions, identification of difficulties related to accessibility, and identification of gaps in services. These data may be evaluated utilizing the field of data science in order to strategically situate healthcare facilities and enhance healthcare accessibility for underprivileged groups. For example, Kihumbe (2019) illustrates the usefulness of Volunteered Geographic Information (VGI) in mapping regions with a high prevalence of HIV, whereas Mooney et al. (2013) evaluated the potential of OpenStreetMap

(OSM) for widespread health computing applications. In addition, Malik & Shaikh (2019) examined the efficacy of VGI data in analyzing the spatial arrangement of healthcare institutions in Pakistan.

Ambulance services are crucial in the provision of healthcare services. The proper management and operation of ambulances is crucial, as it ensures optimal use of these costly and important assets. Ambulance services are essential for providing healthcare services. The importance of efficiently managing and running ambulances cannot be exaggerated, as it guarantees the optimal use of these costly and important assets. (Okyere et al., 2022) developed a VGI-based ambulance management system in Ghana.

Community asset mapping is essential in public health practices as it acknowledges a community's resources, needs, and successful techniques for urban health interventions. Kolak et al. (2020) introduced a novel participatory asset mapping system that utilizes Volunteered Geographic Information (VGI) in the field of urban health. The impact of air quality on public health has been significant for a considerable period of time. In order to successfully address air pollution in metropolitan areas, it is crucial to possess accurate and dependable data on air quality exposure. Gupta et al., (2018) provided useful insights on the systematic deployment of VGI air quality sensors to create precise air quality maps for urban monitoring.

Public Health Awareness Campaigns

Volunteered Geographic Information (VGI) data may be used to discern the population's specific information needs and apprehensions about their health. Data analytics may be used to identify patterns and develop targeted health awareness initiatives to effectively tackle certain health concerns. Noveck et al. (2017) have observed that the lack of public knowledge and misunderstandings considerably impede the efficiency of control efforts against mosquito-borne illnesses (MBDs). Dissemination of myths, rumors, and disinformation increases the likelihood of disease transmission within communities and hinders the effective mobilization of the public for preventative initiatives. Social media serves as a significant provider of Volunteered Geographic Information (VGI), and social media platforms are essential in bridging the information disparities within communities by promoting the interchange of information and raising awareness (Crowley et al., 2012). Noveck et al. (2017) proposed that sentiment analysis and network analysis of social media data obtained via crowdsourcing may be used to evaluate public sentiments on the dissemination of a particular illness, the efficacy of outreach initiatives, and potential areas for improvement.

Acquiring Knowledge and Skills Through Formal Instruction and Learning

School Planning and Allocation refers to the process of strategically organizing and distributing resources within an educational institution.

VGI data may be used to accurately identify areas characterized by high population density and limited access to educational services. Through the use of geographical data analysis, it is possible to identify areas that have limited access to high-quality educational opportunities. This information may then be used by governments and corporations to build and improve educational services for underprivileged populations. Data science methodologies may be used to examine the data and determine optimal sites for new schools or reallocate current resources, therefore promoting equitable access to top-notch education. Xie et al. (2019) observed that Volunteered Geographic Information (VGI) may be used for urban planning in regions where there is a lack of official building data. These projects have the potential to enhance social sustainability by reducing educational inequalities and empowering communities via education (Muzaffar et al., 2017).

Transportation and Accessibility

VGI data may be used to understand students' transportation needs. Data science may be used to create efficient school bus routes, identify areas with insufficient safe pedestrian walkways, and enhance transportation services, all with the aim of facilitating children' access to their schools. Sezer et al. (2018) performed a study that merged OpenStreetMap (OSM) data with demographic data in order to evaluate the level of accessibility to schools.

Educational Resource Mapping refers to the process of systematically identifying and categorizing educational resources available for use in teaching and learning.

Volunteered Geographic Information (VGI) may be used to compile comprehensive databases via the collective efforts of individuals who provide data about educational resources and facilities worldwide. Data science may evaluate this information to develop resource maps that facilitate data-driven decision-making for politicians and educators on resource allocation and improvement plans.In a study done by Filho et al. (2013), they tested the use of OpenStreetMap (OSM) in cartography disciplines to map cities. The findings of the study confirmed that OSM is very successful in improving the learning process. By using "local knowledge," participants were encouraged to actively participate in problem-oriented learning, focusing on real-life challenges within their communities. This method showcased the usefulness of OSM as a helpful instrument for integrating practical and pertinent activities into the learning process.

Means of Conveyance

Transportation Control

VGI data provides real-time information on accidents, road closures, and traffic congestion. These data may be evaluated using data science methodologies to predict traffic patterns, optimize signal timings, and provide alternative routes to enhance traffic flow. OpenStreetMap has shown to be a helpful data source for traffic simulations, offering information that is equivalent to, and in some instances, even better than the proprietary network models provided by government agencies (Rieck et al., 2015; Zilske et al., 2011).

Public Transport Planning

Public transportation is an essential and integral part of the transportation system, acting as a fundamental element for urban mobility. Nevertheless, the rapid development and urbanization have resulted in a significant increase in the need for public transit. Convenient and expeditious availability of both public and private amenities, such as educational institutions, recreational spaces, and retail establishments, plays a pivotal role in assessing the standard of living in metropolitan regions. Volunteered Geographic Information (VGI) may provide insights about the demand for public transportation and the most popular transit routes. Data science may be used to design and improve public transport networks, which involves determining the most efficient routes and identifying areas with high levels of traffic.

Steiniger et al. (2016) developed a web-based framework to evaluate urban accessibility for transportation planning. The findings demonstrated that OSM data may be used to assess urban accessibility, albeit its comprehensiveness may differ across various regions. Tran et al., (2013) proposed a system for the synchronization of transport data between OpenStreetMap (OSM) and a General Transit Feed Specification (GTFS) dataset. Public transport providers were able to easily upload GTFS data to OSM and get valuable crowdsourced data in exchange. This framework facilitates the modification and enhancement of bus stop locations and facilities by using the existing GTFS data as a reference and leveraging online communities.

Shared Transportation and Ride-Sharing

Volunteered Geographic Information (VGI) may be used to advocate and improve initiatives for ride- and carpooling. Data science may be used to develop intuitive tools for facilitating carpooling arrangements and analyzing commuting trends in order to identify potential matches. Hariz et al. (2021) state that Volunteered

Geographic Information (VGI) may improve transportation systems by maximizing passengers' happiness via the real-time interchange of data among the regional manager, public buses, vehicle ride-sharing services, and the riders themselves. In their study, Chao & Wang (2018) devised a model to evaluate the movement of bicycles by identifying optimal locations for docking stations. They accomplished this by using spatial information, including roads, walkways, bicycle lanes, and prominent landmarks from OSM, inside Taipei City.

Waste Management

Optimization of Waste Collection Routes

VGI data contains information on waste-generating trends and the specific locations of trash pickup sites. Data science has the potential to enhance garbage collection routes, hence reducing the environmental footprint and optimizing energy use. In their study, Dias et al. (2019) included Volunteered Geographic Information (VGI) into trash collection routes with the aim of increasing public participation, enhancing the collection rates of recyclable waste, and reducing logistical expenses. In a similar vein, Dowd et al. (2020) showcased the use of OpenStreetMap and Google OR-Tools in optimizing waste management collection routes, specifically tackling the challenges of mixed fleet routing difficulties. In addition, Felício et al. (2022) proposed an architecture that utilizes OpenStreetMap (OSM) for route planning in the specific context of solid waste collection.

Waste Management Facilities for Recycling and Disposing of Materials

VGI data may be used to cartographically represent recycling and disposal facilities and precisely identify areas without enough waste management infrastructures. Data analysis and data science may assist in strategically placing recycling plants in optimal locations and enhancing trash diversion rates. Inadequate planning has led to a significant volume of trash disposal, causing both economic and environmental concerns. In response to this issue, Thompson et al. (2013) proposed a solution for the distribution and movement of garbage containers. This method involves combining recyclable waste with other types of waste in the same containers and creating direct communication channels between residents and waste management authorities. In a similar vein, Mavakala et al. (2017) suggested investigating the use of crowdsourcing as a possible method for identifying, locating, and describing solid waste dumps.

Assessment of the Environmental Effects

Valuable information on illegal dumping and areas of high pollution may be obtained via Volunteered Geographic Information (VGI) data. Data science may be used to examine this data in order to ascertain the environmental impacts of inadequate waste management and to inform specific interventions aimed at mitigating environmental hazards. The use of spatial data may facilitate the implementation of sustainable waste reduction and management strategies, hence improving waste management policies (A. Singh, 2019).Singh et al. (2016) created a WebGIS platform that allows citizens to report, monitor, and visualize solid trash in metropolitan areas. A Geo-locator tool is developed to enable end-users to easily find the facility's locations for reporting and raising complaints.

Figure 3. Potential benefits provided by volunteered geographic information (VGI) and the field of data science

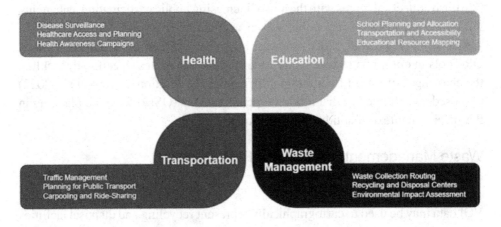

Obstacles

Within the realm of public sector service delivery, Volunteered Geographic Information (VGI) offers many benefits, although it also presents certain obstacles that need thoughtful examination. This section examines notable VGI-related concerns, as emphasized and shown in Figure 4.

Data quality and validation refer to the process of ensuring the accuracy, consistency, and reliability of data. This involves verifying the integrity of the data and confirming that it meets certain standards and criteria.

The dependability of VGI and crowdsourced data, which encompasses correctness, consistency, and completeness, might vary considerably. Therefore, it is crucial to use validation and verification processes to evaluate its quality. When it comes to delivering public services, using unreliable information might impede the efficient allocation of resources and decision-making processes (Ray & Bala, 2020). Inadequate data quality might result in suboptimal allocation of scarce resources and hinder the timely provision of assistance to vulnerable areas. Therefore, precise and verified data is crucial for making educated decisions and taking timely reaction measures.

Robust quality control techniques and data validation methods are essential in order to reduce the dissemination of erroneous information and the possible abuse of data. This includes the use of data cleansing, filtering, and cross-validation methodologies. Partnerships between academic institutions, organizations, and volunteers may be formed to guarantee the precision and dependability of data in diverse public service situations. Moreover, the use of Machine Learning methodologies may be applied to distinguish between spurious and genuine information and automate the identification and elimination of erroneous data (Ray & Bala, 2020).

Ensuring the Protection and Confidentiality of Data

Within the realm of public sector service delivery, the use of Volunteered Geographic Information (VGI) gives rise to apprehensions surrounding the safeguarding of data security and privacy. As the number of community members contributing data increases, it is crucial to protect their privacy and gain express agreement (Yingwei et al., 2020). Insufficient measures to protect data security and privacy may result in the exposure of personal information, undermining public trust and discouraging citizen involvement. Safeguarding privacy is essential for upholding the fundamental values of VGI, which include seizing opportunities, focusing on data, causing disruption, and promoting inclusion (B. T. Haworth et al., 2018).

The privacy issues faced by people may discourage them from sharing crucial information, so impeding the effectiveness of public sector operations. In order to guarantee the protection and confidentiality of data, it is necessary to develop rigorous protocols and rules. Utilizing data encryption techniques and adopting secure data storage protocols may effectively protect confidential information (Muthi Reddy et al., 2018). Moreover, it is essential to provide personnel engaged in VGI collecting with proper education about safe data management protocols.

Engagement and Accessibility

Facilitating the engagement of a wide range of community people in VGI programs might present difficulties. The inclusion of VGI activities may be limited by factors such as technological accessibility, literacy levels, language hurdles, and power imbalances within communities (B. T. Haworth et al., 2018). Limited engagement may lead to incomplete or prejudiced data, since it may neglect the needs and viewpoints of disadvantaged communities (B. T. Haworth et al., 2018). The participation of a diverse range of individuals improves the precision and pertinence of Volunteered Geographic Information (VGI) data, hence enhancing the efficacy of decision-making processes and focused actions.

It is important to make an active attempt to close these gaps and guarantee that underrepresented viewpoints are acknowledged and included in community-led initiatives (Bittner et al., 2016).One may arrange outreach programs to enhance knowledge and stimulate interest in VGI activities, particularly targeting vulnerable populations (B. Haworth et al., 2016). Offering instruction and assistance to persons lacking technology proficiency or digital literacy may significantly boost their involvement in VGI initiatives.

Technological infrastructure refers to the underlying framework of hardware, software, networks, and other technological components that support the functioning of a system or organization.

Restricted technological access may impede the maximum use of VGI in the realm of public sector service delivery (Li & Ulaganathan, 2017). Specific populations may have difficulties in accessing and effectively using the requisite platforms and tools for data input and analysis (Crawford & Finn, 2015). Inadequate technical infrastructure may limit the collection and use of VGI and data science approaches, resulting in delays in real-time monitoring, data transmission, and decision-making. The collection of crucial information may be hindered, which might obstruct the coordination of efficient reaction teams.

In order to surmount these challenges, it is essential to guarantee the presence of the necessary infrastructure and fair accessibility to technology and the Internet, particularly in disadvantaged regions. Creating software and platforms that are easy for users to use, can be used in several languages, and perform well with different hardware and networks helps reduce the negative effects of restricted technical infrastructure. Data science methodologies may also contribute to improving the transmission, storage, and processing of data to guarantee smooth information flow in public sector operations.

Expertise in a Certain Set of Skills

The lack of digital literacy and specialized skill sets among participants might impede the complete usage of Volunteered Geographic Information (VGI) in public sector delivery (Li & Ulaganathan, 2017). Insufficient skills and expertise might hinder people from successfully engaging in data collection, analysis, and interpretation (Sboui & Aissi, 2022). This limitation might undermine the precision and user-friendliness of the produced data. Additionally, the comprehensiveness and dependability of VGI may be constrained by a deficiency of specialized expertise and digital literacy, resulting in the gathering of inaccurate or insufficient data. Moreover, the examination and understanding of data might present difficulties, hindering the acquisition of key insights and informed decision-making in public sector endeavors.

In order to tackle this difficulty, it is essential to provide extensive training and technical assistance to people and communities involved in VGI initiatives (B. Haworth et al., 2016). Capacity-building initiatives may improve data collection techniques, data analysis approaches, and digital literacy proficiencies. Additionally, it is necessary to provide tools and platforms that are easy to use for prospective contributors of Volunteered Geographic Information (VGI), while also considering their varied backgrounds and talents. Data science has the potential to enhance data analysis tools, streamline data processing via automation, and provide valuable insights that may guide decision-making in the public sector.

Figure 4. Challenges of VGI

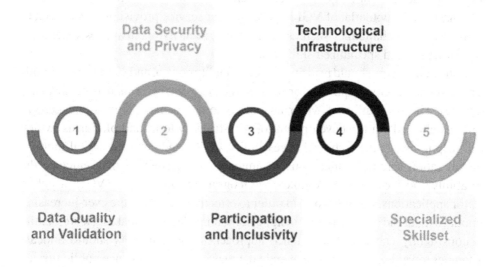

CONCLUSION

The fields of data science and Volunteered Geographic Information (VGI) have emerged as transformative powers in the delivery of public services. VGI, a sort of user-generated content, democratizes geographic information by allowing users to actively contribute to data development and curation. Integrating Volunteered Geographic Information (VGI) into public sector operations might provide novel prospects for enhancing government services in several domains. Data science may enhance VGI by extracting relevant information from several data sources, including administrative borders, surveys, social media, and VGI itself. Data science facilitates the creation of policies based on data and enables decision-making based on evidence by using techniques such as data mining, machine learning, and statistical analysis. Moreover, contemporary technologies such as Artificial Intelligence (AI), Internet of Things (IoT), big data analytics and blockchain have the capability to fundamentally transform the provision of government services.

Volunteered Geographic Information (VGI) may provide immediate disease monitoring within the healthcare domain, hence improving the effectiveness of emergency response efforts. Integrating Volunteered Geographic Information (VGI) into recommender systems may enhance location-based suggestions for people, hence optimizing the delivery of public services. VGI's assistance in urban planning and land use validation enables a more efficient allocation of resources and the advancement of infrastructure development. In addition, VGI's citizen engagement program promotes empowerment and co-creation of public services, ensuring that they align with the authentic needs and preferences of the community. In order to fully harness the potential of VGI in public sector service provision, it is crucial to overcome many challenges such as data quality, security, inclusiveness, technical infrastructure, and specialized skill sets.

Future endeavors should prioritize on data quality control and validation methods for Volunteered Geographic Information (VGI) to further enhance government services. The facilitation of wider and more comprehensive citizen engagement will be achieved via the development of user-friendly tools and platforms, which will help to bridge the technical accessibility, divide and enhance digital literacy. Collaboration across organizations, volunteers, and academics may enhance the reliability and precision of Volunteered Geographic Information (VGI) in public sector applications. Furthermore, in order to effectively manage the ever-increasing amount of data and provide timely insights for prompt decision-making, it is essential to consistently enhance data science approaches. Governments should allocate resources towards data intelligence and analytics in order to enhance public service delivery, promote transparency, and strengthen financial monitoring. The use of data science will enhance efficiency, sustainability, and resource optimization in areas such as education, healthcare, transportation, and waste management.

REFERENCES

Abdulkarim, B., Kamberov, R., & Hay, G. J. (2014). Supporting Urban Energy Efficiency with Volunteered Roof Information and the Google Maps API. *Remote Sensing (Basel)*, *6*(10), 9691–9711. doi:10.3390/rs6109691

Ahmad, M., Khayal, M. S. H., & Tahir, A. (2022). Analysis of Factors Affecting Adoption of Volunteered Geographic Information in the Context of National Spatial Data Infrastructure. *ISPRS International Journal of Geo-Information*, *11*(2), 120. doi:10.3390/ijgi11020120

Ahmad, B. (2015). The UAE Federal Government's E-Participation Roadmap: Developments in UAE Empowerment Initiatives With VGI/PGIS and Location Based Services (LBS). *Canadian Social Science*, *11*(5). doi:10.3968/6919

Annis, A., & Nardi, F. (2019). Integrating VGI and 2D hydraulic models into a data assimilation framework for real time flood forecasting and mapping. *Geo-Spatial Information Science*, *22*(4), 223–236. doi:10.1080/10095020.2019.1626135

Antoniou, V., Fonte, C. C., See, L., Estima, J., Arsanjani, J. J., Lupia, F., Minghini, M., Foody, G., & Fritz, S. (2016). Investigating the feasibility of geo-Tagged photographs as sources of land cover input data. *ISPRS International Journal of Geo-Information*, *5*(5), 64. doi:10.3390/ijgi5050064

Appelgren, E., & Jönsson, A. M. (2021). Engaging Citizens for Climate Change—Challenges for Journalism. *Digital Journalism (Abingdon, England)*, *9*(6), 755–772. doi:10.1080/21670811.2020.1827965

Aprio. (2019). *Artificial Intelligence to Help Resource-Strapped IRS More Efficiently Identify Tax Crimes*. https://www.aprio.com/artificial-intelligence-to-help-resource-strapped-irs-more-efficiency/

Arnaboldi, M., & Azzone, G. (2020). Data science in the design of public policies: Dispelling the obscurity in matching policy demand and data offer. *Heliyon*, *6*(6), e04300. doi:10.1016/j.heliyon.2020.e04300 PMID:32637693

Asamoah, D. A., Doran, D., & Schiller, S. (2020). Interdisciplinarity in Data Science Pedagogy: A Foundational Design. *Journal of Computer Information Systems*, *60*(4), 370–377. doi:10.1080/08874417.2018.1496803

Bittner, C., Michel, B., & Turk, C. (2016). Turning the spotlight on the crowd: Examining the participatory ethics and practices of crisis mapping. *ACME*, *15*(1).

Brodie, M. L. (2019). What Is Data Science? In Applied Data Science: Lessons Learned for the Data-Driven Business. doi:10.1007/978-3-030-11821-1_8

Calcagni, F., Amorim Maia, A. T., Connolly, J. J. T., & Langemeyer, J. (2019). Digital co-construction of relational values: Understanding the role of social media for sustainability. *Sustainability Science, 14*(5), 1309–1321. doi:10.1007/s11625-019-00672-1

Chao, C. Y., & Wang, S. (2018). Using OpenStreetMap data for the location analysis on public bicycle stations – A case study on the Youbike system in downtown Taipei city. *Proceedings - 39th Asian Conference on Remote Sensing: Remote Sensing Enabling Prosperity, ACRS 2018*. Research Gate.

Chen, X., Elmes, G., Ye, X., & Chang, J. (2016). Implementing a Real-Time Twitter-Based System for Resource Dispatch in Disaster Management. *GeoJournal, 81*(6), 863–873. doi:10.1007/s10708-016-9745-8

Crawford, K., & Finn, M. (2015). The limits of crisis data: Analytical and ethical challenges of using social and mobile data to understand disasters. *GeoJournal, 80*(4), 491–502. doi:10.1007/s10708-014-9597-z

Crowley, D. N., Breslin, J. G., Corcoran, P., & Young, K. (2012). Gamification of citizen sensing through mobile social reporting. *4th International IEEE Consumer Electronic Society - Games Innovation Conference, IGiC 2012*. IEEE. 10.1109/IGIC.2012.6329849

Di Vaio, A., Hassan, R., & Alavoine, C. (2022). Data intelligence and analytics: A bibliometric analysis of human–Artificial intelligence in public sector decision-making effectiveness. *Technological Forecasting and Social Change, 174*, 121201. doi:10.1016/j.techfore.2021.121201

Dias, V. E. C., Sperandio, V. G., & Lisboa-Filho, J. (2019). Routes generation for selective collection of urban waste using volunteered geographic information. *Iberian Conference on Information Systems and Technologies, CISTI, 2019-June*. IEEE. 10.23919/CISTI.2019.8760773

Diggle, P. (2005). Applied Spatial Statistics for Public Health Data. *Journal of the American Statistical Association, 100*(470), 702–703. doi:10.1198/jasa.2005.s15

Dowd, M., Dixon, A., & Kinsella, B. (2020). Optimizing waste management collection routes in Urban Haiti: A collaboration between DataKind and SOIL. *ArXiv, 2012*.

Engin, Z., & Treleaven, P. (2019). Algorithmic Government: Automating Public Services and Supporting Civil Servants in using Data Science Technologies. *The Computer Journal, 62*(3), 448–460. doi:10.1093/comjnl/bxy082

Felício, S., Hora, J., Ferreira, M. C., Abrantes, D., Costa, P. D., Dangelo, C., Silva, J., & Galvão, T. (2022). Handling OpenStreetMap georeferenced data for route planning. *Transportation Research Procedia, 62*, 189–196. doi:10.1016/j.trpro.2022.02.024

Filho, H. F., Leite, B. P., Pompermayer, G. A., Werneck, M. G., & Leyh, W. (2013). Teaching VGI as a strategy to promote the production of urban digital cartographic databases. *Joint Urban Remote Sensing Event 2013. JURSE, 2013.* doi:10.1109/JURSE#.2013.6550705

Fonte, C. C., Bastin, L., See, L., Foody, G., & Lupia, F. (2015). Usability of VGI for validation of land cover maps. *International Journal of Geographical Information Science, 29*(May), 1–23. doi:10.1080/13658816.2015.1018266

Gamage, P. (2016). New development: Leveraging 'big data' analytics in the public sector. *Public Money & Management, 36*(5), 385–390. doi:10.1080/09540962.2016.1194087

Georgiadou, Y., Lungo, J. H., & Richter, C. (2014). Citizen sensors or extreme publics? Transparency and accountability interventions on the mobile geoweb. *International Journal of Digital Earth, 7*(7), 516–533. doi:10.1080/17538947.2013.782073

Gomes, M. (2021). Barcelona improves public transport with modelling technology. *PTV Blog.* https://blog.ptvgroup.com/en/city-and-mobility/barcelona-improve-public-transport-modelling/

Goodchild, M. F. (2007). Citizens as sensors: The world of volunteered geography. In GeoJournal. doi:10.1007/s10708-007-9111-y

Grinberger, A. Y., Minghini, M., Juhász, L., Yeboah, G., & Mooney, P. (2022). OSM Science—The Academic Study of the OpenStreetMap Project, Data, Contributors, Community, and Applications. In ISPRS International Journal of Geo-Information, 11(4). doi:10.3390/ijgi11040230

Güiza, F., & Stuart, N. (2018). When citizens choose not to participate in volunteering geographic information to e-governance: a case study from Mexico. In GeoJournal. doi:10.1007/s10708-017-9820-9

Gunapati, S. (2011). Key Features for Designing a Dashboard. *Government Finance Review (0883-7856), 27.*

Gupta, S., Pebesma, E., Degbelo, A., & Costa, A. C. (2018). Optimising citizen-driven air quality monitoring networks for cities. *ISPRS International Journal of Geo-Information, 7*(12), 468. doi:10.3390/ijgi7120468

Haklay, M. (2013). Citizen science and volunteered geographic information: Overview and typology of participation. In Crowdsourcing Geographic Knowledge: Volunteered Geographic Information (VGI) in Theory and Practice. Springer. doi:10.1007/978-94-007-4587-2_7

Hariz, M. (2021). A dynamic mobility traffic model based on two modes of transport in smart cities. *Smart Cities, 4*(1), 253–270. doi:10.3390/smartcities4010016

Haworth, B., Whittaker, J., & Bruce, E. (2016). Assessing the application and value of participatory mapping for community bushfire preparation. *Applied Geography (Sevenoaks, England), 76*, 115–127. doi:10.1016/j.apgeog.2016.09.019

Haworth, B. T., Bruce, E., Whittaker, J., & Read, R. (2018). The good, the bad, and the uncertain: Contributions of volunteered geographic information to community disaster resilience. In Frontiers in Earth Science (Vol. 6). IEEE. doi:10.3389/feart.2018.00183

Honarparvar, S., Forouzandeh Jonaghani, R., Alesheikh, A. A., & Atazadeh, B. (2019). Improvement of a location-aware recommender system using volunteered geographic information. *Geocarto International, 34*(13), 1496–1513. doi:10.1080/10106049.2018.1493155

Hu, S., Ge, Y., Liu, M., Ren, Z., & Zhang, X. (2022). Village-level poverty identification using machine learning, high-resolution images, and geospatial data. *International Journal of Applied Earth Observation and Geoinformation, 107*, 102694. doi:10.1016/j.jag.2022.102694

Huang, H., Yao, X. A., Krisp, J. M., & Jiang, B. (2021). Analytics of location-based big data for smart cities: Opportunities, challenges, and future directions. *Computers, Environment and Urban Systems, 90*, 101712. doi:10.1016/j.compenvurbsys.2021.101712

Keller, C., Glück, F., Gerlach, C. F., & Schlegel, T. (2022). Investigating the Potential of Data Science Methods for Sustainable Public Transport. *Sustainability (Basel), 14*(7), 4211. doi:10.3390/su14074211

Kihumbe. (2019). *Kihumbe- Survey Digitization and Mapping for HIV Monitoring.* Kihumbe.

Kitchin, R., Lauriault, T. P., & Wilson, M. W. (2018). Understanding Spatial Media. In Understanding Spatial Media. Springer. doi:10.4135/9781526425850.n1

Kolak, M., Steptoe, M., Manprisio, H., Azu-Popow, L., Hinchy, M., Malana, G., & Maciejewski, R. (2020). *Extending Volunteered Geographic Information (VGI) with Geospatial Software as a Service: Participatory Asset Mapping Infrastructures for Urban Health*. Springer. doi:10.1007/978-3-030-19573-1_11

Kucukali, A., Pjeternikaj, R., Zeka, E., & Hysa, A. (2022). Evaluating the pedestrian accessibility to public services using open-source geospatial data and QGIS software. *Nova Geodesia*, 2(2), 42. doi:10.55779/ng2242

Li, L., & Ulaganathan, M. N. (2017). Design and development of a crowdsourcing mobile app for disaster response. *International Conference on Geoinformatics, 2017-August*. IEEE. 10.1109/GEOINFORMATICS.2017.8090943

Liming, B., Gavino, A. I., Lee, P., Jungyoon, K., Na, L., Pink Pi, T. H., Xian, T. H., Buay, T. L., Xiaoping, T., Valera, A., Jia, E. Y., Wu, A., & Fox, M. S. (2015). SHINESeniors: Personalized services for active ageing-in-place. *2015 IEEE 1st International Smart Cities Conference*. IEEE. 10.1109/ISC2.2015.7366181

Ma, Q., Wang, L., Gong, X., & Li, K. (2022). Research on the Rationality of Public Toilets Spatial Layout based on the POI Data from the Perspective of Urban Functional Area. *Journal of Geo-Information Science*, 24(1). doi:10.12082/dqxxkx.2022.210331

Maffei, S., Leoni, F., & Villari, B. (2020). Data-driven anticipatory governance. Emerging scenarios in data for policy practices. *Policy Design and Practice*, 3(2), 123–134. doi:10.1080/25741292.2020.1763896

Malik, N. A., & Shaikh, M. A. (2019). Spatial distribution and accessibility to public sector tertiary care teaching hospitals: Case study from Pakistan. *Eastern Mediterranean Health Journal*, 25(6), 431–434. doi:10.26719/emhj.18.049 PMID:31469163

Manikam, S., Sahibudin, S., & Kasinathan, V. (2019). Business intelligence addressing service quality for big data analytics in public sector. *Indonesian Journal of Electrical Engineering and Computer Science*, 16(1), 491. doi:10.11591/ijeecs. v16.i1.pp491-499

Mavakala, B., Mulaji, C., Mpiana, P., Elongo, V., Otamonga, J.-P., Biey, E., Wildi, W., & Pote-Wembonyama, J. (2017). *Citizen Sensing of Solid Waste Disposals : Crowdsourcing As Tool Supporting Waste Management in a. Proceedings Sardinia 2017*. Sixteenth International Waste Management and Landfill Symposium.S. Margherita Di Pula, Cagliari, Italy. https://doi.org/https://archive-ouverte.unige. ch/unige:97650

Mikhaylov, S. J., Esteve, M., & Campion, A. (2018). Artificial intelligence for the public sector: Opportunities and challenges of cross-sector collaboration. *Philosophical Transactions. Series A, Mathematical, Physical, and Engineering Sciences, 376*(2128), 20170357. doi:10.1098/rsta.2017.0357 PMID:30082303

Muneeb, S., & Chandler, T. W. (2021). *Sentiment Analysis for COVID-19 National Vaccination Policy.* PIDE. https://pide.org.pk/blog/sentiment-analysis-for-cov

Muthi Reddy, P., Manjula, S. H., & Venugopal, K. R. (2018). Secured Privacy Data using Multi Key Encryption in Cloud Storage. *Proceedings of 5th International Conference on Emerging Applications of Information Technology, EAIT 2018.* IEEE. 10.1109/EAIT.2018.8470399

Muzaffar, H. M., Tahir, A., Ali, A., Ahmad, M., & McArdle, G. (2017). Quality assessment of volunteered geographic information for educational planning. In *Volunteered Geographic Information and the Future of Geospatial Data.* IGI Global. doi:10.4018/978-1-5225-2446-5.ch005

Namyenya, A., Daum, T., Rwamigisa, P. B., & Birner, R. (2022). E-diary: A digital tool for strengthening accountability in agricultural extension. *Information Technology for Development, 28*(2), 319–345. doi:10.1080/02681102.2021.1875186

Noveck, B. S., Ayoub, R., Hermosilla, M., Marks, J., & Suwondo, P. (2017). *Smarter Crowdsourcing for Zika and Other Mosquito-Borne Diseases.*

Novita, N., & Indrany Nanda Ayu Anissa, A. (2022). The role of data analytics for detecting indications of fraud in the public sector. *International Journal of Research in Business and Social Science (2147- 4478), 11*(7). doi:10.20525/ijrbs.v11i7.2113

Okyere, F., Minnich, T., Sproll, M., Mensah, E., Amartey, L., Otoo-Kwofie, C., & Brunn, A. (2022). Implementation of a low-cost Ambulance Management System. *Dgpf, 30.*

Olteanu-Raimond, A. M., See, L., Schultz, M., Foody, G., Riffler, M., Gasber, T., Jolivet, L., le Bris, A., Meneroux, Y., Liu, L., Poupée, M., & Gombert, M. (2020). Use of automated change detection and VGI sources for identifying and validating urban land use change. *Remote Sensing (Basel), 12*(7), 1186. doi:10.3390/rs12071186

Provost, F., & Fawcett, T. (2013). Data Science and its Relationship to Big Data and Data-Driven Decision Making. *Big Data, 1*(1), 51–59. doi:10.1089/big.2013.1508 PMID:27447038

Qi, Y., Guo, K., Zhang, C., Guo, D., & Zhi, Z. (2018). A VGI-based Foodborn Disease Report and Forecast System. *Proceedings of the 4th ACM SIGSPATIAL International Workshop on Safety and Resilience, EM-GIS 2018*. ACM. 10.1145/3284103.3284124

R, J., & B, S. (2022). Social Impacts of Data Science in Food, Housing And Medical Attention Linked to Public Service. *Technoarete Transactions on Advances in Data Science and Analytics, 1*(1). doi:10.36647/TTADSA/01.01.A004

Rangaswamy, E., Periyasamy, G., & Nawaz, N. (2021). A study on singapore's ageing population in the context of eldercare initiatives using machine learning algorithms. *Big Data and Cognitive Computing, 5*(4), 51. doi:10.3390/bdcc5040051

Ray, A., & Bala, P. K. (2020). Social media for improved process management in organizations during disasters. *Knowledge and Process Management, 27*(1), 63–74. doi:10.1002/kpm.1623

Rieck, D., Schünemann, B., & Radusch, I. (2015). Advanced Traffic Light Information in OpenStreetMap for Traffic Simulations. In Lecture Notes in Mobility. Springer. doi:10.1007/978-3-319-15024-6_2

Rodriguez, G., Torres, H., Fajardo, M., & Medina, J. (2021). Covid-19 in Ecuador: Radiography of Hospital Distribution Using Data Science. *ETCM 2021 - 5th Ecuador Technical Chapters Meeting*. IEEE. 10.1109/ETCM53643.2021.9590641

Rogge, N., Agasisti, T., & De Witte, K. (2017). Big data and the measurement of public organizations' performance and efficiency: The state-of-the-art. *Public Policy and Administration, 32*(4), 263–281. doi:10.1177/0952076716687355

Sangiambut, S., & Sieber, R. (2016). The V in VGI: Citizens or Civic Data Sources. *Urban Planning, 1*(2), 141–154. doi:10.17645/up.v1i2.644

Sboui, T., & Aissi, S. (2022). *A Risk-based Approach for Enhancing the Fitness of use of VGI*. IEEE., doi:10.1109/ACCESS.2022.3201022

Sezer, A., Deniz, M., & Topuz, M. (2018). Analysis of Accessibility of Schools in Usak City via Geographical Information Systems (GIS). *Tarih Kultur Ve Sanat Arastirmalari Dergisi-Journal Of History Culture And Art Research, 7*(5).

Singh, A. (2019). Remote sensing and GIS applications for municipal waste management. *Journal of Environmental Management, 243*, 22–29. doi:10.1016/j.jenvman.2019.05.017 PMID:31077867

Singh, Y. P., Singh, A. K., & Singh, R. P. (2016). *Web GIS based Framework for Citizen Reporting on Collection of Solid Waste and Mapping in GIS for Allahabad City. SAMRIDDHI : A Journal of Physical Sciences.* Engineering and Technology., doi:10.18090/samriddhi.v8i1.11405

Solís, P., McCusker, B., Menkiti, N., Cowan, N., & Blevins, C. (2018). Engaging global youth in participatory spatial data creation for the UN sustainable development goals: The case of open mapping for malaria prevention. *Applied Geography (Sevenoaks, England), 98,* 143–155. doi:10.1016/j.apgeog.2018.07.013

Stahlesq.com. (2018). *How the IRS Uses Artificial Intelligence to Detect Tax Evaders.* Stables HQ. https://stahlesq.com/criminal-defense-law-blog/how-the-irs-uses-artificial-intelligence-to-detect-tax-evaders/

Steiniger, S., Poorazizi, M. E., Scott, D. R., Fuentes, C., & Crespo, R. (2016). Can we use OpenStreetMap POIs for the Evaluation of Urban Accessibility? *International Conference on GIScience Short Paper Proceedings.* IEEE. 10.21433/B31167F0678P

Sturrock, H. J. W., Woolheater, K., Bennett, A. F., Andrade-Pacheco, R., & Midekisa, A. (2018). Predicting residential structures from open source remotely enumerated data using machine learning. *PLoS One, 13*(9), e0204399. doi:10.1371/journal.pone.0204399 PMID:30240429

Subrahmanya, S. V. G., Shetty, D. K., Patil, V., Hameed, B. M. Z., Paul, R., Smriti, K., Naik, N., & Somani, B. K. (2022). The role of data science in healthcare advancements: applications, benefits, and future prospects. In Irish Journal of Medical Science, 191(4). doi:10.1007/s11845-021-02730-z

Thompson, A. F., Afolayan, A. H., & Ibidunmoye, E. O. (2013). Application of geographic information system to solid waste management. *2013 Pan African International Conference on Information Science, Computing and Telecommunications, PACT 2013.* IEEE. 10.1109/SCAT.2013.7055110

To, H., Kim, S. H., & Shahabi, C. (2015). Effectively crowdsourcing the acquisition and analysis of visual data for disaster response. *Proceedings - 2015 IEEE International Conference on Big Data, IEEE Big Data 2015.* IEEE. 10.1109/BigData.2015.7363814

Tran, K., Barbeau, S., Hillsman, E., & Labrador, M. A. (2013). GO_Sync - A Framework to Synchronize Crowd-Sourced Mapping Contributors from Online Communities and Transit Agency Bus Stop Inventories. *International Journal of Intelligent Transportation Systems Research, 11*(2), 54–64. doi:10.1007/s13177-013-0056-x

Tsou, M. H., Jung, C. Te, Allen, C., Yang, J. A., Han, S. Y., Spitzberg, B. H., & Dozier, J. (2017). Building a real-time geo-targeted event observation (Geo) viewer for disaster management and situation awareness. *Lecture Notes in Geoinformation and Cartography*. Springer. doi:10.1007/978-3-319-57336-6_7

Tzavella, K., Fekete, A., & Fiedrich, F. (2018). Opportunities provided by geographic information systems and volunteered geographic information for a timely emergency response during flood events in Cologne, Germany. *Natural Hazards, 91*. doi:10.1007/s11069-017-3102-1

Wahdain, E. A., Baharudin, A. S., & Ahmad, M. N. (2019). Big data analytics in the malaysian public sector: The determinants of value creation. *Advances in Intelligent Systems and Computing, 843*, 139–150. doi:10.1007/978-3-319-99007-1_14

Williamson, B. (2015). Governing methods: Policy innovation labs, design and data science in the digital governance of education. *Journal of Educational Administration and History, 47*(3), 251–271. doi:10.1080/00220620.2015.1038693

Wong, W., & Hinnant, C. C. (2022). Competing perspectives on the Big Data revolution: A typology of applications in public policy. *Journal of Economic Policy Reform*. doi:10.1080/17487870.2022.2103701

Xie, X., Zhou, Y., Xu, Y., Hu, Y., & Wu, C. (2019). OpenStreetMap Data Quality Assessment via Deep Learning and Remote Sensing Imagery. *IEEE Access : Practical Innovations, Open Solutions, 7*, 176884–176895. doi:10.1109/ACCESS.2019.2957825

Yingwei, Y., Dawei, M., & Hongchao, F. (2020). A research framework for the application of volunteered geographic information in post-disaster recovery monitoring. *Tropical Geography, 40*(2). doi:10.13284/j.cnki.rddl.003239

Zilske, M., Neumann, A., & Nagel, K. (2011). OpenStreetMap For Traffic Simulation. M. Schmidt, G. Gartner (Eds.), *Proceedings of the 1st European State of the Map – OpenStreetMap Conference*. Research Gate.

Compilation of References

Abdulkarim, B., Kamberov, R., & Hay, G. J. (2014). Supporting Urban Energy Efficiency with Volunteered Roof Information and the Google Maps API. *Remote Sensing (Basel)*, *6*(10), 9691–9711. doi:10.3390/rs6109691

Acharya, D., Yan, W., & Khoshelham, K. (2018). *Real-time image-based parking occupancy detection using deep learning*. Research Gate.

Aggarwal, K., Singh, S.K., Chopra, M., Kumar, S., & Colace, F. (2022). Deep learning in robotics for strengthening industry 4.0.: opportunities, challenges and future directions. *Robotics and AI for Cybersecurity and Critical Infrastructure in Smart Cities*, 1-19.

Aghbashlo, M., Peng, W., Tabatabaei, M., Kalogirou, S. A., Soltanian, S., Hosseinzadeh-Bandbafha, H., Mahian, O., & Lam, S. S. (2021). Machine learning technology in biodiesel research: A review. *Progress in Energy and Combustion Science*, *85*, 100904. doi:10.1016/j.pecs.2021.100904

Aghbashlo, M., Tabatabaei, M., Hosseinpour, S., Rastegari, H., & Ghaziaskar, H. S. (2018). Multi-objective exergy-based optimization of continuous glycerol ketalization to synthesize solketal as a biodiesel additive in subcritical acetone. *Energy Conversion and Management*, *160*, 251–261. doi:10.1016/j.enconman.2018.01.044

Aghbashlo, M., Tabatabaei, M., Khalife, E., Najafi, B., Mirsalim, S. M., Gharehghani, A., Mohammadi, P., Dadak, A., Roodbar Shojaei, T., & Khounani, Z. (2017). A novel emulsion fuel containing aqueous nano cerium oxide additive in diesel–biodiesel blends to improve diesel engines performance and reduce exhaust emissions: Part II – Exergetic analysis. *Fuel*, *205*, 262–271. doi:10.1016/j.fuel.2017.05.003

Aghbashlo, M., Tabatabaei, M., Rastegari, H., Ghaziaskar, H. S., & Valijanian, E. (2018). Exergy-based optimization of a continuous reactor applied to produce value-added chemicals from glycerol through esterification with acetic acid. *Energy*, *150*, 351–362. doi:10.1016/j.energy.2018.02.151

Aha, D. W., Kibler, D., & Albert, M. K. (1991). Instance-based learning algorithms. *Machine Learning*, *6*(1), 37–66. doi:10.1007/BF00153759

Ahmad, B. (2015). The UAE Federal Government's E-Participation Roadmap: Developments in UAE Empowerment Initiatives With VGI/PGIS and Location Based Services (LBS). *Canadian Social Science*, *11*(5). doi:10.3968/6919

Ahmad, A., Yadav, A. K., & Singh, A. (2023). Application of machine learning and genetic algorithms to the prediction and optimization of biodiesel yield from waste cooking oil. *Korean Journal of Chemical Engineering, 40*(12), 2941–2956. doi:10.1007/s11814-023-1489-9

Ahmad, H., Asghar, M. U., Khan, A., & Mosavi, A. H. (2021). A Hybrid Deep Learning Technique for Personality Trait Classification from Text. *IEEE Access : Practical Innovations, Open Solutions, 9*, 146214–146232. doi:10.1109/ACCESS.2021.3121791

Ahmad, I., Sana, A., Kano, M., Cheema, I. I., Menezes, B. C., Shahzad, J., Ullah, Z., Khan, M., & Habib, A. (2021). Machine learning applications in biofuels' life cycle: Soil, feedstock, production, consumption, and emissions. *Energies, 14*(16), 5072. doi:10.3390/en14165072

Ahmad, M., Khayal, M. S. H., & Tahir, A. (2022). Analysis of Factors Affecting Adoption of Volunteered Geographic Information in the Context of National Spatial Data Infrastructure. *ISPRS International Journal of Geo-Information, 11*(2), 120. doi:10.3390/ijgi11020120

Alazab, M., Layton, R., & Venkatraman, S. (2018). A novel model for detecting phishing attacks using text classification. *Future Generation Computer Systems, 78*, 1086–1097.

Aletras, N., Tsarapatsanis, D., Preotuic-Pietro, D., & Lampos, V. (2016). Predicting judicial decisions of the European Court of Human Rights: A Natural language Processing Perspective. *PeerJ. Computer Science, 2*, 93–99. doi:10.7717/peerj-cs.93

Al-Fuqaha, A., Guizani, M., Mohammadi, M., Aledhari, M., & Ayyash, M. (2015). Internet of Things: A Survey on Enabling Technologies, Protocols and Applications. IEEE Communications Surveys &amp Tutorials. 17. *IEEE Communications Surveys and Tutorials, 2015*(4), 2347–2376. doi:10.1109/COMST.2015.2444095

Alghazzawi, D., Bamasag, O., Albeshri, A., Sana, I., Ullah, H., & Asghar, M. Z. (2022). Efficient prediction of court judgments using an LSTM+ CNN neural network model with an optimal feature set. *Mathematics, 10*(5), 683. doi:10.3390/math10050683

Alguliyev, R., Imamverdiyev, Y., Sukhostat, L., & Bayramov, R. (2021). Plant disease detection based on a deep model. *Soft Computing, 25*(21), 13229–13242. doi:10.1007/s00500-021-06176-4

Ali, R. (2020). *Predictive Modeling: Types, Benefits, and Algorithms.* Oracle Netsuite. https://www. netsuite. com/portal/resource/articles/financial-management/predictive-modeling. shtml

Aliramezani, M., Koch, C. R., & Shahbakhti, M. (2022). Modeling, diagnostics, optimization, and control of internal combustion engines via modern machine learning techniques: A review and future directions. *Progress in Energy and Combustion Science, 88*, 100967. doi:10.1016/j.pecs.2021.100967

Allouch, A., Koubaa, A., Abbes, T., & Ammar, A. (2017). *RoadSense: Smartphone Application to Estimate Road Conditions Using Accelerometer and Gyroscope.* IEEE Sensors Journal. doi:10.1109/JSEN.2017.2702739

Almeida, P. R. D., Oliveira, L. S., Britto, A. S., Silva, E. J., & Koerich, A. L. (2015). PKLot—A robust dataset for parking lot classification. *Expert Systems with Applications*, *42*(11), 4937–4949. doi:10.1016/j.eswa.2015.02.009

Alshamlan, H. M., Badr, G. H., & Alohali, Y. A. (2015). Genetic Bee Colony (GBC) algorithm: A new gene selection method for microarray cancer classification. *Computational Biology and Chemistry*, *56*, 49–60. doi:10.1016/j.compbiolchem.2015.03.001 PMID:25880524

Al-Shanableh, F., Evcil, A., & Savaş, M. A. (2016). Prediction of Cold Flow Properties of Biodiesel Fuel Using Artificial Neural Network. *Procedia Computer Science*, *102*, 273–280. doi:10.1016/j.procs.2016.09.401

Annis, A., & Nardi, F. (2019). Integrating VGI and 2D hydraulic models into a data assimilation framework for real time flood forecasting and mapping. *Geo-Spatial Information Science*, *22*(4), 223–236. doi:10.1080/10095020.2019.1626135

Antoniou, V., Fonte, C. C., See, L., Estima, J., Arsanjani, J. J., Lupia, F., Minghini, M., Foody, G., & Fritz, S. (2016). Investigating the feasibility of geo-Tagged photographs as sources of land cover input data. *ISPRS International Journal of Geo-Information*, *5*(5), 64. doi:10.3390/ijgi5050064

Anwar, M., Sangaiah, A. K., & Farooq, M. S. (2018). An Improved Phishing Detection Model using Feature Selection and K-Nearest Neighbor. *International Journal of Information Management*, *40*, 76–88.

Appalanaidu, M. V., & Kumaravelan, G. (2021). Plant leaf disease detection and classification using machine learning approaches: a review. *Innovations in Computer Science and Engineering: Proceedings of 8th ICICSE*, (pp. 515-525). Research Gate.

Appalanaidu, M. V., & Kumaravelan, G. (2021). Plant leaf disease detection and classification using machine learning approaches: a review. *Innovations in Computer Science and Engineering: Proceedings of 8th ICICSE*, (pp. 515-525). Springer.

Appelgren, E., & Jönsson, A. M. (2021). Engaging Citizens for Climate Change—Challenges for Journalism. *Digital Journalism (Abingdon, England)*, *9*(6), 755–772. doi:10.1080/2167081 1.2020.1827965

Aprio. (2019). *Artificial Intelligence to Help Resource-Strapped IRS More Efficiently Identify Tax Crimes*. https://www.aprio.com/artificial-intelligence-to-help-resource-strapped-irs-more-efficiency/

Araujo, A., Kalebe, R., Girao, G., Filho, I., Goncalves, K., & Neto, B. (2017). Reliability analysis of an IoT-based smart parking application for smart cities. *Proceedings of the 2017 IEEE International Conference on Big Data (Big Data)*. 10.1109/BigData.2017.8258426

Arnaboldi, M., & Azzone, G. (2020). Data science in the design of public policies: Dispelling the obscurity in matching policy demand and data offer. *Heliyon*, *6*(6), e04300. doi:10.1016/j.heliyon.2020.e04300 PMID:32637693

Asamoah, D. A., Doran, D., & Schiller, S. (2020). Interdisciplinarity in Data Science Pedagogy: A Foundational Design. *Journal of Computer Information Systems, 60*(4), 370–377. doi:10.10 80/08874417.2018.1496803

Ashley, K. (2019). A Brief History of the changing roles of case prediction in AI and Law: Law in context. *Socio-Legal Journal, 36*(1), 93–112. doi:10.26826/law-in-context.v36i1.88

Ashley, K., & Brüninghaus, S. (2009). Automatically classifying case texts and predicting outcomes. *Artificial Intelligence and Law, 17*(2), 125–165. doi:10.1007/s10506-009-9077-9

Atadashi, I. M., Aroua, M. K., Aziz, A. R. A., & Sulaiman, N. M. N. (2011). Refining technologies for the purification of crude biodiesel. *Applied Energy, 88*(12), 4239–4251. doi:10.1016/j.apenergy.2011.05.029

Atangana, A., & Gómez-Aguilar, J. F. (2018). Fractional derivatives with no-index law property: Application to chaos and statistics. *Chaos, Solitons, and Fractals, 114*, 516–535. doi:10.1016/j.chaos.2018.07.033

Atangana, A., & Koca, I. (2016). Chaos in a simple nonlinear system with Atangana–Baleanu derivatives with fractional order. *Chaos, Solitons, and Fractals, 89*, 447–454. doi:10.1016/j.chaos.2016.02.012

Awogbemi, O., & Von Kallon, D. V. (2023). Application of machine learning technologies in biodiesel production process—A review. *Frontiers in Energy Research, 11*, 1122638. doi:10.3389/fenrg.2023.1122638

Aydin, I., Karakose, M., & Karakose, E. (2017). A navigation and reservation based smart parking platform using genetic optimization for smart cities. *Proceedings of the 2017 5th International Istanbul Smart Grid and Cities Congress and Fair (ICSG).* 10.1109/SGCF.2017.7947615

Ba, J. (2015). *Multiple Object Recognition with Visual Attention.* CoRR.

Banerjee, A. V. (1993, April). The economics of rumours. *The Review of Economic Studies, 60*(2), 309–327. doi:10.2307/2298059

Barnich, O., & Van Droogenbroeck, M. (2011). ViBe: A universal background subtraction algorithm for video sequences. *IEEE Transactions on Image Processing, 20*(6), 1709–1724. doi:10.1109/TIP.2010.2101613 PMID:21189241

Barth, D. (2009). *The Bright Side of Sitting in Traffic: Crowdsourcing Road Congestion Data.* BlogSpot. https://googleblog.blogspot.com/2009/08/bright-side-of-sitting-in-traffic.html

Basak, R., Sural, S., Ganguly, N., & Ghosh, S. K. (2019, April). Online public shaming on Twitter: Detection, analysis, and mitigation. *IEEE Transactions on Computational Social Systems, 6*(2), 208–220. doi:10.1109/TCSS.2019.2895734

Baswaraju, S., Maheswari, V. U., Chennam, K. K., Thirumalraj, A., Kantipudi, M. P., & Aluvalu, R. (2023, December). Future food production prediction using AROA based hybrid deep learning model in agri-sector. *Human-Centric Intelligent Systems.*, *3*(4), 521–536. doi:10.1007/s44230-023-00046-y

Beeravalli, V., Ashwath, N., Rasul, M., Khan, M., & Capareda, S. (2022). Density, Kinematic Viscosity and Cetane Number Prediction of Biofuel Feedstocks from Fatty Acid Compositions. *2022 International Conference on Futuristic Technologies (INCOFT)*, (pp. 1–6). IEEE. 10.1109/INCOFT55651.2022.10094421

Behrisch, M., Bieker, L., Erdmann, J., & Krajzewicz, D. (2011). SUMO–simulation of urban mobility: An overview. *Proceedings of the SIMUL 2011, The Third International Conference on Advances in System Simulation.*

Ben Lamine, R., Ben Jemaa, R., & Ben Amor, I. A. (2017). Graph Planning Based Composition for Adaptable Semantic Web Services. *Procedia Computer Science*, *112*, 358–368. doi:10.1016/j.procs.2017.08.016

Bevilacqua, V., Mastronardi, G., Menolascina, F., Paradiso, A., & Tommasi, S. (2006). Genetic Algorithms and Artificial Neural Networks in Microarray Data Analysis : A Distributed Approach. *Engineering Letters*, *13*(3), 335–343.

Bezabih, Y. A., Salau, A. O., Abuhayi, B. M., Mussa, A. A., & Ayalew, A. M. (2023). CPD-CCNN: Classification of pepper disease using a concatenation of convolutional neural network models. *Scientific Reports*, *13*(1), 15581. doi:10.1038/s41598-023-42843-2 PMID:37731029

Bhagat, M., Kumar, D., Mahmood, R., Pati, B., & Kumar, M. (2020, February). Bell pepper leaf disease classification using CNN. In *2nd international conference on data, engineering and applications (IDEA)* (pp. 1-5). IEEE. 10.1109/IDEA49133.2020.9170728

Bhagat, M., Kumar, D., & Kumar, S. (2023). Bell pepper leaf disease classification with LBP and VGG-16 based fused features and RF classifier. *International Journal of Information Technology: an Official Journal of Bharati Vidyapeeth's Institute of Computer Applications and Management*, *15*(1), 465–475. doi:10.1007/s41870-022-01136-z

Bhilare, P., Parab, N., Soni, N., & Thakur, B. (2019). Predicting outcome of judicial cases and analysis using machine learning. *International Research Journal in Engineering Technology, 6*, 326-330. https://www.irjet.net/archives/V6/i3/IRJET-V6I362.pdf

Biswas, B. (2020). *Email Spam Classification Dataset CSV*. Kaggle.Com. https://www.kaggle.com/datasets/balaka18/email-spam-classification-dataset-csv

Bittner, C., Michel, B., & Turk, C. (2016). Turning the spotlight on the crowd: Examining the participatory ethics and practices of crisis mapping. *ACME, 15*(1).

Bjørnstad, O. N., Shea, K., Krzywinski, M., & Altman, N. (2020, April). Modeling infectious epidemics. *Nature Methods*, *17*(5), 455–456. doi:10.1038/s41592-020-0822-z PMID:32313223

Bokaba, T., Doorsamy, W., & Paul, B. (2022). Comparative Study of Machine Learning Classifiers for Modelling Road Traffic Accidents. *Applied Sciences (Basel, Switzerland), 12*(2), 828. doi:10.3390/app12020828

Bolton, P. (2021). Petrol and diesel prices. *House of Commons Library, 04712,* 25.

Brady, K. & Brandstein, M. (2020). *An evaluation of audio-visual person recognition on the XM2VTS corpus using the Lausanne protocol.* MIT Lincoln Laboratory.

Brodie, M. L. (2019). What Is Data Science? In Applied Data Science: Lessons Learned for the Data-Driven Business. doi:10.1007/978-3-030-11821-1_8

Bukkarapu, K. R., & Krishnasamy, A. (2023). Biodiesel composition based machine learning approaches to predict engine fuel properties. *Journal of Automobile Engineering.* 10.1177/09544070231158240

Cai, J. & Liu, Z. (2002). Pattern recognition using markov random field models. *Pattern Recognition, 35*(3).

Calcagni, F., Amorim Maia, A. T., Connolly, J. J. T., & Langemeyer, J. (2019). Digital co-construction of relational values: Understanding the role of social media for sustainability. *Sustainability Science, 14*(5), 1309–1321. doi:10.1007/s11625-019-00672-1

Campbell, W. M., & Sturim, D. E. (2006). *The MIT- LL/IBM speaker recognition system using high performance reduced complexity recognition.* MIT Lincoln Laboratory IBM.

CannarellaJ.SpechlerJ. A. (2014). Epidemiological modeling of online social network dynamics. *arXiv:1401.4208.* http://arxiv.org/abs/1401.4208

Celesti, A., Fazio, M., Galán, F., Glikson, A., Mauwa, H., Bagula, A., Celesti, F., & Villari, M. (2019). How to Develop IoT Cloud e-Health Systems Based on FIWARE: A Lesson Learnt. *Journal of Sensor and Actuator Networks., 8*(1), 7. doi:10.3390/jsan8010007

Celesti, A., Galletta, A., Carnevale, L., Fazio, M., Lay-Ekuakille, A., & Villari, M. (2018). 'Lay-Ekuakille, A.; Villari, M. An IoT Cloud System for Traffic Monitoring and Vehicular Accidents Prevention Based on Mobile Sensor Data Processing. *IEEE Sensors Journal, 18*(12), 4795–4802. doi:10.1109/JSEN.2017.2777786

Chalkidis, I., Androutsopoulos, I., & Aletras, N. (2019). Neural Legal Judgement Prediction In English. *Proceedings of the 57th Annual Meeting of the Association for Computational Linguistics,* (pp. 4317-4323). Association for Computational Linguistics. 10.18653/v1/P19-1424

Chang, I. C., Tai, H. T., Yeh, F. H., Hsieh, D. L., & Chang, S. H. A. (2013). VANET-Based A* Route Planning Algorithm for Travelling Time- and Energy-Efficient GPS Navigation App. *International Journal of Distributed Sensor Networks, 9*(7), 794521. doi:10.1155/2013/794521

Chao, C. Y., & Wang, S. (2018). Using OpenStreetMap data for the location analysis on public bicycle stations – A case study on the Youbike system in downtown Taipei city. *Proceedings - 39th Asian Conference on Remote Sensing: Remote Sensing Enabling Prosperity, ACRS 2018.* Research Gate.

Chaudhari, P. R., Jhaveri, R. V., & Maheta, K. V. (2019). K-Nearest Neighbor Algorithm for Phishing Detection. *Procedia Computer Science, 165*, 272–279.

Chen, M., Yang, Q., Li, Q., Wang, G., & Yang, M. (2014). Spatiotemporal background subtraction using minimum spanning tree and optical flow. in *Proc. European Conference on Computer Vision (ECCV)*. Springer. 10.1007/978-3-319-10584-0_34

Chen, B.-H., Shi, L.-F., & Ke, X. (2019). A robust moving object detection in multi-scenario big data for video surveillance. *IEEE Transactions on Circuits and Systems for Video Technology, 29*(4), 982–995. doi:10.1109/TCSVT.2018.2828606

Cheng, J.-J., Liu, Y., Shen, B., & Yuan, W.-G. (2013, January). An epidemic model of rumor diffusion in online social networks. *The European Physical Journal B, 86*(1), 29. doi:10.1140/epjb/e2012-30483-5

Cheng, M., Hu, X., Borji, A., Tu, Z., & Torr, P. (2011). Deeply supervised salient object detection with short connections. *IEEE Transactions on Pattern Analysis and Machine Intelligence, 33*(2), 353–367. PMID:21193811

Chen, H., Zhang, Y., & Gutman, I. (2016). A kernel-based clustering method for gene selection with gene expression data. *Journal of Biomedical Informatics, 62*, 12–20. doi:10.1016/j.jbi.2016.05.007 PMID:27215190

Chen, J., Li, K., Rong, H., Bilal, K., Yang, N., & Li, K. (2018). A disease diagnosis and treatment recommendation system based on big data mining and cloud computing. *Information Sciences, 435*, 124–149. doi:10.1016/j.ins.2018.01.001

Chen, L.-C., Papandreou, G., Kokkinos, I., Murphy, K., & Yuille, A. L. (2018). DeepLab: Semantic image segmentation with deep convolutional nets, atrous convolution, and fully connected CRFs. *IEEE Transactions on Pattern Analysis and Machine Intelligence, 40*(4), 834–848. doi:10.1109/TPAMI.2017.2699184 PMID:28463186

Chen, X., Elmes, G., Ye, X., & Chang, J. (2016). Implementing a Real-Time Twitter-Based System for Resource Dispatch in Disaster Management. *GeoJournal, 81*(6), 863–873. doi:10.1007/s10708-016-9745-8

Chen, Z., Silvestri, F., Tolomei, G., Wang, J., Zhu, H., & Ahn, H. (2022). Explain the Explainer: Interpreting Model-Agnostic Counterfactual Explanations of a Deep Reinforcement Learning Agent. *IEEE Transactions on Artificial Intelligence.*

China Venkaiah, V., & Sesha Phani Deepika, V. (2018). Computational Analysis and Understanding of Natural Languages: Principles, Methods and Applications. In *Handbook of Statistics*. North Holland. https://books.google.com/books?hl=en&lr=&id=gRJrDwAAQBAJ&oi=fnd&pg=PP1&dq=process+mining+approaches+information+security+governance&ots=LYbH5q86TS&sig=4b4o3WEnsUM9dzRagP-GQs6xI88

Chisti, Y. (2018). The saga of algal energy…. *Biotechnology Advances*, *36*(5), 1553. doi:10.1016/j.biotechadv.2018.05.003

Chowdhury, D. N., Agarwal, N., Laha, A. B., & Mukherjee, A. (2018). A Vehicle-to-Vehicle Communication System Using Iot Approach. *Proceedings of the 2018 IEEE Second International Conference on Electronics, Communication and Aerospace Technology (ICECA)*. 10.1109/ICECA.2018.8474909

Cimini, C., Pezzotta, G., Pinto, R., & Cavalieri, S. (2019). Industry 4.0 technologies impacts in the manufacturing and supply chain landscape: An overview. Service Orientation in Holonic and Multi-Agent Manufacturing. *Proceedings of SOHOMA*, *2018*, 109–120.

Corral-Bobadilla, M., Lostado-Lorza, R., Gómez, F.-S., Iñiguez-Macedo, S., & Fraile, C. S. (2023). A novel approach to efficient biodiesel production using waste cooking oil. *2023 8th International Conference on Smart and Sustainable Technologies (SpliTech)*, (pp. 1–4). IEEE. 10.23919/SpliTech58164.2023.10193728

Coşgun, A., Günay, M. E., & Yıldırım, R. (2023). Machine learning for algal biofuels: A critical review and perspective for the future. *Green Chemistry*, *25*(9), 3354–3373. doi:10.1039/D3GC00389B

Crawford, K., & Finn, M. (2015). The limits of crisis data: Analytical and ethical challenges of using social and mobile data to understand disasters. *GeoJournal*, *80*(4), 491–502. doi:10.1007/s10708-014-9597-z

Crowley, D. N., Breslin, J. G., Corcoran, P., & Young, K. (2012). Gamification of citizen sensing through mobile social reporting. *4th International IEEE Consumer Electronic Society - Games Innovation Conference, IGiC 2012*. IEEE. 10.1109/IGIC.2012.6329849

Cui, J., Shen, X., Nie, F., Wang, Z., Wang, J., & Chen, Y. (2022). *A Survey on Legal Judgment Prediction: Datasets, Metrics, Models and Challenges*. https://doi.org//arXiv.2204.04859 doi:10.48550

Da Cruz, T. N., Da Cruz, T. M., & Pinheiro Dos Santos, W. (2018). Detection and classification of mammary lesions using artificial neural networks and morphological wavelets. *Revista IEEE América Latina*, *16*(3), 926–932. doi:10.1109/TLA.2018.8358675

Dagher, S. (2019). *Assad or We Burn Country: How One Family's Lust for Power Destroyed Syria*. London Back Pay Books.

Dalenogare, L. S., Benitez, G. B., Ayala, N. F., & Frank, A. G. (2018). The expected contribution of Industry 4.0 technologies for industrial performance. *International Journal of Production Economics, 204*, 383–394. doi:10.1016/j.ijpe.2018.08.019

Daley, D. J., & Kendall, D. G. (1965). Stochastic rumours. *IMA Journal of Applied Mathematics, 1*(1), 42–55. doi:10.1093/imamat/1.1.42

Damiani, L., Demartini, M., Guizzi, G., Revetria, R., & Tonelli, F. (2018). Augmented and virtual reality applications in industrial systems: A qualitative review towards the industry 4.0 era. *IFAC-PapersOnLine, 51*(11), 624–630. doi:10.1016/j.ifacol.2018.08.388

Daniels, D. J. (2005). *Ground penetrating radar*. Encyclopedia RF Microw. Eng.

de Oliveira, R. S., Reis, J. A., & Sperandio Nascimento, E. G. (2022). Predicting the number of days in court cases using artificial intelligence. *PLoS One, 17*(5), e0269008. doi:10.1371/journal.pone.0269008 PMID:35617285

Deshmukh, A., Patil, D. S., Soni, G., & Tyagi, A. K. (2023). Cyber Security: New Realities for Industry 4.0 and Society 5.0. In Handbook of Research on Quantum Computing for Smart Environments (pp. 299-325). IGI Global.

Devezas, T., & Sarygulov, A. (2017). *Industry 4.0.* Springer. doi:10.1007/978-3-319-49604-7

Devi, S. (2017). *Machine Learning based traffic congestion prediction in a IoT based Smart City*. Academic Press.

Dharmalingam, B., Balamurugan, S., Wetwatana, U., Tongnan, V., Sekhar, C., Paramasivam, B., Cheenkachorn, K., Tawai, A., & Sriariyanun, M. (2023). Comparison of neural network and response surface methodology techniques on optimization of biodiesel production from mixed waste cooking oil using heterogeneous biocatalyst. *Fuel, 340*, 127503. doi:10.1016/j.fuel.2023.127503

Di Vaio, A., Hassan, R., & Alavoine, C. (2022). Data intelligence and analytics: A bibliometric analysis of human–Artificial intelligence in public sector decision-making effectiveness. *Technological Forecasting and Social Change, 174*, 121201. doi:10.1016/j.techfore.2021.121201

Dias, V. E. C., Sperandio, V. G., & Lisboa-Filho, J. (2019). Routes generation for selective collection of urban waste using volunteered geographic information. *Iberian Conference on Information Systems and Technologies, CISTI, 2019-June*. IEEE. 10.23919/CISTI.2019.8760773

Dietz, K. (1967). Epidemics and rumours: A survey. *J. Roy. Stat. Soc., 130*(4), 505–528.

Diggle, P. (2005). Applied Spatial Statistics for Public Health Data. *Journal of the American Statistical Association, 100*(470), 702–703. doi:10.1198/jasa.2005.s15

Distefano, S., Merlino, G., Puliafito, A., Cerotti, D., & Dautov, R. (2017). Crowdsourcing and Stigmergic Approaches for (Swarm) Intelligent Transportation Systems. *Proceedings of the International Conference on Human Centered Computing (HCC 2017)*.

Dogra, A., & Kaur, J. (2022). Moving towards smart transportation with machine learning and Internet of Things (IoT): A review. *Journal of Smart Environments and Green Computing., 2.* doi:10.20517/jsegc.2021.09

Dowd, M., Dixon, A., & Kinsella, B. (2020). Optimizing waste management collection routes in Urban Haiti: A collaboration between DataKind and SOIL. *ArXiv, 2012.*

Dubey, S., Biswas, P., Ghosh, R., Chatterjee, S., Dubey, M. J., Chatterjee, S., Lahiri, D., & Lavie, C. J. (2020, May). Psychosocial impact of covid-19. *Diabetes & Metabolic Syndrome, 14*(5), 779–788. doi:10.1016/j.dsx.2020.05.035 PMID:32526627

Duda, R. O., Hart, P. E., & Stork, D. G. (2020). Unsupervised Learning and Clustering. In *Pattern classification* (2nd ed.). Wiley.

Durgesh, K. (2009). Data Classification using Support Vector Machine. *Journal of Theoretical and Applied Information Technology.*

El Bouchefry, K., & de Souza, R. S. (2020). Learning in Big Data: Introduction to Machine Learning. In Knowledge Discovery in Big Data from Astronomy and Earth Observation: Astrogeoinformatics. Elsevier. doi:10.1016/B978-0-12-819154-5.00023-0

El Naqa, I., & Murphy, M. J. (2015). What is machine learning? In *Machine Learning in Radiation Oncology* (pp. 3–11). Springer. doi:10.1007/978-3-319-18305-3_1

Engin, Z., & Treleaven, P. (2019). Algorithmic Government: Automating Public Services and Supporting Civil Servants in using Data Science Technologies. *The Computer Journal, 62*(3), 448–460. doi:10.1093/comjnl/bxy082

Eser, S. E. R. T. (2021). A deep learning based approach for the detection of diseases in pepper and potato leaves. *Anadolu Tarım Bilimleri Dergisi, 36*(2), 167–178.

Fan, X., Liu, J., Wang, Z., Jiang, Y., & Liu, X. (2017). Crowdsourced Road Navigation: Concept, Design, and Implementation. *IEEE Communications Magazine, 55*(6), 126–128. doi:10.1109/MCOM.2017.1600738

Felício, S., Hora, J., Ferreira, M. C., Abrantes, D., Costa, P. D., Dangelo, C., Silva, J., & Galvão, T. (2022). Handling OpenStreetMap georeferenced data for route planning. *Transportation Research Procedia, 62*, 189–196. doi:10.1016/j.trpro.2022.02.024

Filho, H. F., Leite, B. P., Pompermayer, G. A., Werneck, M. G., & Leyh, W. (2013). Teaching VGI as a strategy to promote the production of urban digital cartographic databases. *Joint Urban Remote Sensing Event 2013. JURSE, 2013.* doi:10.1109/JURSE#.2013.6550705

Fonte, C. C., Bastin, L., See, L., Foody, G., & Lupia, F. (2015). Usability of VGI for validation of land cover maps. *International Journal of Geographical Information Science, 29*(May), 1–23. doi:10.1080/13658816.2015.1018266

Friedman, N., Geiger, D., & Goldszmidt, M. (1997). Bayesian network classifiers. *Machine Learning, 29*(2/3), 131–137. doi:10.1023/A:1007465528199

Fusco, G., Colombaroni, C., Comelli, L., & Isaenko, N. (2015). *Short-term traffic predictions on large urban traffic networks: Applications of network-based machine learning models and dynamic traffic assignment models.* IEEE. . doi:10.1109/MTITS.2015.7223242

Gaikward, S. K. (2010, November). A review on speech recognition technique. *International Journal of Computer Applications, 10*(3).

Gamage, P. (2016). New development: Leveraging 'big data' analytics in the public sector. *Public Money & Management, 36*(5), 385–390. doi:10.1080/09540962.2016.1194087

Geeksforgeeks.org. (2023). *NLP Gensim Tutorial – Complete Guide For Beginners.* Geeksforgeeks. org. https://www.geeksforgeeks.org/nlp-gensim-tutorial-complete-guide-for-beginners/#article-meta-div

Geetha, S., & Cicilia, D. (2017). IoT enabled intelligent bus transportation system. *Proceedings of the 2017 2nd International Conference on Communication and Electronics Systems (ICCES).*

Georgiadou, Y., Lungo, J. H., & Richter, C. (2014). Citizen sensors or extreme publics? Transparency and accountability interventions on the mobile geoweb. *International Journal of Digital Earth, 7*(7), 516–533. doi:10.1080/17538947.2013.782073

Ghobakhloo, M. (2020). Industry 4.0, digitization, and opportunities for sustainability. *Journal of Cleaner Production, 252*, 119869. doi:10.1016/j.jclepro.2019.119869

Ghosh, A., Chatterjee, T., Samanta, S., Aich, J., & Roy, S. (2017). Distracted Driving: A Novel Approach towards Accident Prevention. *Adv. Comput. Sci. Technol., 10*, 2693–2705.

Gibert, K., Pevný, T., & Bourdaillet, J. (2014). Phishstorm: Detecting phishing with streaming analytics. In *Proceedings of the 2014 ACM SIGSAC Conference on Computer and Communications Security* (pp. 1115-1126). ACM.

Girolami, M. & He, C. (2010). Probability density estimation from optimally condensed data samples. *Pattern Analysis and Machine Intelligence, 25*(10), 1253 – 1264.

Girvan, M., & Newman, M. E. J. (2002, June). Community structure in social and biological networks. *Proceedings of the National Academy of Sciences of the United States of America, 99*(12), 7821–7826. doi:10.1073/pnas.122653799 PMID:12060727

Github.Com. (2023). *Pragmatic machine learning and NLP.* Github.Com. https://github.com/RaRe-Technologies/gensim

Giwa, S. O., Adekomaya, S. O., Adama, K. O., & Mukaila, M. O. (2015). Prediction of selected biodiesel fuel properties using artificial neural network. *Frontiers in Energy, 9*(4), 433–445. doi:10.1007/s11708-015-0383-5

Gomes, M. (2021). Barcelona improves public transport with modelling technology. *PTV Blog.* https://blog.ptvgroup.com/en/city-and-mobility/barcelona-improve-public-transport-modelling/

Goodchild, M. F. (2007). Citizens as sensors: The world of volunteered geography. In GeoJournal. doi:10.1007/s10708-007-9111-y

GopalakrishnanK. (2018). Deep Learning in Pavement Image Analysis and Automated Distress Detection: A Review. doi:10.13140/RG.2.2.35354.54728

Goundar, S., Avanija, J., Sunitha, G., Madhavi, K. R., & Bhushan, S. B. (Eds.). (2021). *Innovations in the industrial Internet of Things (IIoT) and smart factory*. IGI Global. doi:10.4018/978-1-7998-3375-8

Gower, J., & Ross, G. (1998). Non-probabilistic Classification. In *Advances in Data Science and Classification. Studies in Classification, Data Analysis, and Knowledge Organization* (pp. 21–28). Springer. doi:10.1007/978-3-642-72253-0_3

Grinberger, A. Y., Minghini, M., Juhász, L., Yeboah, G., & Mooney, P. (2022). OSM Science—The Academic Study of the OpenStreetMap Project, Data, Contributors, Community, and Applications. In ISPRS International Journal of Geo-Information, 11(4). doi:10.3390/ijgi11040230

Guan, X. (2021, April). A novel method of plant leaf disease detection based on deep learning and convolutional neural network. In *2021 6th international conference on intelligent computing and signal processing (ICSP)* (pp. 816-819). IEEE. 10.1109/ICSP51882.2021.9408806

Güiza, F., & Stuart, N. (2018). When citizens choose not to participate in volunteering geographic information to e-governance: a case study from Mexico. In GeoJournal. doi:10.1007/s10708-017-9820-9

Gülseçen, S., Reis, Z. A., Gezer, M., & Erol, Ç. (2019). Industry 4.0 from the MIS Perspective. *Industry 4.0 from the MIS Perspective*, 1–352. doi:10.3726/b15120

Gumzej, R. (2022). Safety and Security Beyond Industry 4.0. [IJAL]. *International Journal of Applied Logistics*, *12*(1), 1–10. doi:10.4018/IJAL.287556

Gunapati, S. (2011). Key Features for Designing a Dashboard. *Government Finance Review (0883-7856), 27*.

Gupta, A., Kulkarni, S., Jathar, V., Sharma, V., & Jain, N. (2017). Smart Car Parking Management System Using IoT. *Am. J. Sci. Eng. Technol.*, *2*, 112.

Gupta, R., Dey, D., & Mukherjee, A. (2013). Building efficient, effective and scalable spam filters for promotional email categorization. *Knowledge-Based Systems*, *53*, 45–57.

Gupta, S., Pebesma, E., Degbelo, A., & Costa, A. C. (2018). Optimising citizen-driven air quality monitoring networks for cities. *ISPRS International Journal of Geo-Information*, *7*(12), 468. doi:10.3390/ijgi7120468

Haeffner, M., & Panuwatwanich, K. (2018). Perceived impacts of Industry 4.0 on manufacturingg industry and its Workforce: Case of Germany. In *8th International Conference on Engineering, Project, and Product Management (EPPM 2017) Proceedings* (pp. 199-208). Springer International Publishing.

Haklay, M. (2013). Citizen science and volunteered geographic information: Overview and typology of participation. In Crowdsourcing Geographic Knowledge: Volunteered Geographic Information (VGI) in Theory and Practice. Springer. doi:10.1007/978-94-007-4587-2_7

Hansen, S. B., Mirkouei, A., & Xian, M. (2019). Cyber-physical control and optimization for biofuel 4.0. *IISE Annual Conference and Expo 2019*. Research Gate.

Hariz, M. (2021). A dynamic mobility traffic model based on two modes of transport in smart cities. *Smart Cities*, 4(1), 253–270. doi:10.3390/smartcities4010016

Haworth, B. T., Bruce, E., Whittaker, J., & Read, R. (2018). The good, the bad, and the uncertain: Contributions of volunteered geographic information to community disaster resilience. In Frontiers in Earth Science (Vol. 6). IEEE. doi:10.3389/feart.2018.00183

Haworth, B., Whittaker, J., & Bruce, E. (2016). Assessing the application and value of participatory mapping for community bushfire preparation. *Applied Geography (Sevenoaks, England)*, 76, 115–127. doi:10.1016/j.apgeog.2016.09.019

He, K., Sun, J., & Tang, X. (2013). Guided image filtering. *IEEE Transactions on Pattern Analysis and Machine Intelligence*, 35(6), 1397–1409. doi:10.1109/TPAMI.2012.213 PMID:23599054

Honarparvar, S., Forouzandeh Jonaghani, R., Alesheikh, A. A., & Atazadeh, B. (2019). Improvement of a location-aware recommender system using volunteered geographic information. *Geocarto International*, 34(13), 1496–1513. doi:10.1080/10106049.2018.1493155

Hosseinpour, S., Aghbashlo, M., Tabatabaei, M., & Khalife, E. (2016). Exact estimation of biodiesel cetane number (CN) from its fatty acid methyl esters (FAMEs) profile using partial least square (PLS) adapted by artificial neural network (ANN). *Energy Conversion and Management*, 124, 389–398. doi:10.1016/j.enconman.2016.07.027

Hou, Y., Edara, P., & Sun, C. (2015). Traffic Flow Forecasting for Urban Work Zones. Intelligent Transportation Systems. *IEEE Transactions on Intelligent Transportation Systems*, 16(4), 1761–1770. doi:10.1109/TITS.2014.2371993

Huang, G.B., Zhu, Q.Y., & Siew, C.K. (2004). Extreme Learning machine: a new learning scheme of feedforward neural network. In *2004 IEEE International Joint Conference on Neural Networks* (pp. 985-990). IEEE.

Huang, H., Yao, X. A., Krisp, J. M., & Jiang, B. (2021). Analytics of location-based big data for smart cities: Opportunities, challenges, and future directions. *Computers, Environment and Urban Systems*, 90, 101712. doi:10.1016/j.compenvurbsys.2021.101712

Huang, Z., Zeng, X., Wang, D., & Fang, S. (2022). Noise Reduction Method of Nanopore Based on Wavelet and Kalman Filter. *Applied Sciences (Basel, Switzerland)*, 12(19), 9517. doi:10.3390/app12199517

Hu, J., Tan, C. W., Wang, W., & Li, J. (2018). A novel feature engineering approach to phishing email detection. *Information Sciences*, 450, 19–31.

Hu, S., Ge, Y., Liu, M., Ren, Z., & Zhang, X. (2022). Village-level poverty identification using machine learning, high-resolution images, and geospatial data. *International Journal of Applied Earth Observation and Geoinformation, 107*, 102694. doi:10.1016/j.jag.2022.102694

Ibrahim, A. T. H., Chang, V., Anuar, N. B., Adewole, K., Yaqoob, I., Gani, A., Ahmed, E., & Chiroma, H. (2016). The role of big data in smart city. *International Journal of Information Management, 36*(5), 748-758. doi:10.1016/j.ijinfomgt.2016.05.002

IEA. (2022). *World Energy Outlook 2022, Part of World Energy Outlook.* IEA. www.iea.org/t&c/%0Ahttps://www.iea.org/reports/world-energy-outlook-2022

Iweka, S. C., Falowo, O. A., Amosun, A. A., & Betiku, E. (2023). Optimization of microwave-assisted biodiesel production from watermelon seeds oil using thermally modified kwale anthill mud as base catalyst. *Heliyon, 9*(7), e17762. doi:10.1016/j.heliyon.2023.e17762 PMID:37539125

Jahirul, M. I., Rasul, M. G., Brown, R. J., Senadeera, W., Hosen, M. A., Haque, R., Saha, S. C., & Mahlia, T. M. I. (2021). Investigation of correlation between chemical composition and properties of biodiesel using principal component analysis (PCA) and artificial neural network (ANN). *Renewable Energy, 168*, 632–646. doi:10.1016/j.renene.2020.12.078

Jahirul, M., Brown, R., Senadeera, W., O'Hara, I., & Ristovski, Z. (2013). The Use of Artificial Neural Networks for Identifying Sustainable Biodiesel Feedstocks. *Energies, 6*(8), 3764–3806. doi:10.3390/en6083764

Jain, A. K. (2010). Data clustering: 50 years beyond K-means. *Pattern Recognition Letters, 31*(8), 651–666. doi:10.1016/j.patrec.2009.09.011

Jain, A. K., Murty, M. N., & Flynn, P. J. (1999). Data clustering: A review. *ACM Computing Surveys, 31*(3), 264–323. doi:10.1145/331499.331504

Jain, R., & Nagel, H.-H. (1979). On the analysis of accumulative difference pictures from image sequences of real-world scenes. *IEEE Transactions on Pattern Analysis and Machine Intelligence, 2*(2), 206–214. doi:10.1109/TPAMI.1979.4766907 PMID:21868850

Jana, S., Begum, A. R., & Selvaganesan, S. (2020). Design and analysis of pepper leaf disease detection using deep belief network. *European Journal of Molecular and Clinical Medicine, 7*(9), 1724–1731.

Jasim, M. A., & Al-Tuwaijari, J. M. (2020, April). Plant leaf diseases detection and classification using image processing and deep learning techniques. In *2020 International Conference on Computer Science and Software Engineering (CSASE)* (pp. 259-265). IEEE. 10.1109/CSASE48920.2020.9142097

Javaid, M., Haleem, A., Singh, R. P., Rab, S., & Suman, R. (2022). Exploring impact and features of machine vision for progressive industry 4.0 culture. *Sensors International, 3*, 100132. doi:10.1016/j.sintl.2021.100132

Javapoint.com. (2021). *K-Nearest Neighbor(KNN) Algorithm for Machine Learning.* JavaPoint. https://www.javatpoint.com/k-nearest-neighbor-algorithm-for-machine-learning

Jayakumar, S., Yusoff, M. M., Rahim, M. H. A., Maniam, G. P., & Govindan, N. (2017). The prospect of microalgal biodiesel using agro-industrial and industrial wastes in Malaysia. *Renewable & Sustainable Energy Reviews*, *72*, 33–47. doi:10.1016/j.rser.2017.01.002

Jeon, P. R., Moon, J.-H., Ogunsola, N. O., Lee, S. H., Ling, J. L. J., You, S., & Park, Y.-K. (2023). Recent advances and future prospects of thermochemical biofuel conversion processes with machine learning. *Chemical Engineering Journal*, *471*, 144503. doi:10.1016/j.cej.2023.144503

Jia, G., Han, G., Li, A., & Du, J. (2018). SSL: Smart Street Lamp Based on Fog Computing for Smarter Cities. *IEEE Transactions on Industrial Informatics*, *14*(11), 4995–5004. doi:10.1109/TII.2018.2857918

Jin, X., Li, S., Ye, H., Wang, J., Wu, Y., Zhang, D., Ma, H., Sun, F., Pugazhendhi, A., & Xia, C. (2023). Investigation and optimization of biodiesel production based on multiple machine learning technologies. *Fuel*, *348*, 128546. doi:10.1016/j.fuel.2023.128546

Kannadhasan, S., & Suresh, R. (2014). EMD Algorithm for Robust Image Watermarking. Recent Advances in Mechanical Engineering and Interdisciplinary Developments. Advanced Materials Research.

Kannadhasan, S., & Rajesh Baba, M. (2016, December). A Novel Approach to detect Text in Various Dynamic-Color Images. In *Mathematics and its Applications*. University College of Engineering, Anna University.

Kanoh, H. (2005). Short-term traffic prediction using fuzzy c-means and cellular automata in a wide-area road network. *Proceedings. 2005 IEEE Intelligent Transportation Systems*. . doi:10.1109/ITSC.2005.1520184

Karadağ, K., Tenekeci, M. E., Taşaltın, R., & Bilgili, A. (2020). Detection of pepper fusarium disease using machine learning algorithms based on spectral reflectance. *Sustainable Computing : Informatics and Systems*, *28*, 100299. doi:10.1016/j.suscom.2019.01.001

Kelbert, F., Shirazi, F., Simo, H., Wüchner, T., Buchmann, J., Pretschner, A., & Waidner, M. (2012). State of online privacy: A technical perspective. In *Internet Privacy* (pp. 189–279). Springer. doi:10.1007/978-3-642-31943-3_4

Keller, C., Glück, F., Gerlach, C. F., & Schlegel, T. (2022). Investigating the Potential of Data Science Methods for Sustainable Public Transport. *Sustainability (Basel)*, *14*(7), 4211. doi:10.3390/su14074211

Kermack, W. O., & McKendrick, A. G. (1927). A contribution to the mathematical theory of epidemics. *Proc. Roy. Soc. london. A. Containing Papers Math. Phys. Character*, *115*(772), 700–721.

Khalid, M., Sarfraz, M. S., Iqbal, U., Aftab, M. U., Niedbała, G., & Rauf, H. T. (2023). Real-Time Plant Health Detection Using Deep Convolutional Neural Networks. *Agriculture*, *13*(2), 510. doi:10.3390/agriculture13020510

Khanna, A., Lamba, B. Y., Jain, S., Bolshev, V., Budnikov, D., Panchenko, V., & Smirnov, A. (2023). Biodiesel Production from Jatropha: A Computational Approach by Means of Artificial Intelligence and Genetic Algorithm. *Sustainability (Basel), 15*(12), 9785. doi:10.3390/su15129785

Kihumbe. (2019). *Kihumbe- Survey Digitization and Mapping for HIV Monitoring.* Kihumbe.

Kim, M., Jang, D., & Yang, Y. (2001). A robust-invariant pattern recognition model using fuzzy art. *Pattern Recognition, 34*(8), 1685-1696.

Kim, H., Ha, Y. J., & Kim, J. (2021). Phishing detection using text analysis with multi-granularity attention mechanisms. *Computers & Security, 106*, 102317.

KingmaD. P.BaJ. (2014). Adam: A method for stochastic optimization. *arXiv:1412.6980.*

Kitchin, R., Lauriault, T. P., & Wilson, M. W. (2018). Understanding Spatial Media. In Understanding Spatial Media. Springer. doi:10.4135/9781526425850.n1

Kokilavani, M., & Malathi, A. (2017). Smart street lighting system using IoT. *Int. J. Adv. Res. Appl. Sci. Technol., 3*, 8–11.

Kolak, M., Steptoe, M., Manprisio, H., Azu-Popow, L., Hinchy, M., Malana, G., & Maciejewski, R. (2020). *Extending Volunteered Geographic Information (VGI) with Geospatial Software as a Service: Participatory Asset Mapping Infrastructures for Urban Health.* Springer. doi:10.1007/978-3-030-19573-1_11

Kolakoti, A., & Satish, G. (2023). Biodiesel production from low-grade oil using heterogeneous catalyst: An optimisation and ANN modelling. *Australian Journal of Mechanical Engineering, 21*(1), 316–328. doi:10.1080/14484846.2020.1842298

Kort, F. (1957). Predicting Supreme Court decisions mathematically: A quantitative analysis of the" right to counsel cases. [Cambridge University Press]. *The American Political Science Review, 51*(1), 1–12. doi:10.2307/1951767

Krizhevsky, A., Sutskever, I., & Hinton, G. E. (2012). Imagenet classification with deep convolutional neural networks. *Proceedings of the Advances in Neural Information Processing Systems (NIPS 2012).*

Kubat, M. (2017). *An introduction to machine learning.* Springer.

Kucukali, A., Pjeternikaj, R., Zeka, E., & Hysa, A. (2022). Evaluating the pedestrian accessibility to public services using open-source geospatial data and QGIS software. *Nova Geodesia, 2*(2), 42. doi:10.55779/ng2242

Kumar, P., Singh, D., & Bhamu, J. (2022). Machine Vision in Industry 4.0: Applications, Challenges and Future Directions. In Machine Vision for Industry 4.0 (pp. 263-284). CRC Press.

Kute, S. S., Tyagi, A. K., & Aswathy, S. U., (2022). Industry 4.0 Challenges in e-Healthcare Applications and Emerging Technologies. *Intelligent Interactive Multimedia Systems for e-Healthcare Applications,* 265-290.

Kwon, D., Park, S., Baek, S., Malaiya, R. K., Yoon, G., & Ryu, J. T. (2018). A study on development of the blind spot detection system for the IoT-based smart connected car. *2018 IEEE International Conference on Consumer Electronics (ICCE)*. 10.1109/ICCE.2018.8326077

Lage-Freitas, A., Allende-Cid, H., Santana, O., & Livia, O. (2022). Predicting Brazilian court decisions. *PeerJ. Computer Science*, 8, e904. doi:10.7717/peerj-cs.904 PMID:35494851

Lebensztayn, E., Machado, F. P., & Rodríguez, P. M. (2011, April). On the behavior of a rumour process with random stifling. *Environmental Modelling & Software*, 26(4), 517–522. doi:10.1016/j.envsoft.2010.10.015

LeCun, Y., Bengio, Y., & Hinton, G. (2015). Deep learning. *Nature*, 521(7553), 436–444. doi:10.1038/nature14539 PMID:26017442

Legon, A., & Alsalman, A. (2020). *How Facebook Can Flatten the Curve of the Coronavirus Infodemic*. AVAAZ. https://secure.avaaz.org/campaign/en/facebook_coronavirus_misinformation/

Leng, J., Sha, W., Wang, B., Zheng, P., Zhuang, C., Liu, Q., Wuest, T., Mourtzis, D., & Wang, L. (2022). Industry 5.0: Prospect and retrospect. *Journal of Manufacturing Systems*, 65, 279–295. doi:10.1016/j.jmsy.2022.09.017

Liang, G., He, W., Xu, C., Chen, L., & Zeng, J. (2015, September). Rumor identification in microblogging systems based on users' behavior. *IEEE Transactions on Computational Social Systems*, 2(3), 99–108. doi:10.1109/TCSS.2016.2517458

Li, D., Xu, L., & Goodman, E. D. (2013). Illumination-robust foreground detection in a video surveillance system. *IEEE Transactions on Circuits and Systems for Video Technology*, 23(10), 1637–1650. doi:10.1109/TCSVT.2013.2243649

Lidkea, V., Muresan, R., Al-Dweik, A., & Zhou, S. (2019). *Improving the Security of Cloud-Based Intelligent Transportation Systems*. Advance online publication. doi:10.1109/CCECE.2019.8861723

Lienhart, R., & Maydt, J. (2002). An extended set of haar-like features for rapid object detection. *Proceedings of the International Conference on Image Processing*. 10.1109/ICIP.2002.1038171

Li, L., & Ulaganathan, M. N. (2017). Design and development of a crowdsourcing mobile app for disaster response. *International Conference on Geoinformatics, 2017-August*. IEEE. 10.1109/GEOINFORMATICS.2017.8090943

Li, L., Zhang, Q., Wang, X., Zhang, J., Wang, T., Gao, T.-L., Duan, W., Tsoi, K. K., & Wang, F.-Y. (2020, April). Characterizing the propagation of situational information in social media during COVID-19 epidemic: A case study on weibo. *IEEE Transactions on Computational Social Systems*, 7(2), 556–562. doi:10.1109/TCSS.2020.2980007

Liming, B., Gavino, A. I., Lee, P., Jungyoon, K., Na, L., Pink Pi, T. H., Xian, T. H., Buay, T. L., Xiaoping, T., Valera, A., Jia, E. Y., Wu, A., & Fox, M. S. (2015). SHINESeniors: Personalized services for active ageing-in-place. *2015 IEEE 1st International Smart Cities Conference*. IEEE. 10.1109/ISC2.2015.7366181

Lin, T. L., Chang, H. Y., & Chen, K. H. (2020). The pest and disease identification in the growth of sweet peppers using faster R-CNN and mask R-CNN. *Journal of Internet Technology, 21*(2), 605–614.

Li, S., Wang, W., Li, Y., & Tan, C. W. (2019). Phishing URL detection based on visual similarity and machine learning. *IEEE Access : Practical Innovations, Open Solutions, 7*, 24854–24864.

Liu, G., Bao, H., & Han, B. (2018). A Stacked Autoencoder-Based Deep Neural Network for Achieving Gearbox Fault Diagnosis. *Mathematical Problems in Engineering, 2018*, 5105709. doi:10.1155/2018/5105709

LiuH. W.LinC. F.ChenY. J. 2018. Beyond State v. Loomis: Artificial Intelligence, Government Algorithmization, and Accountability. International Journal of Law and Information Technology, 27(2):122-141. Available at SSRN: https://ssrn.com/abstract=3313916

Liu, J., Gong, M., Qin, K., & Zhang, P. (2018). A deep convolutional coupling network for change detection based on heterogeneous optical and radar images. *IEEE Transactions on Neural Networks and Learning Systems, 29*(3), 545–559. doi:10.1109/TNNLS.2016.2636227 PMID:28026789

Liu, P., & Zhang, Y. (2023). Optimization of biodiesel production from oil using a novel green catalyst via development of a predictive model. *Arabian Journal of Chemistry, 16*(6), 104785. doi:10.1016/j.arabjc.2023.104785

Liu, W.-M., Levin, S. A., & Iwasa, Y. (1986, February). Influence of nonlinear incidence rates upon the behavior of SIRS epidemiological models. *Journal of Mathematical Biology, 23*(2), 187–204. doi:10.1007/BF00276956 PMID:3958634

Liu, X., Yao, J., Hong, X., Huang, X., Zhou, Z., Qi, C., & Zhao, G. (2018). Background subtraction using spatiotemporal group sparsity recovery. *IEEE Transactions on Circuits and Systems for Video Technology, 28*(8), 1737–1751. doi:10.1109/TCSVT.2017.2697972

Liu, Y., Zhang, L., & Li, W. (2016). Detecting phishing websites with lexical and sentiment features. *Computers & Security, 59*, 158–168.

Liu, Z., & Baghban, A. (2017). Application of LSSVM for biodiesel production using supercritical ethanol solvent. *Energy Sources. Part A, Recovery, Utilization, and Environmental Effects, 39*(17), 1869–1874. doi:10.1080/15567036.2017.1380732

Liu, Z., Lin, Y., Cao, Y., Hu, H., Wei, Y., Zhang, Z., Lin, S., & Guo, B. (2021). *Swin transformer: Hierarchical vision transformer using shifted windows.* In *Proceedings of the IEEE/CVF International Conference on Computer Vision*, Montreal, QC, Canada. 10.1109/ICCV48922.2021.00986

Madden, S. (2012). From Databases to Big Data. *IEEE Internet Computing.* . doi:10.1109/MIC.2012.50

Maffei, S., Leoni, F., & Villari, B. (2020). Data-driven anticipatory governance. Emerging scenarios in data for policy practices. *Policy Design and Practice, 3*(2), 123–134. doi:10.1080/25741292.2020.1763896

Mairizal, A. Q., Awad, S., Priadi, C. R., Hartono, D. M., Moersidik, S. S., Tazerout, M., & Andres, Y. (2020). Experimental study on the effects of feedstock on the properties of biodiesel using multiple linear regressions. *Renewable Energy*, *145*, 375–381. doi:10.1016/j.renene.2019.06.067

Majumdar, A., Garg, H., & Jain, R. (2021). Managing the barriers of Industry 4.0 adoption and implementation in textile and clothing industry: Interpretive structural model and triple helix framework. *Computers in Industry*, *125*, 103372. doi:10.1016/j.compind.2020.103372

Malik, N. A., & Shaikh, M. A. (2019). Spatial distribution and accessibility to public sector tertiary care teaching hospitals: Case study from Pakistan. *Eastern Mediterranean Health Journal*, *25*(6), 431–434. doi:10.26719/emhj.18.049 PMID:31469163

Mamun, M. A. A. (2017). An intelligent smartphone based approach using IoT for ensuring safe driving. In *2017 International Conference on Electrical Engineering and Computer Science (ICECOS)* (pp. 217-223). IEEE. 10.1109/ICECOS.2017.8167137

Manikam, S., Sahibudin, S., & Kasinathan, V. (2019). Business intelligence addressing service quality for big data analytics in public sector. *Indonesian Journal of Electrical Engineering and Computer Science*, *16*(1), 491. doi:10.11591/ijeecs.v16.i1.pp491-499

Ma, Q., Wang, L., Gong, X., & Li, K. (2022). Research on the Rationality of Public Toilets Spatial Layout based on the POI Data from the Perspective of Urban Functional Area. *Journal of Geo-Information Science*, *24*(1). doi:10.12082/dqxxkx.2022.210331

Marković, M., & Gostojić, S. (2018). Open Judicial Data: A Comprehensive Analysis. *Social Science Computer Review*, *38*(3), 295–314. doi:10.1177/0894439318770744

Ma, S. P., Fan, C. Y., Chuang, Y., Liu, I. H., & Lan, C. W. (2019). Graph-based and scenario-driven microservice analysis, retrieval, and testing. *Future Generation Computer Systems*, *100*, 724–735. doi:10.1016/j.future.2019.05.048

Mathew, M. P., & Mahesh, T. Y. (2022). Leaf-based disease detection in bell pepper plant using YOLO v5. *Signal, Image and Video Processing*, *16*(3), 1–7. doi:10.1007/s11760-021-02024-y

Mathur, A., Sah, A., & Rawat, S. (2023). Evolution of Cloud Computing With Blockchain and IoT. In A. Taghipour (Ed.), *Blockchain Applications in Cryptocurrency for Technological Evolution* (pp. 14–32). IGI Global. doi:10.4018/978-1-6684-6247-8.ch002

Mavakala, B., Mulaji, C., Mpiana, P., Elongo, V., Otamonga, J.-P., Biey, E., Wildi, W., & Pote-Wembonyama, J. (2017). *Citizen Sensing of Solid Waste Disposals : Crowdsourcing As Tool Supporting Waste Management in a. Proceedings Sardinia 2017.* Sixteenth International Waste Management and Landfill Symposium.S. Margherita Di Pula, Cagliari, Italy. https://doi.org/ https://archive-ouverte.unige.ch/unige:97650

McHugh, J. M., Konrad, J., Saligrama, V., & Jodoin, P.-M. (2009). Foreground adaptive background subtraction. *IEEE Signal Processing Letters*, *16*(5), 390–393. doi:10.1109/LSP.2009.2016447

Medvedeva, M., Vols, M., & Wieling, M. (2020). Using Machine Learning to predict decisions of the European Court of Human Rights. *Artificial Intelligence and Law, 28*(2), 237–266. doi:10.1007/s10506-019-09255-y

Medvedeva, M., Wieling, M., & Vols, M. (2023). Rethinking the Field of Automatic Prediction of Court Decisions. *Artificial Intelligence and Law, 31*(1), 195–212. doi:10.1007/s10506-021-09306-3

Mehta, S., Kanhangad, V., & Ravi, T. M. (2015). Phishing Detection using Machine Learning Techniques. *International Journal of Computer Applications, 117*(22), 9–13.

Mezair, T., Djenouri, Y., Belhadi, A., Srivastava, G., & Lin, J. C. W. (2022). A sustainable deep learning framework for fault detection in 6G Industry 4.0 heterogeneous data environments. *Computer Communications, 187*, 164–171. doi:10.1016/j.comcom.2022.02.010

Mikhaylov, S. J., Esteve, M., & Campion, A. (2018). Artificial intelligence for the public sector: Opportunities and challenges of cross-sector collaboration. *Philosophical Transactions. Series A, Mathematical, Physical, and Engineering Sciences, 376*(2128), 20170357. doi:10.1098/rsta.2017.0357 PMID:30082303

Miraboutalebi, S. M., Kazemi, P., & Bahrami, P. (2016). Fatty Acid Methyl Ester (FAME) composition used for estimation of biodiesel cetane number employing random forest and artificial neural networks: A new approach. *Fuel, 166*, 143–151. doi:10.1016/j.fuel.2015.10.118

Mohammed, M., Khan, M. B., & Bashier, E. B. M. (2016). *Machine Learning: Algorithms and Applications* (1st ed.). CRC Press. doi:10.1201/9781315371658

Muneeb, S., & Chandler, T. W. (2021). *Sentiment Analysis for COVID-19 National Vaccination Policy.* PIDE. https://pide.org.pk/blog/sentiment-analysis-for-cov

Mustafa, H., Umer, M., Hafeez, U., Hameed, A., Sohaib, A., Ullah, S., & Madni, H. A. (2023). Pepper bell leaf disease detection and classification using optimized convolutional neural network. *Multimedia Tools and Applications, 82*(8), 12065–12080. doi:10.1007/s11042-022-13737-8

Muthi Reddy, P., Manjula, S. H., & Venugopal, K. R. (2018). Secured Privacy Data using Multi Key Encryption in Cloud Storage. *Proceedings of 5th International Conference on Emerging Applications of Information Technology, EAIT 2018.* IEEE. 10.1109/EAIT.2018.8470399

Muzaffar, H. M., Tahir, A., Ali, A., Ahmad, M., & McArdle, G. (2017). Quality assessment of volunteered geographic information for educational planning. In *Volunteered Geographic Information and the Future of Geospatial Data.* IGI Global. doi:10.4018/978-1-5225-2446-5.ch005

Nagel, S. (1960). Using simple calculations to predict judicial decisions. *The American Behavioral Scientist, 4*(4), 24–28. doi:10.1177/000276426000400409

Nagy, M., & Lăzăroiu, G. (2022). Computer vision algorithms, remote sensing data fusion techniques, and mapping and navigation tools in the Industry 4.0-based Slovak automotive sector. *Mathematics, 10*(19), 3543. doi:10.3390/math10193543

Naik, N. (2017). Choice of effective messaging protocols for IoT systems: MQTT, CoAP, AMQP and HTTP. In *2017 IEEE International Systems Engineering Symposium (ISSE)* (pp. 12-18). IEEE. 10.1109/SysEng.2017.8088251

Nair, M. M., Tyagi, A. K., & Sreenath, N. (2021). The future with industry 4.0 at the core of society 5.0: Open issues, future opportunities and challenges. In 2021 international conference on computer communication and informatics (ICCCI). IEEE.

Namyenya, A., Daum, T., Rwamigisa, P. B., & Birner, R. (2022). E-diary: A digital tool for strengthening accountability in agricultural extension. *Information Technology for Development*, *28*(2), 319–345. doi:10.1080/02681102.2021.1875186

Naziya, S. (n.d.). Speech Recognition System-A Review. *IOSR Journal of Computer Engineering*, *18*(4).

Nekovee, M., Moreno, Y., Bianconi, G., & Marsili, M. (2007, January). Theory of rumour spreading in complex social networks. *Physica A*, *374*(1), 457–470. doi:10.1016/j.physa.2006.07.017

Newman, M. E. J. (2013, July). Community detection and graph partitioning. *Europhysics Letters*, *103*(2), 28003. doi:10.1209/0295-5075/103/28003

Ngige, O. C., Ayankoya, F. Y., Balogun, J. A., Onuiri, E., Agbonkhese, C., & Sanusi, F. A. (2023). A dataset for predicting Supreme Court judgments in Nigeria. *Data in Brief, 50*. doi:10.1016/j.dib.2023.109483

Nguyen, T., Wong, Y., & Lechner, B. (2019). Response-based methods to measure road surface irregularity: A state-of-the-art review. *European Transport Research Review*, *11*(1), 43. doi:10.1186/s12544-019-0380-6

Noveck, B. S., Ayoub, R., Hermosilla, M., Marks, J., & Suwondo, P. (2017). *Smarter Crowdsourcing for Zika and Other Mosquito-Borne Diseases*.

Novita, N., & Indrany Nanda Ayu Anissa, A. (2022). The role of data analytics for detecting indications of fraud in the public sector. *International Journal of Research in Business and Social Science (2147- 4478), 11*(7). doi:10.20525/ijrbs.v11i7.2113

O'Neil, C. (2016). *Weapons of Math Destruction: How Big Data increases inequality and threatens democracy*. Crown Publishing Group.

Ogbu, O. (2006). *Modern Nigerian Legal System* (3rd ed.). AP Press.

Ojo, M. O., & Zahid, A. (2023). Improving Deep Learning Classifiers Performance via Preprocessing and Class Imbalance Approaches in a Plant Disease Detection Pipeline. *Agronomy (Basel)*, *13*(3), 887. doi:10.3390/agronomy13030887

Okeke, G. N. (2016). Judicial precedent in the Nigerian legal system and a case for its application under international law. *Nnamdi Azikiwe University Journal of International Law and Jurisprudence*, *1*, 107–115.

Okyere, F., Minnich, T., Sproll, M., Mensah, E., Amartey, L., Otoo-Kwofie, C., & Brunn, A. (2022). Implementation of a low-cost Ambulance Management System. *Dgpf, 30.*

Olteanu-Raimond, A. M., See, L., Schultz, M., Foody, G., Riffler, M., Gasber, T., Jolivet, L., le Bris, A., Meneroux, Y., Liu, L., Poupée, M., & Gombert, M. (2020). Use of automated change detection and VGI sources for identifying and validating urban land use change. *Remote Sensing (Basel), 12*(7), 1186. doi:10.3390/rs12071186

Oluyide, O. M., Tapamo, J. R., & Viriri, S. (2018). Automatic lung segmentation based on Graph Cut using a distance-constrained energy. *IET Computer Vision, 12*(5), 609–615. doi:10.1049/iet-cvi.2017.0226

Oraegbunam, J. C., Ishola, N. B., Sotunde, B. A., Latinwo, L. M., & Betiku, E. (2023). Sandbox oil biodiesel production modeling and optimization with neural networks and genetic algorithm. *Green Technologies and Sustainability, 1*(1), 100007. doi:10.1016/j.grets.2022.100007

Owolabi, K. M., & Atangana, A. (2019). *Numerical Methods for Fractional Differentiation* (Vol. 54). Springer Series in Computational Mathematics. doi:10.1007/978-981-15-0098-5

Ozbayoglu, A. M., Küçükayan, G., & Dogdu, E. (2016). A real-time autonomous highway accident detection model based on big data processing and computational intelligence. In *2016 IEEE International Conference on Big Data (Big Data)*. IEEE. 10.1109/BigData.2016.7840798

Parez, S., Dilshad, N., Alghamdi, N. S., Alanazi, T. M., & Lee, J. W. (2023). Visual intelligence in precision agriculture: Exploring plant disease detection via efficient vision transformers. *Sensors (Basel), 23*(15), 6949. doi:10.3390/s23156949 PMID:37571732

Parihar, S. S., Gupta, J. P., & Kumar, V. (2019). Phishing Detection based on the Features of Phishing Webpages Using K-Nearest Neighbor Algorithm. *International Journal of Computer Applications, 182*(2), 38–43.

Park, M., & Chai, S. (2021). AI Model for Predicting Legal Judgments to Improve Accuracy and Explainability of Online Privacy Invasion Cases. *Applied Sciences (Basel, Switzerland), 11*(23), 11080. doi:10.3390/app112311080

Poornima, S., Kavitha, S., Mohanavalli, S., & Sripriya, N. (2019, April). Detection and classification of diseases in plants using image processing and machine learning techniques. In AIP conference proceedings (Vol. 2095, No. 1). AIP Publishing. doi:10.1063/1.5097529

Popovic, D. (2000). Intelligent Control with Neural Networks. In Soft Computing and Intelligent Systems. doi:10.1016/B978-012646490-0/50021-4

Prasad. (2016). *Top 20 Python Machine Learning Open Source Projects, updated.* KD nuggets. https://www.kdnuggets.com/2016/11/top-20-python-machine-learning-opensource-updated.html

Pratap, R. (2023). Rudra Pratap Controlling of Fake Information Dissemination in Online Social Networks: An Epidemiological Approach. *IEEE Access : Practical Innovations, Open Solutions, 11*(April), 32229–32240.

Provost, F., & Fawcett, T. (2013). Data Science and its Relationship to Big Data and Data-Driven Decision Making. *Big Data*, *1*(1), 51–59. doi:10.1089/big.2013.1508 PMID:27447038

Qi, Y., Guo, K., Zhang, C., Guo, D., & Zhi, Z. (2018). A VGI-based Foodborn Disease Report and Forecast System. *Proceedings of the 4th ACM SIGSPATIAL International Workshop on Safety and Resilience, EM-GIS 2018*. ACM. 10.1145/3284103.3284124

Quadri, N. N., Alqahtani, H., Khan, R., Almakdi, S., Alshehri, M., & Mohammed, A. (2022). An Intelligent Traffic Surveillance System Using Integrated Wireless Sensor Network and Improved Phase Timing Optimization. *Sensors (Basel)*, *22*(9), 3333. doi:10.3390/s22093333 PMID:35591023

R, J., & B, S. (2022). Social Impacts of Data Science in Food, Housing And Medical Attention Linked to Public Service. *Technoarete Transactions on Advances in Data Science and Analytics*, *1*(1). doi:10.36647/TTADSA/01.01.A004

Rabiner, L. R. (1990). A tutorial on hidden Markov models and selected applications in speech recognition. In *Readings in Speech Recognition* (pp. 267–296). Elsevier. doi:10.1016/B978-0-08-051584-7.50027-9

Ramya, S., Madhubala, P., Sushmitha, E. C., Manivannan, D., & Al Firthous, A. (2023). Machine Learning and Image Processing Based Computer Vision in Industry 4.0. In Handbook of Research on Computer Vision and Image Processing in the Deep Learning Era (pp. 211-222). IGI Global.

Rangaswamy, E., Periyasamy, G., & Nawaz, N. (2021). A study on singapore's ageing population in the context of eldercare initiatives using machine learning algorithms. *Big Data and Cognitive Computing*, *5*(4), 51. doi:10.3390/bdcc5040051

Rawat, S., & Sah, A. (2012). An approach to Enhance the software and services of Health care centre. 3(7), 126–137.

Rawat, S., & Kumar, R. (2020). Direct-Indirect Link Matrix: A Black Box Testing Technique for Component-Based Software. *International Journal of Information Technology Project Management*, *11*(4), 56–69. doi:10.4018/IJITPM.2020100105

Rawat, S., & Sah, A. (2013a). An Approach to Integrate Heterogeneous Web Applications. *International Journal of Computer Applications*, *70*(23), 7–12. doi:10.5120/12205-7639

Rawat, S., & Sah, A. (2013b). Prime and Essential Prime Implicants of Boolean Functions through Cubical Representation. *International Journal of Computer Applications*, *70*(23), 1–6. doi:10.5120/12204-7638

Ray, A., & Bala, P. K. (2020). Social media for improved process management in organizations during disasters. *Knowledge and Process Management*, *27*(1), 63–74. doi:10.1002/kpm.1623

Reimann, R., Zeng, B., Jakopec, M., Burdukiewicz, M., Petrick, I., Schierack, P., & Rödiger, S. (2020). Classification of dead and living microalgae Chlorella vulgaris by bioimage informatics and machine learning. *Algal Research*, *48*, 101908. doi:10.1016/j.algal.2020.101908

Ren, F., Li, S.-P., & Liu, C. (2017, March). Information spreading on mobile communication networks: A new model that incorporates human behaviors. *Physica A, 469*, 334–341. doi:10.1016/j.physa.2016.11.027

Ribeiro, J., Lima, R., Eckhardt, T., & Paiva, S. (2021). Robotic process automation and artificial intelligence in industry 4.0–a literature review. *Procedia Computer Science, 181*, 51–58. doi:10.1016/j.procs.2021.01.104

Rieck, D., Schünemann, B., & Radusch, I. (2015). Advanced Traffic Light Information in OpenStreetMap for Traffic Simulations. In Lecture Notes in Mobility. Springer. doi:10.1007/978-3-319-15024-6_2

Rizvi, S. R., Zehra, S., & Olariu, S. (2018). ASPIRE: An Agent-Oriented Smart Parking Recommendation System for Smart Cities. *IEEE Intelligent Transportation Systems Magazine*.

Rodriguez, G., Torres, H., Fajardo, M., & Medina, J. (2021). Covid-19 in Ecuador: Radiography of Hospital Distribution Using Data Science. *ETCM 2021 - 5th Ecuador Technical Chapters Meeting*. IEEE. 10.1109/ETCM53643.2021.9590641

Rodriguez-Mier, P., Pedrinaci, C., Lama, M., & Mucientes, M. (2016). An integrated semantic web service discovery and composition framework. *IEEE Transactions on Services Computing, 9*(4), 537–550. doi:10.1109/TSC.2015.2402679

Rogge, N., Agasisti, T., & De Witte, K. (2017). Big data and the measurement of public organizations' performance and efficiency: The state-of-the-art. *Public Policy and Administration, 32*(4), 263–281. doi:10.1177/0952076716687355

Ruiz, L. R. (2010). *Interactive Pattern Recognition applied to Natural Language Processing*. Thesis.

Ryder, B., & Wortmann, F. (2017). Autonomously detecting and classifying traffic accident hotspots. In *Proceedings of the 2017 ACM International Joint Conference on Pervasive and Ubiquitous Computing and Proceedings of the 2017 ACM International Symposium on Wearable Computers (UbiComp '17)*. Association for Computing Machinery. 10.1145/3123024.3123199

Saarika, P., Sandhya, K., & Sudha, T. (2017). Smart transportation system using IoT. *Proceedings of the 2017 IEEE International Conference on Smart Technologies for Smart Nation (SmartTechCon)*. 10.1109/SmartTechCon.2017.8358540

Saberi, M., Azadeh, A., Nourmohammadzadeh, A., & Pazhoheshfar, P. (2011). Comparing performance and robustness of SVM and ANN for fault diagnosis in a centrifugal pump. *19th International Congress on Modelling and Simulation*, Perth, Australia.

Sabri, T. M. (2020). Study of transmission dynamics of COVID-19 mathematical model under ABC fractional order derivative. *Results in Physics, 19*, 103507. doi:10.1016/j.rinp.2020.103507

Saeesian, M., Khalighi, M., Azimi-Tafreshi, N., Jafari, G. R., & Ausloos, M. (2017, February). Memory effects on epidemic evolution: The susceptible-infected-recovered epidemic model. *Physical Review. E, 95*(2). PMID:28297983

Sah, A., Bhadula, S. J., Dumka, A., & Rawat, S. (2018). A software engineering perspective for development of enterprise applications. Handbook of Research on Contemporary Perspectives on Web-Based Systems. IGI Global. doi:10.4018/978-1-5225-5384-7.ch001

Sah, A., Dumka, A., & Rawat, S. (2018). Web technology systems integration using SOA and web services. Handbook of Research on Contemporary Perspectives on Web-Based Systems, (pp. 24–45). doi:10.4018/978-1-5225-5384-7.ch002

Sah, A., Vanshika, Tyagi, S., Singla, P., & Rawat, S. (2023). Health Chain. In A. Taghipour (Ed.), Blockchain Applications in Cryptocurrency for Technological Evolution (pp. 160-172). IGI Global. doi:10.4018/978-1-6684-6247-8.ch010

Sah, A., Choudhury, T., Rawat, S., & Tripathi, A. (2020). A Proposed Gene Selection Approach for Disease Detection. *Advances in Intelligent Systems and Computing, 1120*, 199–206. doi:10.1007/978-981-15-2449-3_16

Sah, A., Rawat, S., Choudhury, T., & Dewangan, B. K. (2022). An Extensive Review of Web-Based Multi-Granularity Service Composition. *International Journal of Web-Based Learning and Teaching Technologies, 17*(4), 1–19. doi:10.4018/IJWLTT.285570

Samudravijaya, K. (2010). *Speech and Speaker recognition tutorial.* TIFR Mumbai.

Sangiambut, S., & Sieber, R. (2016). The V in VGI: Citizens or Civic Data Sources. *Urban Planning, 1*(2), 141–154. doi:10.17645/up.v1i2.644

Sankar, K., Krishnan, V. G., Saradhi, M. V., Priya, K. H., & Vijayaraja, V. (2023). Tom and Jerry Based Multi-path Routing with Optimal K-medoids for choosing Best Cluster head in MANET. *International Journal of Communication Networks and Information Security, 15*(1), 59–65.

Santosh, S. (2007). Bayesian Quadratic Discriminant Analysis. *Journal of Machine Learning Research, 8*, 1277–1305.

Satyanarayanan, M. (2017, January). The Emergence of Edge Computing. *Computer, 50*(1), 30–39. doi:10.1109/MC.2017.9

Sboui, T., & Aissi, S. (2022). *A Risk-based Approach for Enhancing the Fitness of use of VGI.* IEEE., doi:10.1109/ACCESS.2022.3201022

Sebayang, A. H., Kusumo, F., Milano, J., Shamsuddin, A. H., Silitonga, A. S., Ideris, F., Siswantoro, J., Veza, I., Mofijur, M., & Reen Chia, S. (2023). Optimization of biodiesel production from rice bran oil by ultrasound and infrared radiation using ANN-GWO. *Fuel, 346*, 128404. doi:10.1016/j.fuel.2023.128404

Sezer, A., Deniz, M., & Topuz, M. (2018). Analysis of Accessibility of Schools in Usak City via Geographical Information Systems (GIS). *Tarih Kultur Ve Sanat Arastirmalari Dergisi-Journal Of History Culture And Art Research, 7*(5).

Shaikh, R. A., Sahu, T. P., & Anand, V. (2020). Predicting outcomes of legal cases based on legal factors using classifiers. *Procedia Computer Science*, *167*, 2393–2402. doi:10.1016/j.procs.2020.03.292

Shandilya, S., & Chandankhede, C. (2018). Survey on recent cancer classification systems for cancer diagnosis. *Proceedings of the 2017 International Conference on Wireless Communications, Signal Processing and Networking*. IEEE. 10.1109/WiSPNET.2017.8300231

Sharma, D., & Gomase, V. (2017). An Approach for Detecting Phishing Websites Based on K-Nearest Neighbors Algorithm. *International Journal of Computer Applications*, *176*(3), 22–26.

Sharma, V., Tsai, M.-L., Chen, C.-W., Sun, P.-P., Nargotra, P., & Dong, C.-D. (2023). Advances in machine learning technology for sustainable biofuel production systems in lignocellulosic biorefineries. *The Science of the Total Environment*, *886*, 163972. doi:10.1016/j.scitotenv.2023.163972 PMID:37164089

Shelare, S. D., Belkhode, P. N., Nikam, K. C., Jathar, L. D., Shahapurkar, K., Soudagar, M. E. M., Veza, I., Khan, T. M. Y., Kalam, M. A., Nizami, A.-S., & Rehan, M. (2023). Biofuels for a sustainable future: Examining the role of nano-additives, economics, policy, internet of things, artificial intelligence and machine learning technology in biodiesel production. *Energy*, *282*, 128874. doi:10.1016/j.energy.2023.128874

Sheng, S., Holbrook, M., Kumaraguru, P., Cranor, L. F., & Downs, J. (2010). Who falls for phishing scams? A demographic analysis of phishing susceptibility and effectiveness of interventions. In *Proceedings of the SIGCHI Conference on Human Factors in Computing Systems (CHI)* (pp. 373-382). ACM. 10.1145/1753326.1753383

Shereesha, M., Hemavathy, C., Teja, H., Reddy, G. M., Kumar, B. V., & Sunitha, G. (2022). *Precision Mango Farming: Using Compact Convolutional Transformer for Disease Detection.* In International Conference on Innovations in Bio-Inspired Computing and Applications (pp. 458-465). Cham: Springer Nature Switzerland.

Shi, J., Jin, L., Li, J., & Fang, Z. (2017). A smart parking system based on NB-IoT and third-party payment platform. *Proceedings of the 2017 17th International Symposium on Communications and Information Technologies (ISCIT)*. 10.1109/ISCIT.2017.8261235

Shrivastava, G., Kumar, P., Ojha, R. P., Srivastava, P. K., Mohan, S., & Srivastava, G. (2020, October). Defensive Modeling of Fake News Through Online Social Networks. *IEEE Transactions on Computational Social Systems*, *7*(5), 1159–1167. doi:10.1109/TCSS.2020.3014135

Shu, K., Bernard, H. R., & Liu, H. (2019). Studying fake news via network analysis: Detection and mitigation. Emerging Research Challenges and Opportunities in Computational Social Network Analysis and Mining. Springer.

Siddique, N., Arefin, M. S., Ahad, M. A. R., & Dewan, M. A. A. (Eds.). (2023). *Computer Vision and Image Analysis for Industry 4.0*. CRC Press. doi:10.1201/9781003256106

Simmons, R. (2018). Big Data, Machine Judges, and the Legitimacy of the Criminal Justice System. *SSRN*, *52*(2), 1067–1118. doi:10.2139/ssrn.3156510

Simon, O. (2015). Short-term Travel-time Prediction on Highway: A Review of the Data-driven Approach. *Transport Reviews, 35*.

Singh, A. (2019). Remote sensing and GIS applications for municipal waste management. *Journal of Environmental Management, 243*, 22–29. doi:10.1016/j.jenvman.2019.05.017 PMID:31077867

Singh, B., Srivastava, A. K., & Prakash, O. (2023a). Experimental analysis of biodiesel production from used cooking oil and its combustion, performance and emission analysis at different blending ratios in diesel engine. *International Journal of Renewable Energy Technology, 14*(3), 259–277. doi:10.1504/IJRET.2023.132976

Singh, B., Srivastava, A. K., & Prakash, O. (2023b). *A Comprehensive Review on Rare Biodiesel Feedstock Availability, Fatty Acid Composition, Physical Properties, Production, Engine Performance and Emission.* Process Integration and Optimization for Sustainability., doi:10.1007/s41660-023-00343-w

Singh, Y. P., Singh, A. K., & Singh, R. P. (2016). *Web GIS based Framework for Citizen Reporting on Collection of Solid Waste and Mapping in GIS for Allahabad City. SAMRIDDHI : A Journal of Physical Sciences.* Engineering and Technology., doi:10.18090/samriddhi.v8i1.11405

Sittón-Candanedo, I., Alonso, R. S., Rodríguez-González, S., García Coria, J. A., & De La Prieta, F. (2020). Edge computing architectures in industry 4.0: A general survey and comparison. In 14th International Conference on Soft Computing Models in Industrial and Environmental Applications. Springer.

Sivalingam, S. M. (2023). A neural networks–based numerical method for the generalized Caputo-type fractional differential equations. *Science Direct, 213*. doi:10.1016/j.matcom.2023.06.012

Sivalingam, S. M., & Pushpendra Kumar, V. (2023). Govindaraj, A novel optimization – based physics–informed neural network scheme for solving fractional differential equations. *Engineering with Computers*. doi:10.1007/s00366-023-01830-x

Smith, M., Banerjee, I., & Laskowski, S. (2017). A novel machine learning approach to detect phishing URLs using natural language processing. *Journal of Computer and System Sciences, 86*, 13–26.

Solís, P., McCusker, B., Menkiti, N., Cowan, N., & Blevins, C. (2018). Engaging global youth in participatory spatial data creation for the UN sustainable development goals: The case of open mapping for malaria prevention. *Applied Geography (Sevenoaks, England), 98*, 143–155. doi:10.1016/j.apgeog.2018.07.013

Soltanolkottabi, M., Ben-Arieh, D., & Wu, C.-H. (2019, April). Modeling behavioral response to vaccination using public goods game. *IEEE Transactions on Computational Social Systems, 6*(2), 268–276. doi:10.1109/TCSS.2019.2896227 PMID:32391406

Sommariva, S., Vamos, C., Mantzarlis, A., Dào, L. U.-L., & Martinez Tyson, D. (2018, July). Spreading the (fake) news: Exploring health messages on social media and the implications for health professionals using a case study. *American Journal of Health Education, 49*(4), 246–255. doi:10.1080/19325037.2018.1473178

Sony, M., & Naik, S. (2020). Key ingredients for evaluating Industry 4.0 readiness for organizations: A literature review. *Benchmarking, 27*(7), 2213–2232. doi:10.1108/BIJ-09-2018-0284

Soultana, A., Benabbou, F., & Sael, N. (2020). *Providing Context Awareness in the Smart Car Environment: State of the Art.* Springer. . doi:10.1007/978-3-030-37629-1_59

Stahlesq.com. (2018). *How the IRS Uses Artificial Intelligence to Detect Tax Evaders.* Stables HQ. https://stahlesq.com/criminal-defense-law-blog/how-the-irs-uses-artificial-intelligence-to-detect-tax-evaders/

Steiniger, S., Poorazizi, M. E., Scott, D. R., Fuentes, C., & Crespo, R. (2016). Can we use OpenStreetMap POIs for the Evaluation of Urban Accessibility? *International Conference on GIScience Short Paper Proceedings.* IEEE. 10.21433/B31167F0678P

Sturrock, H. J. W., Woolheater, K., Bennett, A. F., Andrade-Pacheco, R., & Midekisa, A. (2018). Predicting residential structures from open source remotely enumerated data using machine learning. *PLoS One, 13*(9), e0204399. doi:10.1371/journal.pone.0204399 PMID:30240429

Subrahmanya, S. V. G., Shetty, D. K., Patil, V., Hameed, B. M. Z., Paul, R., Smriti, K., Naik, N., & Somani, B. K. (2022). The role of data science in healthcare advancements: applications, benefits, and future prospects. In Irish Journal of Medical Science, 191(4). doi:10.1007/s11845-021-02730-z

Sukpancharoen, S., Katongtung, T., Rattanachoung, N., & Tippayawong, N. (2023). Unlocking the potential of transesterification catalysts for biodiesel production through machine learning approach. *Bioresource Technology, 378*, 128961. doi:10.1016/j.biortech.2023.128961 PMID:36972805

Sultana, N., Hossain, S. M. Z., Abusaad, M., Alanbar, N., Senan, Y., & Razzak, S. A. (2022). Prediction of biodiesel production from microalgal oil using Bayesian optimization algorithm-based machine learning approaches. *Fuel, 309*, 122184. doi:10.1016/j.fuel.2021.122184

Sumayli, A. (2023). Development of advanced machine learning models for optimization of methyl ester biofuel production from papaya oil: Gaussian process regression (GPR), multilayer perceptron (MLP), and K-nearest neighbor (KNN) regression models. *Arabian Journal of Chemistry, 16*(7), 104833. doi:10.1016/j.arabjc.2023.104833

Sunitha, G., Arunachalam, R., Abd-Elnaby, M., Eid, M. M., & Rashed, A. N. Z. (2022). A comparative analysis of deep neural network architectures for the dynamic diagnosis of COVID-19 based on acoustic cough features. *International Journal of Imaging Systems and Technology, 32*(5), 1433–1446. doi:10.1002/ima.22749 PMID:35941929

Suvarna, M., Jahirul, M. I., Aaron-Yeap, W. H., Augustine, C. V., Umesh, A., Rasul, M. G., Günay, M. E., Yildirim, R., & Janaun, J. (2022). Predicting biodiesel properties and its optimal fatty acid profile via explainable machine learning. *Renewable Energy, 189*, 245–258. doi:10.1016/j.renene.2022.02.124

Swan, M. (2012). Sensor mania! the internet of things, wearable computing, objective metrics, and the quantified self 2.0. *J. Sens. Actuator Netw., 1*(3), 217–253. doi:10.3390/jsan1030217

Szegedy, C., Liu, W., Jia, Y., Sermanet, P., Reed, S., Anguelov, D., Erhan, D., Vanhoucke, V., & Rabinovich, A. (2015). Going deeper with convolutions. *Proceedings of the IEEE Conference on Computer Vision and Pattern Recognition.*

Tafidis, P., Teixeira, J., Bahmankhah, B., Macedo, E., Coelho, M. C., & Bandeira, J. (2017). Exploring crowdsourcing information to predict traffic-related impacts. *Proceedings of the 2017 IEEE International Conference on Environment and Electrical Engineering and 2017 IEEE Industrial and Commercial Power Systems Europe (EEEIC/I&CPS Europe)*. 10.1109/EEEIC.2017.7977595

Talari, S., Shafie-khah, M., Siano, P., Loia, V., Tommasetti, A., & Catalão, J. P. S. (2017). A Review of Smart Cities Based on the Internet of Things Concept. *Energies, 10*(4), 1–23. doi:10.3390/en10040421

Tang, J., Abbas, A. K., Koka, N. A., Sadoon, N., Abbas, J. K., Abdalhuseen, R. A., Abosaooda, M., Ahmed, N. M., & Abbas, A. H. (2023). Optimization of thermal biofuel production from biomass using CaO-based catalyst through different algorithm-based machine learning approaches. *Case Studies in Thermal Engineering, 50*, 103419. doi:10.1016/j.csite.2023.103419

Tarek, R. (2018). Fog Computing: Data Streaming Services for Mobile End-Users. *Procedia Computer Science, 134.*

Tchameni, A. P., Zhao, L., Ribeiro, J. X. F., & Li, T. (2019). Predicting the rheological properties of waste vegetable oil biodiesel-modified water-based mud using artificial neural network. *Geosystem Engineering, 22*(2), 101–111. doi:10.1080/12269328.2018.1490209

Thangaraja, J., Zigan, L., & Rajkumar, S. (2023). A machine learning framework for evaluating the biodiesel properties for accurate modeling of spray and combustion processes. *Fuel, 334*, 126573. doi:10.1016/j.fuel.2022.126573

Thompson, A. F., Afolayan, A. H., & Ibidunmoye, E. O. (2013). Application of geographic information system to solid waste management. *2013 Pan African International Conference on Information Science, Computing and Telecommunications, PACT 2013*. IEEE. 10.1109/SCAT.2013.7055110

To, H., Kim, S. H., & Shahabi, C. (2015). Effectively crowdsourcing the acquisition and analysis of visual data for disaster response. *Proceedings - 2015 IEEE International Conference on Big Data, IEEE Big Data 2015*. IEEE. 10.1109/BigData.2015.7363814

Toufik, M., & Atangana, A. (2017). New numerical approximation of fractional derivative with non-local and non-singular kernel: Application to chaotic models. *The European Physical Journal Plus, 132*(10), 444. doi:10.1140/epjp/i2017-11717-0

Tran, K., Barbeau, S., Hillsman, E., & Labrador, M. A. (2013). GO_Sync - A Framework to Synchronize Crowd-Sourced Mapping Contributors from Online Communities and Transit Agency Bus Stop Inventories. *International Journal of Intelligent Transportation Systems Research, 11*(2), 54–64. doi:10.1007/s13177-013-0056-x

Tripathy, A. K., Mishra, A. K., & Das, T. K. (2017). Smart lighting: Intelligent and weather adaptive lighting in street lights using IOT. *Proceedings of the 2017 International Conference on Intelligent Computing, Instrumentation and Control Technologies (ICICICT)*. 10.1109/ICICICT1.2017.8342746

Tsou, M. H., Jung, C. Te, Allen, C., Yang, J. A., Han, S. Y., Spitzberg, B. H., & Dozier, J. (2017). Building a real-time geo-targeted event observation (Geo) viewer for disaster management and situation awareness. *Lecture Notes in Geoinformation and Cartography*. Springer. doi:10.1007/978-3-319-57336-6_7

Turing.Com. (2023). *A Guide on Word Embeddings in NLP*. Turing.com. https://www.turing.com/kb/guide-on-word-embeddings-in-nlp

Tyagi, A. K., Fernandez, T. F., Mishra, S., & Kumari, S. (2020). Intelligent automation systems at the core of industry 4.0. In *International conference on intelligent systems design and applications* (pp. 1-18). Cham: Springer International Publishing.

Tyagi, A. K., Dananjayan, S., Agarwal, D., & Thariq Ahmed, H. F. (2023). Blockchain—Internet of Things Applications: Opportunities and Challenges for Industry 4.0 and Society 5.0. *Sensors (Basel), 23*(2), 947. doi:10.3390/s23020947 PMID:36679743

Tzavella, K., Fekete, A., & Fiedrich, F. (2018). Opportunities provided by geographic information systems and volunteered geographic information for a timely emergency response during flood events in Cologne, Germany. *Natural Hazards, 91*. doi:10.1007/s11069-017-3102-1

Ulmer, S. S. (1963). Quantitative analysis of judicial processes: Some practical and theoretical applications. *Law and Contemporary Problems, 28*(1), 164–184. https://scholarship.law.duke.edu/cgi/viewcontent.cgi?article=2952&context=lcp. doi:10.2307/1190728

Utgoff, P. E. (1989). Incremental induction of decision trees. *Machine Learning, 4*(2), 161–186. doi:10.1023/A:1022699900025

Vangelista, L., Zanella, A., & Zorzi, M. (2015). *Long-Range IoT Technologies: The Dawn of LoRa*. FABULOUS.

Vapnik, V. (1999). An overview of statistical learning theory. *IEEE Transactions on Neural Networks, 10*(5).

Vishnoi, V. K., Kumar, K., & Kumar, B. (2021). Plant disease detection using computational intelligence and image processing. *Journal of Plant Diseases and Protection, 128*(1), 19–53. doi:10.1007/s41348-020-00368-0

Waelen, R. A. (2023). The ethics of computer vision: An overview in terms of power. *AI and Ethics*, 1–10. doi:10.1007/s43681-023-00272-x

Wahdain, E. A., Baharudin, A. S., & Ahmad, M. N. (2019). Big data analytics in the malaysian public sector: The determinants of value creation. *Advances in Intelligent Systems and Computing, 843*, 139–150. doi:10.1007/978-3-319-99007-1_14

Wang, J., Wang, C., Song, X., & Raghavan, V. (2017). Automatic intersection and traffic rule detection by mining motor-vehicle GPS trajectories. *Computers, Environment and Urban Systems, 64*, 19–29. doi:10.1016/j.compenvurbsys.2016.12.006

Wang, T., He, J., & Wang, X. (2018, January). An information spreading model based on online social networks. *Physica A, 490*, 488–496. doi:10.1016/j.physa.2017.08.078

Wang, W. (2006, January). Epidemic models with nonlinear infection forces. *Mathematical Biosciences and Engineering, 3*(1), 267–279. doi:10.3934/mbe.2006.3.267 PMID:20361823

Wang, Y., Zhang, L., Zhang, D., & Li, W. (2018). Detecting phishing emails using a hierarchical classification framework. *IEEE Transactions on Information Forensics and Security, 13*(8), 1906–1919.

Watanabe, S. (1985). *Pattern Recognition: Human and Mechanical.* Wiley.

Watkins, C. J., & Dayan, P. (1992). Q-learning. *Machine Learning, 8*(3-4), 279–292. doi:10.1007/BF00992698

Wazid, M., Das, A. K., Chamola, V., & Park, Y. (2022). Uniting cyber security and machine learning: Advantages, challenges and future research. *ICT Express, 8*(3), 313–321. doi:10.1016/j.icte.2022.04.007

Wen, S., Zhou, W., Zhang, J., Xiang, Y., Zhou, W., & Jia, W. (2013, August). Modeling propagation dynamics of social network worms. *IEEE Transactions on Parallel and Distributed Systems, 24*(8), 1633–1643. doi:10.1109/TPDS.2012.250

Werbos, P. J. (1990). Backpropagation through time: What it does and how to do it. *Proceedings of the IEEE, 78*(10), 1550–1560. doi:10.1109/5.58337

Williamson, B. (2015). Governing methods: Policy innovation labs, design and data science in the digital governance of education. *Journal of Educational Administration and History, 47*(3), 251–271. doi:10.1080/00220620.2015.1038693

Wong, W., & Hinnant, C. C. (2022). Competing perspectives on the Big Data revolution: A typology of applications in public policy. *Journal of Economic Policy Reform.* doi:10.1080/17487870.2022.2103701

Wu, Q., Huang, C., Wang, S.-Y., Chiu, W.-C., & Chen, T. (2007). Robust parking space detection considering inter-space correlation. *Proceedings of the 2007 IEEE International Conference on Multimedia and Expo.* 10.1109/ICME.2007.4284736

Wu, S., Das Sarma, A., Fabrikant, A., Lattanzi, S., & Tomkins, A. (2013). Arrival and departure dynamics in social networks. *Proc. 6th ACM Int. Conf. Web Search Data Mining (WSDM)* (pp. 233–242). ACM. 10.1145/2433396.2433425

Xenakis, A., Karageorgos, A., Lallas, E., Chis, A. E., & González-Vélez, H. (2019). Towards Distributed IoT/Cloud based Fault Detection and Maintenance in Industrial Automation. *Procedia Computer Science, 151.*

Xie, X., Zhou, Y., Xu, Y., Hu, Y., & Wu, C. (2019). OpenStreetMap Data Quality Assessment via Deep Learning and Remote Sensing Imagery. *IEEE Access : Practical Innovations, Open Solutions, 7,* 176884–176895. doi:10.1109/ACCESS.2019.2957825

Xing, Y., Zheng, Z., Sun, Y., & Agha Alikhani, M. (2021). A Review on Machine Learning Application in Biodiesel Production Studies. *International Journal of Chemical Engineering, 2021,* 1–12. doi:10.1155/2021/2154258

Yingwei, Y., Dawei, M., & Hongchao, F. (2020). A research framework for the application of volunteered geographic information in post-disaster recovery monitoring. *Tropical Geography, 40*(2). doi:10.13284/j.cnki.rddl.003239

Yisheng, L., Duan, Y., Kang, W., & Li, Z. (2014). Traffic Flow Prediction With Big Data: A Deep Learning Approach. *IEEE Transactions on Intelligent Transportation Systems, 16,* 865–873. doi:10.1109/TITS.2014.2345663

Zantalis, F., Koulouras, G., Karabetsos, S., & Kandris, D. (2019). future internet A Review of Machine Learning and IoT in Smart Transportation. *Future Internet, 11*(4), 94. doi:10.3390/fi11040094

Završnik, A. (2018). Algorithmic justice: Algorithms and big data in criminal justice settings. *European Journal of Criminology, 18*(5), 623–642. doi:10.1177/1477370819876762

Zhang, L., Sun, L., Li, W., Zhang, J., Cai, W., Cheng, C., & Ning, X. (2021). A joint Bayesian framework based on partial least squares discriminant analysis for finger vein recognition. *IEEE Sensors Journal, 22*(1), 785–794. doi:10.1109/JSEN.2021.3130951

Zhang, Y., Sheng, M., Liu, X., Wang, R., Lin, W., Ren, P., Wang, X., Zhao, E., & Song, W. (2022). A heterogeneous multi-modal medical data fusion framework supporting hybrid data exploration. *Health Information Science and Systems, 10*(1), 22. doi:10.1007/s13755-022-00183-x PMID:36039096

Zhang, Y., Wu, S., Li, Q., & Hu, J. (2020). Detecting phishing emails with lexical and syntactic features. *Information Sciences, 509,* 48–60.

Zhang, Z., Wang, H., Wang, C., & Fang, H. (2015, September). Modeling epidemics spreading on social contact networks. *IEEE Transactions on Emerging Topics in Computing*, *3*(3), 410–419. doi:10.1109/TETC.2015.2398353 PMID:27722037

Zhou, L., Zhang, L., & Konz, N. (2022). Computer vision techniques in manufacturing. *IEEE Transactions on Systems, Man, and Cybernetics. Systems*.

Zhou, X., Yang, C., & Yu, W. (2013). Moving object detection by detecting contiguous outliers in the low-rank representation. *IEEE Transactions on Pattern Analysis and Machine Intelligence*, *35*(3), 597–610. doi:10.1109/TPAMI.2012.132 PMID:22689075

Zhou, Z. H. (2012). *Ensemble Methods: Foundations and Algorithms*. Chapman and Hall/CRC. doi:10.1201/b12207

Zilske, M., Neumann, A., & Nagel, K. (2011). OpenStreetMap For Traffic Simulation. M. Schmidt, G. Gartner (Eds.), *Proceedings of the 1st European State of the Map – OpenStreetMap Conference*. Research Gate.

Zilvan, V., Ramdan, A., Suryawati, E., Kusumo, R. B. S., Krisnandi, D., & Pardede, H. F. (2019, October). Denoising convolutional variational autoencoders-based feature learning for automatic detection of plant diseases. In *2019 3rd International Conference on Informatics and Computational Sciences (ICICoS)* (pp. 1-6). IEEE. 10.1109/ICICoS48119.2019.8982494

Ziyai, M. R., Mehrpooya, M., Aghbashlo, M., Omid, M., Alsagri, A. S., & Tabatabaei, M. (2019). Techno-economic comparison of three biodiesel production scenarios enhanced by glycerol supercritical water reforming process. *International Journal of Hydrogen Energy*, *44*(33), 17845–17862. doi:10.1016/j.ijhydene.2019.05.017

About the Contributors

G. Ananthi is currently working as an Assistant Professor (Senior Grade), in the Department of Computer Science and Engineering, Mepco Schlenk Engineering College, Sivakasi. She completed her UG in CSE and PG in CSE at Mepco Schlenk Engineering College respectively on 2001 and 2010. She completed her Ph.D in Information and Communication Engineering under Anna University, Chennai during July 2022. She has 19 years of teaching experience. She has 23 publications in Journals and conferences. She is a life member in CSI and ISTE. Her areas of specialization are image processing, machine learning and soft computing.

Rakesh Chandrashekar did his BE in mechanical engineering, M. Tech in Thermal Power Engineering and Pursuing PhD in energy-efficient space Cooling Systems. He is associated with New Horizon College of Engineering from the Department of Mechanical Engineering, since 2011. He is actively involved in research published many papers in indexed journals, and worked on Government and Industry-funded projects. The research area includes- smart space cooling systems, Building heat transfer, Design of heat exchangers, renewable energy, Internet of Things and Industry 4.0.

Monica Janet Clifford is associated with the Department of Commerce, as a research scholar, Christ University, Bangalore, India. She also works as an Assistant Professor with the Department of Commerce, UG studies, Mount Carmel College-Autonomous, Bangalore, India. She has completed her Master of Commerce in St Joseph's College of Commerce and has completed her Post Graduate Diploma in Business Administration. She has presented research papers in various National and International conferences on Contextual Marketing. Adding to this, she has actively been a part of various national level workshops and seminars for research advancements. She is an aspiring candidate to publish quality research work in her area of interest in reputed journals.

Navnath D. Kale working as Sr. Assistant Professor in School of Computer Engineering at MIT Academy of Engineering, Alandi, Pune. He completed Master of Technology in Computer Science and Engineering from Visveswaraya Technological University, Belgaum, India and Ph.D.(CSE) in the field of Wireless Sensor Networks from Koneru Lakshmaiah Education Foundation (K. L. University), Vijayawada, India. He is in teaching profession for more than 19 years. He has presented number of papers in National and International Journals, Conference and Symposiums and published books as well. His main area of interest includes Wireless sensor Networks, Computer Network and Information Security.

Vijaykumar P. Mantri is working as a Senior Assistant Professor in the School of Computer Engineering at MIT Academy of Engineering, Alandi, Pune, India. He completed his Master of Technology in Computer Science and Engineering from Visveswaraya Technological University, Belgaum, India and presently pursuing Ph.D. (CSE) from Vishwakarma University, Pune, India. He has more than 24 Years of teaching experience. He presented and published many Research and Technical Papers in National and International Journals and Conferences. His main research interests are Machine Learning and Deep Learning.

R. Nagarajan received his B.E. in Electrical and Electronics Engineering from Madurai Kamarajar University, Madurai, India, in 1997. He received his M.E. in Power Electronics and Drives from Anna University, Chennai, India, in 2008. He received his Ph.D in Electrical Engineering from Anna University, Chennai, India, in 2014. He has worked in the industry as an Electrical Engineer. He is currently working as Professor of Electrical and Electronics Engineering at Gnanamani College of Technology, Namakkal, Tamilnadu, India. His current research interest includes Power Electronics, Power System, Network Security, Cloud Computing, Wireless Sensor Communication, Digital Image Processing, Data Mining, Soft Computing Techniques and Renewable Energy Sources. He is published more than 120 Research Articles in various referred International Journals and he is published more than 60 Books & Book Chapter in various referred international Publications.

Preeti Patil working as Associate Professor and Head of Department, Information Technology at D Y Patil College of Engineering, Akurdi Pune. She completed Ph.D.(Computer Engineering).She is in teaching profession for more than 22 years. she has presented number of papers in National and International Journals, Conference and Symposiums and published books as well. Her main area of interest includes Database Mining, Business Intelligence, Big Data

Mohit Payal was born in Dehradun, Uttarakhand, India, in 1986. He received the PhD degree in electronics and communication engineering from G. B. Pant Engineering College, Pauri Garhwal, India (Affiliated to Uttarakhand technical University), in 2021. He received the MTech degree in digital signal processing from the G. B. Pant Engineering College, Pauri Garhwal, India, in 2012. He received the BTech degree in electronics and communication engineering from Graphic Era University (formerly known as Graphic Era Institute of Technology), Dehradun, India, in 2009. His research area are simulation & modelling of semiconductor devices, VLSI, Internet of Things.

Sabyasachi Pramanik is a professional IEEE member. He obtained a PhD in Computer Science and Engineering from Sri Satya Sai University of Technology and Medical Sciences, Bhopal, India. Presently, he is an Associate Professor, Department of Computer Science and Engineering, Haldia Institute of Technology, India. He has many publications in various reputed international conferences, journals, and book chapters (Indexed by SCIE, Scopus, ESCI, etc). He is doing research in the fields of Artificial Intelligence, Data Privacy, Cybersecurity, Network Security, and Machine Learning. He also serves on the editorial boards of several international journals. He is a reviewer of journal articles from IEEE, Springer, Elsevier, Inderscience, IET and IGI Global. He has reviewed many conference papers, has been a keynote speaker, session chair, and technical program committee member at many international conferences. He has authored a book on Wireless Sensor Network. He has edited 8 books from IGI Global, CRC Press, Springer and Wiley Publications.

Kavitha R. works with the Department of Commerce, Christ University, Bangalore, India. She holds a PhD in Commerce from Bharathiyar University, Coimbatore, Tamil Nadu. Her area of focus in on marketing, brand management, consumer behaviour and buying process. Her doctoral dissertation was on 'A study on the mind of nouveau shoppers of pandora's box in Indian shopping malls'. Her other research focus is on entrepreneurship, women entrepreneurship, retailing and banking. She has published papers in scopus indexed journals and in many other reputed journals. She has also been a part of many international conferences and is also a member of the review committee of many international journals

Saurabh Rawat is conscientious and self motivated individual with great enthusiasm and determination to succeed through his pupils. The author is highly experienced professional with more than 20 years in the field of computers and Mathematics. An alumnus of IIT, specializes in Vedic Mathematics, believes in concept based learning along with innovative techniques. Every year author is guiding many students through on and off campus recruitment in various multinational companies like Infosys, Accenture, TCS, Wipro and many more. Author has also assisted aspirants in various examinations like GRE, GMAT, CAT, MAT, SSC and many more. He has appeared in CAT examinations many times himself. He has several research papers and conference proceeding in reputed journals.

Anushree Sah is highly experienced IT professional having an experience of more than 15 years in the field of IT industry and education. The author has worked with the renowned companies like Oracle Financial Services & Software Ltd., Western Union, Dencare Ltd. etc. Having experience of multinational companies, the author has used all her experience in preparing this book with short cuts and concepts. The author has completed her bachelor's in Computer Science and Engineering and has Master's degree from University of Greenwich, London, U.K. She holds various academic and administrative responsibilities in her current working place. Verbal ability is her passion, and penned down many books on verbal ability. The author specializes in Mathematical based subjects. She has several research papers and conference proceedings in reputed journals.

K.G. Suma is working as an Associate Professor in the Department of Computer Science and Engineering, VIT-AP, India. She has received her Ph.D. degree from Anna University Chennai, INDIA in 2017. Her research areas include Image Processing, Medical Imaging, Machine Learning and Soft Computing. She carried several administrative roles in academics. She has won Young Women Engineer from IET in the year of 2020. She has published several Scopus and SCI indexed Journal publications, Book chapters, and attended national and international conferences and won prizes. She has 2 national/ international patents.

Gurram Sunitha (Academician, Researcher, Author) is currently working as a Professor at Department of AI & ML, School of Computing, Mohan Babu University, Tirupati, A.P., India. She received her Ph.D. degree in Computer Science and Engineering from S.V.University, Tirupati. She has 23 years of experience in academia. Her research interests include Data Mining, Spatio-Temporal Analytics, Machine Learning and Artificial Intelligence. She has 13 patents and 6 books (International & National, Edited & Authored) published to her credit. She has published around 70+ research papers in various International Refereed Journals (SCIE/Scopus/Web of Science) and International Conferences indexed in Springer, IEEEXplore etc. She has been serving as reviewer for several reputed journals; She has been acting as Technical Program/Organizing/ Advisory/ Reviewer Committee Member and has been serving on the program committees and co-chaired various International Conferences across the world.

Arunadevi Thirumalraj did her BE in Computer Science Engineering in Government college of Engineering, Bodinayakanur and she has worked as a Research associate in various industrial and academic research institutes for past 6 years. Now she is pursing ME Computer Science Engineering in K.Ramakrishnan College of Technology, (KRCT), Tiruchirappalli. She is actively involved in the field of innovative teaching and Learning. She has publishing a good number of papers in indexed journals.

Index

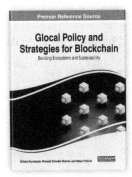
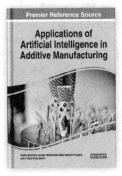

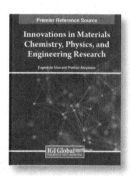
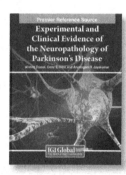
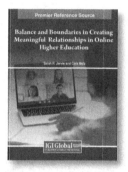